STUDY GUIDE

STUDY GUIDE

Richard O. Straub

University of Michigan, Dearborn

to accompany

David G. Myers

PSYCHOLOGY
in everyday life

SECOND EDITION

WORTH PUBLISHERS

Study Guide
by Richard O. Straub
to accompany
Myers: **Psychology in Everyday Life,** Second Edition

© 2012, 2009 by Worth Publishers

Printed in the United States of America

ISBN 13: 978-1-4292-8321-2
ISBN 10: 1-4292-8321-1

First printing

Worth Publishers
41 Madison Avenue
New York, NY 10010
www.worthpublishers.com

contents

preface

This Study Guide is designed for use with *Psychology in Everyday Life,* Second Edition, by David G. Myers. It is intended to help you to learn material in the textbook, to evaluate your understanding of that material, and then to review any problem areas. Many students will also benefit from reading "Time Management: Or, How to Be a Great Student and Still Have a Life!" in the text. This essay offers proven study suggestions for useful note-taking, evaluating your exam performance, and improving your comprehension while studying from textbooks.

Features

This Study Guide offers many useful features. Each chapter begins with a Chapter Review that is organized by major text section and one or more learning objectives. Each objective is followed by a brief summary of important concepts from the text, including all key terms. Under each objective are a number of fill-in and essay-type questions, art to be labeled, photos from the text as reminders of important concepts, and summary tables to be completed or that are already completed for you. Also included are practical study tips and applications. These tips and applications are designed to help you evaluate your understanding of the text chapter's broader concepts, and make the text material more meaningful by relating it to your own life. Following the Chapter Review is a Progress Test consisting of multiple-choice, matching, and essay questions that focus on

facts and definitions. For all questions, the correct answers are given, followed by textbook page references (so you can easily go back and reread the material) and explanations of why the answer is correct as well as why the other choices are incorrect. Most chapters also include at least one Summing Up concept map in the form of a flow chart. Designed to promote a deeper understanding of the conceptual relationships among chapter issues, these review charts follow the lead of the text in emphasizing the importance of viewing human behavior as a product of biological, psychological, and social-cultural influences. Some tell a story, so that you are learning the concepts as applied to real-life situations.

Acknowledgments

Special thanks are due to Betty Shapiro Probert for her extraordinary editorial contributions and to Don Probert for his skill and efficiency in the composition of this guide. I would also like to thank Sharon Prevost, Jenny Chiu, and Stacey Alexander of Worth Publishers for their dedication and energy in skillfully coordinating various aspects of production. Most important, I want to thank Jeremy, Rebecca, Melissa, and Pam for their enduring love and support.

Richard O. Straub

STUDY GUIDE

1

PSYCHOLOGY'S ROOTS, BIG IDEAS, AND CRITICAL THINKING TOOLS

Chapter 1 first traces the roots of psychology back to the early Greek philosophers. The chapter then discusses four big ideas that penetrate psychology: the importance of critical thinking and the biopsychosocial approach, as well as the ideas that we operate with a two-track mind and that psychology explores both human strengths and challenges. The core of the chapter describes the methods of research: the case study, surveys, naturalistic observation, and experimentation. The final section answers some common questions about psychology.

CHAPTER REVIEW

First, skim each text section, noting headings and bold-face items. Review the section by reading the objectives and summaries provided here, then answer the questions that follow. In some cases, STUDY TIPS explain how best to learn a difficult concept and APPLICATIONS help you to know how well you understand the material. Check your understanding of the material by consulting the answers beginning on page 14. Do not continue with the next section until you understand each answer. If you need to, review or reread the section in the textbook before continuing.

Psychology's Roots

Objective 1: Describe the growth of scientific psychology from its early pioneers to contemporary concerns.

Early philosophers such as Aristotle theorized about learning and memory, motivation and emotion, perception and personality. Their thinking about thinking continued until Wilhelm Wundt established the first psychological laboratory in 1879 in Leipzig, Germany. He sought to measure the fastest and simplest mental processes. William James brought psychology to America, writing a psychology textbook in 1890 and mentoring Mary Whiton Calkins, the first female president of APA. Margaret Floy Washburn was the first psychology Ph.D. and the second female president of APA.

Psychology developed from philosophy and biology. Its pioneers included Russian physiologist Ivan Pavlov, Austrian personality theorist Sigmund Freud, and Swiss biologist Jean Piaget. Until the 1920s, psychology was defined as the science of mental life. From the 1920s through the 1960s, American psychologists, led by John Watson and later by B. F. Skinner, both *behaviorists,* redefined psychology as the science of observable behavior. In responding to Freudian psychology and behaviorism, *humanistic psychology* emphasized our growth potential and the importance of meeting our needs for love and acceptance. In the 1960s, psychology began to recapture its initial interest in mental processes, as a result of the *cognitive revolution.* More recently, **cognitive neuroscience** has increased our understanding of the brain's role in mental activities. Today, *psychology* is defined as the *scientific study of behavior and mental processes.* Behavior is anything an organism does. Mental processes are the internal subjective experiences we infer from behavior, for example, perceptions, thoughts, and feelings.

1. The Greek philosopher _____ developed early theories about _____ and _____ , _____ and _____ , and _____ and _____ .

2. The historical roots of psychology include the fields of _____ and _____ .

3. The first psychological laboratory was founded in 1879 by Wilhelm _____ .

4. Some early psychologists included Ivan Pavlov, who pioneered the study of _____ ; the personality theorist _____ ; Jean Piaget, who studied _____ ; and _____ , author of an 1890 psychology textbook.

5. The first female president of the American Psychological Association was _____ . The first woman to receive a Ph.D. in psychology was _____ .

6. In its earliest years, psychology was defined as the science of _____ life. From the 1920s into the 1960s, psychology in America was redefined as the science of _____ behavior. This second major force in psychology's history was _____ .

7. As a response to Freudian psychology and to _____ , which they considered

too limiting, pioneers _____ and _____ forged _____ psychology, which emphasized ways that a _____ environment can enhance personal _____ .

8. During the 1960s, psychology underwent a _____ revolution as it began to recapture interest in _____ processes. The study of the brain processes underlying thought is called _____ .

9. Today, we define psychology as the scientific study of _____ and _____ processes.

APPLICATION: Dharma has to write a term paper on the history of psychology. As part of her paper, she notes that "psychology has been defined in various ways depending on the researchers' perspective, but today it is generally defined as the 'scientific study of behavior and mental processes.'"

10. In identifying the different definitions, Dharma explains that Wilhelm Wundt would have omitted the phrase "_____ _____ " from the definition.

11. In concluding her paper, Dharma recaps by saying that
   a. psychology began as the science of mental life.
   b. from the 1920s into the 1960s, psychology was defined as the scientific study of observable behavior.
   c. contemporary psychologists study both overt behavior and covert thoughts.
   d. all of these statements are true.

Objective 2: Describe psychology's current perspectives, and identify some of its subfields.

Psychology's varied perspectives complement one another. The *neuroscience perspective* studies how the body and brain work to create emotions, memories, and sensory experiences. The *evolutionary perspective* considers how evolution influences behavior tendencies. The *behavior genetics perspective* considers how heredity and experience influence our individual differences. The *psychodynamic perspective* views behavior as springing from unconscious drives and conflicts. The *behavioral perspective* examines how observable responses are acquired and changed. The *cognitive perspective* studies how we encode, process, store, and retrieve information. The *social-cultural perspective* examines how behavior and thinking vary with the situation and culture.

Psychologists work in a variety of fields. *Biological psychologists* explore the link between brain and behavior; *developmental psychologists* study our changing abilities from womb to tomb; *personality psychologists* investigate our persistant traits; *industrial-organizational psychologists* study and advise on behavior in the workplace; *counseling psychologists* assist people with problems in living and in achieving greater well-being; *clinical psychologists* study, assess, and treat people with psychological disorders; and *social psychologists* explore how we view and affect one another.

....

STUDY TIP: This section describes a number of perspectives in psychology. Keep in mind that each perspective is nothing more than how certain psychologists feel behavior and mental processes should be investigated. For example, a clinical psychologist could approach the study of abnormal behavior from any of the perspectives discussed. Typically, however, psychologists work from a combination of perspectives rather than exclusively from only one. To deepen your understanding of the various perspectives, review the following chart. In the first column are listed psychology's contemporary perspectives. In the second column are listed historical roots and the pioneers who contributed to each modern-day perspective and the subfield that derives from it. As you work through the chapters, you might want to annotate this chart to include what you know about these psychologists.

Perspective	Historical Roots and Pioneers
Neuroscience	Aristotle (perception, emotion), Wundt
Evolutionary	Darwin, Freud
Behavior Genetics	Darwin
Psychodynamic	Aristotle (personality), Freud
Behavioral	Aristotle (learning), Pavlov, Watson, Skinner
Cognitive	Aristotle (memory), Wundt (quantifying mental processes), Piaget
Social-Cultural	Piaget, Rogers, Maslow

APPLICATION:

12. Match each psychological perspective and subfield with its definition or description.

Perspective or Subfield

_e_	1. neuroscience perspective
_b_	2. social-cultural perspective
_I_	3. psychiatry
_J_	4. clinical psychology
_M_	5. behavior genetics perspective
_d_	6. behavioral perspective
_a_	7. industrial-organizational psychology
_f_	8. cognitive perspective
_L_	9. personality psychology
_c_	10. developmental psychology
	11. evolutionary perspective
	12. psychodynamic perspective
_g_	13. counseling psychology
_n_	14. social psychology

Definitions or Descriptions

a. the study of behavior in the workplace

b. how people differ as products of different environments

c. the study of how people change over the life span

d. the mechanisms by which observable responses are acquired and changed

e. how the body and brain create emotions, memories, and sensations

f. how the mind encodes, processes, stores, and retrieves information

g. helping people to cope with personal and career chellenges

h. how natural selection favors traits that promote the perpetuation of one's genes

i. the study, assessment, and treatment of troubled people

j. the medical treatment of psychological disorders

k. the disguised effects of unfulfilled wishes and childhood traumas

l. the analysis of people's persistent traits

m. how much genes and environment contribute to individual differences

n. how people affect one another

Four Big Ideas in Psychology

Objective 3: Identify four big ideas that run throughout psychology.

The four big ideas that run through psychology, and thus this text, are the following.
- *Critical thinking* is smart thinking. Critical thinkers do not blindly accept arguments and conclusions. They examine assumptions, uncover hidden values, weigh evidence, and assess conclusions.
- Behavior is a *biopsychosocial* event. To understand behavior, we need several levels of analysis—biological, psychological, and social-*cultural*. The *nature-nurture issue*—the relative contributions of biology and environment—is a major issue.
- We operate with a two-track mind (*dual processing*)—that is, information is processed both consciously and unconsciously.
- Psychology explores human strengths as well as challenges. The scientific study of human strengths is called *positive psychology*.

1. Psychology's first big idea is that _critical thinking_ is smart thinking. This means that this type of thinker examines _assumptions_, uncovers hidden _values_, weighs _evidence_, and tests _conclusions_.

2. Each person is a complex _____ that is part of a larger _____ _____ and at the same time composed of smaller systems. For this reason, psychologists work from three main _____ of _____— biological, _____, and _____-_____— which together form an integrated _____ approach to the study of behavior and mental processes.

3. Culture refers to the _____ _____, _____, _____, and _____ shared by a large group of people that one generation passes on to the next.

4. The nature-nurture issue is the controversy over the relative contributions of _____ and _____ .

STUDY TIP: The nature-nurture issue is psychology's biggest and most persistent debate. Psychologists explore the issue by asking, for example, how differences in intelligence, personality, and psychological disorders are influenced by heredity and by environment. Today, contemporary science recognizes that *nurture works on what nature endows.* Our species is biologically endowed with an enormous capacity to learn and to adapt. Moreover, every *psychological event is simultaneously a biological event.*

• •

5. Psychology's third big idea is that that information is often processed simultaneously on separate _____ and _____ tracks. This principle is called _____ _____ .

6. Psychology's fourth big idea is that psychology explores human _____ and _____ .

7. The scientific study of positive _____ , positive _____ traits, and positive _____ , communities, and cultures is called _____ _____ .

Why Do Psychology?

Objective 4: Explain how hindsight bias and overconfidence can make research findings seem like mere common sense.

The **hindsight bias,** also known as the *I-knew-it-all-along phenomenon,* is the tendency to believe, after learning an outcome, that one would have foreseen it. Finding out that something has happened makes it seem inevitable. Thus, after learning the results of a study in psychology, it may seem to be obvious common sense. However, experiments have found that events seem far less obvious and predictable beforehand than in hindsight. Sometimes psychological findings even jolt our common sense.

Our everyday thinking is also limited by our tendency to think we know more than we do. Asked how sure we are of our answers to factual questions, we tend to be more confident than correct. Students' predictions of their future behaviors are similarly *overconfident.*

1. Although human _____ is important, research shows that our gut feelings lead us astray.

2. The tendency to perceive an outcome that has occurred as being obvious and predictable is called the _____ _____ . This phenomenon is _____ (rare/common).

3. Because it is _____ (after the fact/usually wrong), this tendency makes research findings seem like mere common sense.

4. Our everyday thinking is also limited by _____ in what we think we know.

5. Most people are _____ (better/worse/equally wrong) in predicting their social behavior.

Objective 5: Explain how the three key elements of the scientific attitude make scientific inquiry so useful.

The scientific attitude reflects a hard-headed *curiosity* to explore and understand the world without being fooled by it. The eagerness to *skeptically* scrutinize competing claims requires *humility* because it means we may have to reject our own ideas. This attitude, coupled with scientific principles for sifting reality from fantasy, helps us separate sense from nonsense, and thus makes modern science possible.

6. The scientific approach is characterized by the attitudes of _____ , _____ , and _____ .

APPLICATION:

7. In psychology, the motto that "the rat is always right" expresses a humble attitude. Explain.

_____

_____

_____

How Do Psychologists Ask and Answer Questions?

Objective 6: Describe how psychological theories guide scientific research.

A useful *theory* effectively organizes a wide range of observations and implies testable predictions, called *hypotheses.* By enabling us to test and reject or revise a particular theory, such predictions give direction to research. They specify in advance what results would support the theory and what results would disconfirm it. As a check on their biases, psychologists report their results precisely with clear *operational definitions* of concepts. Such statements of the procedures used to define research variables allow others to *replicate,* or repeat, their observations. Often, research leads to a revised theory that better organizes and predicts observable behaviors or events.

1. Psychologists use the _____ _____ to guide their study of behavior and mental processes.

2. An explanation using an integrated set of principles that organizes observations and predicts behaviors or events is a _____ . Testable predictions that allow a scientist to evaluate a theory are called _____ . These predictions give direction to _____ .

3. To prevent theoretical biases from influencing scientific observations, research must be reported precisely—using clear _____
_____ of all concepts—so that
others can _____ the findings.

4. The test of a useful theory is the extent to which it
effectively _____ a range of obser-
vations and leads to clear _____ .
A good theory also often leads to new
_____ and a revised theory.

5. Psychologists conduct research using

_____ , _____ ,
and _____ .

Objective 7: Compare and contrast case studies, surveys,
and naturalistic observation, and explain the importance
of random sampling.

The *case study* is the method by which psychologists
analyze one or more individuals in great depth in the
hope of revealing things true of us all. While individual
cases can suggest fruitful ideas, any given individual
may be atypical, making the case misleading.

The *survey* looks at many cases in less depth and
asks people to report their behavior or opinions. Asking
questions is tricky because even subtle changes in the
order or wording of questions can dramatically affect
responses. In everyday experience, we are tempted to
generalize from a few vivid but unrepresentative cases.
The survey ascertains the self-reported attitudes or
behaviors of a *population* by questioning a *representative,
random sample.*

Naturalistic observation consists of observing and
recording the behavior of organisms in their natural
environment. Like the case study and survey methods,
this research strategy describes behavior but does not
explain it.

6. The research strategy in which one or more individuals is studied in depth in order to reveal universal
principles of behavior is the

_____ _____ .

7. Although case studies can suggest directions for further study, a potential problem with this method is
that any given individual may be _____ .

8. The method in which a group of people is questioned about their attitudes or behavior is the

_____ .

9. An important factor in the validity of survey
research is the _____ of questions.

10. Surveys try to obtain a _____
sample, one that will be representative of the
_____ being studied. In such a
sample, every person _____
(does/does not) have a chance of being included.

11. Large, representative samples _____
(are/are not) better than small ones.

12. The research method in which people or animals are
directly observed in their natural environments is
called _____

_____ .

13. Case studies, surveys, and naturalistic observation
do not explain behavior; they simply
_____ it.

Objective 8: Describe positive and negative correlations,
and explain how correlational measures can aid the
process of prediction but not provide evidence of cause-
effect relationships.

When surveys and naturalistic observations reveal that
one trait or behavior accompanies another, we say the
two **correlate**. A *correlation coefficient* is a mathematical
measure of relationship. A *positive correlation* indicates a
direct relation-
ship, meaning
that two things
increase togeth-
er or decrease
together. A *nega-
tive correlation*
indicates an
inverse relationship: As one thing increases, the other
decreases. The correlation coefficient helps us to see the
world more clearly by revealing the extent to which two
things relate.

	Factor A	Factor B
Positive correlation	air temperature ↑ ↓	ice cream sales ↑ ↓
Negative correlation	TV viewing ↑ ↓	reading ↓ ↑

Perhaps the most irresistible thinking error is to
assume that correlation proves causation. Correlation
reveals how closely two things vary together and thus
how well one predicts the other. However, the fact that
events are correlated does not mean that one causes the
other. Thus, while correlation enables prediction, it does
not provide explanation.

• •
STUDY TIP: Many students find the concept of correlation
confusing. A common mistake is the belief that a negative correlation indicates a weak or absent relationship between two
variables. Remember that correlation does not prove causation; rather, it indicates the degree to which you can predict
changes in one variable from another. The *strength* of a correlation, indicated by a numerical value, is independent of the
direction (positive [+] or negative [–]) of the relationship. A
negative correlation simply means that two variables change in
opposite directions, such as when sales of hot chocolate
decrease as the average daily temperature increases.
• •

14. When changes in one factor are accompanied by
changes in another, the two factors are said to be

_____ , and one is thus able to
_____ the other. The statistical
expression of this relationship is called a

_____ _____ .

15. If two factors increase or decrease together, they are

    _____ _____ .

    If, however, one decreases as the other increases,

    they are _____ _____ .

    Another way to state the latter is that the two vari-

    ables relate _____ .

16. A negative correlation between two variables does

    not indicate the _____ or

    _____ of the relationship. Nor

    does correlation prove _____ ;

    rather, it merely indicates the possibility of a

    _____ - _____

    relationship.

17. A correlation between two events or behaviors

    means only that one event can be

    _____ from the other.

18. Because two events may both be caused by some

    other _____ , a correlation does

    not mean that one _____ the

    other. For this reason, correlation thus does not

    enable _____ .

Objective 9: Describe how people form illusory correlations, and explain the human tendency to perceive order
in random sequences.

Illusory correlation, the perception of a relationship where
none exists, often occurs because our belief that a relationship exists leads us to notice and recall confirming
instances of that belief. Because we are sensitive to
unusual events, we are especially likely to notice and
remember the occurrence of two such events in
sequence, even though those events are most likely *random.*

19. A perceived correlation that does not really exist is

    an _____

    _____ .

20. We are especially likely to remember a premonition

    of an unlikely phone call followed by that call, but in

    fact the two events occurring in sequence are

    _____ .

APPLICATIONS: Test your understanding of correlational
research by answering these questions.

21. If your level of test anxiety goes down as your time spent

    studying for the exam goes up, you would say these

    events are _____ (positively/negatively)

    correlated.

Explain your reasoning. _____

_____

_____

22. If eating saturated fat and the likelihood of contracting

    cancer are positively correlated, what could you say about

    the relationship between saturated fat and cancer? _____

    _____

    _____

23. Knowing that height and body weight are positively corre-

    lated means that as height increases, weight _____

    (increases/decreases).

24. Joe believes that his basketball game is always best when

    he wears his old gray athletic socks. Joe is a victim of the

    phenomenon called _____

    _____ .

Objective 10: Explain how experiments help researchers
isolate cause and effect, focusing on the characteristics
of experimentation that make this possible.

The *experiment* is a research method in which the investigator manipulates one or more factors to observe their
effect on some behavior or mental process while controlling other factors. If a behavior changes when we vary
an experimental factor, then we know the factor is having a causal effect.

In many experiments, control is achieved by *randomly assigning* people either to an *experimental group,* in
which they are exposed to the treatment, or a *control
group,* in which they are not exposed.

Often, the research participants are blind (unin-
formed) about what treatment, if any, they are receiving.
One group might receive the treatment, while the other
group receives a *placebo* (an inactive substance or condition). Often both the participant and the research assistant who collects the data will not know which group the
participant is in (the *double-blind procedure*). The *placebo
effect* is well-documented. Just thinking one is receiving
treatment can lead to symptom relief.

The *independent variable* is the experimental factor
that is being manipulated. It is the variable whose effect
is being studied. The *dependent variable* is the variable
that may change in response to the manipulations of the
independent variable. It is the outcome factor.

25. To isolate _____ and

    _____ , researchers have to sim-

    plify our complex world. They do this by using the

    _____ method.

26. Using this method, a researcher _____

    the factor of interest while _____

    _____ (controlling) other factors.

    By _____ assigning participants

to groups, researchers are able to hold
_____ all factors except the one
being investigated.

27. Research studies have found that breast-fed infants
_____ (do/do not) grow up with
higher intelligence scores than those of infants who
are bottle-fed with formula. Experiments such as
this must involve at least two groups: the
_____ group, who receive the
treatment (are breast-fed), and the
_____ group, who do not receive
the treatment (are bottle-fed).

28. To ensure that the two groups are identical, experimenters rely on the _____
_____ of individuals to the two
groups.

29. Researchers sometimes give certain participants an
inactive substance or treatment, called a
_____ , and compare their behav-
ior with that of participants who receive the actual
treatment. When merely thinking that one is receiving a treatment produces results, a

_____ _____

is said to occur.

30. When neither the participants nor the person collecting the data knows which condition a participant
is in, the researcher is making use of the

_____-_____

procedure.

STUDY TIP: Students often confuse *independent variables*
and *dependent variables*. Remember that independent variables are manipulated (controlled) directly by the researcher to
determine how they affect dependent variables. Dependent
variables are the behaviors and mental processes that psychologists are trying to understand. In a sense, dependent
variables *depend* on the actions of independent variables.
When you are struggling to distinguish two variables, ask
yourself, "Which of these two variables can affect the other?"
Consider, for example, a researcher investigating caffeine and
reaction time. After randomly assigning different students to
groups that drink a highly caffeinated drink and a weakly caffeinated drink, she measures each student's speed in pushing
a button in response to a signal light. Which variable is the
independent variable, and which is the dependent variable? If
the answer is not obvious, try the test question, "Which variable can affect the other?" Clearly, reaction time cannot affect
caffeine. So in this example, the dose of caffeine is the independent variable and reaction time is the dependent variable.

31. The factor that is being manipulated in an experiment is called the _____ variable.
The measurable factor that may change as a result
of these manipulations is called the
_____ variable.

32. The aim of an experiment is to _____
a(n) _____ variable,
_____ the _____
variable, and _____ all other
_____ .

Explain at least one advantage of the experiment as a
research method.

STUDY TIP/APPLICATIONS: The concepts of control
and operational definition are important in experimental
research. In an experiment, researchers strive to hold constant
(*control*) the possible effects of all variables on the dependent
variable, except the one that is being manipulated (independent variable). Operational definitions, which were explained
earlier, are like recipes for measuring a variable so that other
researchers can replicate your results. They are much more
precise than dictionary definitions. For example, the dictionary
might define intelligence as "the capacity to reason." Because
this definition is too vague for research purposes, a psychologist might create the operational definition of intelligence as "a
person's answers to a specific set of IQ test questions." Test
your understanding of these important concepts by completing the following exercises.

33. The concept of control is important in psychological
research because it allows researchers to study the influence of one or two _____ variables
on a _____ variable while holding
other potential influences _____ .

34. Martina believes that high doses of caffeine slow a person's reaction time. To test this belief, she has five friends
each drink three 8-ounce cups of coffee and then measures their reaction time on a learning task. What is
wrong with Martina's research strategy?
    a. No independent variable is specified.
    b. No dependent variable is specified.
    c. There is no control group.
    d. There is no provision for replication of the findings.

35. How would you operationally define the following variables?

    Exercise:

    Anger:

    Stress:

Frequently Asked Questions About Psychology

Objective 11: Explain the value of simplified laboratory conditions in discovering general principles of behavior.

The experimenter intends the laboratory experiment to be a simplified reality, one in which important features can be simulated and controlled. The experiment's purpose is not to re-create the exact behaviors of everyday life but to test theoretical principles. It is the resulting principles—not the specific findings—that help explain everyday behavior.

1. In laboratory experiments, psychologists' concern is not with specific behaviors but with the underlying theoretical _____ .

2. Psychologists conduct experiments on simplified behaviors in a laboratory environment in order to gain _____ over the many variables present in the "real world." In doing so, they are able to test general _____ of behavior that also operate in the real world.

Objective 12: Explain why psychologists study animals, and discuss the ethics of experimentation with both animals and humans.

Some psychologists study animals out of an interest in animal behaviors. Others do so because knowledge of the physiological and psychological processes of animals enables them to better understand the similar processes that operate in humans.

Because psychologists follow ethical and legal guidelines, animals used in psychological experiments rarely experience pain. The debate between animal protection organizations and researchers has raised two important issues: Is it right to place the well-being of humans above that of animals, and what safeguards are in place to protect the well-being of animals in research? Many professional organizations and funding agencies have developed extensive guidelines for the humane use of animals.

Ethical principles for the treatment of human participants urge investigators to obtain informed consent, protect participants from harm and discomfort, treat information about individuals confidentially, and fully explain the research afterward.

3. Many psychologists study animals because they are fascinating. More important, they study animals because of the _____ (similarities/differences) between humans and other animals. These studies have led to treatments for human _____ and to a better understanding of human functioning.

4. Some people question whether experiments with animals are _____ . They wonder whether it is right to place the _____ of humans over those of animals.

5. Opposition to animal experimentation also raises the question of what _____ should protect the well-being of animals.

Describe the goals of the ethical guidelines for psychological research.

Objective 13: Describe how personal values can influence psychologists' research and its application, and discuss psychology's potential to manipulate people.

Psychologists' values can influence their choice of research topic, their theories and observations, their labels for behavior, and their professional advice.

Knowledge is power that can be used for good or evil. Applications of psychology's principles have so far been mostly for the good, and psychology addresses some of humanity's greatest problems and deepest longings.

6. Psychologists' values _____ (do/do not) influence their theories, observations, and professional advice.

7. Although psychology _____ (can/cannot) be used to manipulate people, its purpose is to _____ .

(Close-Up) How to Be a Better Student

To master information, you must actively process it. People learn and remember material best when they put it in their own words, rehearse it, and then review and rehearse it again. An acronym for Survey, Question, Read, Rehearse, and Review, *SQ3R* is a study method that encourages active processing of new information.

Objective 14: Describe several effective study techniques.

1. In order to master any subject, you must _____ process it.

2. The _____ study method incorporates five steps: **a.** _____ , **b.** _____ , **c.** _____ , **d.** _____ , and **e.** _____ .

List five more study tips identified in the text.

a. _____

b. _____

c. _____

d. _____

e. _____

PROGRESS TEST

Multiple-Choice Questions

Circle your answers to the following questions and check them with the answers beginning on page 15. If your answer is incorrect, read the explanation for why it is incorrect and then consult the text.

1. In its earliest days, *psychology* was defined as the
   a. science of mental life.
   b. study of conscious and unconscious activity.
   c. scientific study of observable behavior.
   d. scientific study of behavior and mental processes.

2. Who would be most likely to agree with the statement, "Psychology should investigate only behaviors that can be observed"?
   a. Wilhelm Wundt
   b. Sigmund Freud
   c. John B. Watson
   d. William James

3. Today, *psychology* is defined as the
   a. scientific study of mental phenomena.
   b. scientific study of conscious and unconscious activity.
   c. scientific study of behavior.
   d. scientific study of behavior and mental processes.

4. Who wrote an early psychology textbook?
   a. Wilhelm Wundt   c. Jean Piaget
   b. Ivan Pavlov   d. William James

5. Psychologists who study the degree to which genes influence our personality are working from the _____ perspective.
   a. behavioral   c. behavior genetics
   b. evolutionary   d. neuroscience

6. Which of the following best describes the issue of the relative importance of nature and nurture on our behavior?
   a. the issue of the relative influence of biology and experience on behavior
   b. the issue of the relative influence of rewards and punishments on behavior
   c. the debate as to the relative importance of heredity and instinct in determining behavior

   d. the debate as to whether mental processes are a legitimate area of scientific study

7. Raoul is a psychologist studying the brain's role in human emotions. Which psychological perspective is he working from?
   a. neuroscience
   b. cognitive
   c. behavioral
   d. behavior genetics

8. A psychologist who explores how Asian and North American definitions of attractiveness differ is working from the _____ perspective.
   a. behavioral   c. cognitive
   b. evolutionary   d. social-cultural

9. Manuel has had several anxiety attacks over the last month. Which type of psychologist would treat Manuel?
   a. counseling psychologist
   b. personality psychologist
   c. clinical psychologist
   d. psychiatrist

10. After detailed study of a gunshot wound victim, a psychologist concludes that the brain region destroyed is likely to be important for memory functions. Which type of research did the psychologist use to deduce this?
    a. the case study   c. correlation
    b. a survey   d. experimentation

11. In an experiment to determine the effects of loud noise on studying, the loud noise is the
    a. control condition.
    b. intervening variable.
    c. independent variable.
    d. dependent variable.

12. To determine the effects of a new drug on memory, researchers give one group of people a pill that contains the drug. A second group is given a pill that does not contain the drug. This second group constitutes the
    a. random sample.   c. control group.
    b. experimental group. d. test group.

13. *Theories* are defined as
    a. testable propositions.
    b. factors that may change in response to manipulation.
    c. statements of the procedures used to describe research variables.
    d. principles that help to organize, predict, and explain facts.

14. A psychologist studies the play behavior of third-grade children by watching groups during recess at school. Which type of research is she using?
    a. correlation
    b. case study
    c. experimentation
    d. naturalistic observation

15. To ensure that other researchers can repeat their work, psychologists use
    a. control groups.
    b. random assignment.
    c. double-blind procedures.
    d. operational definitions.

16. The scientific attitude of skepticism is based on the belief that
    a. people are rarely candid in revealing their thoughts.
    b. mental processes can't be studied objectively.
    c. the scientist's intuition about behavior is usually correct.
    d. ideas need to be tested against observable evidence.

17. Psychologists' personal values
    a. have little influence on how their experiments are conducted.
    b. do not influence the interpretation of experimental results because of the use of statistical techniques that guard against subjective bias.
    c. can bias both scientific observation and interpretation of data.
    d. have little influence on investigative methods but a significant effect on interpretation.

18. If shoe size and IQ are negatively correlated, which of the following is true?
    a. People with large feet tend to have high IQs.
    b. People with small feet tend to have high IQs.
    c. People with small feet tend to have low IQs.
    d. IQ is unpredictable based on a person's shoe size.

19. Which of the following would be best for determining whether alcohol impairs memory?
    a. case study   c. survey
    b. naturalistic observation   d. experiment

20. Well-done surveys measure attitudes in a representative subset, or _____ , of an entire group, or _____ .
    a. population; random sample
    b. control group; experimental group
    c. experimental group; control group
    d. random sample; population

21. The first psychology laboratory was established by _____ in the year _____ .
    a. Wundt; 1879   c. Freud; 1900
    b. James; 1890   d. Watson; 1913

22. Who would be most likely to agree with the statement, "Psychology is the science of mental life"?
    a. Wilhelm Wundt
    b. John Watson
    c. Ivan Pavlov
    d. virtually any American psychologist during the 1960s

23. In psychology, *behavior* is best defined as
    a. anything a person says, does, or feels.
    b. any action we can observe and record.
    c. any action, whether observable or not.
    d. anything we can infer from a person's actions.

24. Carl Rogers and Abraham Maslow are most closely associated with
    a. cognitive psychology.
    b. behaviorism.
    c. psychodynamic theory.
    d. humanistic psychology.

25. Two historical roots of psychology are the disciplines of
    a. philosophy and chemistry.
    b. physiology and chemistry.
    c. philosophy and biology.
    d. philosophy and physics.

26. A teacher was interested in knowing whether her students' test performance could be predicted from their proximity to the front of the classroom. So she matched her students' scores on a math test with their seating position. This is an example of
    a. experimentation.
    b. correlational research.
    c. a survey.
    d. naturalistic observation.

27. The way the mind encodes, processes, stores, and retrieves information is the primary concern of the _____ perspective.
    a. neuroscience   c. social-cultural
    b. evolutionary   d. cognitive

28. Of the following, who is also a physician?
    a. clinical psychologist
    b. experimental psychologist
    c. psychiatrist
    d. biological psychologist

29. Dr. Jones is researching the relationship between changes in our thinking over the life span and changes in moral reasoning. He is most likely a
    a. clinical psychologist.
    b. personality psychologist.
    c. psychiatrist.
    d. developmental psychologist.

30. Which psychologist is most directly concerned with suggesting ways to improve worker productivity in a computer factory?
    a. clinical psychologist
    b. personality psychologist
    c. industrial-organizational psychologist
    d. psychiatrist

31. Dr. Ernst explains behavior in terms of different situations. Dr. Ernst is working from the _____ perspective.
    a. behavioral   c. social-cultural
    b. evolutionary   d. cognitive

32. Which perspective emphasizes the learning of observable responses?
    a. behavioral
    b. social-cultural
    c. neuroscience
    d. cognitive

33. The biopsychosocial approach emphasizes the importance of
    a. different levels of analysis in exploring behavior and mental processes.
    b. observable behavior over mental processes.
    c. the environment over heredity.
    d. having a single academic perspective to guide research.

34. To prevent the possibility that a placebo effect or researchers' expectations will influence a study's results, scientists use
    a. control groups.
    b. experimental groups.
    c. random assignment.
    d. the double-blind procedure.

35. In an experiment to determine the effects of attention on memory, memory is the
    a. control condition.
    b. intervening variable.
    c. independent variable.
    d. dependent variable.

36. Which of the following *best* describes hindsight bias?
    a. Events seem more predictable before they have occurred.
    b. Events seem more predictable after they have occurred.
    c. A person's intuition is usually correct.
    d. A person's intuition is usually not correct.

37. The procedure designed to ensure that the experimental and control groups do not differ in any way that might affect the experiment's results is called
    a. variable controlling.
    b. random assignment.
    c. representative sampling.
    d. stratification.

38. Illusory correlation refers to
    a. the perception that two negatively correlated variables are positively correlated.
    b. the perception of a nonexistent correlation.
    c. an insignificant correlation.
    d. a correlation that equals –1.0.

39. Which type of research would allow you to determine whether students' college grades accurately predict later income?
    a. case study
    b. naturalistic observation
    c. experimentation
    d. correlation

40. In a test of the effects of air pollution, groups of students performed a reaction time task in a polluted or an unpolluted room. To what condition were students in the unpolluted room exposed?
    a. experimental
    b. control
    c. randomly assigned
    d. dependent

41. To study the effects of lighting on mood, Dr. Cooper had students fill out questionnaires in brightly lit or dimly lit rooms. In this study, the independent variable consisted of
    a. the number of students assigned to each group.
    b. the students' responses to the questionnaire.
    c. the room lighting.
    d. the subject matter of the questions asked.

42. You decide to test your belief that men drink more soft drinks than women by finding out whether more soft drinks are consumed per day in the men's dorm than in the women's dorm. Your belief is a(n) _____ , and your research prediction is a(n) _____ .
    a. hypothesis; theory
    b. theory; hypothesis
    c. independent variable; dependent variable
    d. dependent variable; independent variable

43. To examine assumptions, discern hidden values, evaluate evidence, and assess conclusions is to
    a. conduct a survey.
    b. develop a theory.
    c. experiment.
    d. think critically.

44. Which of the following procedures is an example of the use of a placebo?
    a. In a test of the effects of a drug on memory, a participant is led to believe that a harmless pill actually contains an active drug.
    b. A participant in an experiment is led to believe that a pill, which actually contains an active drug, is harmless.
    c. Participants in an experiment are not told which treatment condition is in effect.
    d. Neither the participants nor the experimenter knows which treatment condition is in effect.

45. The psychologist who has called for a more positive psychology is
    a. William James.
    b. Martin Seligman.
    c. B. F. Skinner.
    d. Sigmund Freud.

46. A major principle underlying the SQ3R study method is that
    a. people learn and remember material best when they actively process it.
    b. many students overestimate their mastery of text and lecture material.
    c. study time should be spaced over time rather than crammed into one session.
    d. overlearning disrupts efficient retention.

47. To say that we operate with a two-track mind means that we
    a. can think of several things at once.
    b. process information at conscious and unconscious levels.
    c. think both objectively and subjectively.
    d. examine assumptions and assess conclusions.

Matching Items

Match each term with its definition or description.

Terms

_____ **1.** hypothesis
_____ **2.** theory
_____ **3.** independent variable
_____ **4.** dependent variable
_____ **5.** experimental group
_____ **6.** control group
_____ **7.** case study
_____ **8.** survey
_____ **9.** replication
_____ **10.** random assignment
_____ **11.** experiment
_____ **12.** double-blind
_____ **13.** culture

Definitions or Descriptions

a. an in-depth observational study of one person
b. the variable being manipulated in an experiment
c. the variable being measured in an experiment
d. the "treatment-absent" group in an experiment
e. testable proposition
f. repeating an experiment to see whether the same results are obtained
g. the process in which research participants are selected by chance for different groups in an experiment
h. an explanation using an integrated set of principles that organizes observations and predicts behavior
i. the research strategy in which the effects of one or more variables on behavior are tested
j. shared ideas and behaviors passed from one generation to the next
k. the "treatment-present" group in an experiment
l. the research strategy in which a representative sample of individuals is questioned
m. experimental procedure in which neither the research participant nor the experimenter knows which condition the participant is in

Application Essay

Elio has a theory that regular exercise can improve thinking. Help him design an experiment evaluating this theory. (Use the space below to list the points you want to make, and organize them. Then write the essay on a separate piece of paper.)

SUMMING UP

See the facing page.

TERMS AND CONCEPTS

Using your own words, on a separate piece of paper write a brief definition or explanation of each of the following.

1. behaviorism
2. humanistic psychology
3. cognitive neuroscience
4. psychology
5. critical thinking
6. biopsychosocial approach
7. culture
8. nature-nurture issue
9. dual processing
10. positive psychology
11. hindsight bias
12. theory
13. hypothesis
14. operational definition
15. replication
16. case study
17. survey
18. random sample
19. naturalistic observation
20. correlation
21. illusory correlation
22. experiment
23. random assignment
24. experimental group
25. control group
26. placebo
27. double-blind procedure
28. placebo effect
29. independent variable
30. dependent variable
31. SQ3R

SUMMING UP

To study increased suicide rates among teenagers, a researcher develops a hypothesis that anxiety leads to depression, which may lead to suicidal behavior. She has a variety of research methods to choose from.

She can focus on one or two extreme situations to educate herself about depression among young people, a method called the
_____ _____ ,

which can

suggest _____ for further study,

but

the information generated may not be _____ of all young people.

The researcher could also conduct a _____ ,

interviewing _____ (a few/many) teenagers in _____ (more/less) depth, creating questions carefully to avoid _____ _____ .

Yet another alternative would be for the researcher to study teenagers at school or at play, a method called _____ _____ .

However, like the two other _____ methods described on this page, this method does not _____ behavior.

If the researcher finds that these traits occur together—as anxiety increases, so does depression—she can say that they are positively _____ .

To determine whether anxiety *causes* depression, the researcher conducts an _____ ,

randomly assigning participants to two groups,

teens who are exposed to an anxiety-arousing movie, the _____ group,

and

teens who see a romantic movie, the _____ group.

Both groups then take a test to measure depression.

In this study, the movie is the _____ variable, the variable that is manipulated,

in order to see the effect on

the teens' level of depression, which is the _____ variable.

ANSWERS

Chapter Review

Psychology's Roots

1. Aristotle; learning; memory; motivation; emotion; perception; personality
2. biology; philosophy
3. Wundt
4. learning; Sigmund Freud; children; William James
5. Mary Calkins; Margaret Floy Washburn
6. mental; observable; behaviorism
7. behaviorism; Carl Rogers; Abraham Maslow; humanistic; positive; growth
8. cognitive; mental; cognitive neuroscience
9. behavior; mental
10. Wundt would have omitted "behavior and." In performing the first experiment, Wundt was attempting to measure the fastest and simplest *mental processes.*
11. All of these statements about psychology's history are true, so **d.** is the answer.
12. Matching

1. e	**6.** d	**11.** h
2. b	**7.** a	**12.** k
3. j	**8.** f	**13.** g
4. i	**9.** l	**14.** n
5. m	**10.** c	

Four Big Ideas in Psychology

1. critical thinking; assumptions; values; evidence; conclusions
2. system; social system; levels; analysis; psychological; social-cultural; biopsychosocial
3. enduring behaviors; attitudes; ideas; traditions
4. genes; experience
5. conscious; unconscious; dual processing
6. strengths; challenges
7. emotions; character; groups; positive psychology

Why Do Psychology?

1. intuition
2. hindsight bias; common
3. after the fact
4. overconfidence
5. equally wrong
6. curiosity; skepticism; humility
7. This expression suggests that if research does not support our predictions, we must revise our predictions and do more research. "The rat [the research subject in many experiments] is always right [it tells us so]."

How Do Psychologists Ask and Answer Questions?

1. scientific method
2. theory; hypotheses; research
3. operational definitions; replicate
4. organizes; predictions; research
5. description; correlation; experimentation
6. case study
7. atypical
8. survey
9. wording
10. random; population; does
11. are
12. naturalistic observation
13. describe
14. correlated; predict; correlation coefficient
15. positively correlated; negatively correlated; inversely
16. strength; weakness; causation; cause-effect
17. predicted
18. event; caused; explanation
19. illusory correlation
20. random
21. negatively. This is an example of a negative correlation. As one factor (time spent studying) increases, the other factor (anxiety level) decreases.
22. A positive correlation simply means that two factors tend to increase or decrease together; so the more saturated fat you eat, the more likely you are to contract cancer. However, eating saturated fat doesn't necessarily cause cancer; other factors may be involved.
23. increases. If height and weight are positively correlated, increased height is associated with increased weight. Thus, one can predict a person's weight from his or her height.
24. illusory correlation. It is a correlation that is perceived but doesn't actually exist, as in Joe's belief that he plays better when he wears these socks.
25. cause; effect; experimental
26. manipulates; holding constant; randomly; constant
27. do; experimental; control
28. random assignment
29. placebo; placebo effect
30. double-blind
31. independent; dependent
32. manipulate; independent; measure; dependent; control; variables

Experimentation has the advantage of increasing the investigator's control of both relevant and irrelevant variables that might influence behavior. Experiments also permit the investigator to go beyond observation and description to uncover cause-effect relationships in behavior.

33. independent; dependent; constant. By being able to control the variables and hold other possible factors constant, the experimenter is able to demonstrate cause and effect, rather than simply describe the situation.

34. **c.** is the answer. To determine the effects of caffeine on reaction time, Martina needs to measure reaction time in a control, or comparison, group that does not receive caffeine. Note that caffeine is the independent variable, and reaction time is the dependent variable.

35. Some possible operational definitions would be:

    Exercise: Jogging 30 minutes at a pace of 9 minutes per mile.

    Anger: Observable attack behavior, such as hitting someone.

    Stress: Number of negative life events.

Frequently Asked Questions About Psychology

1. principles
2. control; principles
3. similarities; diseases
4. ethical; well-being
5. safeguards

Ethical guidelines require investigators to (1) obtain informed consent of potential participants, (2) protect them from harm and discomfort, (3) treat information about participants confidentially, and (4) fully explain the research afterward.

6. do
7. can; enlighten

(Close-Up) How to Be a Better Student

1. actively
2. SQ3R; a. survey; b. question; c. read; d. rehearse; e. review
   a. Distribute study time.
   b. Learn to think critically.
   c. In class, listen actively.
   d. Overlearn.
   e. Be a smart test-taker.

Progress Test

Multiple-Choice Questions

1. **a.** is the answer.
   b. Psychology has never been defined in terms of conscious and unconscious activity.
   c. From the 1920s into the 1960s, psychology was defined as the scientific study of observable behavior.
   d. *Psychology* today is defined as the scientific study of behavior and mental processes. In its earliest days, however, psychology focused exclusively on mental phenomena.

2. **c.** is the answer.
   a. Wilhelm Wundt, the founder of the first psychology laboratory, was seeking to measure the simplest mental processes.
   b. Sigmund Freud developed an influential theory of personality that focused on unconscious processes.

   d. William James, author of an 1890 textbook, was a philosopher and was more interested in mental phenomena than observable behavior.

3. **d.** is the answer.
   a. In its earliest days, psychology was defined as the science of mental phenomena.
   b. Psychology has never been defined in terms of conscious and unconscious activity.
   c. From the 1920s into the 1960s, psychology was defined as the scientific study of behavior.

4. **d.** is the answer.
   a. Wilhelm Wundt founded the first psychology laboratory.
   b. Ivan Pavlov pioneered the study of learning.
   c. Jean Piaget was this century's most influential observer of children.

5. **c.** is the answer.

6. **a.** is the answer. Biology and experience are internal and external influences, respectively.
   b. Rewards and punishments are both external influences on behavior.
   c. Heredity and instinct are both internal influences on behavior.
   d. The legitimacy of the study of mental processes does not relate to the internal/external issue.

7. **a.** is the answer.
   b. The cognitive perspective would be concerned with how information was encoded, processed, stored, and retrieved.
   c. The behavioral perspective studies the mechanisms by which observable responses are acquired and changed.
   d. The behavior genetics perspective focuses on the relative contributions of genes and environment to individual differences.

8. **d.** is the answer.
   a. Behavioral psychologists investigate how learned behaviors are acquired. They generally do not focus on subjective opinions, such as attractiveness.
   b. The evolutionary perspective studies how natural selection favors traits that promote the perpetuation of one's genes.
   c. Cognitive psychologists study the mechanisms of thinking and memory, and generally do not investigate attitudes. Also, because the question specifies that the psychologist is interested in comparing two cultures, d. is the best answer.

9. **c.** is the answer.
   a. Counseling psychologists help people cope with personal and vocational challenges.
   b. Personality psychologists study people's traits.
   d. Psychiatrists are medical doctors who can prescribe drugs.

10. **a.** is the answer. In a case study, one person is studied in depth.
    b. In survey research, a group of people is interviewed.
    c. Correlations identify whether two factors are related.
    d. In an experiment, an investigator manipulates one variable to observe its effect on another.

11. **c.** is the answer. The loud noise is the variable being manipulated in the experiment.
    a. A control condition for this experiment would be a group of people studying in a quiet room.
    b. An intervening variable is a variable other than those being manipulated that may influence behavior.
    d. The dependent variable is the behavior measured by the experimenter—in this case, the effects of loud noise.

12. **c.** is the answer. The control group is the group for which the experimental treatment (the new drug) is absent.
    a. A random sample is a subset of a population in which every person has an equal chance of being selected.
    b. The experimental group is the group for which the experimental treatment (the drug) is present.
    d. "Test group" is an ambiguous term; both the experimental and control group are tested.

13. **d.** is the answer.
    a. Hypotheses are testable propositions.
    b. Dependent variables are factors that may change in response to manipulated independent variables.
    c. This refers to an operational definition.

14. **d.** is the answer.

15. **d.** is the answer.

16. **d.** is the answer.

17. **c.** is the answer.
    a., b., & d. Psychologists' personal values can influence all of these.

18. **b.** is the answer.
    a. & c. These answers would have been correct had the question stated that there is a *positive* correlation between shoe size and IQ. Actually, there is probably no correlation at all!

19. **d.** is the answer. In an experiment, it would be possible to manipulate alcohol consumption and observe the effects, if any, on memory.
    a., b., & c. These answers are incorrect because only by directly controlling the variables of interest can a researcher uncover cause-effect relationships.

20. **d.** is the answer.
    a. A sample is a subset of a population.
    b. & c. Control and experimental groups are used in experimentation, not in survey research.

21. **a.** is the answer.

22. **a.** is the answer.
    b. & d. John Watson, like many American psychologists during this time, believed that psychology should focus on the study of observable behavior.
    c. Because he pioneered the study of learning, Pavlov focused on observable behavior and would certainly have *disagreed* with this statement.

23. **a.** is the answer.

24. **d.** is the answer.

25. **c.** is the answer.

26. **b.** is the answer.
    a. This is not an experiment because the teacher is not manipulating the independent variable (seating position); she is merely measuring whether variation in this factor predicts test performance.
    c. If the study were based entirely on students' self-reported responses, this would be a survey.
    d. This study goes beyond naturalistic observation, which merely describes behavior as it occurs, to determine if test scores can be predicted from students' seating position.

27. **d.** is the answer.
    a. The neuroscience perspective studies the biological bases for a range of psychological phenomena.
    b. The evolutionary perspective studies how natural selection favors traits that promote the perpetuation of one's genes.
    c. The social-cultural perspective is concerned with variations in behavior across situations and cultures.

28. **c.** is the answer. Psychiatrists are the only ones with medical degrees.

29. **d.** is the answer. The emphasis on change during the life span indicates that Dr. Jones is most likely a developmental psychologist.
    a. Clinical psychologists study, assess, and treat people who are psychologically troubled.
    b. Personality psychologists study our traits.
    c. Psychiatrists are medical doctors.

30. **c.** is the answer.
    a. Clinical psychologists study, assess, and treat people with psychological disorders.
    b. & d. Personality psychologists and psychiatrists do not usually study people in work situations.

31. **c.** is the answer.
    a. Psychologists who follow the behavioral perspective emphasize observable, external influences on behavior.
    b. The evolutionary perspective focuses on how natural selection favors traits that promote the perpetuation of one's genes.
    d. The cognitive perspective places emphasis on conscious, rather than unconscious, processes.

32. **a.** is the answer.

33. **a.** is the answer.
    b. & c. The biopsychosocial approach has nothing to do with the relative importance of basic research and applied research and is equally applicable to both.
    d. On the contrary, the biopsychosocial approach is based on the idea that single academic perspectives are often limited.

34. **d.** is the answer.
    a. & b. The double-blind procedure is one way to create experimental and control groups.
    c. Research participants are randomly assigned to either an experimental or a control group.

35. **d.** is the answer.
    a. The control condition is the comparison group, in which the experimental treatment (the treatment of interest) is absent.
    b. There is no such term as "intervening variable."

c. Attention is the independent variable, which is being manipulated.

36. **b.** is the answer.
    a. The phenomenon is related to hindsight rather than foresight.
    c. & d. The phenomenon doesn't involve whether or not the intuitions are correct but rather people's attitude that they had the correct intuition.

37. **b.** is the answer. If enough participants are used in an experiment and they are randomly assigned to the two groups, any differences that emerge between the groups should stem from the experiment itself.
    a., c., & d. None of these terms describes precautions taken in setting up groups for experiments.

38. **b.** is the answer.

39. **d.** is the answer. Correlations show how well one factor can be predicted from another.
    a. Because a case study focuses in great detail on the behavior of an individual, it's probably not useful in showing whether predictions are possible.
    b. Naturalistic observation is a method of describing, rather than predicting, behavior.
    c. In experimental research, the effects of manipulated independent variables on dependent variables are measured. It is not clear how an experiment could help determine whether college grades predict later income.

40. **b.** is the answer. The control condition is the one in which the treatment—in this case, pollution—is absent.
    a. Students in the polluted room would be in the experimental condition.
    c. Presumably, all students in both conditions were randomly assigned to their groups. Random assignment is a method for establishing groups, rather than a condition.
    d. The word *dependent* refers to a kind of variable in experiments; conditions are either experimental or control.

41. **c.** is the answer. The lighting is the factor being manipulated.
    a. & d. These answers are incorrect because they involve aspects of the experiment other than the variables.
    b. This answer is the dependent, not the independent, variable.

42. **b.** is the answer. A general belief such as this one is a theory; it helps organize, explain, and generate testable predictions (called hypotheses) such as "men drink more soft drinks than women."
    c. & d. Independent and dependent variables are experimental treatments and behaviors, respectively. Beliefs and predictions may involve such variables, but are not themselves those variables.

43. **d.** is the answer.

44. **a.** is the answer.
    b. Use of a placebo tests whether the behavior of a research participant, who mistakenly believes that a treatment (such as a drug) is in effect, is the same as it would be if the treatment were actually present.
    c. & d. These are examples of *blind* and *double-blind* control procedures.

45. **b.** is the answer.
    a. William James, author of an important 1890 textbook, was a philosopher and was more interested in mental phenomena than observable behavior.
    c. B. F. Skinner was a behaviorist who believed that only observable behavior could be studied scientifically.
    d. Sigmund Freud developed an influential theory of personality that focused on unconscious processes.

46. **a.** is the answer.
    b. & c. Although each of these is true, SQ3R is based on the more general principle of active learning.
    d. In fact, just the opposite is true.

47. **b.** is the answer.

Matching Items

1. e	**5.** k	**9.** f	**13.** j
2. h	**6.** d	**10.** g	
3. b	**7.** a	**11.** i	
4. c	**8.** l	**12.** m	

Application Essay

Elio's hypothesis is that daily aerobic exercise for one month will improve memory. Exercise is the independent variable. The dependent variable is memory. Exercise could be manipulated by having people in an experimental group jog for 30 minutes each day. Memory could be measured by comparing the number of words they recall from a test list studied before the exercise experiment begins, and again afterward. A control group that does not exercise is needed so that any improvement in the experimental group's memory can be attributed to exercise, and not to some other factor, such as the passage of one month's time or familiarity with the memory test. The control group should engage in some nonexercise activity for the same amount of time each day that the experimental group exercises. The participants should be randomly selected from the population at large, and then randomly assigned to the experimental and control groups.

Summing Up

To study increased suicide rates among teenagers, a researcher develops a hypothesis that anxiety leads to depression, which may lead to suicidal behavior. She has a variety of research methods to choose from.

She can focus on one or two extreme situations to educate herself about depression among young people, a method called the *case study*, which can suggest *hypotheses* for further study, but the information generated may not be *representative* of all young people.

The researcher could also conduct a *survey*, interviewing *many* teenagers in *less* depth, creating questions carefully to avoid *wording effects*.

Yet another alternative would be for the researcher to study teenagers at school or at play, a method called *naturalistic observation*. However, like the two other *descriptive* methods described on this page, this method does not *explain* behavior.

If the researcher finds that these traits occur together—as anxiety increases, so does depression—she can say that they are positively *correlated*.

To determine whether anxiety *causes* depression, the researcher conducts an *experiment,* randomly assigning participants to two groups, teens who are exposed to an anxiety-arousing movie, the *experimental* group, and teens who see a romantic movie, the *control* group. Both groups then take a test to measure depression. In this study, the movie is the *independent* variable, the variable that is manipulated, in order to see the effect on the teens' level of depression, the *dependent* variable.

Terms and Concepts

1. **Behaviorism** is the view that psychology should focus only on the scientific study of observable behaviors without reference to mental phenomena.

2. **Humanistic psychology** is the branch of psychology that emphasizes the growth potential of healthy people.

3. **Cognitive neuroscience** is the study of how brain activity is linked with memory, language, and other forms of mental activity.

4. **Psychology** is the scientific study of behavior and mental processes.

5. **Critical thinking** is careful reasoning that examines assumptions, discerns hidden values, evaluates evidence, and assesses conclusions.

6. The **biopsychosocial approach** is an integrated approach that focuses on biological, psychological, and social-cultural levels of analysis for a given behavior or mental process.

7. **Culture** is the enduring behaviors, ideas, attitudes, and traditions shared by a large group of people and transmitted from one generation to the next.

8. The **nature-nurture issue** is the controversy over the relative contributions that genes (nature) and experience (nurture) make to the development of psychological traits and behaviors.

9. **Dual processing** is the principle that we often process information simultaneously on separate conscious and unconscious tracks.

10. **Positive psychology** is the scientific study of human strengths and virtues.

11. **Hindsight bias** refers to the tendency to believe, after learning an outcome, that one would have foreseen it; also called the *I-knew-it-all-along phenomenon*.

12. A **theory** is an explanation using an integrated set of principles that organizes observations and predicts behaviors or events.

13. A **hypothesis** is a testable prediction, often implied by a theory; testing the hypothesis helps scientists to test the theory.

    Example: In order to test his theory of why people conform, Solomon Asch formulated the testable **hypothesis** that an individual would be more likely to go along with the majority opinion of a large group than with that of a smaller group.

14. An **operational definition** is a precise statement of the procedures (operations) used to define research variables.

15. **Replication** is the process of repeating an experiment, often with different participants and in different situations, to see whether the basic finding generalizes to other people and circumstances.

16. The **case study** is an observation technique in which one person is studied in great depth, often with the intention of revealing universal principles.

17. The **survey** is a technique for ascertaining the self-reported attitudes or behaviors of a representative, random sample of people.

18. A **random sample** is one that is representative because every member of the population has an equal chance of being included.

19. **Naturalistic observation** involves observing and recording behavior in naturally occurring situations without trying to manipulate and control the situation.

20. **Correlation** is a measure of the extent to which two factors vary together, and thus of how well either factor predicts the other. The correlation coefficient is a statistical measure of the relationship; it can be positive or negative.

    Example: If there is a positive correlation between air temperature and ice cream sales, the warmer (higher) it is, the more ice cream is sold. If there is a negative correlation between air temperature and sales of cocoa, the cooler (lower) it is, the more cocoa is sold.

21. **Illusory correlation** is the perception of a relationship where none exists.

22. An **experiment** is a research method in which a researcher manipulates one or more factors (independent variables) in order to observe their effect on some behavior or mental process (the dependent variable); experiments therefore make it possible to establish cause-effect relationships.

23. **Random assignment** is the procedure of assigning participants to the experimental and control conditions by chance in order to minimize preexisting differences between those assigned to the different groups.

24. The **experimental group** of an experiment is the one that is exposed to the independent variable being studied.

Example: In the study of the effects of a new drug on reaction time, participants in the **experimental group** would actually receive the drug being tested.

25. The **control group** of an experiment is the one that is not exposed to the treatment of interest, or independent variable, so a comparison to the experimental condition can be made.

    Example: The **control group** for an experiment testing the effects of a new drug on reaction time would be a group of participants given a placebo (inactive drug or sugar pill) instead of the drug being tested.

26. **Placebos** are inert substances or conditions that are assumed to be active agents.

27. A **double-blind procedure** is an experimental procedure in which neither the experimenter nor the research participants are aware of which condition is in effect. It is used to prevent experimenters' and participants' expectations from influencing the results of an experiment.

28. The **placebo effect** occurs when the results of an experiment are caused by a participant's expectations about what is really going on.

29. The **independent variable** of an experiment is the factor being manipulated and tested by the investigator.

    Example: In the study of the effects of a new drug on reaction time, the drug is the **independent variable**.

30. The **dependent variable** of an experiment is the factor being measured by the investigator.

    Example: In the study of the effects of a new drug on reaction time, the participants' reaction time is the **dependent variable.**

31. **SQ3R** is a study method consisting of five steps: Survey, Question, Read, Rehearse, and Review.

2

THE BIOLOGY OF MIND AND CONSCIOUSNESS

Chapter 2 is concerned with the functions of the brain and its component neural systems, which provide the basis for all human behavior. Under the direction of the brain, the nervous and endocrine systems coordinate a variety of voluntary and involuntary behaviors and serve as the body's mechanisms for communication with the external environment. Consciousness—our awareness of ourselves and our environment—can be experienced in various states. Chapter 2 examines normal consciousness as well as sleep and dreaming,

CHAPTER REVIEW

First, skim each text section, noting headings and bold-face items. Review the section by reading the objectives and summaries provided here, then answer the questions that follow. In some cases, STUDY TIPS explain how best to learn a difficult concept and APPLICATIONS help you to know how well you understand the material. Check your understanding of the material by consulting the answers beginning on page 36. Do not continue with the next section until you understand each answer. If you need to, review or reread the section in the textbook before continuing.

Biology and Behavior

Objective 1: Explain why psychologists are concerned with human biology.

Everything psychological is simultaneously biological. We think, feel, and act with our bodies. By studying the links between biology and psychology, *biological psychologists* are gaining a better understanding of how our thinking and emotions can influence our brain and our health. This is key to the biopsychosocial approach.

1. In the most basic sense, every idea, mood, memory, and behavior that an individual has ever experienced is a _____ phenomenon.

2. Researchers who study the links between biology and behavior are called _____

    _____ .

••

STUDY TIP: Many students find the technical material in this chapter difficult to master. Not only are there many terms for you to remember, but you must also know the organization and function of the various divisions of the nervous system. Learning this material will require a great deal of rehearsal. Working the chapter review several times, drawing and labeling brain diagrams, making flash cards, and mentally reciting terms are all useful techniques for rehearsing this type of material.

••

APPLICATION:

3. Cite some possible areas a biological psychologist would be likely to study.

Neural Communication

Objective 2: Describe the parts of a neuron.

A *neuron* consists of a cell body and branching fibers: The *dendrite* fibers receive information from sensory receptors or other neurons and transmit it to the cell body, and the *axon* fibers pass that information along to other neurons.

1. Our body's neural system is built from billions of nerve cells, or _____ .

2. The extensions of a neuron that receive messages from other neurons are the _____ .

3. The extension of a neuron that transmits information to other neurons is the _____ .

4. The neural impulse, or _____

    _____ , is a brief electrical charge that travels down a(n) _____ .

5. The junction between two neurons is called a

    _____ .

6. Identify the major parts of the neuron and the activity diagrammed below:

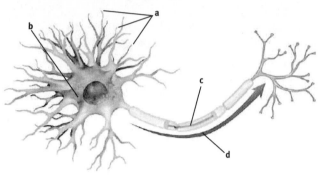

a. _____   c. _____
b. _____   d. _____

Objective 3: Explain how nerve cells communicate.

A nerve impulse fires when the neuron is stimulated by signals from sensory receptors or when triggered by chemical signals from adjacent neurons. Received signals trigger an impulse only if the excitatory signals minus the inhibitory signals exceeds a minimum intensity called the *threshold*. The neuron's reaction is an *all-or-none response*. The impulse, called the *action potential,* is a brief electrical signal that travels down the axon.

When the action potential reaches the axon's end, your neural system converts an electrical impulse into a chemical message. The action potential triggers the release of chemical messengers called *neurotransmitters,* which cross the junction between neurons called the *synapse.* They then combine with receptor sites on neighboring neurons, thus passing on their excitatory or inhibitory messages. The sending neuron, in a process called *reuptake,* normally absorbs the excess neurotransmitter molecules in the gap.

7. To trigger a neural impulse,
   _____ signals minus
   _____ signals must exceed a certain intensity, called the _____ .
   Increasing a stimulus above this level
   _____ (will/will not) increase the neural impulse's intensity. This phenomenon is called an _____-
   _____-_____
   response.

8. The strength of a stimulus _____ (does/does not) affect the speed of a neural impulse.

STUDY TIP/APPLICATION: To understand the relationships among excitatory and inhibitory synapses, threshold, and the all-or-none response, you should think of the neuron as a simple switch that is always either "on" or "off." This "all-or-

none" response is in contrast to the graded, "partially on" response of the more complex dimmer switch. Whether the all-or-none response occurs depends on whether the input to the neuron is sufficient to allow it to reach its threshold—much as a simple light switch requires a certain amount of force to operate. In the neuron's case, the "force" refers to the combination of excitatory inputs (which promote a response) and inhibitory inputs (which promote the neuron's remaining in its resting state).

9. Several shy neurons send an inhibitory message to neighboring neuron Joni. At the same time, a larger group of party-going neurons send Joni excitatory messages. What will Joni do? _____
   _____
   _____

10. At the synapse, the neural impulse triggers the release of chemical messengers called _____ . These chemicals cross the synaptic gap and bind to _____ sites on the receiving neuron.

11. Neurotransmitters influence neurons either by _____ or _____ their readiness to fire. Excess neurotransmitters are reabsorbed by the sending neuron in a process called _____ .

Outline the sequence of reactions that occur when a neural impulse is generated and transmitted from one neuron to another.

Objective 4: Describe how neurotransmitters influence mood and behavior, and explain how drugs and other chemicals affect neurotransmitters.

Different neurotransmitters have different effects on behavior and emotion. For example, the neurotransmitter serotonin affects mood, hunger, sleep, and arousal. Dopamine influences movement, learning, attention, and emotion. The brain's *endorphins,* natural *opiates* released in response to pain and vigorous exercise, explain the "runner's high" and the indifference to pain in some injured people.

When the brain is flooded with opiate drugs such as heroin and morphine, it may stop producing its own natural opiates, and withdrawal of these drugs may deprive the brain of any form of relief.

12. The neurotransmitter serotonin affects our

_____ , _____ , and

_____ . Dopamine influences

_____ . A

neurotransmitter that is important in muscle action

is _____ ; it is also important in

learning and _____ .

13. Naturally occurring opiatelike neurotransmitters

that are present in the brain are called

_____ . When the brain is flooded

with drugs such as _____ or

_____ , it may stop producing

these neurotransmitters.

APPLICATIONS:

14. Lolita is feeling depressed for no particular reason. It is

possible that she has an undersupply of _____ .

15. Punjab had lunch at the local Chinese restaurant.

Afterward, he suffered a migraine, most likely caused by

an _____ of _____ .

The Nervous System

Objective 5: Identify the two major divisions of the nervous system, and describe their basic functions.

Neurons communicating with other neurons form our body's *nervous system*. The brain and spinal cord form the *central nervous system (CNS)*. The *peripheral nervous system (PNS)* links the central nervous system with the body's sense receptors, muscles, and glands. The axons carrying this PNS information are bundled into the electrical cables we know as *nerves*.

Sensory neurons carry information from the body's tissues and sensory organs inward to the brain and spinal cord, which process the information. *Motor neurons* carry outgoing information from the central nervous system to the body's tissues. *Interneurons* in the CNS communicate internally and intervene between the sensory inputs and the motor outputs.

The peripheral nervous system consists of two subsystems. The *somatic nervous system* enables voluntary control of our skeletal muscles. The *autonomic nervous system* is a dual self-regulating system that influences our glands and the muscles of our internal organs. The *sympathetic nervous system* arouses; the *parasympathetic nervous system* calms.

In the central nervous system, the brain enables our thinking, feeling, and acting. Its billions of neurons cluster into work groups called *neural networks*. The spinal cord is a two-way highway connecting the PNS and the brain. Nerve fibers carry information from the senses to the brain, and others carry motor-control information to body parts.

1. Taken altogether, the neurons of the body form the

_____ _____ .

2. The brain and spinal cord comprise the

_____ nervous system. The neurons that link the brain and spinal cord to the body's sense receptors, muscles, and glands form the

_____ nervous system.

3. Sensory and motor axons are bundled into electrical

cables called _____ .

4. Information arriving in the central nervous system from the body travels in _____

neurons. The central nervous system sends instructions to the body's muscles by means of

_____ neurons.

5. The neurons that enable internal communication within the central nervous system are called

_____ .

6. The division of the peripheral nervous system that enables voluntary control of the skeletal muscles is

the _____ nervous system.

7. Responses of the glands and muscles of internal organs are controlled by the _____

nervous system.

8. The body is made ready for action by the

_____ division of the autonomic

nervous system.

9. The _____ division of the autonomic nervous system produces relaxation.

10. Neurons cluster into work groups called

_____ _____ .

....

STUDY TIP/APPLICATION: To keep the various functions of the peripheral nervous system (PNS) straight, remember that the PNS consists of two main divisions: somatic and autonomic. The somatic ("S") division primarily regulates "S functions," such as the senses and skeletal muscles. The autonomic ("A") division regulates automatic ("A") physical systems that do not require conscious attention. These include breathing, heart rate, and digestion, to name a few.

11. You are sitting at your desk at home, studying for an exam. No one else is home, but you hear creaking floorboards. You sneak downstairs, only to discover your parents have returned home early. Describe and explain the sequence of physical reactions that occurred in your body as you felt fear and then relief.

....

The Endocrine System

Objective 6: Describe the nature and functions of the endocrine system and its interaction with the nervous system.

The *endocrine system*'s glands secrete *hormones,* chemical messengers produced in one tissue that travel through the bloodstream and affect other tissues, including the brain. Compared with the speed at which messages move through the nervous system, endocrine messages move more slowly but their effects are usually longer-lasting. The endocrine system's hormones influence many aspects of our lives, including growth, reproduction, metabolism, and mood, working with our nervous system to keep everything in balance while responding to stress, exertion, and thoughts. In a moment of danger, the *adrenal glands* release the hormones *epinephrine* and *norepinephrine,* which increase heart rate, blood pressure, and blood sugar, providing us with a surge of energy known as the *fight-or-flight response.* The **pituitary gland** is the endocrine system's control center. Under the influence of the brain's *hypothalamus,* the pituitary's secretions influence growth and the release of hormones by other endocrine glands. These may in turn influence both the brain and behavior and thus reveal the intimate connection of the nervous and endocrine systems.

1. The body's chemical communication network is called the _____ _____ . This system transmits information through chemical messengers called _____ at a much _____ (faster/slower) rate than the nervous system, and its effects last _____ (a longer time/a shorter time).

2. In a moment of danger, the _____ glands release _____ and _____ .

3. The control center is the _____ gland, which, under the control of an adjacent brain area called the _____ , helps regulate _____ and the release of hormones by other endocrine glands.

4. The feedback system linking the nervous and endocrine systems is thus:

   brain's _____ → _____ → other glands → _____ → brain.

APPLICATION:

5. A bodybuilder friend suddenly seems to have grown several inches in height. You suspect that your friend's growth spurt has occurred because he has been using drugs that affect the _____ gland(s).

The Brain

Objective 7: Describe several techniques for studying the brain.

Powerful techniques now reveal brain structures and activities in the living brain. By recording electrical activity on the brain's surface (*EEG [electroencephalograph]*) and by looking inside the living brain to see its activity using the *PET (positron emission tomography) scan,* MRI *(magnetic resonance imaging),* and *fMRI (functional MRI),* neuroscientists examine the connections between brain, mind, and behavior.

1. (Close-Up) The _____ is a recording of the electrical activity of the whole brain.

2. (Close-Up) The technique depicting the level of activity of brain areas by measuring the brain's consumption of glucose is called the

   _____ _____ .

(Close-Up) Briefly explain the purpose of the PET scan.

3. (Close-Up) A technique that produces clearer images of the brain (and other body parts) by using magnetic fields and radio waves is known as

   _____ .

4. (Close-Up) By taking pictures less than a second apart, the _____ _____ detects blood rushing to the part of the cortex thought to control the bodily activity being studied.

• •

STUDY TIP/APPLICATIONS: To help keep the various research methods for studying the brain straight, think of the methods as falling into two categories: (1) those that measure ongoing electrical or metabolic brain activity in real time (EEG, PET scan, fMRI) and (2) those that merely provide a momentary picture of the brain's anatomical structure (MRI).

5. **a.** Which method would be most useful to a neurologist attempting to locate a tumor in a patient's brain? _____

   b. Which method would be most useful to a researcher attempting to pinpoint the area of the brain that is most critical to speaking aloud? _____

   c. What are some other instances when a researcher would be best advised to use methods that give a picture of the brain's structure?

d. What are some other instances when a researcher would be best advised to use methods that measure brain activity?

••

Objective 8: Describe the functions of the brainstem and its related structures.

The **brainstem** is the brain's oldest and innermost region. It includes the **medulla,** which controls heartbeat and breathing, and the **reticular formation,** which plays an important role in controlling arousal. Atop the brainstem is the **thalamus,** the brain's sensory switchboard. It receives information from all the senses except smell and sends it to the brain regions that deal with seeing, hearing, tasting, and touching. The **cerebellum,** attached to the rear of the brainstem, coordinates movement output and balance. It helps process and store memories that we cannot consciously recall. Like the other older brain structures, it processes most information outside of our awareness (part of our two-track brain). It also helps us judge time, control our emotions, and discriminate sounds and textures.

6. The oldest and innermost region of the brain is the

_____ .

7. At the base of the brainstem, where the spinal cord enters the skull, lies the _____ , which controls _____ and

_____ .

8. Nerves from each side of the brain cross over to connect with the body's opposite side in the

_____ .

9. At the top of the brainstem sits the

_____ , which serves as the brain's sensory switchboard, receiving information from all the senses except _____ and routing it to the regions dealing with those senses. These egg-shaped structures also receive replies from the higher regions, which they direct to the

_____ and the _____ .

10. The _____ _____

is a nerve network inside the brainstem that plays an important role in controlling _____ . Electrically stimulating this area will produce a(n) _____ animal. Severing this area from higher brain regions will cause an animal to lapse into a(n) _____ .

11. At the rear of the brainstem lies the

_____ . It helps process and store _____ for things we cannot consciously recall, but its major function is coordination of voluntary movement and _____ control.

12. The lower brain functions occur without _____ effort, indicating that our two-track brain processes most information _____ (inside/outside) of our awareness.

APPLICATIONS:

13. The part of the human brain that is most like that of a shark is the _____ .

14. Dr. Frankenstein made a mistake during neurosurgery on his monster. After the operation, the monster "saw" with his ears and "heard" with his eyes. It is likely that Dr. Frankenstein "rewired" neural connections in the monster's _____ .

Objective 9: Describe the structures and functions of the limbic system, and explain the relationship of the hypothalamus to the pituitary gland.

The **limbic system** has been linked primarily to memory, emotions, and drives. For example, one of its neural centers, the **hippocampus,** processes conscious memories. Another, the **amygdala,** influences aggression and fear. A third, the **hypothalamus,** has been linked to various bodily maintenance functions and to pleasurable rewards. Its hormones influence the pituitary gland and thus it provides a major link between the nervous and endocrine systems.

15. Between the brainstem and cerebral hemispheres is the _____ system. One component of this system that processes conscious memory is the _____ (see a in the above drawing).

16. Aggression or fear will result from stimulation of different regions of the _____ (see b).

17. We must remember, however, that the brain _____ (is/is not) neatly organized into structures that correspond to our categories of behavior. For example, aggressive behavior _____ (does/does not) involve neural activity in all brain levels.

18. Below the thalamus is the _____ (c), which regulates bodily maintenance behaviors such as _____ , _____ ,

_____ _____ ,

and _____ _____ . This area also regulates behavior by secreting _____ that enable it to control the nearby "master gland," the _____ gland. Olds and Milner discovered that this region also contains _____ centers, which organisms will work hard to have stimulated.

APPLICATIONS:

19. If Dr. Rogers wishes to conduct an experiment on the effects of stimulating the reward centers of a rat's brain, he should insert an electrode into the

    _____ .

20. A scientist from another planet wishes to study the simplest brain mechanisms underlying emotion and memory. You recommend that the scientist study the

    _____ .

Objective 10: Identify the four lobes of the cerebral cortex, noting the location of each.

The *cerebral cortex*, a thin surface layer of interconnected neural cells that covers the two hemispheres of the *cerebrum*, is our body's ultimate control and information-processing center. Each hemisphere has four lobes. The *frontal lobes* are just behind the forehead. The *parietal lobes* are at the top of the head and toward the rear. The *occipital lobes* are at the back of the head. The *temporal lobes* are just above the ears. Each lobe performs many functions, and many functions require the cooperation of several lobes.

21. The most complex functions of human behavior are linked to the most developed part of the brain, the

    _____ _____ .

    This thin layer of interconnected neural cells is the body's ultimate control and

    _____-_____

    center.

22. List the four lobes of the brain.

    a. _____   c. _____

    b. _____   d. _____

Objective 11: Describe the functions of the motor cortex, sensory cortex, and association areas.

The *motor cortex*, an arch-shaped region at the rear of the frontal lobes, controls voluntary muscle movements on the opposite side of the body. Body parts requiring the most precise control occupy the greatest amount of cortical space. The *sensory cortex*, a region at the front of

the parietal lobes, registers and processes our senses of touch and movement. The most sensitive body parts require the largest amount of space in the sensory cortex. Other senses send input to other parts of the cortex. Visual information goes to the occipital lobes, and sounds go to the temporal lobes. People with schizophrenia sometimes experience auditory *hallucinations* in the auditory cortex.

The *association areas* are not involved in primary motor or sensory functions. Rather, they interpret, integrate, and act on sensory information and link it with stored memories. They are involved in higher mental functions, such as learning, remembering, thinking, and speaking. Association areas are found in all four lobes. Complex human abilities, such as language, result from the intricate coordination of many brain areas.

23. Electrical stimulation of one side of the _____ cortex, an arch-shaped region at the back of the _____ lobe, will produce movement on the opposite side of the body. The more precise the control needed, the _____ (smaller/ greater) amount of cortical space occupied.

24. At the front of the parietal lobes lies the _____ cortex, which, when stimulated, elicits a sensation of _____ .

25. The more sensitive a body region, the greater the area of _____ _____ devoted to it.

26. Visual information is received in the _____ lobes; auditory information is received in the _____ lobes.

27. People with schizophrenia sometimes have false sensory experiences called _____ .

28. Areas of the brain that don't receive sensory information or direct movement but, rather, integrate and interpret information received by other regions are known as _____ _____ . Approximately _____ of the human cortex is of this type. Such areas in the _____ lobe are involved in judging, planning, and processing of new memories and in some aspects of personality. In the _____ lobe, these areas enable mathematical and spatial reasoning, and an area of the _____ lobe enables us to recognize faces.

APPLICATION:

29. In the diagrams to the right, the numbers refer to brain locations that have been damaged. Based on the text explanation of each area's function, match each location with its probable effect on behavior.

Location

_____ **1.**
_____ **2.**
_____ **3.**
_____ **4.**
_____ **5.**
_____ **6.**
_____ **7.**
_____ **8.**
_____ **9.**

Behavioral Effect

a. vision disorder
b. insensitivity to touch
c. motor paralysis
d. hearing problem
e. lack of coordination
f. abnormal hunger
g. split brain
h. sleep/arousal disorder
i. altered personality

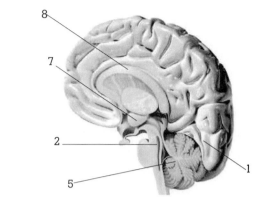

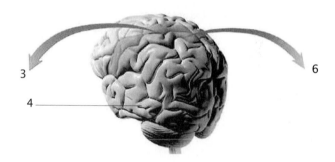

Objective 12: Explain how the brain processes language.

Language depends on a chain of events in several brain regions. When we read a sentence aloud, the words (1) register in the visual area, (2) are relayed to the *angular gyrus,* which transforms the words into an auditory code, which is (3) received and understood in nearby *Wernicke's area* and (4) sent to *Broca's area,* which (5) controls the motor cortex as it creates the pronounced word. Depending on which link in this chain is damaged, a different form of speech impairment occurs: Damage to the angular gyrus leaves the person able to speak and understand but unable to read, damage to Wernicke's area disrupts understanding, and damage to Broca's area disrupts speaking.

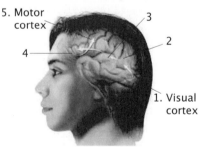

30. Studies of people with language impairments have shown that _____ _____ (4 in drawing above) is involved in producing speech, _____ _____ (3) is involved in understanding speech, and the

_____ _____ (2) is involved in recoding printed words into auditory form.

31. Although the mind's subsystems are localized in particular brain regions, the brain _____ (does/does not) act as a unified whole. Two principles— _____ and _____ —describe the way our brain functions.

APPLICATIONS:

32. Your roommate Bruce plays the guitar and is part of a band that works at local clubs on weekends. Your musical talent is restricted to "listening to his band." You would expect that Bruce has more cortical space dedicated to "finger control" in the _____ lobes of his brain.

33. Gustav has been diagnosed with a brain tumor. To pinpoint the location of that tumor, his doctor electrically stimulated parts of his sensory cortex. If Gustav was conscious during the procedure, he probably experienced _____ .

Objective 13: Discuss the brain's plasticity following injury or illness.

Research indicates that some neural tissue can reorganize in response to damage. When one brain area is damaged, others may in time take over some of its function. For example, if you lose a finger, the sensory cortex that received its input will begin to receive input from the adjacent fingers, which become more sensitive. Our brains are most **plastic** when we are young children. In fact, children who have had an entire hemisphere removed still lead normal lives.

34. The quality of the brain that makes it possible for undamaged brain areas to take over the functions of damaged regions is known as _____ . This quality is especially apparent in the brains of _____ (young children/adolescents/adults).

35. Some brain neural tissue can _____ in response to damage. Also, the brain sometimes attempts to mend itself by producing new neurons, a process called _____ .

Objective 14: Describe split-brain research, and explain how it helps us understand the functions of our left and right hemispheres.

A **split brain** is one whose **corpus callosum,** the wide band of axon fibers that connects the two brain hemispheres, has been severed. Experiments on split-brain patients have refined our knowledge of interactions between the brain's two hemispheres, as well as each hemisphere's special functions (called hemispheric specialization). In the laboratory, investigators ask a split-brain patient to look at a designated spot, then send information to either the left or right hemisphere (by flashing it to the right or left visual field). Quizzing each hemisphere separately, the researchers have confirmed that for most people the left hemisphere is the more verbal and the right hemisphere excels in visual perception and the recognition of emotion. Studies of people with intact brains have confirmed that the right and left hemispheres each make unique contributions to the integrated functioning of the brain.

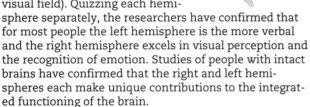

corpus callosum

36. In treating patients with severe epilepsy, neurosurgeons separated the two hemispheres of the brain by cutting the _____ . When this structure is severed, the result is referred to as a _____ _____ .

37. In a split-brain patient, only the _____ hemisphere will be aware of

an unseen object held in the left hand. In this case, the person would not be able to _____ the object.

Explain why a split-brain patient would be able to read aloud the word *pencil* flashed to his or her right visual field but would be unable to identify a *pencil* by touch using only the left hand.

38. When the "two minds" of a split brain are at odds, the _____ hemisphere tries to rationalize what it doesn't understand.

39. Deaf people use the _____ hemisphere to process sign language.

40. Although the _____ hemisphere is better at making quick, literal interpretations of language, the _____ hemisphere excels at high-level language processing and at copying drawings, _____ _____ , perceiving differences, and perceiving and expressing _____ .

APPLICATIONS:

41. A split-brain patient has a picture of a knife flashed to her left hemisphere and that of a fork to her right hemisphere. She will be able to identify the _____ with her _____ hand. She would then be able to verbally report that she had seen the _____ .

42. Anton is applying for a technician's job with a neurosurgeon. In trying to impress his potential employer with his knowledge of the brain, he says, "After my father's stroke I knew immediately that the blood clot had affected his left cerebral hemisphere because he no longer recognized his friend." Should Anton be hired? _____ Explain your answer. _____ _____

Brain States and Consciousness

Objective 15: Define *consciousness,* and discuss how our perceptions are directed by selective attention.

The subfield of *cognitive neuroscience* studies, among other things, states of **consciousness.**
Selective attention means that at any moment, awareness focuses on only a limited aspect of all that we experience. In one study, students whose attention was diverted by cell-phone conversations were slower to

respond to traffic signals than those not talking on the phone. Selective attention limits our perception, as many stimuli will pass by unnoticed. This lack of awareness is evident in studies of *inattentional blindness*. One form of this is *change blindness*.

1. Consciousness, which is studied by the subfield of _____ _____ , is defined as _____ _____ .

2. When we focus our conscious awareness on a particular stimulus we are using _____ _____ . Normally, our attention _____ (is/is not) divided.

3. When researchers told participants to press a key each time they saw a black-shirted basketball player, they displayed _____ _____ and failed to notice a gorilla-suited assistant who passed through. One form of this phenomenon, in which people don't notice a change that occurs after a brief visual interruption, is called _____ _____ .

Objective 16: Describe the cycle of our circadian rhythm, focusing on the stages of our sleep cycle.

Our daily schedule of waking and sleeping is governed by a biological clock known as *circadian rhythm.* Our body temperature rises as morning approaches, peaks during the day, dips for a time in early afternoon, and then begins to drop again before we go to sleep. Thinking is sharpest and memory most accurate when people are at their peak in circadian arousal.

We pass through a cycle of five sleep stages that total about 90 minutes. As we lie awake and relaxed, before we *sleep,* our EEG shows relatively slow *alpha waves. Stage 1 sleep* is characterized by fantastic images resembling *hallucinations. Stage 2 sleep* (the stage in which we spend about half the night) follows for about 20 minutes, with its characteristic *sleep spindles.* For the next few minutes, you go through the *transitional Stage 3* to the *deep sleep* of *Stage 4,* when the brain emits large, slow *delta* waves. These two slow-wave stages last about 30 minutes, during which we are hard to awaken. Reversing course, we retrace our path through these stages with one difference. About an hour after falling asleep, we begin approximately 10 minutes of **REM (rapid eye movement) sleep** in which most dreaming occurs. In this fifth stage (also known as *paradoxical sleep),* we are internally aroused but outwardly paralyzed. The sleep cycle repeats several times during a normal night's sleep, with periods of Stage 4 sleep progressively shortening and periods of REM sleep lengthening.

4. Our bodies' internal "clocks" control several _____ _____ .

5. The sleep-waking cycle follows a 24-hour clock called the _____ _____ .

6. Body temperature _____ (rises/falls) as morning approaches and begins to _____ (rise/fall) again before we go to sleep.

7. When people are at their daily peak in circadian arousal, _____ is sharpest and _____ is most accurate.

8. Our circadian rhythm is altered by _____ and _____ . Before age 20, we tend to be_____-energized "owls"; we then become _____-loving "larks".

9. The sleep cycle consists of _____ distinct stages.

10. The rhythm of sleep cycles was discovered when Aserinsky noticed that, at periodic intervals during the night, the _____ of a sleeping child moved rapidly. This stage of sleep, during which _____ occur, is called _____ _____ .

11. The relatively slow brain waves of the awake but relaxed state are known as _____ waves.

12. During Stage 1 sleep, people often experience fantastic sensations similar to _____ .

13. The bursts of brain-wave activity that occur during Stage 2 sleep are called _____ _____ .

14. Stage _____ is a transitional stage, leading to the deep sleep of Stage _____ . A person in these stages of _____-_____ sleep generally will be _____ (easy/difficult) to awaken. Even during these stages, your brain monitors events, confirming that we process most information outside our conscious awareness (_____ _____).

Describe the bodily changes that accompany REM sleep.

15. During REM sleep, the motor cortex is
_____ (active/relaxed), while the
muscles are _____ (active/
relaxed). For this reason, REM is often referred to as
_____ sleep.

16. The rapid eye movements generally signal the
beginning of a _____ , which dur-
ing REM sleep is often storylike, _____ ,
and more richly hallucinatory.

APPLICATION:

18. Match the sleep stage with a description of that stage or
an activity that occurs then.

Sleep Stage

_____   **1.** Stage 1 sleep
_____   **2.** Stage 2 sleep
_____   **3.** Stage 3 sleep
_____   **4.** Stage 4 sleep
_____   **5.** REM sleep

Objective 17: Describe individual differences in sleep
duration, noting four theories about why we need to
sleep.

People differ in their individual sleep requirements. For
example, newborns sleep twice as much as adults. These
age-related changes are rivaled by differences in the normal amount of sleep among individuals of any age. Twin
studies suggest that these differences may be partially
genetic. Sleep patterns are also culturally influenced.
People in modern industrialized nations get less sleep
because of shift work and social diversions, for example.
The first theory of why we sleep is that sleep may
have played a protective role in keeping our distant
ancestors safe during potentially dangerous times. A
second theory is that sleep may help us recover, restoring and repairing brain tissue. Third, sleep restores and
rebuilds our fading memories of the day's experiences.
After working on a task, then sleeping on it, people solve
problems more insightfully than do those who stay
awake. Finally, sleep is linked with the release of pituitary growth hormone and so may play a role in the
growth process.

19. Newborns spend nearly _____
(how much?) of their day asleep, while adults spend
no more than _____ .

20. Sleep patterns are influenced by
_____ , as indicated by the fact
that sleep patterns among _____

17. The sleep cycle repeats itself about every
_____ minutes. As the night pro-
gresses, Stage 4 sleep becomes _____
(longer/briefer) and REM periods become
_____ (longer/briefer).
Approximately _____ percent of a
night's sleep is spent in REM sleep.

Description or Example

a. Bonita dreams that she's dancing with Orlando Bloom at
a grand ball.
b. Manfred feels like he's floating above the bed.
c. Little Alex gets out of bed and starts toward the door,
mumbling fearfully that someone is trying to stab him.
d. Rapid, rhythmic brain-wave activity indicates you are
clearly asleep.
e. You are in slow-wave sleep and you do not awaken
easily.

(identical/fraternal) twins are very similar. Sleep is
also influenced by _____ , as indi-
cated by the fact that people in industrialized
nations now sleep _____
(more/less) than they did a century ago.

State four possible reasons sleep may have evolved.

21. Animals that need to sleep a lot produce an abundance of chemical _____
_____ that are toxic to our
_____ . Sleep also stimulates
_____ thinking.

22. During sleep a growth hormone is released by the
_____ gland. Adults spend
_____ (more/less) time in deep
sleep than children and so release _____
(more/less) growth hormone.

APPLICATIONS:

23. Arsenio is participating in a sleep experiment. While he sleeps, a PET scan of his brain reveals increased activity in the amygdala of the limbic system. This most likely indicates that Arsenio is in _____ sleep.

24. Concluding her presentation on contemporary theories of why sleep is necessary, Marilynn makes all of the following points except that
    a. sleep may have evolved because it kept our ancestors safe during potentially dangerous periods.
    b. sleep gives the brain time to heal, as it restores and repairs damaged neurons.
    c. sleep encourages growth through a hormone secreted during Stage 4.
    d. slow-wave sleep provides a "psychic safety valve" for stressful waking experiences.

Objective 18: Describe the effects of sleep loss, and identify the major sleep disorders.

People today suffer from sleep patterns that thwart their having an energized feeling of well-being. Findings suggest that sleep deprivation suppresses immune cells that fight off viral infections and cancer; impair concentration, creativity, and communication; make us irritable; and slow performance with greater vulnerability to accidents. Chronic sleep deprivation can also alter metabolic and hormonal function, creating conditions that may contribute to obesity, high blood pressure, and memory impairment.

Some 1 in 10 adults, and 1 in 4 older adults, complain of *insomnia,* problems in falling or staying asleep. Rarer but more severe than insomnia are the sleep disorders narcolepsy and sleep apnea. People with *narcolepsy* suffer periodic, overwhelming sleepiness, sometimes at the most inopportune times. The person sometimes collapses directly into a brief period of REM sleep. Those who suffer *sleep apnea* (mostly obese men) intermittently stop breathing during sleep. After an airless minute or so, decreased blood oxygen arouses the sleeper to snort in air for a few seconds. Still other sleepers, mostly children, experience *night terrors.* They sit up or walk around, talk nonsense, experience a doubling of heart and breathing rates, and appear terrified. Sleepwalking and sleeptalking are also usually childhood disorders.

25. Sleep deprivation has a number of effects, including difficulty studying, _____ _____ , a tendency to make mistakes, _____ , and fatigue. It can also make you fatter by increasing _____ , a hunger-arousing hormone, and decreasing _____ , a hunger-suppressing hormone. It also increases _____ , a stress hormone that stimulates fat production.

26. A persistent difficulty in falling or staying asleep is characteristic of _____ . Sleeping pills and alcohol may make the problem worse since they tend to _____ (increase/reduce) REM sleep.

27. The sleep disorder in which a person experiences uncontrollable sleep attacks is _____ . People with severe cases of this disorder may collapse directly into _____ sleep and experience a loss of _____ _____ .

28. Individuals suffering from _____ _____ stop breathing while sleeping. This disorder is especially prevalent among _____ men.

29. The sleep disorder characterized by extreme fright and a doubling of heart and breathing rates is called _____ _____ . These episodes usually happen during Stage _____ sleep. The same is true of episodes of _____ and _____ , problems that _____ (run/do not run) in families. These sleep episodes are most likely to be experienced by _____ (young children/adolescents/older adults), in whom this stage tends to be the lengthiest and deepest.

Objective 19: Describe the most common content of dreams, and compare the five major perspectives on why we dream.

REM dreams are vivid, emotional, and bizarre. Common themes are failing, being attacked and pursued, and experiencing misfortune. The story line of our dreams—what Sigmund Freud called their *manifest content*—sometimes incorporates traces of previous days' experiences and preoccupations. Only 1 in 10 dreams among young men and 1 in 30 among young women have sexual overtones. Sensory stimuli may also intrude on our dreams as our two-track mind monitors our environment.

In his wish-fulfillment theory, Freud suggested that a dream's manifest content is a censored version of its *latent content,* which gratifies our unconscious wishes. The information-processing perspective suggests that dreams help us process information and fix it in memory. Some physiological theories propose that REM-induced regular brain stimulation helps develop and preserve neural pathways in the brain. The activation-synthesis explanation is that REM sleep triggers impulses in brain areas that process visual images, but not the visual cortex area, evoking visual images that our brain weaves into a story line. The cognitive-development perspective maintains that dreams represent the dreamer's level of brain maturation and cognitive development. Despite their differences, most theorists agree that REM sleep and its associated dreams serve an important function, as shown by the **REM rebound** that occurs following REM deprivation.

30. Dreams experienced during _____ sleep are vivid, emotional, and bizarre.

31. For both men and women, 8 in 10 dreams are marked by _____ (positive/negative) emotions, such as fears of being _____ .

32. Freud referred to the actual content of a dream as its _____ content. Freud believed that this is a censored, symbolic version of the true meaning, or _____ content, of the dream.

33. According to Freud, most of the dreams of adults reflect _____ wishes and are the key to understanding inner wishes that cannot be expressed publicly. To Freud, dreams serve as _____ _____ that discharges otherwise unacceptable feelings.

34. Researchers who believe that dreams serve an _____-processing function receive support from the fact that REM sleep facilitates _____ . Brain scans confirm this link.

35. Other theories propose that dreaming serves some _____ function, for example, that REM sleep provides the brain with needed _____ . Such an explanation is supported by the fact that _____ (infants/adults) spend the most time in REM sleep.

36. Still other theories propose that dreams are elicited by random bursts of _____ activity originating in lower regions of the brain, such as the _____ . According to the _____-_____ theory, dreams are the brain's attempt to make sense of this activity. According to another theory, the _____-_____ theory, dreams are a natural part of brain _____ and _____ development.

37. Researchers agree that we _____ (need/do not need) REM sleep. After being deprived

of REM sleep, a person spends more time in REM sleep; this is the _____ _____ effect.

APPLICATIONS:

38. Barry has participated in a sleep study for the last four nights. He was awakened each time he entered REM sleep. Now that the experiment is over, Barry will most likely show a(n) _____ (increase/decrease) in REM sleep, a phenomenon known as _____ _____ .

39. Bahara dreams that she trips and falls as she walks up the steps to the stage to receive her college diploma. Her psychoanalyst suggests that the dream might symbolize her fear of moving on to the next stage of her life—a career. The analyst is evidently attempting to interpret the _____ content of Bahara's dream.

PROGRESS TEST

Multiple-Choice Questions

Circle your answers to the following questions and check them with the answers beginning on page 39. If your answer is incorrect, read the explanation for why it is incorrect and then consult the text.

1. Heartbeat, digestion, and other self-regulating bodily functions are governed by the
   a. voluntary nervous system.
   b. autonomic nervous system.
   c. sympathetic division of the autonomic nervous system.
   d. somatic nervous system.

2. A strong stimulus can increase the
   a. speed of the impulse the neuron fires.
   b. intensity of the impulse the neuron fires.
   c. number of times the neuron fires.
   d. threshold that must be reached before the neuron fires.

3. The pain of heroin withdrawal occurs because
   a. under the influence of heroin the brain ceases production of endorphins.
   b. under the influence of heroin the brain ceases production of all neurotransmitters.
   c. during heroin withdrawal the brain's production of all neurotransmitters is greatly increased.
   d. heroin destroys endorphin receptors in the brain.

4. The brain research technique that involves monitoring the brain's use of glucose is called the
   a. PET scan.   **c.** EEG.
   b. fMRI.   **d.** MRI.

5. Although there is no single "control center" for emotions, their regulation is primarily attributed to the brain region known as the
   a. limbic system.   **c.** brainstem.
   b. reticular formation.   **d.** cerebellum.

6. Damage to _____ will usually cause a person to lose the ability to understand language.
   a. the angular gyrus
   b. Broca's area
   c. Wernicke's area
   d. frontal lobe association areas

7. Which of the following is typically controlled by the right hemisphere?
   a. language
   b. learned voluntary movements
   c. arithmetic reasoning
   d. perceptual tasks

8. Dr. Hernandez is studying neurotransmitter abnormalities in depressed patients. She would most likely describe herself as a
   a. personality psychologist.
   b. behaviorist.
   c. psychoanalyst.
   d. biological psychologist.

9. Voluntary movements, such as writing with a pencil, are directed by the
   a. sympathetic nervous system.
   b. somatic nervous system.
   c. parasympathetic nervous system.
   d. autonomic nervous system.

10. A neuron will generate action potentials when
    a. it remains below its threshold.
    b. it receives an excitatory input.
    c. excitatory minus inhibitory inputs exceed a minimum intensity.
    d. it is stimulated by a neurotransmitter.

11. Which is the correct sequence in the transmission of a neural impulse?
    a. axon, dendrite, cell body, synapse
    b. dendrite, axon, cell body, synapse
    c. synapse, axon, dendrite, cell body
    d. dendrite, cell body, axon, synapse

12. Chemical messengers produced by endocrine glands are called
    a. lobes.   **c.** hormones.
    b. neurotransmitters.   **d.** enzymes.

13. Following a head injury, a person has ongoing difficulties staying awake. Most likely, the damage occurred to the
    a. thalamus.   **c.** reticular formation.
    b. corpus callosum.   **d.** cerebellum.

14. An experimenter flashes the word FLYTRAP onto a screen facing a split-brain patient so that FLY projects to her right hemisphere and TRAP to her left hemisphere. When asked what she saw, the patient will
    a. say she saw FLY.
    b. say she saw TRAP.
    c. point to FLY using her right hand.
    d. point to TRAP using her left hand.

15. Cortical areas that are NOT primarily concerned with sensory, motor, or language functions are
    a. called projection areas.
    b. called association areas.
    c. located mostly in the parietal lobe.
    d. located mostly in the temporal lobe.

16. The visual cortex is located in the
    a. occipital lobe.   **c.** frontal lobe.
    b. temporal lobe.   **d.** parietal lobe.

17. Which of the following is typically controlled by the left hemisphere?
    a. spatial reasoning
    b. word recognition
    c. the left side of the body
    d. perceptual skills

18. When Sandy scalded her toe in a tub of hot water, the pain message was carried to her spinal cord by the _____ nervous system.
    a. somatic   **c.** parasympathetic
    b. sympathetic   **d.** central

19. Melissa has just completed running a marathon. She is so elated that she feels little fatigue or discomfort. Her lack of pain is probably the result of the release of
    a. ACh.   **c.** dopamine.
    b. endorphins.   **d.** norepinephrine.

20. I am a relatively fast-acting chemical messenger that affects mood, hunger, sleep, and arousal. What am I?
    a. acetylcholine   **c.** norepinephrine
    b. dopamine   **d.** serotonin

21. The gland that regulates body growth is the
    a. adrenal.   **c.** hypothalamus.
    b. thyroid.   **d.** pituitary.

22. Epinephrine and norepinephrine are _____ that are released by the _____ gland.
    a. neurotransmitters; pituitary
    b. hormones; pituitary
    c. neurotransmitters; thyroid
    d. hormones; adrenal

23. Jessica experienced difficulty keeping her balance after receiving a blow to the back of her head. It is likely that she injured her
    a. medulla.
    b. thalamus.
    c. hypothalamus.
    d. cerebellum.

24. Researchers caused a cat to lapse into a coma by severing neural connections between the cortex and the
    a. reticular formation.
    b. hypothalamus.
    c. thalamus.
    d. cerebellum.

25. Research has found that the amount of representation in the motor cortex reflects the
    a. size of the body parts.
    b. degree of precise control required by each of the parts.
    c. sensitivity of the body region.
    d. area of the occipital lobe being stimulated by the environment.

26. The nerve fibers that enable communication between the right and left cerebral hemispheres and that have been severed in split-brain patients form a structure called the
    a. reticular formation.
    b. association areas.
    c. corpus callosum.
    d. parietal lobes.

27. Beginning at the front of the brain and moving toward the back of the head, then down the skull and back around to the front, which of the following is the correct order of the cortical regions?
    a. occipital lobe; temporal lobe; parietal lobe; frontal lobe
    b. temporal lobe; frontal lobe; parietal lobe; occipital lobe
    c. frontal lobe; occipital lobe; temporal lobe; parietal lobe
    d. frontal lobe; parietal lobe; occipital lobe; temporal lobe

28. Following a nail gun wound to his head, Jack became more uninhibited, irritable, dishonest, and profane. It is likely that his personality change was the result of injury to his
    a. parietal lobe.
    b. temporal lobe.
    c. occipital lobe.
    d. frontal lobe.

29. Three-year-old Marco suffered damage to the speech area of the brain's left hemisphere when he fell from a swing. Research suggests that
    a. he may never speak again.
    b. his motor abilities may improve so that he can easily use sign language.

    c. his right hemisphere may take over much of the language function.
    d. his earlier experience with speech may enable him to continue speaking.

30. Sleep spindles predominate during which stage of sleep?
    a. Stage 2
    b. Stage 3
    c. Stage 4
    d. REM sleep

31. During which stage of sleep does the body experience increased heart rate, rapid breathing, and genital arousal?
    a. Stage 2
    b. Stage 3
    c. Stage 4
    d. REM sleep

32. The sleep cycle is approximately _____ minutes.
    a. 30
    b. 50
    c. 75
    d. 90

33. The effects of chronic sleep deprivation include
    a. difficulty studying.
    b. diminished productivity.
    c. a tendency to gain weight.
    d. all of these answers.

34. One effect of sleeping pills is to
    a. decrease REM sleep.
    b. increase REM sleep.
    c. decrease Stage 2 sleep.
    d. increase Stage 2 sleep.

35. According to Freud, dreams are
    a. a symbolic fulfillment of erotic wishes.
    b. the result of random neural activity in the brainstem.
    c. the brain's mechanism for self-stimulation.
    d. the disguised expressions of wishes we can't fulfill in public.

36. Which of the following is NOT a theory of dreaming mentioned in the text?
    a. Dreams facilitate information processing.
    b. Dreaming stimulates the developing brain.
    c. Dreams result from random neural activity originating in the brainstem.
    d. Dreaming is an attempt to escape from social stimulation.

37. Which of the following statements regarding REM sleep is true?
    a. Adults spend more time than infants in REM sleep.
    b. REM sleep deprivation results in a REM rebound.
    c. People deprived of REM sleep adapt easily.
    d. Sleeping medications tend to increase REM sleep.

38. The perceptual error in which we fail to see an object when our attention is directed elsewhere is
    a. neurogenesis.
    b. inattentional blindness.
    c. narcolepsy.
    d. an all-or-none response.

39. A person whose EEG shows a high proportion of alpha waves is most likely
  a. dreaming.
  b. in Stage 2 sleep.
  c. in Stage 3 or 4 sleep.
  d. awake and relaxed.

40. Circadian rhythms are the
  a. brain waves that occur during Stage 4 sleep.
  b. muscular tremors that occur during opiate withdrawal.
  c. regular body cycles that occur on a 24-hour schedule.
  d. brain waves that are indicative of Stage 2 sleep.

41. Which of the following is NOT an example of a biological rhythm?
  a. the circadian rhythm
  b. the 90-minute sleep cycle
  c. the five sleep stages
  d. sudden sleep attacks during the day

42. Which of the following is characteristic of REM sleep?
  a. genital arousal
  b. increased muscular tension
  c. night terrors
  d. alpha waves

43. *Consciousness* is defined in the text as
  a. mental life.
  b. selective attention to ongoing perceptions, thoughts, and feelings.
  c. information processing.
  d. our awareness of ourselves and our environment.

44. According to the activation-synthesis theory, dreaming represents
  a. the brain's efforts to integrate unrelated bursts of activity in visual brain areas with the emotional tone provided by limbic system activity.
  b. a mechanism for coping with the stresses of daily life.
  c. a symbolic depiction of a person's unfulfilled wishes.
  d. an information-processing mechanism for converting the day's experiences into long-term memory.

Matching Items 1

Match each structure or technique with its corresponding function or description.

Structures

_____ **1.** hypothalamus
_____ **2.** EEG
_____ **3.** fMRI
_____ **4.** reticular formation
_____ **5.** MRI
_____ **6.** thalamus
_____ **7.** corpus callosum
_____ **8.** cerebellum
_____ **9.** amygdala
_____ **10.** medulla

Functions or Descriptions

a. amplified recording of brain waves
b. technique that uses radio waves and magnetic fields to image brain anatomy
c. serves as sensory switchboard
d. contains reward centers
e. technique that uses radio waves and magnetic fields to show brain function
f. helps control arousal
g. links the cerebral hemispheres
h. influences aggression and fear
i. regulates breathing and heartbeat
j. enables coordinated movement

Matching Items 2

Match each term with its appropriate definition or description.

Definitions or Descriptions

_____ **1.** surface meaning of dreams
_____ **2.** deeper meaning of dreams
_____ **3.** stage of sleep associated with delta waves
_____ **4.** stage of sleep associated with muscular relaxation
_____ **5.** sleep disorder in which breathing stops
_____ **6.** sleep disorder occurring in Stage 4 sleep
_____ **7.** twilight stage of sleep associated with imagery resembling hallucinations
_____ **8.** disorder in which sleep attacks occur

Terms

a. Stage 1 sleep
b. night terrors
c. manifest content
d. narcolepsy
e. sleep apnea
f. Stage 4 sleep
g. REM sleep
h. latent content

Application Essay

Discuss how the endocrine and nervous systems become involved when a student feels stress—such as that associated with an upcoming final exam. (Use the space below to list the points you want to make, and organize them. Then write the essay on a separate sheet of paper.)

TERMS AND CONCEPTS

Using your own words, on a separate piece of paper write a brief definition or explanation of each of the following terms.

1. biological psychology
2. neuron
3. dendrite
4. axon
5. action potential
6. synapse
7. threshold
8. all-or-none response
9. neurotransmitters
10. opiates
11. endorphins
12. nervous system
13. central nervous system (CNS)
14. peripheral nervous system (PNS)
15. nerves
16. sensory neurons
17. motor neurons
18. interneurons
19. somatic nervous system
20. autonomic nervous system
21. sympathetic nervous system
22. parasympathetic nervous system
23. endocrine system
24. hormones
25. adrenal glands
26. pituitary gland
27. electroencephalograph (EEG)
28. PET (positron emission tomography) scan
29. MRI (magnetic resonance imaging)
30. fMRI (functional magnetic resonance imaging)
31. brainstem
32. medulla
33. thalamus
34. reticular formation
35. cerebellum
36. limbic system
37. amygdala
38. hypothalamus
39. cerebral cortex
40. frontal lobes
41. parietal lobes
42. occipital lobes
43. temporal lobes
44. motor cortex
45. sensory cortex
46. hallucinations
47. association areas
48. Broca's area
49. Wernicke's area
50. plasticity
51. neurogenesis
52. corpus callosum
53. split brain
54. consciousness
55. selective attention
56. inattentional blindness
57. circadian rhythm
58. REM sleep
59. alpha waves
60. sleep
61. insomnia
62. narcolepsy
63. sleep apnea
64. dream
65. manifest content
66. latent content
67. REM rebound

ANSWERS
Chapter Review

Introduction

1. biological
2. biological psychologists

3. A biological psychologist might study chemical changes that accompany emotions, how muscle tension varies with facial expression, how heart rate changes as people become angry, and so on.

Neural Communication

1. neurons
2. dendrites
3. axon
4. action potential; axon
5. synapse
6. **a.** dendrites
   b. cell body
   c. axon
   d. neural impulse (action potential)
7. excitatory; inhibitory; threshold; will not; all-or-none
8. does not
9. Because she has reached her threshold, she will probably fire.
10. neurotransmitters; receptor
11. exciting; inhibiting; reuptake

A neural impulse is generated by excitatory signals minus inhibitory signals exceeding a certain threshold. The stimuli are received through the dendrites, combined in the cell body, and electrically transmitted in an all-or-none fashion down the length of the axon. When the combined signal reaches the end of the axon, chemical messengers called neurotransmitters are released into the synaptic gap between two neurons. Neurotransmitter molecules bind to receptor sites on the dendrites of neighboring neurons and have either an excitatory or inhibitory influence on that neuron's tendency to generate its own neural impulse.

12. mood; hunger; sleepiness; arousal, movement, learning, and attention; acetylcholine (ACh); memory
13. endorphins; heroin; morphine
14. norepinephrine. An undersupply can cause depression.
15. oversupply; glutamate. Glutamate is in MSG, which is commonly used in Chinese cooking. Glutamate can cause migraines because an oversupply can overstimulate the brain.

The Nervous System

1. nervous system
2. central; peripheral
3. nerves
4. sensory; motor
5. interneurons
6. somatic
7. autonomic
8. sympathetic
9. parasympathetic
10. neural networks

11. When you hear the creaking, you become afraid. The sympathetic division of your autonomic nervous system becomes aroused, causing these physiological changes: accelerated heartbeat, elevated blood sugar, dilation of arteries, slowing of digestion, and increased perspiration to cool the body. When you realize it's only your parents, your parasympathetic nervous system produces the opposite physical reactions, calming your body.

The Endocrine System

1. endocrine system; hormones; slower; a longer time
2. adrenal; epinephrine; norepinephrine
3. pituitary; hypothalamus; growth
4. hypothalamus → pituitary → other glands → hormones → brain.
5. pituitary

The Brain

1. EEG (electroencephalograph)
2. PET scan

By depicting the brain's consumption of a temporarily radioactive form of glucose, the PET scan allows researchers to see which brain areas are most active as a person performs various tasks. This provides additional information on the specialized functions of various regions of the brain.

3. MRI (magnetic resonance imaging)
4. functional MRI
5. **a.** MRI
   b. PET scan
   c. to study developmental changes in brain structure, to compare brain anatomy in women and men
   d. to learn which areas of the brain become active during strong emotions, to determine whether brain activity is abnormal in people suffering from dementia (memory and language problems)
6. brainstem
7. medulla; breathing; heartbeat
8. brainstem
9. thalamus; smell; medulla; cerebellum
10. reticular formation; arousal; alert (awake); coma
11. cerebellum; memories; balance
12. conscious; outside
13. brainstem. The brainstem is the oldest and most primitive region of the brain. It is found in lower vertebrates, such as the shark, as well as in humans and other mammals.
14. thalamus. The thalamus relays sensory messages from the eyes, ears, and other receptors to the appropriate projection areas of the cortex. "Rewiring" the thalamus, theoretically, could have the effects stated in this question.
15. limbic; hippocampus
16. amygdala
17. is not; does

18. hypothalamus; hunger; thirst; body temperature; sexual behavior; hormones; pituitary; reward
19. hypothalamus. As Olds and Milner discovered, electrical stimulation of the hypothalamus is a highly reinforcing event because it is the location of the animal's reward centers.
20. limbic system. The hippocampus of the limbic system is involved in processing memory. The amygdala of the limbic system influences fear and anger.
21. cerebral cortex; information-processing
22. **a.** frontal lobe   **c.** occipital lobe
    b. parietal lobe   **d.** temporal lobe
23. motor; frontal; greater
24. sensory; touch
25. sensory cortex
26. occipital; temporal
27. hallucinations
28. association areas; three-fourths; frontal; parietal; temporal
29. Brain Damage Diagram
    1. a   **4.** d   **7.** f
    2. h   **5.** e   **8.** g
    3. c   **6.** b   **9.** i
30. Broca's area; Wernicke's area; angular gyrus
31. does; specialization; integration
32. frontal. The motor cortex, which determines the precision with which various parts of the body can be moved, is located in the frontal lobes.
33. a sense of touch. Stimulation of the sensory cortex elicits a sense of touch, as the experiments of Wilder Penfield demonstrated.
34. plasticity; young children
35. reorganize; neurogenesis
36. corpus callosum; split brain
37. right; name

The word *pencil,* when flashed to a split-brain patient's right visual field, would project only to the opposite, or left, hemisphere of the patient's brain. Because the left hemisphere contains the language control centers of the brain, the patient would be able to read the word aloud. The left hand is controlled by the right hemisphere of the brain. Because the right hemisphere would not be aware of the word, it would not be able to guide the left hand in identifying a pencil by touch.

38. left
39. left
40. left; right; recognizing faces; emotion
41. fork; left; knife. The left hand, controlled by the right hemisphere, would be able to identify the fork, the picture of which is flashed to the right hemisphere. She would verbally report she had seen the knife because it was flashed to her left hemisphere.
42. no. The left hemisphere does not specialize in facial recognition. And blood clots can form anywhere in the brain.

Brain States and Consciousness

1. cognitive neuroscience; our awareness of ourselves and our environment

2. selective attention; is
3. inattentional blindness; change blindness
4. biological rhythms
5. circadian rhythm
6. rises; fall
7. thinking; memory
8. age; experience; evening; morning
9. 5
10. eyes; dreams; REM sleep
11. alpha
12. hallucinations
13. sleep spindles
14. 3; 4; slow-wave; difficult; dual processing

During REM sleep, brain waves become as rapid as those of Stage 1 sleep, heart rate and breathing become more rapid and irregular, and genital arousal and rapid eye movements occur.

15. active; relaxed; paradoxical
16. dream; emotional
17. 90; briefer; longer; 20 to 25
18. **1.** b   **4.** c
    2. d   **5.** a
    3. e
19. two-thirds; one-third
20. genes; identical; culture; less

Sleep may have played a protected our distant ancestors during potentially dangerous times. A second theory is that sleep may help us recuperate, restoring and repairing brain tissue. Third, sleep restores and rebuilds our fading memories of the day's experiences. Finally, sleep may have evolved because it promotes growth.

21. free radicals; neurons; creative
22. pituitary; less; less
23. REM. The amygdala is involved in emotion, and dreams during REM sleep often tend to be emotional.
24. **d.** is the answer. Freud's theory proposed that dreams, which occur during fast-wave, REM sleep, serve as a psychic safety valve.
25. diminished productivity; irritability; ghrelin; leptin; cortisol
26. insomnia; reduce
27. narcolepsy; REM; muscle control
28. sleep apnea; obese
29. night terrors; 4; sleepwalking; sleeptalking; run; young children
30. REM
31. negative; attacked, pursued, or rejected, or of experiencing misfortune
32. manifest; latent
33. erotic; safety valve
34. information; memory
35. physiological; stimulation; infants
36. neural; brainstem; activation-synthesis; cognitive-development; maturation; cognitive
37. need; REM rebound

38. increase; REM rebound. The existence of REM rebound is evidence of our need for REM sleep.

39. latent. The analyst is evidently trying to go beyond the events in the dream and understand the dream's hidden meaning, or the dream's latent content.

Progress Test

Multiple-Choice Questions

1. **b.** is the answer. The autonomic nervous system controls internal functioning, including heartbeat, digestion, and glandular activity.
a. The functions mentioned are all automatic, not voluntary, so this answer cannot be correct.
c. This answer is incorrect because most organs are affected by both divisions of the ANS.
d. The somatic nervous system transmits sensory input to the central nervous system and enables voluntary control of skeletal muscles.

2. **c.** is the answer. Stimulus strength can affect only the number of times a neuron fires or the number of neurons that fire.
a., b., & d. These answers are incorrect because firing is an all-or-none response, so intensity remains the same regardless of stimulus strength. Nor can stimulus strength change the neuronal threshold or the impulse speed.

3. **a.** is the answer. Endorphins are neurotransmitters that function as natural painkillers. When the body has a supply of artificial painkillers such as heroin, endorphin production stops.
b. The production of neurotransmitters other than endorphins does not cease.
c. Neurotransmitter production does not increase during withdrawal.
d. Heroin makes use of the same receptor sites as endorphins.

4. **a.** is the answer. The PET scan measures glucose consumption in different areas of the brain to determine their levels of activity.
b. The fMRI compares MRI scans taken less than a second apart to reveal brain anatomy and function.
c. The EEG is a measure of electrical activity in the brain.
d. MRI uses magnetic fields and radio waves to produce computer-generated images of soft tissues of the body.

5. **a.** is the answer.
b. The reticular formation is linked to arousal.
c. The brainstem governs the mechanisms of basic survival—heartbeat and breathing, for example—and has many other roles.
d. The cerebellum coordinates movement output and balance.

6. **c.** is the answer. Wernicke's area is involved in comprehension, and people who have damage to Wernicke's area are unable to understand what is said to them.
a. The angular gyrus translates printed words into speech sounds; damage would result in the inability to read aloud.

b. Broca's area is involved in the physical production of speech; damage would result in the inability to speak fluently.
d. The cortex's association areas are involved in, among other things, processing language; damage to these areas wouldn't specifically affect comprehension.

7. **d.** is the answer.
a. In most persons, language is primarily a left hemisphere function.
b. Learned movements are unrelated to hemispheric specialization.
c. Arithmetic reasoning is generally a left hemisphere function.

8. **d.** is the answer. Biological psychologists study the links between biology (in this case, neurotransmitters) and psychology (depression, in this example).

9. **b.** is the answer.
a., c., & d. The autonomic nervous system, which is divided into the sympathetic and parasympathetic divisions, is concerned with regulating basic bodily maintenance functions.

10. **c.** is the answer.
a. An action potential will occur only when the neuron's threshold is *exceeded*.
b. An excitatory input that does not reach the neuron's threshold will not trigger an action potential.
d. This answer is incorrect because some neurotransmitters inhibit a neuron's readiness to fire.

11. **d.** is the answer. A neuron receives incoming stimuli on its dendrites and cell body. These electrochemical signals are combined in the cell body, generating an impulse that travels down the axon, causing the release of neurotransmitter substances into the synaptic cleft or gap.

12. **c.** is the answer.
a. Each hemisphere of the brain is divided into four lobes.
b. Neurotransmitters are the chemicals involved in synaptic transmission in the nervous system.
d. Enzymes are chemicals that facilitate various chemical reactions throughout the body but are not involved in communication within the endocrine system.

13. **c.** is the answer. The reticular formation plays an important role in arousal.
a. The thalamus relays sensory input.
b. The corpus callosum links the two cerebral hemispheres.
d. The cerebellum is involved in coordination of movement output and balance.

14. **b.** is the answer.

15. **b.** is the answer. Association areas interpret, integrate, and act on information from other areas of the cortex.

16. **a.** is the answer. The visual cortex is located at the very back of the brain.

17. **b.** is the answer.
a., c., & d. Spatial reasoning, perceptual skills, and the left side of the body are primarily influenced by the right hemisphere.

18. **a.** is the answer. Sensory neurons in the somatic nervous system relay such messages.
    b. & c. These divisions of the autonomic nervous system are concerned with the regulation of bodily maintenance functions such as heartbeat, digestion, and glandular activity.
    d. The spinal cord itself is part of the central nervous system, but the message is carried to the spinal cord by the somatic division of the peripheral nervous system.

19. **b.** is the answer. Endorphins are neurotransmitters that function as natural painkillers and are evidently involved in the "runner's high" and other situations in which discomfort or fatigue is expected but not experienced.
    a. ACh is a neurotransmitter involved in muscular control.
    c. Dopamine is a neurotransmitter involved in, among other things, motor control.
    d. Norepinephrine is an adrenal hormone released to help us respond in moments of danger.

20. **d.** is the answer.

21. **d.** is the answer. The pituitary regulates body growth, and some of its secretions regulate the release of hormones from other glands.
    a. The adrenal glands are stimulated by the autonomic nervous system to release epinephrine and norepinephrine.
    b. The thyroid gland affects metabolism, among other things.
    c. The hypothalamus regulates the pituitary but does not itself directly regulate growth.

22. **d.** is the answer. Also known as adrenaline and noradrenaline, epinephrine and norepinephrine are hormones released by the adrenal glands.

23. **d.** is the answer. The cerebellum is involved in the coordination of voluntary muscular movements.
    a. The medulla regulates breathing and heartbeat.
    b. The thalamus relays sensory inputs to the appropriate higher centers of the brain.
    c. The hypothalamus is concerned with the regulation of basic drives and emotions.

24. **a.** is the answer. The reticular formation controls arousal via its connections to the cortex. Thus, separating the two produces a coma.
    b., c., & d. None of these structures controls arousal. The hypothalamus regulates hunger, thirst, sexual behavior, and other basic drives; the thalamus is a sensory relay station; and the cerebellum is involved in the coordination of voluntary movement.

25. **b.** is the answer.
    c. & d. These refer to the sensory cortex.

26. **c.** is the answer. The corpus callosum is a large band of neural fibers linking the right and left cerebral hemispheres. To sever the corpus callosum is in effect to split the brain.

27. **d.** is the answer. The frontal lobe is in the front of the brain. Just behind is the parietal lobe. The occipital lobe is located at the very back of the head and

just below the parietal lobe. Next to the occipital lobe and toward the front of the head is the temporal lobe.

28. **d.** is the answer. As demonstrated in the case of Phineas Gage, injury to the frontal lobe may produce such changes in personality.
    a. Damage to the parietal lobe might disrupt functions involving the sensory cortex.
    b. Damage to the temporal lobe might impair hearing.
    c. Occipital damage might impair vision.

29. **c.** is the answer.

30. **a.** is the answer.
    b. & c. Delta waves predominate during Stages 3 and 4. Stage 3 is the transition between Stages 2 and 4 and is associated with a pattern that has elements of both stages.
    d. Faster, nearly waking brain waves occur during REM sleep.

31. **d.** is the answer.
    a., b., & c. During non-REM Stages 1–4 heart rate and breathing are slow and regular and the genitals are not aroused.

32. **d.** is the answer.

33. **d.** is the answer.

34. **a.** is the answer. Like alcohol, sleeping pills carry the undesirable consequence of reducing REM sleep and may make insomnia worse in the long run.
    b., c., & d. Sleeping pills do not produce these effects.

35. **a.** is the answer. Freud saw dreams as psychic safety valves that discharge unacceptable feelings that are often related to erotic wishes.
    b. & c. These physiological theories of dreaming are not associated with Freud.
    d. According to Freud, dreams represent the individual's conflicts and wishes but in disguised, rather than transparent, form.

36. **d.** is the answer.
    a., b., & c. Each of these describes a valid theory of dreaming that was mentioned in the text.

37. **b.** is the answer. Following REM deprivation, people temporarily increase their amount of REM sleep, in a phenomenon known as REM rebound.
    a. Just the opposite is true: The amount of REM sleep is greatest in infancy.
    c. Deprived of REM sleep by repeated awakenings, people return more and more quickly to the REM stages after falling back to sleep. They by no means adapt easily to the deprivations.
    d. Just the opposite occurs: They tend to suppress REM sleep.

38. **b.** is the answer.
    a. Neurogenesis is the formation of new neurons.
    c. Narcolepsy is a sleep disorder in which the person falls asleep at inopportune times.
    d. The all-or-none response refers to the fact that neurons either respond or do not respond.

39. **d.** is the answer.
    a. The brain waves of REM sleep (dream sleep) are more like those of Stage 1 sleepers.
    b. Stage 2 is characterized by sleep spindles.
    c. Stages 3 and 4 are characterized by slow, rolling delta waves.

40. **c.** is the answer.

41. **d.** is the answer.

42. **a.** is the answer.
    b. During REM sleep, muscular tension is low.
    c. Night terrors are associated with Stage 4 sleep.
    d. Alpha waves are characteristic of the relaxed, awake state.

43. **d.** is the answer.

44. **a.** is the answer.
    b. & c. These essentially Freudian explanations of the purpose of dreaming are based on the idea that a dream is a psychic safety valve that harmlessly discharges otherwise inexpressible feelings.
    d. This explanation of the function of dreaming is associated with the information-processing viewpoint.

Matching Items 1

1. d   5. b   9. h
2. a   6. c   10. i
3. e   7. g
4. f   8. j

Matching Items 2

1. c   5. e
2. h   6. b
3. f   7. a
4. g   8. d

Application Essay

The body's response to stress is regulated by the nervous system. As the date of the exam approaches, the stressed student's cerebral cortex activates the hypothalamus, triggering the release of hormones that in turn activate the sympathetic branch of the autonomic nervous system and the endocrine system. The autonomic nervous system controls involuntary bodily responses such as breathing, heartbeat, and digestion. The endocrine system's glands secrete hormones into the bloodstream that regulate the functions of body organs.

In response to activation by the hypothalamus, the student's pituitary gland would secrete a hormone, which in turn triggers the release of epinephrine, norepinephrine, and other stress hormones from the adrenal glands. These hormones would help the student's body manage stress by making nutrients available to meet the increased demands for energy stores the body often faces in coping with stress. As these hormones activate the sympathetic division of the autonomic system, the body's fight-or-flight response occurs, including increased heart rate, breathing, and blood pressure and the suppression of digestion. After the exam date has passed, the student's body would attempt to restore its normal, pre-stress state. The parasympathetic branch of the autonomic system would slow the student's heart-

beat and breathing and digestive processes would no longer be suppressed, perhaps causing the student to feel hungry.

Terms and Concepts

1. **Biological psychology** is the study of the links between biology and behavior.

2. The **neuron**, or nerve cell, is the basic building block of the nervous system.

3. The **dendrites** of a neuron are the bushy, branching extensions that receive messages from other nerve cells and conduct impulses toward the cell body.

4. The **axon** of a neuron is the extension that sends impulses to other nerve cells or to muscles or glands.

5. An **action potential** is a neural impulse that travels down the nerve cell's axon.

6. A **synapse** is the junction between the axon tip of the sending neuron and the dendrite or cell body of the receiving neuron. The tiny gap at this junction is called the *synaptic gap* or *cleft*.

7. A neuron's **threshold** is the level of stimulation that must be exceeded in order for the neuron to fire, or generate an electrical impulse.

8. The **all-or-none response** is a neuron's reaction of either firing (with a full-strength response) or not firing.

9. **Neurotransmitters** are chemicals that are released into synaptic gaps and so *transmit neural messages* from neuron to neuron.

10. **Opiates** are chemicals, such as morphine, that depress neural activity, temporarily lessening pain and anxiety.

11. **Endorphins** are natural, opiatelike neurotransmitters linked to pain control and to pleasure.

    Memory aid: <u>End</u>orphins *end* pain.

12. The **nervous system** is the speedy, electrochemical communication system, consisting of all the nerve cells in the peripheral and central nervous systems.

13. The **central nervous system (CNS)** consists of the brain and spinal cord; it is located at the *center*, or internal core, of the body.

14. The **peripheral nervous system (PNS)** includes the sensory and motor neurons that connect the central nervous system to the body's sense receptors, muscles, and glands; it is at the *periphery* of the body relative to the brain and spinal cord.

15. **Nerves** are bundles of neural axons, which are part of the PNS, that connect the central nervous system with muscles, glands, and sense organs.

16. **Sensory neurons** carry information from the sense receptors to the central nervous system for processing.

17. **Motor neurons** carry information and instructions for action from the central nervous system to muscles and glands.

18. **Interneurons** are the neurons of the central nervous system that link the sensory and motor neurons in the transmission of sensory inputs and motor outputs.

19. The **somatic nervous system** is the division of the peripheral nervous system that enables voluntary control of the skeletal muscles; also called the *skeletal nervous system*.

20. The **autonomic nervous system** is the division of the peripheral nervous system that controls the glands and the muscles of internal organs and thereby controls internal functioning; it regulates the *automatic* behaviors necessary for survival.

21. The **sympathetic nervous system** is the division of the autonomic nervous system that arouses the body, mobilizing its energy in stressful situations.

22. The **parasympathetic nervous system** is the division of the autonomic nervous system that calms the body, conserving its energy.

23. The **endocrine system**, the body's "slower" chemical communication system, consists of glands that secrete hormones into the bloodstream.

24. **Hormones** are chemical messengers, mostly those manufactured by the endocrine glands, that are produced in one tissue and circulate through the bloodstream to their target tissues, on which they have specific effects.

25. The **adrenal glands** produce epinephrine and norepinephrine, hormones that prepare the body to deal with emergencies or stress.

26. The **pituitary gland**, under the influence of the hypothalamus, regulates growth and controls other endocrine glands; sometimes called the "master gland."

27. An **EEG (electroencephalograph)** is an apparatus, using electrodes placed on the scalp, that records waves of electrical activity that sweep across the brain's surface. *Encephalo* comes from a Greek word meaning "related to the brain."

28. The **PET (positron emission tomography) scan** measures the levels of activity of different areas of the brain by tracing their consumption of a radioactive form of glucose, the brain's fuel.

29. **MRI (magnetic resonance imaging)** uses magnetic fields and radio waves to produce computer-generated images that show brain structures more clearly.

30. In a **fMRI (functional magnetic resonance imaging)**, MRI scans taken less than a second apart are compared to reveal bloodflow and, therefore, brain anatomy and function.

31. The **brainstem**, the oldest and innermost region of the brain, is an extension of the spinal cord and is the central core of the brain; its structures direct automatic survival functions.

32. Located in the brainstem, the **medulla** controls breathing and heartbeat.

33. Located atop the brainstem, the **thalamus** routes incoming messages to the appropriate cortical centers and transmits replies to the medulla and cerebellum.

34. Also part of the brainstem, the **reticular formation** is a nerve network that plays an important role in controlling arousal.

35. The **cerebellum** processes sensory input and coordinates movement output and balance.

36. The **limbic system** is the neural system associated with emotions such as fear and aggression and basic physiological drives.

    Memory aid: Its name comes from the Latin word *limbus*, meaning "border"; the **limbic system** is at the border of the brainstem and cerebral hemispheres.

37. The **amygdala** is part of the limbic system and influences the emotions of fear and aggression.

38. Also part of the limbic system, the **hypothalamus** regulates hunger, thirst, body temperature, and sex; helps govern the endocrine system via the pituitary gland; and contains the so-called reward centers of the brain.

39. The **cerebral cortex** is a thin intricate covering of interconnected neural cells atop the cerebral hemispheres. The seat of information processing, the cortex is responsible for those complex functions that make us distinctively human.

    Memory aid: Cortex in Latin means "bark." As bark covers a tree, the **cerebral cortex** is the "bark of the brain."

40. Located at the front of the brain, just behind the forehead, the **frontal lobes** are involved in speaking and muscle movements and in making plans and judgments.

41. Situated between the frontal and occipital lobes, the **parietal lobes** contain the sensory cortex.

42. Located at the back and base of the brain, the **occipital lobes** contain the visual cortex, which receives information from the eyes.

43. Located on the sides of the brain, the **temporal lobes** contain the auditory areas, which receive information from the ears.

    Memory aid: The **temporal lobes** are located near the *temples.*

44. Located at the back of the frontal lobe, the **motor cortex** controls voluntary movement.

45. The **sensory cortex** is located at the front of the parietal lobes, just behind the motor cortex. It registers and processes body touch and movement sensations.

46. **Hallucinations** are false sensory experiences that occur without any sensory stimulus.

47. Located throughout the cortex, **association areas** of the brain are involved in higher mental functions, such as learning, remembering, and abstract thinking.

Memory aid: Among their other functions, **association areas** of the cortex are involved in integrating, or *associating*, information from different areas of the brain.

=**48.Broca's area**, located in the left frontal lobe, is involved in controlling the motor ability to produce speech.

49. **Wernicke's area,** located in the left temporal lobe, is involved in language comprehension and expression.

50. **Plasticity** is the brain's capacity for modification, as evidenced by brain reorganization following damage (especially in children).

51. **Neurogenesis** is the formation of new neurons.

52. The **corpus callosum** is the large band of neural fibers that links the right and left cerebral hemispheres. Without this band of nerve fibers, the two hemispheres could not interact.

53. **Split brain** is a condition in which the major connections between the two cerebral hemispheres (the corpus callosum) are severed, literally resulting in a split brain.

54. For most psychologists, **consciousness** is our awareness of ourselves and our environment.

55. **Selective attention** is the focusing of our awareness on a particular stimulus.

56. **Inattentional blindness** is a perceptual error in which we fail to see a visible object when our attention is directed elsewhere.

57. A **circadian rhythm** is any regular bodily rhythm, such as body temperature and sleep-wakefulness, that follows a 24-hour cycle.

    Memory aid: In Latin, *circa* means "about" and *dies* means "day." A **circadian rhythm** is one that is about a day, or 24 hours, in duration.

58. **REM (rapid eye movement) sleep** is the sleep stage in which the brain and eyes are active, the muscles are relaxed, and vivid dreaming occurs; also known as *paradoxical sleep.*

    Memory aid: **REM** is an acronym for rapid eye movement, the distinguishing feature of this sleep stage that led to its discovery.

59. **Alpha waves** are the relatively slow brain waves characteristic of an awake, relaxed state.

60. **Sleep** is the natural, periodic, reversible loss of consciousness, on which the body and mind depend for healthy functioning.

61. **Insomnia** is a sleep disorder in which the person regularly has difficulty in falling or staying asleep.

62. **Narcolepsy** is a sleep disorder in which the victim suffers sudden, uncontrollable sleep attacks, often characterized by entry directly into REM.

63. **Sleep apnea** is a sleep disorder in which the person ceases breathing while asleep, briefly arouses to gasp for air, falls back asleep, and repeats this cycle throughout the night.

    Example: One theory of the sudden infant death syndrome is that it is caused by **sleep apnea.**

64. **Dreams** are vivid sequences of images, emotions, and thoughts, the most vivid of which occur during REM sleep.

65. In Freud's theory of dreaming, the **manifest content** is the remembered story line.

66. In Freud's theory of dreaming, the **latent content** is the underlying but censored meaning of a dream.

    Memory aids for 65 and 66: Manifest means "clearly apparent, obvious"; *latent* means "hidden, concealed." A dream's **manifest content** is that which is obvious; its **latent content** remains hidden until its symbolism is interpreted.

67. **REM rebound** is the tendency for REM sleep to increase following REM sleep deprivation.

3

DEVELOPING THROUGH THE LIFE SPAN

Developmental psychologists study the life cycle, from conception to death. Chapter 3 covers physical, cognitive, and social development over the life span and introduces three major issues in developmental psychology: (1) how our genetic heritage, or nature, interacts with our individual experiences, or nurture, to shape who we are; (2) whether development is best described as gradual and continuous or as a discontinuous sequence of stages; and (3) whether the individual's personality remains stable or changes over the life span.

CHAPTER REVIEW

First, skim each text section, noting headings and boldface items. Review the section by reading the objectives and summaries provided here, then answer the questions that follow. In some cases, STUDY TIPS explain how best to learn a difficult concept and APPLICATIONS help you to know how well you understand the material. Check your understanding of the material by consulting the answers beginning on page 59. Do not continue with the next section until you understand each answer. If you need to, review or reread the section in the textbook before continuing.

Introduction

Objective 1: State three areas of change that developmental psychologists study, and identify the three major issues in developmental psychology.

Developmental psychologists study physical, cognitive, and social changes throughout the life cycle. Three issues pervade this study: (1) the relative impact of genes and experience on behavior, (2) whether development is best described as gradual and continuous or as a sequence of separate stages, and (3) whether personality traits remain stable or change over the life span.

1. Scientists who study physical, cognitive, and social changes throughout the life cycle are called

   _____ _____ .

2. One of the major issues in developmental psychology concerns how our genes interact with our experience to influence our development; this is the issue of _____ and _____ .

3. A second developmental issue concerns whether developmental changes are gradual or abrupt; this is the issue of _____ or

   _____ .

4. A third controversial issue concerns the consistency of personality and whether development is characterized more by _____ over time or by change.

Prenatal Development and the Newborn

Objective 2: Describe conception, and define *chromosome, DNA, gene,* and *genome,* noting how they relate.

A total of 200 million or more sperm deposited during intercourse approach the egg 85,000 times their own size. The few that make it to the egg release digestive enzymes that eat away the egg's protective coating, allowing a sperm to penetrate. The egg's surface blocks out all others and within a half day, the egg nucleus and the sperm nucleus fuse.

Every cell contains the genetic master code for the body. Within each cell are **chromosomes,** threadlike structures composed of molecules called **DNA (deoxyribonucleic acid).** *Genes* are DNA segments that, when "turned on," guide your development. These elements make up your *heredity.* The *genome* provides the complete instructions for making an organism, consisting of all the genetic material in the organism's chromosomes. Variations at particular gene sites in the DNA define each person's uniqueness. Human traits are influenced by many genes *interacting* with the *environment.*

1. Conception begins when a woman's

   _____ releases a mature

   _____ .

2. The few _____ from the man that reach the egg release digestive _____ that eat away the egg's protective covering. As soon as one sperm penetrates the egg, the egg's surface _____ all other sperm.

3. The egg and sperm _____ fuse and become one.

4. The master plans for development are stored in the _____ . Each is composed of molecules of _____ .

5. The biochemical units that influence development are called _____ . Together, these are the elements of _____ .

6. The complete instructions for making an organism are referred to as the human _____ .

STUDY TIP: To keep the various elements of heredity (chromosomes, genes, and DNA) straight, you might find it helpful to think of a metaphor. The chromosomes would be the "books" of heredity, with the "words" that make each of us a distinctive human being the genes, and the "letters," the DNA. You can also keep the relationship among genes, DNA, and chromosomes straight by thinking visually. Chromosomes are the largest of the units. They are made of up genes, which are in turn made up of DNA. Test your understanding by identifying the elements of heredity in the drawing below. Note that c. is the unit that contains the code for proteins, and d. is the spiraling, complex molecule.

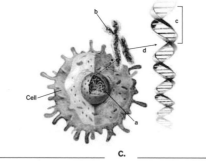

7. a. _____   **c.** _____
   b. _____   **d.** _____

8. Human differences are also shaped by external influences in the _____ . In psychology, an _____ occurs when the effect of one factor (such as _____) depends on another factor (such as _____).

APPLICATION:

9. Which of the following is an example of an interaction?
   a. Swimmers swim fastest during competition against other swimmers.
   b. Swimmers with certain personality traits swim fastest during competition, while those with other personality traits swim fastest during solo time trials.
   c. As the average daily temperature increases, sales of ice cream decrease.
   d. As the average daily temperature increases, sales of lemonade increase.

Objective 3: Discuss the course of prenatal development and the destructive impact of teratogens.

The fertilized egg is called a **zygote.** Fewer than half of these zygotes survive. In the first week, cell division produces a zygote of some 100 identical cells, which then begin to specialize. About 10 days after conception, the zygote's outer cells attach to the uterine wall and become the placenta through which nourishment and oxygen passes. The inner cells become the **embryo.** If the zygote has split in two, **identical twins** develop. If two eggs have been fertilized, **fraternal twins** develop.

By 9 weeks after conception, the embryo looks unmistakably human and is now a **fetus.** During the sixth month, internal organs such as the stomach have

become sufficiently formed and functional to allow a prematurely born fetus a chance of survival. At each prenatal stage, genetic and environmental factors affect development. Along with nutrients and oxygen, **teratogens** ingested by the mother can reach the developing child. The teratogens can place the fetus at risk. If the mother drinks heavily, the effects may be visible as **fetal alcohol syndrome (FAS).**

10. Fertilized human eggs are called _____ . During the first week, the cells in this cluster begin to _____ . The outer part of the fertilized egg attaches to the _____ wall, forming the _____ .

11. From about 2 until 8 weeks of age the developing human, formed from the inner cells of the fertilized egg, is called a(n) _____ .

12. Twins who developed from a single egg are genetically _____ . Twins who developed from different fertilized eggs are no more genetically alike than siblings and are called _____ twins.

13. During the final stage of prenatal development, the developing human is called a(n) _____ .

14. Along with nutrients and oxygen, a range of harmful substances known as _____ can pass through the placenta.

15. If a woman drinks during pregnancy, the alcohol enters her and her fetus' bloodstream, depressing activity in both their _____ nervous systems. If a mother drinks heavily, her baby is at risk for the birth defects and mental retardation that accompany _____ _____ .

Objective 4: Describe some abilities and traits of the newborn.

Newborns are surprisingly competent. They are born with sensory equipment and **reflexes** that facilitate their interacting with adults and securing nourishment. Touched on its cheek, a baby opens its mouth and *roots* for a nipple. Newborns turn their heads in the direction of human voices and gaze longer at a drawing of a face-like image. They prefer to look at objects 8 to 12 inches away, the approximate distance between a nursing infant's eyes and the mother's. Within days after birth, the newborn distinguishes its mother's odor, and at 3 weeks, the newborn prefers its mother's voice.

Similar as newborns are, they also differ. This difference is **temperament,** or emotional excitability. Temperament, which is one aspect of our personality, seems to be rooted in our biology.

16. Newborns come equipped with automatic
_____ responses suited to their
survival. When an infant's cheek is touched, for
example, it will vigorously _____
for a nipple.

Give some evidence supporting the claim that a newborn's sensory equipment is biologically prewired to
facilitate social responsiveness.

17. The term that refers to the inborn personality, especially the child's emotional excitability, is
_____ , which _____
(does/does not) endure over time.

18. From the first weeks of life, _____
babies are more _____ ,
_____ , and _____ .
In contrast, _____ babies are
_____ , _____ ,
and _____ in feeding and sleeping.

19. Faced with a new or strange situation, high-strung
infants become _____ (more/less)
physiologically aroused than less excitable infants.

Objective 5: Explain how twin and adoption studies help
us understand the effects of nature and nurture.

20. (Close-Up) To study the power and limits of genetic
influences on behavior, researchers use
_____ and _____
studies.

21. (Close-Up) In terms of abilities, personal traits, and
interests, identical twins are _____
(more/no more) alike than are fraternal twins.

22. (Close-Up) Through research on identical twins
raised apart, psychologists are able to study the
influence of the _____ .

23. (Close-Up) Studies tend to show that the personalities of adopted children _____
(do/do not) closely resemble those of their adoptive
parents. In traits such as _____
and _____ , they are more similar
to their biological parents.

24. Despite growing up in the same home environment, Karen
and her brother John have personalities as different from
each other as two people selected randomly from the
population. This is because of the _____
of their individual _____ and nonshared
_____ .

25. Dr. Gonzalez is conducting research on whether people
who do well in school can thank their genes or their environment for their success. To distinguish how much
genetic and environmental factors affect school success,
Dr. Gonzalez should compare children with _____
(the same/different) genes and _____
(the same/different) environments.

Infancy and Childhood

Objective 6: Describe some developmental changes in
brain and motor abilities during infancy and childhood.

Within the brain, nerve cells form before birth. After
birth, the neural networks that enable us to walk, talk,
and remember have a wild growth spurt. From ages 3 to
6, growth occurs most rapidly in the frontal lobes, which
enable rational planning. The association areas of the
cortex, which are linked to thinking, memory, and language, are the last brain areas to develop. *Maturation,*
the biological growth processes that enable orderly
changes in behavior, sets the basic course of development and experience adjusts it. Maturation accounts for
common sequences, from standing before walking to
using nouns before adjectives. We seem to have a **critical
period** for some skills. Lacking certain experiences, the
brain cells normally assigned to the relevant skills may
be *pruned.*

As infants' muscles and nervous systems mature,
they begin to control their movements. With occasional
exceptions, the sequence is universal. Babies roll over
before they sit unsupported, and they usually walk
before they run. Heredity plays a major role. Identical
twins typically begin sitting up and walking on nearly
the same day. Experience has a limited effect for other
physical skills as well, including those that enable bowel
and bladder control.

1. Biological growth processes that enable orderly
changes in behavior are called _____ .

2. The developing brain _____
(over/under)produces neurons. At birth, the human
nervous system _____ (is/is not)
fully mature.

3. Between 3 and 6 years of age, the brain is developing
most rapidly in the _____
lobes, which enable _____
_____ . The last cortical areas to

develop are the _____

_____ .

4. After puberty, a process of _____ shuts down some neural connections and strengthens others. For some skills there is a

_____ _____ during which exposure to certain experiences is needed for normal development to occur.

5. Infants pass the milestones of _____ development at different rates, but the basic

_____ of stages is fixed. For example, they walk before they _____ .

6. Heredity plays a _____ (major/minor) role in motor development.

7. Until the necessary muscular and neural maturation is complete, including the rapid development of the brain's _____ , experience has a _____ (large/small) effect on behavior.

APPLICATION:

8. Calvin, who is trying to impress his psychology professor with his knowledge of infant motor development, asks why some infants learn to roll over before they lift their heads from a prone position, while others develop these skills in the opposite order. What should Calvin's professor conclude from this question?
   a. Calvin clearly understands that the sequence of motor development is not the same for all infants.
   b. Calvin doesn't know what he's talking about. Although some infants reach these developmental milestones ahead of others, the order is the same for all infants.
   c. Calvin needs to be reminded that rolling over is an inherited reflex, not a learned skill.
   d. Calvin understands an important principle: Motor development is unpredictable.

Objective 7: State Piaget's understanding of how the mind develops, and outline Piaget's four stages of cognitive development, noting current thinking regarding cognitive stages.

Jean Piaget maintained that the mind of the child is not a miniature model of the adult's. He theorized that the mind tries to make sense of experience by forming *schemas,* concepts or frameworks that organize and interpret information.

Cognition refers to all the mental activities associated with thinking, knowing, remembering, and communicating. During the *sensorimotor stage* (birth to nearly age 2) of cognitive development, children experience the world through their senses and actions. By about 8 months, an infant exhibits *object permanence,* an awareness that things still exist even when they are out of sight.

Piaget maintained that up to about age 6 or 7, children are in a *preoperational stage*—too young to perform mental operations. They are *egocentric,* that is, they cannot perceive things from another's point of view and lack a *theory of mind.* (*Autism* is also marked by impaired ability to infer others' mental states.) Piaget thought that at about age 6 or 7, children become capable of performing *concrete operations,* for example, those required to understand the principle of *conservation.* They think logically about concrete events and understand reversing mathematical operations. By age 12, reasoning expands from the purely concrete to encompass abstract thinking, which Piaget called *formal operational thinking.* At about the same time as Piaget was developing his theory, Lev Vygotsky proposed that children learn in part by talking to themselves and from *scaffolding* by parents.

Today's research shows that young children are more capable and their development more continuous than Piaget believed. Nonetheless, studies support his idea that human cognition unfolds basically in the sequence he proposed.

9. The first researcher to show that the thought processes of adults and children are very different was _____ . He believed that children are _____ thinkers as they try to make sense of their experiences.

10. To organize and interpret his or her experiences, the developing child constructs concepts or mental molds called _____ .

11. The term for all the mental activities associated with thinking, remembering, communicating, and knowing is _____ .

12. In Piaget's first stage of development, the _____ stage, children experience the world through their motor and sensory interactions with objects.

13. The awareness that things continue to exist even when they are removed from view is called

_____ _____ .

14. Developmental researchers have found that Piaget and his followers _____ (overestimated/underestimated) young children's competence and that development is more _____ than Piaget believed.

15. The principle that the quantity of a substance remains the same even when the shape of its container changes is called _____ . Piaget believed that preschoolers, who are in the _____ stage, _____ (have/have not) developed this concept.

16. Preschoolers have difficulty perceiving things from another person's point of view. This inability is called _____ .

17. The child's growing ability to take another's perspective is evidence that the child is acquiring a _____ _____ . Between about 3½ and 4½, children come to realize that others may hold _____ _____ .

18. The disorder characterized by deficient _____ and _____ interaction and an impaired _____ _____ is _____ . This disorder is related to poor communication among brain areas that normally work together to enable taking another's _____ .

19. Piaget believed that children acquire the mental abilities needed to understand simple math and conservation by about _____ years of age. At this time, they enter the _____ _____ stage.

20. Russian psychologist _____ noted that by age _____ children stop thinking aloud and instead rely on _____ _____ . When parents give children words, they provide, according to this theorist, a _____ upon which the child can build higher-level thinking.

21. In Piaget's final stage, the _____ _____ stage, reasoning expands from the purely concrete to encompass _____ thinking.

22. Piaget identified significant milestones in cognitive development; his emphasis was less on the _____ at which children typically reach these milestones than on their _____ .

. . . .

STUDY TIP: Jean Piaget was the first major theorist to realize that each stage of life has its own characteristic way of thinking. To deepen your understanding of Jean Piaget's stages of cognitive development, fill in the blanks in the chart below. Do as much as you can without reviewing the text. To get you started, the first stage has been completed.

23. Typical Age Range	Stage	New Developments	Test to Determine if Someone Is in This Stage
Birth to nearly 2 years	Sensorimotor	Stranger anxiety Object permanence	Have the child's mother leave the room Hide a toy under a blanket
2 to _____	_____		
	Concrete _____		
About 12 through _____	_____		

APPLICATIONS:

24. Compared with when he was younger, 4-year-old Antonio is better able to empathize with his friend's feelings. This growing ability to take another's perspective indicates that Antonio is acquiring a _____ _____ .

25. As 8-year-old Gabriella observes, liquid is transferred from a tall, thin tube into a short, wide jar. She is asked if there is now less liquid in order to determine if she has mastered the concept of _____ .

26. Caleb is 14 months old and he behaves as though "out of sight is out of existence." He is in Piaget's _____ stage of cognitive development.

27. Makayla is 3 years old, can use language, and has trouble taking another person's perspective. She is in Piaget's _____ stage of cognitive development.

28. Four-year-old Jamail has a younger sister. When asked if he has a sister, he is likely to answer _____ (yes/no); when asked if his sister has a brother, Jamail is likely to answer _____ (yes/no).

Objective 8: Explain how the bonds of attachment form between parents and infants.

Stranger anxiety is the fear of unfamiliar faces that infants commonly display, beginning by about 8 months of age (soon after object permanence emerges). They greet strangers by crying and reaching for their familiar caregivers.

The *attachment* bond is a survival impulse that keeps infants close to their caregivers. The Harlows found that infant monkeys became attached to "mothers" that provided contact comfort rather than nourishment. Human infants also become attached to their parents or primary caregivers not simply because they gratify biological needs (nourishment) but because they provide body contact that is soft and warm.

29. Soon after _____

    _____ emerges and children

    become mobile, a new fear, called

    _____ _____ ,

    emerges. This fear emerges at about age _____ .

30. The development of a strong emotional bond

    between infant and parent is called

    _____ .

31. The Harlows' studies of monkeys have shown that

    mother-infant attachment does not depend on the

    mother providing nourishment as much as it does

    on her providing _____ _____ .

32. Human attachment involves one person providing

    another with a _____

    _____ when distressed and a

    _____ _____ from

    which to explore.

Objective 9: Contrast secure and insecure attachment, and discuss the roles of parents and infants in the development of attachment and an infant's feelings of basic trust.

When placed in a *strange situation* such as a laboratory playroom, about 60 percent of children display *secure attachment;* they play comfortably in their mother's presence, are distressed when she leaves, and seek contact when she returns. Other infants, who are *insecurely attached,* are less likely to explore their surroundings and, when their mother leaves, cry loudly and remain upset or seem indifferent to her going and returning. Sensitive, responsive parents tend to have securely attached children. Insensitive, unresponsive parents have infants who often become insecurely attached. Although genetically influenced temperament may elicit responsive parenting, parental sensitivity has been taught and does increase secure attachment to some extent. Erik Erikson attributed the child's development of

basic trust—a sense that the world is predictable and reliable—to sensitive, loving caregivers. Adult relationships tend to reflect the attachment styles of early childhood.

Infants who experience abuse or extreme neglect often become withdrawn, frightened, even speechless. Young monkeys who are deprived of attachment may, as adults, cower in fright or lash out in aggression when placed with other monkeys their age. In humans, too, the unloved sometimes become the unloving. But children are *resilient* and can go on to a better life.

Severe and prolonged abuse places children at increased risk for nightmares, depression, and an adolescence troubled by substance abuse, binge eating, and aggression.

33. Placed in a research setting called the

    _____ _____ ,

    children show one of two patterns of attachment:

    _____ attachment or

    _____ attachment.

Contrast the responses of securely and insecurely attached infants to strange situations.

Discuss the impact of responsive parenting on infant attachment.

34. Attachment style _____ (is/is not)

    entirely the result of parenting. Equally important is

    the infant's inborn _____ .

35. Separation anxiety peaks in infants around

    _____ months, then

    _____ (gradually declines/remains

    constant for about a year). This is true of children

    _____ (in North America/through-

    out the world).

36. According to Erikson, securely attached infants

    approach life with a sense of _____

    _____ .

37. Although abused children _____

    (are/are not) at risk for certain problems, some

    abused children show great _____

    and go on to lead better lives.

APPLICATION:

38. Layla and Christian Bishop have a 13-month-old boy. According to Erikson, the Bishops' sensitive, loving care of their child contributes to the child's _____ _____ .

Objective 10: Identify three primary parenting styles, and assess their impact on development.

Authoritarian parents impose rules and expect obedience. *Permissive* parents submit to their children's desires, make few demands, and use little punishment. *Authoritative* parents are both demanding and responsive. Children with the highest self-esteem, self-reliance, and social competence generally have warm, concerned, authoritative parents. However, other forces, such as **culture,** are also factors in how parents rear their children.

39. Parents who impose rules and expect obedience are exhibiting a(n) _____ style of parenting.

40. Parents who make few demands of their children and tend to submit to their children's desires are identified as _____ parents.

41. Setting and enforcing standards after discussion with their children is the approach taken by _____ parents.

42. Studies have shown that children with high self-esteem, self-restraint, and social competence tend to have _____ parents. Remember that these correlational studies _____ (do/do not) prove causation.

43. Culture refers to the set of _____ , _____ , _____ , and _____ shared by a group of people and transmitted from one _____ to the next.

44. The _____ approach to development reminds us that individual development is the product of biological influences such as _____ _____ ; psychological influences such as _____ ; and social-cultural influences such as _____ .

Adolescence

Objective 11: Define *adolescence,* and identify the major physical changes that occur during this period.

Adolescence, the transition period from childhood to adulthood, typically begins at **puberty** with the onset of rapid growth and developing sexual maturity. A surge of hormones triggers a two-year period of growth that begins in girls at about age 11 and in boys at about age 13. Just as in earlier stages, the sequence of changes is the same for everyone, but the timing is not. The landmarks of puberty are the first ejaculation (*spermarche*) in boys, which usually occurs by about age 14, and the first menstrual period (**menarche**) in girls, usually within a year of age 12.

Frontal lobe maturation that improves judgment and impulse control lags the emotional limbic system. The pubertal hormonal surge, early development of the emotional limbic system, and later maturation of the frontal lobe help explain teens' occasional impulsiveness, risky behaviors, and emotional storms.

1. *Adolescence* is defined as the transition period between _____ and _____ .

2. Adolescence begins with the time of developing sexual maturity known as _____ . A two-year period of rapid physical development begins in girls at about the age of _____ and in boys at about the age of _____ .

3. The first menstrual period is called _____ . In boys, the first ejaculation is called _____ .

4. The _____ (timing/sequence) of pubertal changes is more predictable than their _____ (timing/sequence).

5. Teens' occasional impulsiveness and risky behaviors may be due, in part, to the fact that development in the brain's _____ _____ lags behind that of the _____ _____ .

Objective 12: Describe adolescents' reasoning abilities and moral development, according to Piaget and Kohlberg.

During the early teen years, reasoning is often self-focused. Adolescents may think their private experiences are unique. Gradually, adolescents develop the capacity for what Piaget called *formal operations,* the capacity to reason abstractly. This includes the ability to test hypotheses and deduce conclusions. The new reasoning power is evident in adolescents' pondering and debating such abstract topics as human nature, good and evil, and truth and justice.

Lawrence Kohlberg contended that moral thinking likewise proceeds through a series of stages, from a *preconventional morality* of self-interest, to a *conventional morality* that cares for others and upholds laws and rules, to (in some people) a *postconventional morality* of agreed-upon rights or basic ethical principles. Kohlberg's critics argue that the postconventional level represents morality from the perspective of individualistic males and is biased against the moral reasoning of those in collectivist societies. Character-education programs teach children to empathize with others and to delay gratification. As thinking matures, behavior also becomes less selfish and more caring.

6. During the early teen years, reasoning is often _____ , as adolescents often feel their experiences are unique.

7. Piaget's final stage of cognitive development is the stage of _____ _____ . The adolescent in this stage is capable of thinking logically about _____ as well as concrete propositions. This enables them to detect _____ in others' reasoning and to spot hypocrisy.

8. The theorist who proposed that moral thought progresses through stages is _____ . These stages are divided into three basic levels: _____ , _____ , and _____ .

9. In the preconventional stages of morality, characteristic of children, the emphasis is on obeying rules in order to avoid _____ or gain _____ .

10. Conventional morality usually emerges by early _____ . The emphasis is on gaining social _____ or upholding the social _____ .

11. Individuals who base moral judgments on their own perceptions of basic ethical principles are said by Kohlberg to employ _____ morality.

12. Critics of Kohlberg's theory argue that the _____ level is found mostly among people of the European and North American educated _____ _____ . His theory is biased against _____ societies.

13. Morality involves doing the right thing. Today's _____-_____ _____ focus on moral issues and doing the right thing. They teach children _____ for others' feelings.

14. Children who learn to delay _____ become more socially responsible, _____ successful, and productive.

APPLICATIONS:

15. Jake, a junior in high school, regularly attends church because his family and friends think he should. Jake is in Kohlberg's _____ stage of moral reasoning.

16. In Jada's country, people believe in family togetherness above all else. Because her culture does not give priority to _____ , Kohlberg would say that she is not at his highest level of moral reasoning, the _____ level.

Objective 13: Identify Erikson's eight stages of psychosocial development and their accompanying issues.

Erik Erikson theorized eight stages of life, each with its own *psychosocial* task. In infancy (the first year), the issue is *trust* versus mistrust. In toddlerhood (the second year), the challenge is *autonomy* versus shame and doubt. Preschoolers (age 3 to 5) learn *initiative* or guilt, and elementary school children (age 6 to puberty) develop *competence* or inferiority. A chief task of adolescence is to solidify one's sense of self—one's *identity.* Part of this self-concept is their *social identity,* their sense of group membership. Adolescents usually try out different "selves" in different situations. Most adolescents eventually unify the various selves into a consistent and comfortable sense of themselves. For young adults (twenties to early forties) the issue is *intimacy,* the ability to form emotionally close relationships, versus isolation, and for middle-aged adults (forties to sixties), generativity versus stagnation. Late adulthood's (late sixties and older) challenge is integrity versus despair.

17. To refine their sense of identity, adolescents in Western cultures experiment with different _____ in different situations. The result may be role _____ , which is resolved by forming a self-definition, or _____ .

18. Cultures that place less value on _____ inform adolescents about who they are, rather than letting them decide on their own. Some adolescents may form an identity early, taking on their _____ values and expectations.

19. During the early to mid-teen years, self-esteem generally _____ (rises/falls/remains stable). During the late teens and twenties, self-esteem generally _____ (rises/falls/remains stable).

20. Erikson saw the formation of identity as a prerequisite for the development of _____ in young adulthood.

STUDY TIP: Summary tables can help clarify all the stages of a theory such as Erikson's. Complete the missing information in the following table of Erikson's stages of psychosocial development and use it as a study guide.

Group Age	Psychosocial Stage
Infancy	_____
_____	Autonomy vs. shame and doubt
Preschooler	_____
_____	Competence vs. inferiority
Adolescence	_____
_____	Intimacy vs. isolation
Middle adulthood	_____
_____	Integrity vs. despair

••

Objective 14: Contrast parental and peer influences during adolescence.

As adolescents in Western cultures form their own identities, they become increasingly independent of their parents. Nonetheless, researchers have found that most teenagers relate to their parents reasonably well. Positive relations with parents support positive peer relations. Teens are herd animals, and they talk, dress, and act more like their peers than their parents. Although adolescence is a time of increasing peer influence, parents continue to influence teens in shaping their religious faith as well as college and career choices.

21. Adolescence is typically a time of increasing influence from one's _____ and decreasing influence from _____ .

22. Most adolescents report that they _____ (do/do not) like their parents. Positive parent-teen relations tend to go with _____ (positive/negative) peer relations.

23. When rejected adolescents withdraw, they are vulnerable to _____ , low _____ , and _____ . Peer approval matters.

Objective 15 Discuss the value of parenting in adolescent development.

Although parents do not determine their children's personality, they do influence their attitudes, values, manners, faith, and politics. Child neglect, abuse, and parental divorce are rare in adoptive homes. And adopted children tend to be more self-giving than average.

24. (Thinking Critically) Twin and adoption studies show that shared environmental influences account for less than _____ (how many?) percent of children's personality differences.

25. (Thinking Critically) Adoption studies show that par-

enting _____ (does/does not) matter. For example, adopted children often score _____ (higher/lower) than their biological parents on intelligence tests.

26. (Thinking Critically) Parents influence their children's attitudes, values, manners, _____ , and _____ . Peer influence is primarily a result of the desire to fit in, and similarities among peers may result from a _____ _____ , as kids seek out peers with similar attitudes and interests.

Objective 16: Discuss the characteristics of emerging adulthood.

Clearly, the graduation from adolescence to adulthood is now taking longer. In the United States, the average age at first marriage has increased four years since 1960. The time from 18 to the mid-twenties is an increasingly not-yet-settled phase of life which is now called *emerging adulthood.* During this time, many young people attend college or work but continue to live with their parents.

27. In earlier times, society marked the transition to adulthood with an elaborate initiation called a public _____ _____ _____ . As a result of increased _____ _____ and weakened _____ - _____ bonds, sexual maturity is beginning _____ (earlier/later) than in the past.

28. Because the time from 18 to the mid-twenties is increasingly a not-yet-settled phase of life, some psychologists refer to this period as _____ _____ .

29. Researchers who emphasize _____ and _____ view development as a slow, ongoing process. Those who emphasize _____ see development more as a process of maturation.

Adulthood

Objective 16: Identify the major changes in physical and sensory abilities that occur in middle adulthood and later life.

Muscular strength, reaction time, sensory keenness, and cardiac output crest by the mid-twenties and then slowly begin to decline. These barely perceptible physical declines of early adulthood begin to accelerate during middle adulthood. For women, a significant physical change of adult life is *menopause,* the end of the menstrual cycle. A woman's attitudes and expectations influence the impact of menopause. Men experience no equivalent of menopause and no sharp drop in sex hormones. After middle age, most men and women remain capable of satisfying sexual activity.

In later life, vision, muscle strength, reaction time, stamina, hearing, and smell diminish. Short-term ailments are fewer, but a weakened immune system makes life-threatening ailments more likely.

1. During adulthood, age _____ (is/is not) a very good predictor of people's traits.

2. The mid-twenties are the peak years for

    _____ _____ ,

    _____ _____ ,

    _____ _____ , and

    _____ _____ .

    Because they mature earlier, _____ (women/men) also peak earlier.

3. During early and middle adulthood, physical vigor has less to do with _____ than with a person's _____ and _____ habits.

4. The end of the menstrual cycle, known as _____ , occurs within a few years of _____ . A woman's experience during this time depends largely on her _____ and _____ .

5. Although men do not go through any kind of menopause, they do experience a more gradual decline in _____ count, level of the hormone _____ , and speed of erection and ejaculation during later life.

6. With age, the eye's pupil _____ (shrinks/enlarges) and its lens becomes cloudy. As a result, the amount of light that reaches the retina is _____ (increased/reduced).

7. Although older adults are _____ (more/less) susceptible to life-threatening ailments, they suffer from short-term ailments such as flu _____ (more/less) often than younger adults.

8. Aging causes a gradual loss of _____ _____ . The brain regions that shrink during aging are the areas important to _____ .

Objective 17: Assess the impact of aging on memory and intelligence.

Neural processes slow, and, compared with teens and young adults, older people take a bit longer time to react, to solve perceptual puzzles, and to remember names.

Exercising the body feeds the brain and helps compensate for the loss of brain cells. As the years pass, recognition memory shows minimal decline; recall shows greater decline.

Crystallized intelligence—one's accumulated knowledge and verbal skills as reflected in vocabulary and analogies tests—increases into middle age. *Fluid intelligence* —one's ability to reason speedily and abstractly, as when solving novel logic problems—declines slowly up to age 75, then more rapidly, especially after age 85.

Cross-cultural research indicates that nearness to death—the *terminal-decline phenomenon*—tells more about mental ability than age does.

9. The speed of neural processing _____ (slows/does not slow) during late adulthood. Studies of developmental changes in learning and memory show that during adulthood there is a decline in the ability to _____ (recall/recognize) new information but not in the ability to _____ (recall/recognize) such information.

10. The accumulation of stored information that comes with education and experience is called _____ intelligence, which tends to _____ with age.

11. The ability to reason abstractly is referred to as _____ intelligence, which tends to _____ with age.

12. Physical exercise stimulates _____ _____ development and _____ connections, thanks to increased _____ and nutrient flow.

APPLICATIONS:

13. Deborah is a mathematician and Willie is a philosopher. Considering their professions, Deborah will make her most significant career accomplishments _____ (at about the same time as/at an earlier age than/at a later age than) Willie will.

14. Sixty-five-year-old Jordan cannot reason as well as he could when he was younger. Most likely, Jordan's _____ intelligence has declined.

15. Which statement illustrates cognitive development during the course of adult life?
    a. Forty-three-year-old Sophia has better recognition memory than 72-year-old Kylie.
    b. Both Sophia and Kylie have strong recall and recognition memory.
    c. Kylie's recognition memory decreased sharply at age 50.
    d. Forty-three-year-old Sophia has better recall memory than 72-year-old Kylie.

Objective 18: Discuss the importance of love, marriage, children, and work in adulthood.

Two basic aspects of our lives dominate adulthood. Erik Erikson called them *intimacy* (forming close relationships) and *generativity* (being productive and supporting future generations). Evolutionary psychologists suggest that marriage had survival value for our ancestors in that parents who stayed together and raised children to a child-bearing age had a greater chance of passing their genes on. Compared with their counterparts of 50 years ago, people in Western countries are better educated and marrying later. Yet they are twice as likely to divorce. Nonetheless, more than 9 in 10 heterosexual adults marry; research indicates that married people are generally happier when compared with the unmarried. Often, love bears children. Most parents are happy to see their children grow up, leave home, marry, and have careers.

For adults, a large part of the answer to "Who are you?" is the answer to "What do you do?" Choosing a career path is difficult, especially in today's changing work environment. Although chance events may alter our course, the **social clock** still defines the best time to leave home, get a job, marry, and so on.

16. According to Erikson, the two basic tasks of adulthood are achieving _____ and _____ . According to Freud, the healthy adult is one who can _____ and _____ .

17. One factor that promotes lasting bonds of love in couples is _____ , which refers to the willingness to reveal intimate aspects of oneself to others. The chances of a marriage lasting increase when couples marry after age _____ and are well _____ .

18. Marriages today are _____ (half/twice) as likely to end in divorce as they were in the 1960s. Couples who live together before marrying have a _____ (higher/lower) divorce rate than those who do not.

19. Marriage is a predictor of _____ , _____ _____ , _____ , and _____ .

20. For most couples, the children's leaving home produces a(n) _____ (increase/decrease) in marital satisfaction.

21. For men and women, happiness is having work that fits their interests and provides them with a sense of _____ and _____ .

22. The term used to refer to the culturally preferred timing for leaving home, getting a job, marrying, and so on is the _____ _____ .

Objective 19: Identify the range of reactions to the death of a loved one.

Usually, the most difficult separation is from one's spouse or partner. Grief is especially severe when the death of a loved one comes before its expected time on the social clock. The normal range of reactions to a loved one's death is wider than most people suppose. Some cultures encourage public weeping and wailing; others hide grief. Within any culture, some individuals grieve more intensely and openly. Research discounts the popular idea that terminally ill and bereaved people go through predictable stages.

23. Grief over a loved one's death is especially severe when it comes _____ .

24. Reactions to a loved one's death _____ (do/do not) vary according to cultural norms. Those who express the strongest grief immediately _____ (do/do not) purge their grief more quickly.

25. Terminally ill and grief-stricken people _____ (do/do not) go through identical stages.

Objective 20: Describe trends in people's life satisfaction across the life span.

People of all ages report similar feelings of happiness and satisfaction with life. If anything, positive feelings grow after midlife and negative feelings subside. Older adults increasingly express positive emotions. Moreover, the bad feelings we associate with negative events fade faster than do the good feelings we associate with positive events. As the years pass, feelings mellow. Life itself can be affirmed even at death, especially if one's life has been meaningful and worthwhile, what Erikson called a sense of *integrity*.

26. From early adulthood to midlife, people typically experience a strengthening sense of _____ , _____ , and _____ .

27. According to studies, older people _____ (do/do not) report as much happiness and satisfaction with life as younger people do. In addition, their feelings _____ (do/do not) mellow.

28. As we age, the brain shows _____ (increased/decreased) activity in response to negative events.

29. According to Erikson, the final task of adulthood is to achieve a sense of _____ .

30. The first two years of life _____ (do/do not) provide a good basis for predicting a person's eventual traits.

31. Research on the consistency of personality shows that some traits, such as those related to _____ , are more stable than others, such as social attitudes. Life requires both _____ and _____ .

APPLICATIONS:

32. The text discusses well-being across the life span. Which of the following people is likely to report the greatest life satisfaction?
    a. Billy, a 7-year-old second-grader
    b. Kathy, a 17-year-old high-school senior
    c. Mildred, a 70-year-old retired teacher
    d. too little information to tell

33. In thinking about stability and change over the life span, most developmental psychologists believe that
    a. Development occurs in a series of sharply defined stages.
    b. The first two years are the most crucial in determining the individual's personality.
    c. The consistency of personality in most people tends to increase over the life span.
    d. Social and emotional style are among the characteristics that show the least stability over the life span.

PROGRESS TEST

Multiple-Choice Questions

Circle your answers to the following questions and check them with the answers beginning on page 62. If your answer is incorrect, read the explanation for why it is incorrect and then consult the text.

1. Of the following, the best way to separate the effects of genes and environment in research is to study
   a. fraternal twins.
   b. identical twins.
   c. adopted children and their adoptive parents.
   d. identical twins raised in different environments.

2. Unlike _____ twins, who develop from a single fertilized egg, _____ twins develop from separate fertilized eggs.
   a. fraternal; identical
   b. identical; fraternal
   c. placental; nonplacental
   d. nonplacental; placental

3. Temperament refers to a person's characteristic
   a. emotional reactivity and intensity.
   b. attitudes.
   c. behaviors.
   d. role-related traits.

4. Physiological tests reveal that anxious, inhibited infants
   a. become less physically aroused when facing new situations.
   b. have slow, steady heart rates.
   c. have high and variable heart rates.
   d. have underreactive nervous systems.

5. The human genome is best defined as
   a. a complex molecule containing genetic information that makes up the chromosomes.
   b. a segment of DNA.
   c. the complete instructions for making an organism.
   d. the inner cells of the zygote.

6. Most human traits are
   a. learned.
   b. determined by a single gene.
   c. influenced by many genes acting together.
   d. unpredictable.

7. (Close-Up) Several studies of long-separated identical twins have found that these twins
   a. have little in common, due to the different environments in which they were raised.
   b. have many similarities, in everything from medical histories to personalities.
   c. have similar personalities, but very different likes, dislikes, and life-styles.
   d. are no more similar than are fraternal twins reared apart.

8. (Close-Up) Adoption studies show that the personalities of adopted children
   a. closely match those of their adoptive parents.
   b. are more similar to their biological parents than to their adoptive parents.
   c. closely match those of the biological children of their adoptive parents.
   d. closely match those of other children reared in the same home, whether or not they are biologically related.

9. Chromosomes are composed of small segments of
   a. DNA called genes.
   b. DNA called neurotransmitters.
   c. DNA called endorphins.
   d. DNA called enzymes.

10. When the effect of one factor (such as environment) depends on another (such as heredity), we say there is a(n) _____ between the two factors.
    a. attachment
    b. positive correlation
    c. negative correlation
    d. interaction

11. Dr. Joan Goodman is studying how memory changes as people get older. She is most likely a(n) _____ psychologist.
    a. social
    b. cognitive
    c. developmental
    d. experimental

12. In Piaget's concrete operational stage, the child is able to understand the principle of
    a. conservation.
    b. schemas.
    c. attachment.
    d. object permanence.

13. Piaget held that egocentrism is characteristic of the
   a. sensorimotor stage.
   b. preoperational stage.
   c. concrete operational stage.
   d. formal operational stage.

14. During which stage of cognitive development do children begin to show object permanence?
   a. sensorimotor   **c.** concrete operational
   b. preoperational   **d.** formal operational

15. Babies will vigorously root for a nipple when
   a. their foot is tickled.
   b. their cheek is touched.
   c. they hear a loud noise.
   d. they make eye contact with their caregiver.

16. The Harlows' studies of attachment in monkeys showed that
   a. nourishment was the single most important factor motivating attachment.
   b. a cloth mother produced the greatest attachment response.
   c. whether a cloth or wire mother was present mattered less than the presence or absence of other infants.
   d. attachment in monkeys is based on stability.

17. When psychologists discuss maturation, they are referring to stages of growth that are NOT influenced by
   a. conservation.   **c.** nurture.
   b. nature.   **d.** continuity.

18. The developmental theorist who suggested that securely attached children develop an attitude of basic trust is
   a. Piaget.   **c.** Vygotsky.
   b. Harlow.   **d.** Erikson.

19. Research findings on infant motor development are consistent with the idea that
   a. cognitive development lags behind motor skills development.
   b. maturation of physical skills is relatively unaffected by experience.
   c. motor-skill development is slowed down by lack of useful experience.
   d. in humans, the process of maturation may be significantly altered by cultural factors.

20. According to Erikson, the central psychological challenges related to adolescence, young adulthood, and middle age, respectively, are
   a. identity formation, intimacy, generativity.
   b. intimacy, identity formation, generativity.
   c. generativity, intimacy, identity formation.
   d. intimacy, generativity, identity formation.

21. In preconventional morality, the person
   a. obeys out of a sense of social duty.
   b. conforms to gain social approval.
   c. obeys to avoid punishment or to gain concrete rewards.
   d. follows his or her conscience.

22. A person's general ability to think abstractly is called _____ intelligence. This ability generally _____ with age.
   a. fluid; increases
   b. fluid; decreases
   c. crystallized; decreases
   d. crystallized; increases

23. Among the hallmarks of growing up are a boy's first ejaculation and a girl's first menstrual period, which also is called
   a. puberty.   **c.** menarche.
   b. menopause.   **d.** generativity.

24. An older person who can remember his or her life with a sense of satisfaction and completion has attained Erikson's stage of
   a. generativity.   **c.** isolation.
   b. intimacy.   **d.** integrity.

25. According to Piaget, the ability to reason abstractly is characteristic of the stage of
   a. preoperational thought.
   b. concrete operations.
   c. formal operations.
   d. fluid intelligence.

26. The cognitive ability that has been shown to decline during adulthood is the ability to
   a. recall new information.
   b. recognize new information.
   c. learn meaningful new material.
   d. use judgment in dealing with daily life problems.

27. Which of the following statements concerning the effects of aging is true?
   a. Aging will probably lead to total memory failure if an individual lives long enough.
   b. Aging increases susceptibility to short-term ailments such as the flu.
   c. Significant increases in life satisfaction are associated with aging.
   d. The aging process can be significantly affected by the individual's activity patterns.

28. The average age at which puberty begins is _____ in boys; in girls, it is _____ .
   a. 14; 13   **c.** 11; 10
   b. 13; 11   **d.** 10; 9

29. Adolescence is marked by the onset of
   a. an identity crisis.
   b. parent-child conflict.
   c. the concrete operational stage.
   d. puberty.

30. The end of menstruation is called
   a. menarche.   **c.** genome.
   b. menopause.   **d.** generativity.

31. The idea that terminally ill and grief-stricken people go through identical stages, such as denial, anger, and so forth,
    a. is widely supported by research.
    b. more accurately describes grieving in some cultures than others.
    c. is true of women but not men.
    d. is not supported by research studies.

32. Stranger anxiety develops soon after
    a. the concept of conservation.
    b. egocentrism.
    c. a theory of mind.
    d. the concept of object permanence.

33. Before Piaget, people were more likely to believe that
    a. the child's mind is a miniature model of the adult's.
    b. children think about the world in radically different ways from adults.
    c. the child's mind develops through a series of stages.
    d. children interpret their experiences in terms of their current understandings.

34. Which is the correct sequence of stages in Piaget's theory of cognitive development?
    a. sensorimotor, preoperational, concrete operational, formal operational
    b. sensorimotor, preoperational, formal operational, concrete operational
    c. preoperational, sensorimotor, concrete operational, formal operational
    d. preoperational, sensorimotor, formal operational, concrete operational

35. A child whose mother drank heavily when she was pregnant is at heightened risk of
    a. being emotionally excitable during childhood.
    b. becoming insecurely attached.
    c. being born with the physical and cognitive abnormalities of fetal alcohol syndrome.
    d. addiction to a range of drugs throughout life.

36. Which is the correct order of stages of prenatal development?
    a. zygote, fetus, embryo
    b. zygote, embryo, fetus
    c. embryo, zygote, fetus
    d. embryo, fetus, zygote

37. The term *critical period* refers to
    a. prenatal development.
    b. the initial 2 hours after a child's birth.
    c. the preoperational stage.
    d. a restricted time for learning.

38. Which of the following was NOT found by the Harlows in socially deprived monkeys?
    a. They had difficulty mating.
    b. They showed extreme fear or aggression when first seeing other monkeys.
    c. They showed abnormal physical development.
    d. The females were abusive mothers.

39. Insecurely attached infants who are left by their mothers in an unfamiliar setting often will
    a. hold fast to their mothers on their return.
    b. explore the new surroundings confidently.
    c. be indifferent toward their mothers on their return.
    d. display little emotion at any time.

40. Whose stage theory of moral development was based on how people reasoned about ethical dilemmas?
    a. Erikson   c. Harlow
    b. Piaget   d. Kohlberg

41. The social clock refers to
    a. an individual or society's distribution of work and leisure time.
    b. adulthood responsibilities.
    c. typical ages for starting a career, marrying, and so on.
    d. age-related changes in one's circle of friends.

42. At which of Kohlberg's levels is moral reasoning based on the existence of fundamental human rights?
    a. preconventional morality
    b. conventional morality
    c. postconventional morality
    d. generative morality

43. In Erikson's theory, individuals generally focus on developing _____ during adolescence and then _____ during young adulthood.
    a. identity; intimacy
    b. intimacy; identity
    c. basic trust; identity
    d. identity; basic trust

44. The emotional impact of menopause on a woman depends on
    a. whether she is still married.
    b. whether she is working.
    c. how supportive her children are.
    d. her expectations and attitudes.

45. Notable achievements in fields such as _____ _____ are often made by younger adults in their late twenties or early thirties, when _____ intelligence is at its peak.
    a. mathematics; fluid
    b. philosophy; fluid
    c. science; crystallized
    d. literature; crystallized

46. After their grown children have left home, most couples experience
    a. distress because the "nest is empty."
    b. increased strain in their marital relationship.
    c. the desire to start another family.
    d. greater happiness and enjoyment in their relationship.

47. A person's accumulation of stored information, called _____ intelligence, generally _____ with age.
  a. fluid; decreases
  b. fluid; increases
  c. crystallized; decreases
  d. crystallized; increases

48. Stage theories have been criticized because they fail to consider that development may be significantly affected by
  a. variations in the social clock.
  b. each individual's experiences.
  c. each individual's historical and cultural setting.
  d. all of these factors.

Application Essay

Sheryl is a 12-year-old living in the United States. She is in the sixth grade. Describe the developmental changes she is likely to be experiencing according to Piaget, Kohlberg, and Erikson. (Use the space below to list the points you want to make, and organize them. Then write the essay on a separate sheet of paper.)

TERMS AND CONCEPTS

Using your own words, on a piece of paper write a brief definition or explanation of each of the following terms.

1. developmental psychology
2. chromosomes
3. DNA
4. genes
5. heredity
6. genome
7. environment
8. interaction
9. zygote
10. embryo
11. identical twins
12. fraternal twins
13. fetus
14. teratogens
15. fetal alcohol syndrome (FAS)
16. reflex

17. temperament
18. maturation
19. critical period
20. schema
21. cognition
22. sensorimotor stage
23. object permanence
24. preoperational stage
25. conservation
26. egocentrism
27. theory of mind
28. autism
29. concrete operational stage
30. formal operational stage
31. stranger anxiety
32. attachment
33. basic trust
34. adolescence
35. puberty
36. menarche
37. identity
38. social identity
39. intimacy
40. emerging adulthood
41. menopause
42. crystallized intelligence
43. fluid intelligence
44. social clock

SUMMING UP
See the next page.

ANSWERS

Chapter Review

Introduction
1. developmental psychologists
2. nature; nurture
3. continuity; stages
4. stability

Prenatal Development and the Newborn
1. ovary; egg
2. sperm; enzymes; blocks
3. nuclei
4. chromosomes; DNA
5. genes; heredity
6. genome
7. **a.** cell nucleus
  b. chromosome
  c. gene
  d. DNA

SUMMING UP

Jorge and Sonya Nuñez have conceived a male child, who they will name Felipe.

Felipe started out as a fertilized egg, or _____ , whose cells quickly begin to _____ .

Two weeks into _____ development, his organs begin to form and function, and he is referred to as an _____ .

As Felipe becomes more human in appearance, about 9 weeks after conception, he is called a _____ .

Throughout this process,

Felipe's genes interact with the _____ and Felipe is protected by Sonya's _____ , which prevents many harmful substances from reaching him,

and

because Sonya doesn't drink alcohol, Felipe will NOT be exposed to this harmful _____

and

will not be at risk of developing _____ _____ _____ .

As a newborn,

Felipe comes equipped with a variety of _____ suited to survival,

including

the tendency to root for a nipple, quickly close in on it, and _____ .

Felipe is now an infant, and his biological and psychological development continues,

which depends to a large extent on the rapid development of his brain's _____ lobes,

with

the last areas of the brain to develop being those linked with thinking, memory, and language—the _____ areas of the cortex.

Also,

as his genes continue to direct his biological growth through the process called _____ ,

Felipe begins to sit, to crawl, then to stand, walk, and run. This _____ of motor development is universal; the _____ is not.

8. environment; interaction; nurture; nature
9. **b.** is the answer. It describes an interaction between heredity (personality trait) and environment (swim competition).
10. zygotes; specialize; uterine; placenta
11. embryo
12. identical; fraternal
13. fetus
14. teratogens
15. central; fetal alcohol syndrome
16. reflex; root

Newborns reflexively turn their heads in the direction of human voices. They gaze longer at a drawing of a face-like image. They focus best on objects about 8 to 12 inches away, which is about the distance between a nursing infant's eyes and the mother's. Within days, they recognize their mother's smell and voice.

17. temperament; does
18. difficult; irritable; intense; unpredictable; easy; cheerful; relaxed; predictable
19. more
20. twin; adoption
21. more
22. environment
23. do not; outgoingness; agreeableness
24. interaction; genes; experiences
25. same; different

Infancy and Childhood

1. maturation
2. over; is not
3. frontal; rational planning; association areas
4. pruning; critical period
5. motor; sequence; run
6. major
7. cerebellum; small
8. **b.** is the answer. Although the rate of motor development varies from child to child, the basic sequence is universal and, therefore, predictable.
9. Piaget; active
10. schemas
11. cognition
12. sensorimotor
13. object permanence
14. underestimated; continuous
15. conservation; preoperational; have not
16. egocentrism
17. theory of mind; false beliefs
18. communication; social; theory of mind; autism; viewpoint (perspective)
19. 6 or 7; concrete operational
20. Lev Vygotsky; 7; inner speech; scaffold
21. formal operational; abstract
22. age; sequence
23. Piaget's stages summarized

Typical Age Range	Stage	New Developments	Test to Determine If Someone Is in This Stage
Birth to nearly 2 years	Sensorimotor	Stranger anxiety Object permanence	Have the child's mother leave the room Hide a toy under a blanket
2 to 6 or 7 years	Preoperational	Egocentrism Not yet logical	Ask questions to determine child's ability to take another's perspective
6 or 7 to 11 years	Concrete operational	Conservation Simple math	Transfer liquid from a tall, thin glass into a short, wide glass
About 12 through adulthood	Formal operational	Abstract logic	Give child a hypothetical reasoning problem

24. theory of mind
25. conservation
26. sensorimotor
27. preoperational
28. yes; no
29. object permanence; stranger anxiety; 8 months
30. attachment
31. contact comfort
32. safe haven; secure base
33. strange situation; secure; insecure

Placed in a strange situation, securely attached infants play comfortably, happily exploring their new environment. In contrast, insecurely attached infants are less likely to explore their surroundings and may even cling to their mothers. When separated from their mothers, insecurely attached infants are much more distressed than securely attached infants. When reunited with their mothers, insecurely attached infants may be indifferent.

Research studies conducted by Mary Ainsworth have revealed that sensitive, responsive mothers tend to have securely attached infants, whereas insensitive, unresponsive mothers often have insecurely attached infants. Other studies have found that temperamentally difficult infants whose mothers receive training in responsive parenting are more likely to become securely attached than are control infants.

34. is not; temperament
35. 13; gradually declines; throughout the world
36. basic trust
37. are; resilience
38. basic trust
39. authoritarian
40. permissive
41. authoritative
42. authoritative; do not
43. behaviors; attitudes; values; traditions; generation
44. biopsychosocial; genes and prenatal environment; beliefs, expectations, and feelings; parental and peer influences

Adolescence

1. childhood; adulthood
2. puberty; 11; 13
3. menarche; spermarche
4. sequence; timing
5. frontal lobe; limbic system
6. self-focused
7. formal operations; abstract; inconsistencies
8. Kohlberg; preconventional; conventional; postconventional
9. punishment; rewards
10. adolescence; approval; order
11. postconventional
12. postconventional; middle class; collectivist
13. character-education programs; empathy
14. gratification; academically
15. preconventional
16. individualism; postconventional
17. selves; confusion; identity
18. individualism; parents'
19. falls; rises
20. intimacy

Erikson's stages of psychosocial development

Group Age	Psychosocial Stage
Infancy	Trust vs. mistrust
Toddlerhood	Autonomy vs. shame and doubt
Preschooler	Initiative vs. guilt
Elementary school	Competence vs. inferiority
Adolescence	Identity vs. role confusion
Young adulthood	Intimacy vs. isolation
Middle adulthood	Generativity vs. stagnation
Late adulthood	Integrity vs. despair

21. peers; parents
22. do; positive
23. loneliness; self-esteem; depression
24. 10
25. does; higher
26. faith; politics; selection effect
27. rite of passage; body fat; parent-child; earlier
28. emerging adulthood
29. experience; learning; biology

Adulthood

1. is not
2. muscular strength; reaction time; sensory keenness; cardiac output; women
3. age; health; exercise
4. menopause; 50; expectations; attitudes
5. sperm; testosterone
6. shrinks; reduced
7. more; less
8. brain cells; memory
9. slows; recall; recognize
10. crystallized; increase
11. fluid; decrease
12. brain cell; neural; oxygen
13. at an earlier age than. Mathematical and philosophical reasoning involve fluid and crystallized intelligence, respectively. Because fluid intelligence generally declines with age while crystallized intelligence increases, it is likely that significant mathematical accomplishments will occur at an earlier age than philosophical accomplishments.
14. fluid. Fluid intelligence refers to a person's ability to reason speedily and abstractly, an ability that declines with age.
15. d. is the answer. In tests of recognition memory, the performance of older persons shows little decline. The ability to recall material, especially meaningless material, declines with age.
16. intimacy; generativity; love; work
17. self-disclosure; 20; educated
18. twice; higher
19. happiness; sexual satisfaction; health; income
20. increase
21. competence; accomplishment
22. social clock
23. suddenly and before its expected time on the social clock
24. do; do not
25. do not
26. identity; confidence; self-esteem
27. do; do
28. decreased
29. integrity
30. do not
31. temperament; stability; change

32. **d.** is the answer. Research has not uncovered a tendency for people of any particular age group to report greater feelings of satisfaction or well-being.

33. **c.** is the answer. Although some researchers emphasize consistency and others emphasize potential for change, they all agree that consistency increases over the life span. Research has shown that development does not occur in neatly defined stages and that the first two years do not predict later personality.

Progress Test

Multiple-Choice Questions

1. **d.** is the answer.

2. **b.** is the answer.
   c. & d. There are no such things as "placental" or "nonplacental" twins. All twins have a placenta during prenatal development.

3. **a.** is the answer.

4. **c.** is the answer.
   a., b., & d. The reactions of these infants are the opposite of what these choices describe.

5. **c.** is the answer.
   a. This defines DNA.
   b. This is a gene.
   d. These become the embryo.

6. **c.** is the answer.

7. **b.** is the answer.
   a., c., & d. Despite being raised in different environments, long-separated identical twins often have much in common, including likes, dislikes, and lifestyles. This indicates the significant heritability of many traits.

8. **b.** is the answer.
   a., c., & d. The personalities of adopted children do not much resemble those of their adoptive parents (therefore, not a.) or other children reared in the same home (therefore, not c. or d.).

9. **a.** is the answer.
   b. Neurotransmitters are the chemicals involved in synaptic transmission in the nervous system.
   c. Endorphins are the brain's naturally occurring opiatelike neurotransmitters that are responsible for the "runner's high," for example.
   d. Enzymes are chemicals that facilitate various chemical reactions throughout the body but are not involved in heredity.

10. **d.** is the answer.
    a. Attachment is an emotional tie between two people.
    b. & c. When two factors are correlated, it means either that increases in one factor are accompanied by increases in the other (positive correlation) or that increases in one factor are accompanied by decreases in the other (negative correlation).

11. **c.** is the answer. Developmental psychologists study physical, cognitive (memory, in this example), and social change throughout the life span.

   a. Social psychologists study how people influence and are influenced by others.
   b. Cognitive psychologists *do* study memory; because Dr. Goodman is interested in life-span *changes* in memory, she is more likely a developmental psychologist.
   d. Experimental psychologists study physiology, sensation, perception, learning, and other aspects of behavior. Only developmental psychologists focus on developmental changes.

12. **a.** is the answer.
    b. Schemas are mental concepts or frameworks that organize and interpret information.
    c. Piaget's theory is not concerned with attachment.
    d. Attaining object permanence is the hallmark of sensorimotor thought.

13. **b.** is the answer. The preoperational child sees the world from his or her own viewpoint.
    a. As immature as egocentrism is, it represents a significant cognitive advance over the sensorimotor child, who knows the world only through senses and actions. Even simple self-awareness takes a while to develop.
    c. & d. As children attain the operational stages, they become more able to see the world through the eyes of others.

14. **a.** is the answer. Before object permanence is attained, "out of sight" is truly "out of mind."
    b., c., & d. Developments during the preoperational, concrete operational, and formal operational stages include the use of language, conservation, and abstract reasoning, respectively.

15. **b.** is the answer. The infant turns its head and begins sucking when its cheek is stroked.
    a., c., & d. These stimuli produce other reflexes in the newborn.

16. **b.** is the answer.
    a. When given the choice between a wire mother with a bottle and a cloth mother without, the monkeys preferred the cloth mother.
    c. The presence of other infants made no difference.
    d. Stability was not a factor in this experiment.

17. **c.** is the answer. Through maturation—an orderly sequence of biological growth processes that are relatively unaffected by experience—all humans develop.
    a. Conservation is the cognitive awareness that objects do not change with changes in shape.
    b. The forces of nature *are* those that direct maturation.
    d. The continuity-stages debate has to do with whether development is a gradual and continuous process or a distinct stagelike process. Those who emphasize maturation see development as occurring in stages, not continuously.

18. **d.** is the answer. Erikson proposed that development occurs in a series of stages. During the first stage the child develops an attitude of either basic trust or mistrust.

a. Piaget's theory is concerned with cognitive development.
b. Harlow conducted research on attachment.
c. Vygotsky focused on the influence of social factors on cognitive development.

19. **b.** is the answer.
20. **a.** is the answer.
21. **c.** is the answer. At the preconventional level, moral reasoning centers on self-interest, whether this means obtaining rewards or avoiding punishment.
    a. & b. Moral reasoning based on a sense of social duty or a desire to gain social approval is associated with the conventional level of moral development.
    d. Reasoning based on ethical principles is characteristic of the postconventional level of moral development.
22. **b.** is the answer.
    a. Fluid intelligence tends to decrease with age.
    c. & d. Crystallized intelligence refers to the accumulation of facts and general knowledge that takes place during a person's life. Crystallized intelligence generally *increases* with age.
23. **c.** is the answer.
    a. Puberty refers to the early adolescent period during which accelerated growth and sexual maturation occur, not to the first menstrual period.
    b. Menopause is the cessation of menstruation, which typically occurs in the early fifties.
    d. In Erikson's theory, generativity, or the sense of contributing and being productive, is the task of middle adulthood.
24. **d.** is the answer.
    a. Generativity is associated with middle adulthood.
    b. & c. Intimacy and isolation are associated with young adulthood.
25. **c.** is the answer. Once formal operational thought has been attained, thinking is no longer limited to concrete events.
    a. & b. Preoperational thought and concrete operational thought emerge before, and do not include, the ability to think logically about abstractions.
    d. Fluid intelligence refers to abstract reasoning abilities; however, it is unrelated to Piaget's theory and stages.
26. **a.** is the answer.
    b., c., & d. These cognitive abilities remain essentially unchanged as the person ages.
27. **d.** is the answer. "Use it or lose it" seems to be the rule: Often, changes in activity patterns contribute significantly to problems regarded as being part of usual aging.
    a. Most older people suffer some memory loss but remember some events very well.
    b. Although older adults are more subject to long-term ailments than younger adults, they actually suffer fewer short-term ailments.
    c. People of all ages report equal happiness or satisfaction with life.
28. **b.** is the answer.
29. **d.** is the answer. The physical changes of puberty mark the onset of adolescence.

a. & b. An identity crisis or parent-child conflict may or may not occur during adolescence; neither of these formally marks its onset.
c. Formal operational thought, rather than concrete reasoning, typically develops in adolescence.
30. **b.** is the answer.
    a. Menarche refers to the onset of menstruation.
    c. The human genome is the complete genetic instructions for making an organism.
    d. Generativity is Erikson's term for productivity during middle adulthood.
31. **d.** is the answer.
32. **d.** is the answer. With object permanence, a child develops schemas for familiar objects, including faces, and may become upset by a stranger who does not fit any of these schemas.
    a. The concept of conservation develops during the concrete operational stage, whereas stranger anxiety develops during the sensorimotor stage.
    b. & c. Egocentrism and a theory of mind both develop during the preoperational stage. This follows the sensorimotor stage, when stranger anxiety develops.
33. **a.** is the answer.
    b., c., & d. Each of these is an understanding developed by Piaget.
34. **a.** is the answer.
35. **c.** is the answer.
    a., b., & d. A child's emotional temperament, attachment, and addiction have not been linked to the mother's drinking while pregnant.
36. **b.** is the answer.
37. **d.** is the answer. A critical period is a restricted time during which an organism must be exposed to certain influences or experiences for a particular kind of learning to occur.
    a. Critical periods refer to developmental periods after birth.
    b. Critical periods vary from behavior to behavior, but they are not confined to the hours following birth.
    c. Critical periods are not specifically associated with the preoperational period.
38. **c.** is the answer. Deprived monkeys were impaired in their social behaviors but not in their physical development.
    a., b., & d. Each of these was found in socially deprived monkeys.
39. **c.** is the answer.
    a. Insecurely attached infants often cling to their mothers when placed in a new situation; yet, when the mother returns after an absence, the infant's reaction tends to be one of indifference.
    b. These behaviors are characteristic of securely attached infants.
    d. Insecurely attached infants in unfamiliar surroundings will often exhibit a range of emotional behaviors.
40. **d.** is the answer.
    a. Erikson studied psychosocial development.
    b. Piaget studied cognitive development.
    c. Harlow is known for his studies of attachment in infant monkeys.

41. **c.** is the answer. Different societies and eras have somewhat different ideas about the age at which major life events should ideally occur.

42. **c.** is the answer.
   a. Preconventional morality is based on avoiding punishment and obtaining rewards.
   b. Conventional morality is based on gaining the approval of others and/or on following the law and social convention.
   d. There is no such thing as generative morality.

43. **a.** is the answer.
   b. According to Erikson, identity develops before intimacy.
   c. & d. Forming basic trust is the task of infancy.

44. **d.** is the answer.

45. **a.** is the answer. A mathematician's skills are likely to reflect abstract reasoning, or fluid intelligence, which declines with age.
   b. & d. Philosophy and literature are fields in which individuals often do their most notable work later in life, after more experiential knowledge (crystallized intelligence) has accumulated.
   c. Scientific achievements generally reflect fluid, rather than crystallized, intelligence.

46. **d.** is the answer.
   a., b., & c. Most couples do not feel a loss of purpose or marital strain following the departure of grown children.

47. **d.** is the answer.
   a. & b. Fluid intelligence, which decreases with age, refers to the ability to reason abstractly.
   c. Crystallized intelligence increases with age.

48. **d.** is the answer.

Application Essay

Sheryl's age would place her at the beginning of Piaget's stage of formal operations. Although her thinking is probably still somewhat self-focused, Sheryl is becoming capable of abstract, logical thought. Because her logical thinking also enables her to detect inconsistencies in others' reasoning and between their ideals and actions, Sheryl and her parents may be having some heated debates about now.

According to Kohlberg, Sheryl is probably at the beginning of postconventional morality. When she was younger, Sheryl probably abided by rules to gain social approval, or simply because "rules are rules" (conventional morality). Now that she is older, Sheryl's moral reasoning will increasingly be based on her own personal code of ethics and an affirmation of people's agreed-upon rights.

According to Erikson, psychosocial development occurs in eight stages, each of which focuses on a particular task. As an adolescent, Sheryl's psychosocial task is to develop a sense of self by testing roles, then integrating them to form a single identity. Erikson called this stage "identity versus role confusion."

Summing Up

Jorge and Sonya Nuñez have conceived a male child, who they will name Felipe. Felipe begins his life as a fertilized egg, or *zygote*, whose cells quickly begin to *divide*. Two weeks into *prenatal* development, his organs begin to form and function, and he is referred to as an *embryo*. As Felipe becomes more human, about 9 weeks after conception, he is a *fetus*.

Throughout this process, Felipe's genes interact with the *environment*, and Felipe is protected by Sonya's *placenta*, which prevents many harmful substances from reaching him, and because Sonya doesn't drink alcohol, Felipe will NOT be exposed to this harmful *teratogen* and will not be at risk of developing birth defects such as *fetal alcohol syndrome*.

As a newborn, Felipe comes equipped with a variety of *reflexes* suited to survival, including the tendency to root for a nipple, quickly close in on it, and *suck*.

Felipe is now an infant, and his biological development continues, preparing the way for psychological development, which depends to a large extent on the rapid development of his brain's *frontal lobes,* with the last areas of the brain to develop being those linked with thinking, memory, and language—the *association* areas of the cortex. Also, as his genes continue to direct his biological growth through the process called *maturation,* Felipe begins to sit, to crawl, then to stand, walk, and run. This *sequence* of motor development is universal; the *timing* is not.

Terms and Concepts

1. **Developmental psychology** is the branch of psychology concerned with physical, cognitive, and social change throughout the life span.

2. **Chromosomes** are threadlike structures made of DNA molecules, which contain the genes. In conception, the 23 chromosomes in the egg are paired with the 23 chromosomes in the sperm.

3. **DNA** (deoxyribonucleic acid) is a complex molecule containing the genetic information that makes up the chromosomes.

4. **Genes** are the biochemical units of heredity that make up the chromosomes; they are segments of the DNA molecules capable of synthesizing a protein.

5. **Heredity** is the genetic transfer of characteristics from parents to offspring.

6. A **genome** is the complete genetic instructions for making an organism.

7. **Environment** is every external influence, from prenatal nutrition to social support in later life.

8. An **interaction** occurs when the effects of one factor (such as environment) depend on another factor (such as heredity).
   Example: Because the way people react to us (an environmental factor) depends on our genetically influenced temperament (a genetic factor), there is an **interaction** between environment and heredity.

9. The **zygote** (a term derived from the Greek word for "joint") is the fertilized egg, that is, the cluster of cells formed during conception by the union of sperm and egg.

10. The **embryo** is the developing prenatal organism from about 2 weeks through 2 months after conception.

11. **Identical twins** develop from a single fertilized egg that splits in two, creating two genetically identical siblings.

12. **Fraternal twins** develop from two separate eggs fertilized by different sperm and therefore are no more genetically similar than ordinary siblings.

13. The **fetus** is the developing prenatal human from 9 weeks after conception to birth.

14. **Teratogens** (literally, poisons) are any chemicals and viruses that cross the mother's placenta and can harm the developing embryo or fetus.

15. **Fetal alcohol syndrome (FAS)** refers to the physical and cognitive abnormalities that heavy drinking by a pregnant woman may cause in the developing child.

16. A **reflex** is an unlearned and automatic response to a sensory stimulus.

17. **Temperament** refers to a person's characteristic emotional reactivity and intensity.

18. **Maturation** refers to the biological growth processes that enable orderly changes in behavior, relatively uninfluenced by experience or other environmental factors.

    Example: The ability to walk depends on a certain level of neural and muscular **maturation**. For this reason, until the toddler's body is physically ready to walk, practice "walking" has little effect.

19. A **critical period** is a limited time early in life during which an organism must be exposed to certain stimuli or experiences if it is to develop properly.

20. In Piaget's theory of cognitive development, **schemas** are mental concepts or frameworks that organize and interpret information.

21. **Cognition** refers to all the mental processes associated with thinking, knowing, remembering, and communicating.

22. In Piaget's theory of cognitive stages, the **sensorimotor stage** lasts from birth to about age 2. During this stage, infants gain knowledge of the world through their senses and their motor activities.

23. **Object permanence,** which develops during the sensorimotor stage, is the awareness that things do not cease to exist when not perceived.

24. In Piaget's theory, the **preoperational stage** lasts from about 2 to 6 or 7 years of age. During this stage, language development is rapid, but the child is unable to understand the mental operations of concrete logic.

25. **Conservation** is the principle that properties such as number, volume, and mass remain constant despite changes in the forms of objects; it is acquired during the concrete operational stage.

26. In Piaget's theory, **egocentrism** refers to the difficulty that preoperational children have in considering another's viewpoint. *Ego* means "self," and *centrism* indicates "in the center"; the preoperational child is "self-centered."

27. Our ideas about our own and others' thoughts, feelings, and perceptions and the behaviors these might predict constitute our **theory of mind**.

28. **Autism** is a disorder that appears in childhood and is marked by deficient communication, social interaction, and understanding of others' states of mind.

29. During the **concrete operational stage,** lasting from about ages 6 or 7 to 11, children can think logically about concrete events and objects.

30. In Piaget's theory, the **formal operational stage** normally begins about age 12. During this stage people begin to think logically about abstract concepts.

    Memory aid: To help differentiate Piaget's stages remember that "operations" are mental transformations. *Pre*operational children, who lack the ability to perform transformations, are "before" this developmental milestone. *Concrete* operational children can operate on real, or concrete, objects. *Formal* operational children can perform logical transformations on abstract concepts.

31. **Stranger anxiety** is the fear of strangers that infants begin to display by about 8 months of age.

32. **Attachment** is an emotional tie with another person, shown in young children by their seeking closeness to a caregiver and showing distress on separation.

33. According to Erikson, **basic trust** is a sense that the world is predictable and trustworthy—a concept that infants form if their needs are met by responsive caregiving.

34. **Adolescence** refers to the life stage from puberty to independent adulthood.

35. **Puberty** is the early adolescent period of sexual maturation, during which a person becomes capable of reproduction.)

36. **Menarche** is the first menstrual period.

37. In Erikson's theory, establishing an **identity,** or a sense of self, is the primary task of adolescence.

38. **Social identity** is our sense of who we are that comes from the groups to which we belong.

39. In Erikson's theory, **intimacy,** or the ability to establish close, loving relationships, is the primary task of late adolescence and early adulthood.

40. **Emerging adulthood** refers to the period between age 18 and the mid-twenties, when many in Western cultures are no longer adolescents but have not yet achieved full independence as adults.

41. **Menopause** is the natural end of menstruation and typically occurs in the early fifties. It also can mean the biological transition a woman experiences from before to after the end of menstruation.

42. **Crystallized intelligence** refers to those aspects of intellectual ability, such as vocabulary and general knowledge, that reflect accumulated learning. Crystallized intelligence tends to increase with age.

43. **Fluid intelligence** refers to a person's ability to reason speedily and abstractly. Fluid intelligence tends to decline with age.

44. The **social clock** refers to the culturally preferred timing of social events, such as leaving home, marrying, having children, and retiring.

4

GENDER AND SEXUALITY

Chapter 4 is concerned with the ways in which genes and environment interact to shape both the biological and social aspects of our gender and sexual behavior. Men and women are more alike than different, but they do differ in certain areas, such as aggression, social power, and social connectedness. Sexual motivation in men and women is triggered less by physiological factors and more by external incentives. Even so, research studies demonstrate that sexual orientation is neither willfully chosen nor easily changed.

CHAPTER REVIEW

First, skim each text section, noting headings and bold-face items. Review the section by reading the objectives and summaries provided here, then answer the questions that follow. In some cases, STUDY TIPS explain how best to learn a difficult concept and APPLICATIONS help you to know how well you understand the material. Check your understanding of the material by consulting the answers beginning on page 77. Do not continue with the next section until you understand each answer. If you need to, review or reread the section in the textbook before continuing.

Gender Development

Objective 1: Discuss gender similarities and differences in psychological traits such as aggression, social power, and social connectedness.

Gender refers to the biologically and socially influenced characteristics by which members of a culture define *male* and *female*. Although males and females are similar in most ways, they differ in body fat, muscle, height, and life expectancy. Females are more vulnerable to depression, anxiety, and eating disorders. In contrast, males are more likely to commit suicide and become dependent on alcohol. They are also much more likely to be diagnosed with autism, color-blindness, ADHD as children, and antisocial personality disorder as adults.

In surveys, men admit to more *aggression* than do women, and experiments confirm that men tend to behave more aggressively such as by delivering what they believe are painful shocks. The same difference is reflected in violent crime rates. The gender gap in physical aggression appears in many cultures and at various ages.

Throughout the world, men are perceived as more dominant, forceful, and independent, while women are viewed as more submissive, nurturing, and socially connected. In groups, leadership tends to go to males. In everyday behavior, men are more likely to talk assertively, to interrupt, to initiate touching, to smile less, and to stare.

In comparison to men, women are more concerned with making social connections. This gender difference surfaces early, in children's play. As teens, girls spend more time with friends and on social networking Internet sites and less time alone. Women emphasize caring, often assuming responsibility for the very young and very old. Both men and women indicate that their friendships with women tend to be more intimate, enjoyable, and nurturing.

1. The characteristics by which people define *male* and *female* constitute _____ .

2. Among your _____ (how many?) chromosomes, _____ (how many?) are unisex.

3. Compared with the average man, an average woman has more _____ , less _____ , and is a few inches _____ . Women are more likely than men to suffer from _____ , _____ , and _____ _____ .

4. Compared with women, men are more likely to commit _____ and to become dependent on _____ . They are also more likely to be diagnosed with _____ , _____ - _____ , _____ , and _____ _____ .

5. *Aggression* is defined as _____ or _____ behavior that is _____ to hurt someone.

6. The aggression gender gap pertains to harmful _____ rather than verbal _____ aggression.

7. Throughout the world, men are more likely than women to engage in _____ , _____ , and _____ .

8. Compared with women, men are perceived as being more _____ , _____ , and _____ . As leaders, they tend to be more _____ , while women are more _____ .

9. Compared with men, women are perceived as being more _____ , _____ , and _____ _____ .

10. Gender differences in power generally _____ (increase/decrease) as we age.

11. According to Carol Gilligan, women are more concerned than men in making _____ with others.

12. This difference is noticeable in how children _____ , and it continues throughout the teen and adult years. Girls play in groups that are _____ and less _____ than boys' groups, and they are more open to _____ .

13. Because they are more _____ , women are likely to use conversation to _____ _____ , while men are likely to use conversation to _____ _____ .

14. Gender diversity is the byproduct of the interplay among our _____ , our _____ _____ , and our _____ _____ .

APPLICATION:

15. Mackenzie and Zachary live next door to Ella and Michael. They've become good friends, and every Sunday they get together for dinner. Zachary and Michael discuss the best way to clean their roofs, demonstrating the male tendency to _____ . Mackenzie and Ella talk about how to make their new neighbors feel welcome, demonstrating the female tendency to _____ .

Objective 2: Explain how biological sex is determined, and describe the role of sex hormones in biological development and gender differences.

Biological sex is determined by the twenty-third pair of chromosomes, the two sex chromosomes. The member of the pair inherited from the mother is an **X chromosome.** The X (female) or Y (male) chromosome that comes from the father determines the child's sex. The **Y chromosome** triggers the production of the principal male sex hormone, **testosterone,** which in turn triggers the development of external male sex organs.

During the fourth and fifth prenatal months, the male's greater testosterone and the female's ovarian hormones have an impact on the brain's wiring. In adulthood, male and female brains differ in some areas. For example, the part of the frontal lobes involved in verbal fluency is thicker in women and part of the parietal lobes involved in space perception is thicker in men.

16. The twenty-third pair of chromosomes determines the developing person's _____ . The mother always contributes a(n) _____ chromosome. When the father contributes a(n) _____ chromosome, the testes begin producing the hormone _____ . In about the _____ (what week?), this hormone initiates the development of external male sex organs.

17. Sex chromosomes control _____ that influence the brain's wiring. In adulthood, part of the _____ lobe, an area involved in _____ fluency, is thicker in women. Part of the brain's _____ lobe, a key area for _____ perception, is thicker in men.

Objective 3: Discuss the importance of gender roles in development.

Although biology influences our gender, gender is also socially constructed. Culture shapes our **roles.** For example, **gender roles**—our expectations about the way men and women behave—vary across cultures and time. For instance, in nomadic societies of food-gathering people, there is little division of labor by sex. In agricultural societies, women stay close to home while men often roam more freely. Such societies typically socialize children into more distinct gender roles. Even among industrialized countries, gender roles vary greatly, for example, in the expectation that life will be more satisfying when both spouses work and share child care.

Society assigns each of us to the social category of male and female. The result is our **gender identity,** our sense of being male or female. To varying degrees, we also undergo **gender typing,** acquiring a traditional male or female role. **Social learning theory** assumes that children learn gender-linked behaviors by observing and imitating significant others and by being rewarded and punished. Thinking also matters. As children, we form **gender schemas,** frameworks for organizing boy-girl characteristics.

18. Our expectations about the way people in a certain social position should behave defines their _____ . Our culture's definition of how

males and females should behave is their

_____ _____ .

19. Gender roles _____ (are/are not) rigidly fixed, as evidenced by the fact that they vary across _____ and over _____ . For instance, in _____ societies there tends to be minimal division of labor by sex; by contrast, in _____ societies, women remain close to home while men roam freely, herding cattle or sheep.

20. Our individual sense of being male or female is called our _____ _____ . The degree to which we exhibit traditionally male or female traits and interests is called _____ _____ .

21. According to _____ _____ theory, children learn gender-linked behaviors by observing and imitating others and being rewarded or punished. Even when their families discourage traditional gender typing, children _____ (do/do not) organize themselves into "boy worlds" and "girl worlds."

22. As young children, we formed _____ that helped us make sense of the world. To organize boy-girl characteristics, we formed a _____ _____ , which became a gender lens through which we viewed our experiences.

APPLICATIONS:

23. Rod has always felt pressure to be the driver when traveling in a car with Sue because he learned that this was expected of men. Rod's feelings illustrate the influence of _____ _____ .

24. Pat and Alex have been married for about 10 years. During that time, Alex is the one most likely to spend less time at work, more time with household chores, and more time caring for the very young and the very old. Alex is most likely _____ (male/female).

25. When his son cries because another child has taken his favorite toy, Brandon admonishes him by saying, "Big boys don't cry." Evidently, Brandon is an advocate of _____ _____ in accounting for the development of gender-linked behaviors.

26. Three-year-old Caleb shares a toy chest with his 18-month-old sister Elena. Caleb has put all cars, trucks, and superheros to his side of the chest and all the dolls, stuffed animals, and miniature furniture to Elena's side. Caleb has clearly formed a _____ _____ about gender-linked behaviors.

Human Sexuality

Objective 4: Discuss the impact of hormones on our sexuality, and describe the stages of the human sexual response cycle.

The sex hormones direct the physical development of male and female sex characteristics and, especially in nonhuman animals, activate sexual behavior. Although testosterone and the *estrogens* are present in both sexes, males have a higher level of testosterone and females a higher level of estrogens such as estradiol.

In humans, the hormones influence sexual behaviors more loosely. Large hormonal shifts, such as occurs at puberty, have a greater effect. Also, in later life, as sex hormones decline, the frequency of sexual fantasies and intercourse also declines. Chance events, such as surgery or drugs, may cause hormonal shifts that affect sexual behavior.

The human *sexual response cycle* normally follows a pattern of *excitement, plateau, orgasm* (which seems to involve similar feelings and brain activity in males and females), and *resolution*, followed in males by a **refractory period,** during which renewed arousal and orgasm are not possible.

Unprotected sex has led to increased rates of *sexually transmitted infections (STIs)*, including **AIDS.** Teenage girls, because of their less mature biological development and lower levels of protective antibodies, seem especially vulnerable to STIs. Although condoms do not protect against all STIs, they do reduce the risk of getting *HIV (human immunodeficiency virus)*.

1. In most mammals, females are sexually receptive only during ovulation, when the female sex hormones, the _____ , such as _____ , peak.

2. The importance of the hormone _____ to male sexual arousal is confirmed by the fact that sexual interest declines in animals if their _____ are surgically removed. In women, low levels of the hormone _____ may cause a waning of sexual interest.

3. Normal hormonal fluctuations in humans have _____ (little/significant) effect on sexual motivation—except at two predictable points in the life span. During _____, a surge in _____ hormones triggers the development of _____ _____ . In later life, levels of the hormone _____ fall, and women experience _____ .

4. A third possibility is that hormonal shifts may be caused by _____ or drugs, resulting in a _____ (increase/decrease) in the sex drive as _____ levels decline.

5. The two researchers who identified a four-stage sexual response cycle are _____ and _____ . In order, the stages of the cycle are the _____ phase, the _____ phase, _____ , and the _____ phase.

6. During resolution, males experience a _____ _____ , during which they are incapable of another orgasm.

7. Unprotected sex has led to an increase in rates of _____ _____ _____ . Teenage girls, because of their lower levels of protective _____ , may be especially vulnerable to STIs.

8. Condom use reduces the risk of getting _____ , the virus that causes _____ . This virus is passed more often from _____ (male to female/female to male) than from _____ (male to female/female to male).

Objective 5: Discuss some factors that influence teenagers' sexual behavior and use of contraceptives.

Although American teens have lower rates of intercourse than European teens, they also have lower rates of condom use and thus higher pregnancy and abortion rates. Reasons for this failure include ignorance of which birth control methods will protect them and a tendency to overestimate the sexual activity of their friends. Guilt related to sexual activity sometimes results in lack of planned birth control. When passion overwhelms intentions, the result may be conception. Often there is mini-mal communication about birth control, as many teenagers are uncomfortable discussing contraception with either parents or partners. Sexually active teens also tend to use alcohol, which can break down normal restraints. Finally, television and movies foster sexual norms of unprotected promiscuity.

Attempts to protect teens through comprehensive sex education programs include a greater emphasis on teen abstinence. Teens with high rather than average intelligence more often delay sex. Religious engagement, father's presence, and participation in service learning programs are also predictors of sexual restraint.

9. Compared with European teens, American teens have _____ (higher/lower) rates of intercourse, _____ (higher/lower) rates of contraceptive use, and thus _____ (higher/lower) rates of teen pregnancy and abortion.

State five factors that contribute to the high rate of unprotected sex among teenagers.

State several predictors of sexual restraint (reduced teen sexuality and pregnancy).

10. Which of the following teens is most likely to delay the initiation of sex?
    a. Jack, who has below-average intelligence
    b. Jason, who is not religiously active
    c. Ron, who regularly volunteers his time in community service
    d. It is impossible to predict.

Objective 6: Discuss the impact of external and imagined stimuli on sexual motivation and behavior.

External stimuli, such as sexually explicit materials, can trigger arousal in both men and women. Sexually coercive material tends to increase viewers' acceptance of rape and violence toward women. Images of sexually attractive men and women may lead people to be less satisfied with their own partners and relationships. Our imaginations also influence sexual motivation.

Wide-awake people become sexually aroused both by memories of prior sexual activities and by fantasies. About 95 percent of both men and women say they have had sexual fantasies.

11. Research has shown that erotic stimuli
_____ (are/are not) nearly as
arousing for women as for men.

12. With repeated exposure, the emotional response to
an erotic stimulus often grows
_____ .

Explain some of the possible harmful consequences of
sexually explicit material.

13. Most women and men _____
(have/do not have) sexual fantasies. Compared to
women's fantasies, men's sexual fantasies are more
_____ .

Sexual Orientation

Objective 7: Summarize current views on the number of
people whose sexual orientation is homosexual, and discuss the research on environmental and biological influences on sexual orientation.

Sexual orientation is our enduring sexual attraction
toward members of either our own sex (*homosexual*) or
the other sex (*heterosexual*). Estimates based on data
from the 2000 U.S. Census suggest that 2.5 percent of
the population is gay or lesbian. About 3 or 4 percent
of men and 1 or 2 percent of women are exclusively
homosexual.

Sexual orientation is neither willfully chosen nor
willfully changed. Women's sexual orientation tends to
be less strongly felt and potentially more changeable
than men's. Men's lesser *erotic plasticity* is apparent
across time, cul-
tures, situa-
tions, and other
factors.

Although
we are still
unsure why one
person becomes
homosexual
and another

heterosexual, it is beginning to look as though biological
factors are involved. No links have been found between
homosexuality and a child's relationships with parents,

father-absent homes, fear or hatred of people of the
other gender, childhood sexual experience, peer relationships, or dating experiences. On the other hand, biological influences are evident in studies of same-sex
relations in several hundred species, straight-gay differences in brain characteristics, genetic studies of family
members and twins, and the effect of exposure to certain hormones during critical periods of prenatal development.

1. A person's sexual attraction toward members of a
particular gender is referred to as
_____ _____ .

2. Historically, _____ (all/a slight
majority) of the world's cultures have been predomi-
nantly heterosexual.

3. Estimates indicate that approximately _____
percent of men and _____ percent of
women are exclusively homosexual. Fewer than 1
percent report being actively _____ .

4. A person's sexual orientation _____
(does/does not) appear to be voluntarily chosen.
Several research studies reveal that sexual orientation among _____
(women/men) tends to be less strongly felt and
potentially more variable than among the other gender. This phenomenon has been called the
gender difference in _____
_____ .

5. Gays and lesbians suffer elevated rates of
_____ and risk of
_____ attempts, but this may
result from their experiences with harassment and
discrimination.

6. Childhood events and family relationships
_____ (are/are not) important
factors in determining a person's sexual orientation.

7. Homosexuality _____
(does/does not) involve a fear of the other gender
that leads people to direct their sexual desires
toward members of their own gender.

8. Sex hormone levels _____
(do/do not) predict sexual orientation.

9. As children, most homosexuals
_____ (were/were not)
sexually victimized.

10. Same-sex attraction _____
(does/does not) occur among many species.

11. Researcher Simon LeVay discovered a cluster of cells in the _____ that is larger in _____ men than in all others. Gays and lesbians differ from their straight counterparts in their preference for sex-related _____ . Other studies have found a section of the brain's _____ _____ that is one-third larger in homosexual men than in heterosexual men.

12. Studies of twins suggest that genes probably _____ (do/do not) play a role in homosexuality. Research has confirmed that homosexual men have more homosexual relatives on their _____ (mother's/father's) side than on their _____ (mother's/father's) side.

13. In animals and some rare human cases, sexual orientation has been altered by abnormal _____ conditions during prenatal development. In humans, prenatal exposure to hormone levels typical of _____ , particularly between _____ and _____ months after conception, may predispose an attraction to males.

14. Men who have older brothers are somewhat _____ (more/less) likely to be gay. This phenomenon, which has been called the _____ _____- _____ _____ , may represent a defensive maternal _____ response to substances produced by _____ (male/female) fetuses.

15. There are several behavioral and biological traits on which homosexuals appear to fall midway between _____ females and males. These include _____ _____ .

An Evolutionary Explanation of Human Sexuality

Objective 8: Discuss how evolutionary psychologists use natural selection to explain human sexuality.

Evolutionary psychologists use the principles of *natural selection* to understand human behavior and mental processes. They explain how natural selection favors behavioral tendencies that contributed to the survival and spread of our genes. The principle helps us understand gender differences and similarities and important aspects of human sexuality.

One of the largest reported gender differences is women's greater disapproval of and lesser willingness to engage in casual, uncommitted sex. In comparison to women, men think more about sex, masturbate more often, are more likely to initiate sex, and make more sacrifices to gain sex.

Evolutionary psychologists apply the principle of natural selection to explain women's more relational and men's more recreational approaches to sex. While most women incubate and nurse one infant at a time, a man can spread his genes by mating with many females. Women most often send their genes into the future by pairing wisely, men by pairing widely. Women increase their own and children's chances of survival by searching for mates who are mature, dominant, bold, and affluent. Being attracted to fertile-appearing partners increases men's chances of spreading their genes widely.

1. Researchers who use natural selection to explain the adaptive nature of human behavior are called _____ _____ .

2. According to the principle of _____ _____ , traits that contribute to _____ and _____ will be most likely to be passed on to succeeding generations.

3. According to this view, men who were most likely to pass on their genes were attracted to women with features that implied _____ .

4. Compared with women, men masturbate _____ (more/less) and initiate _____ (more/less) sex.

5. According to evolutionary psychology, men have a more _____ approach to sex, while women have a more _____ approach.

6. According to the evolutionary perspective, over ancestral time men were selected for behaviors that promoted pairing _____ (widely/wisely). This perspective also explains why women often feel attracted to men who are _____ , _____ , _____ , and _____ .

THINK ABOUT IT: A key concept closely related to the principle of natural selection is fitness. We've all heard about "survival of the fittest," but the phrase is often misunderstood. It is not always true that "only the strong survive." From the standpoint of evolutionary psychology, "fitness" most directly refers to reproductive success. Traits and behaviors that have a genetic basis obviously cannot be passed on to succeeding generations if individuals do not have offspring. As you think about gender issues and sexuality, it may be helpful to consider the question, "How might this trait or behavior have promoted reproductive success over evolutionary time?"

Objective 9: Summarize the criticisms of evolutionary explanations of human behaviors, and describe the evolutionary psychologists' responses to those criticisms.

Critics argue that evolutionary psychologists start with an effect (e.g., gender sexuality difference) and work backward to propose an explanation. In addition, much of who we are is not hard-wired. Cultural expectations can bend the genders. Still others suggest that evolutionary explanations may undercut moral responsibility for sexual behavior. In response, evolutionary psychologists point to the explanatory power of their theoretical principles, especially those offering testable predictions. They also note that understanding what we are capable of doing can help us become better people.

State several criticisms of evolutionary psychology.

APPLICATION:

7. Responding to the argument that gender differences are often by-products of a culture's social and family structures, an evolutionary psychologist is most likely to point to our great human capacity to _____ and to _____ and to survive.

Thinking About Gender, Sexuality, and Nature-Nurture Interaction

1. We are the product of our _____ and _____ , but we are also a system that is _____ .

PROGRESS TEST

Multiple-Choice Questions

Circle your answers to the following questions and check them with the answers beginning on page 78. If your answer is incorrect, read the explanation for why it is incorrect and then consult the text.

1. Dr. Ross believes that principles of natural selection help explain why infants come to fear strangers about the time they become mobile. Dr. Ross is most likely a(n)
   a. behavior geneticist.
   b. molecular geneticist.
   c. evolutionary psychologist.
   d. molecular biologist.

2. Through natural selection, the traits that are most likely to be passed on to succeeding generations are those that contribute to
   a. reproduction.   c. aggressiveness.
   b. power.   d. connectedness.

3. Which of the following is NOT true regarding gender and sexuality?
   a. Men are more likely than women to masturbate.
   b. Women are more likely than men to cite affection as a reason for first intercourse.
   c. Men are more likely than females to initiate sexual activity.
   d. Gender differences in sexuality are noticeably absent among gay men and lesbian women.

4. Evolutionary psychologists attribute gender differences in sexuality to the fact that women have
   a. greater reproductive potential than do men.
   b. lower reproductive potential than do men.
   c. weaker sex drives than men.
   d. stronger sex drives than men.

5. According to evolutionary psychology, men are drawn sexually to women who seem _____ , while women are attracted to men who seem _____ .
   a. nurturing; youthful
   b. youthful and fertile; mature and affluent
   c. slender; muscular
   d. exciting; dominant

6. Gender refers to
   a. the biological and social characteristics by which people define male and female.
   b. the biological definition of male and female.
   c. our sense of being male or female.
   d. the extent to which we exhibit traditionally male or female traits.

7. The fertilized egg will develop into a boy if, at conception,
   a. the sperm contributes an X chromosome.
   b. the sperm contributes a Y chromosome.
   c. the egg contributes an X chromosome.
   d. the egg contributes a Y chromosome.

8. Which theory states that gender becomes a lens through which children view their experiences?
   a. social learning theory
   b. sociocultural theory
   c. cognitive theory
   d. gender schema theory

9. The hormone testosterone
   a. is found only in females.
   b. determines the sex of the developing person.
   c. stimulates growth of the female sex organs.
   d. stimulates growth of the male sex organs.

10. Each cell of the human body has a total of
    a. 23 chromosomes.   c. 46 chromosomes.
    b. 23 genes.   d. 46 genes.

11. Evolutionary explanations of gender differences in sexuality have been criticized because
    a. they offer "after-the-fact" explanations.
    b. standards of attractiveness vary with time and place.
    c. they underestimate cultural influences on sexuality.
    d. of all of these reasons.

12. Children who are raised by parents who discourage traditional gender typing
    a. are less likely to display gender-typed behaviors themselves.
    b. often become confused and develop an ambiguous gender identity.
    c. nevertheless organize themselves into "girl worlds" and "boy worlds."
    d. display excessively masculine and feminine traits as adults.

13. The correct order of the stages of Masters and Johnson's sexual response cycle is
    a. plateau; excitement; orgasm; resolution.
    b. excitement; plateau; orgasm; resolution.
    c. excitement; orgasm; resolution; refractory.
    d. plateau; excitement; orgasm; refractory.

14. Which of the following is NOT true regarding sexual orientation?
    a. Sexual orientation is neither willfully chosen nor willfully changed.
    b. All cultures in all times have been predominantly heterosexual.
    c. Men's sexual orientation is potentially more fluid and changeable than women's.
    d. Women, regardless of sexual orientation, respond to both female and male erotic stimuli.

15. Surgically removing the testes of male rats results in
    a. reduced testosterone and sexual interest.
    b. reduced testosterone, but no change in sexual interest.
    c. reduced estrogen and sexual interest.
    d. reduced estrogen, but no change in sexual interest.

16. Of the following parts of the world, teen intercourse rates are higher in
    a. Western Europe.   c. The United States.
    b. Canada.   d. Asia.

17. Exposing a fetus to the hormones typical of females between _____ and _____ months after conception may predispose the developing human to become attracted to males.
    a. 1; 3   c. 4; 7
    b. 2; 5   d. 6; 9

18. Which of the following statements concerning homosexuality is true?
    a. Homosexuals have abnormal hormone levels.
    b. As children, most homosexuals were molested by an adult homosexual.
    c. Homosexuals had a domineering opposite-sex parent.
    d. Research indicates that sexual orientation may be at least partly physiological.

19. Sexual orientation refers to
    a. a person's tendency to display behaviors typical of males or females.
    b. a person's sense of identity as a male or female.
    c. a person's enduring sexual attraction toward members of a particular gender.
    d. characteristics defined by society as male or female.

20. According to Masters and Johnson, the sexual response of males is most likely to differ from that of females during
    a. the excitement phase.
    b. the plateau phase.
    c. orgasm.
    d. the resolution phase.

21. Which of the following was NOT identified as a contributing factor in the high rate of unprotected sex among adolescents?
    a. alcohol use
    b. thrill-seeking
    c. mass media sexual norms
    d. ignorance

22. The *fraternal birth-order effect* refers to the fact that
    a. men who have younger brothers are somewhat more likely to be gay.
    b. men who have older brothers are somewhat more likely to be gay.
    c. women with older sisters are somewhat more likely to be gay.
    d. women with younger sisters are somewhat more likely to be gay.

Application Essay

Lakia's new boyfriend has been pressuring her to become more sexually intimate than she wants to at this early stage in their relationship. Strongly gender-typed and "macho" in attitude, Jerome is becoming increasingly frustrated with Lakia's hesitation, while Lakia is starting to wonder if a long-term relationship with this type of man is what she really wants. In light of your understanding of the evolutionary explanation of gender differences in sexuality, explain why the tension between Lakia and Jerome would be considered understandable. (Use the space below to list points you want to make, and organize them. Then write the essay on a separate piece of paper.)

SUMMING UP

See the next page.

TERMS AND CONCEPTS

Using your own words, on a piece of paper write a brief definition or explanation of each of the following terms.

1. gender
2. aggression
3. X chromosome
4. Y chromosome
5. testosterone
6. role
7. gender role
8. gender identity
9. social learning theory
10. gender typing
11. estrogens
12. sexual response cycle
13. refractory period
14. AIDS
15. sexual orientation
16. evolutionary psychology
17. natural selection

SUMMING UP

Belle and Bruno are an average female and male. Compared with Bruno, Belle

| has a body with more _____ and less _____ , | begins puberty about _____ years earlier, and | is expected to outlive him by about _____ years. |

Psychologically, Belle and Bruno are different in several ways:

Belle is

Bruno is

| more vulnerable to _____ , _____ , and _____ disorders. | more likely to commit _____ , to become dependent on _____ , and to have _____ as a child. |

In terms of social power,

Belle is

while

Bruno is

| perceived as (any traits perceived as "feminine") _____ , _____ , and _____ , | more likely to dominate, to be more _____ , even _____ , and to talk _____ . |

In terms of social connectedness,

| Belle is more concerned with _____ , with making connections, and less concerned with viewing herself as a separate _____ . | This is seen early in their play: Bruno plays in _____ (larger/smaller) groups, while Belle plays in _____ (larger/smaller) groups. |

ANSWERS

Chapter Review

Gender Development

1. gender

2. 46; 45

3. fat; muscle; shorter; depression; anxiety; eating disorders

4. suicide; alcohol; autism, color-blindness, ADHD, antisocial personality disorder

5. physical; verbal; intended

6. physical; relational

7. hunting; fighting; warring

8. dominant; forceful; independent; directive; democratic

9. submissive; nurturing; socially connected

10. decrease

11. connections

12. play; smaller; competitive; feedback

13. interdependent; explore relationships; communicate solutions

14. biology; personal history; current situation

15. talk with others to communicate solutions; talk with others to explore relationships. Men prefer side-by-side activities and coming up with solutions. Women prefer face-to-face activities, such as trying to make another woman feel welcome.

16. sex; X; Y; testosterone; seventh

17. hormones; frontal; verbal; parietal; space

18. roles; gender roles

19. are not; cultures; time; nomadic; agricultural

20. gender identity; gender typing

21. social learning; do

22. schemas; gender schema

23. gender roles

24. female. Males such as Pat are more likely to spend more time at work and less time at home doing household chores.

25. social learning. Following social learning theory, Brandon is using verbal punishment to discourage what he believes to be an inappropriate gender-linked behavior in his son.

26. gender schema. Even when parents raise children in a gender-neutral environment, the children automatically divide things into a "girls' world" and a "boys' world."

Human Sexuality

1. estrogens; estradiol

2. testosterone; testes; testosterone

3. little; puberty; sex; sex characteristics; estrogen; menopause

4. surgery; decrease; testosterone

5. Masters; Johnson; excitement; plateau; orgasm; resolution

6. refractory period

7. sexually transmitted infections (STIs); antibodies

8. HIV; AIDS; male to female; female to male

9. lower; lower; higher

Among the factors that contribute to unprotected sex among adolescents are (1) ignorance about the safe and risky times of the menstrual cycle, (2) guilt related to sexual activity, (3) minimal communication about birth control, (4) alcohol use that influences judgment, and (5) mass media norms of unprotected promiscuity.

High intelligence, religious engagement, father's presence, and participation in service learning programs predict sexual restraint in teens.

10. **c.** is the answer. Teens with high rather than average intelligence (therefore, not a.) and those who are religiously active (therefore, not b.) are most likely to delay sex.

11. are

12. weaker

Erotic material may increase the viewer's acceptance of the false idea that women enjoy rape, may increase men's willingness to hurt women, may lead people to devalue their partners and relationships, and may diminish people's satisfaction with their own sexual partners.

13. have; frequent, physical, and less romantic

Sexual Orientation

1. sexual orientation

2. all

3. 3 or 4; 1 or 2; bisexual

4. does not; women; erotic plasticity

5. depression; suicide

6. are not

7. does not

8. do not

9. were not

10. does

11. hypothalamus; heterosexual; odors; anterior commissure

12. do; mother's; father's

13. hormone; females; 2; 5

14. more; fraternal birth-order effect (older-brother effect); immune; male

15. heterosexual; spatial abilities, fingerprint ridge counts, handedness, and gender nonconformity

An Evolutionary Explanation of Human Sexuality

1. evolutionary psychologists

2. natural selection; survival; reproduction

3. fertility

4. more; more

5. recreational; relational

6. widely; mature, dominant, bold, affluent

Evolutionary psychology has been criticized for starting with an effect and working backward, for ignoring the impact of culture, and for implying that because genes are destiny men don't need to take responsibility for their sexual behaviors.

7. adapt; learn

Thinking About Gender, Sexuality, and Nature-Nurture Interaction

1. nature; nurture; open

Progress Test

Multiple-Choice Questions

1. c. is the answer.
a., b., & d. Whereas evolutionary psychologists attempt to explain universal human tendencies, these researchers investigate genetic differences among individuals.

2. a. is the answer.
b., c., & d. Natural selection favors traits that send one's genes into the future, such as surviving longer and reproducing more often. Aggression, power, and connectedness do not necessarily promote either.

3. d. is the answer. Such gender differences characterize both heterosexual and homosexual people.

4. b. is the answer. Most women incubate and nurse only one infant at a time.
c. & d. The text does not suggest that there is a gender difference in the strength of the sex drive.

5. b. is the answer.
a. According to this perspective, women prefer mates with the potential for long-term nurturing investment in their joint offspring.
c. Men are drawn to women who suggest fertility, which is not necessarily a slender body.
d. Excitement was not mentioned as a criterion for mating.

6. a. is the answer.
b. This definition is incomplete.
c. This defines gender identity.
d. This defines gender typing.

7. b. is the answer.
a. In this case, a female would develop.
c. & d. The egg can contribute only an X chromosome. Thus, the sex of the child is determined by which chromosome the sperm contributes.

8. d. is the answer.
a. According to social learning theory, gender typing evolves through imitation and reinforcement.
b. & c. Neither theory focuses on gender typing.

9. d. is the answer.
a. Although testosterone is the principal male hormone, it is present in both females and males.
b. This is determined by the sex chromosomes.
c. In the absence of testosterone, female sex organs will develop.

10. c. is the answer.
b. & d. Each cell of the human body contains hundreds of genes.

11. d. is the answer.

12. c. is the answer.
b. & d. There is no evidence that being raised in a "gender neutral" home confuses children or fosters a backlash of excessive gender typing.

13. b. is the answer.

14. c. is the answer. Research studies suggest that women's sexual orientation is potentially more fluid and changeable than men's.

15. a. is the answer.
c. & d. Surgically removing the testes, which produce testosterone, does not alter estrogen levels.

16. a. is the answer.

17. b. is the answer. The time between the middle of the second and fifth months after conception may be a critical period for the brain's neuro-hormonal control system. Exposure to abnormal hormonal conditions at other times has no effect on sexual orientation.

18. d. is the answer. Researchers have not been able to find any clear differences, psychological or otherwise, between homosexuals and heterosexuals. Thus, the basis for sexual orientation remains unknown, although recent evidence points more to a physiological basis.

19. c. is the answer.

20. d. is the answer. During the resolution phase males experience a refractory period.
a., b., & c. The male and female responses are very similar in each of these phases.

21. b. is the answer.

22. b. is the answer.

Application Essay

Evolutionary psychologists would not be surprised by the tension between Lakia and Jerome and would see it as a reflection of women's more relational and men's more recreational approach to sex. Since eggs are expensive, compared with sperm, women prefer mates who will be committed to caring for their joint offspring. According to this perspective, this may be why Lakia is not in a hurry to become sexually intimate with Jerome. Men, on the other hand, are selected for "pairing widely" but not necessarily wisely in order to maximize the spreading of their genes. This is especially true of men like Jerome, who have traditional masculine attitudes.

Summing Up

Belle and Bruno are an average female and male. Compared with Bruno, Belle has a body with more *fat* and less *muscle*, begins puberty about *two* years earlier, and is expected to outlive him by about *five* years.

Psychologically, Belle and Bruno are different in several ways: Belle is more vulnerable to *depression, anxiety,* and *eating disorders.* Bruno is more likely to commit *suicide,* to become dependent on *alcohol,* and to have *ADHD* as a child.

In terms of social power, Belle is perceived as (any traits considered feminine) *submissive, nurturing,* and *socially connected,* while Bruno is more likely to dominate, to be more *directive,* even *autocratic,* and to talk *assertively.*

In terms of social connectedness, Belle is more concerned with *relationships,* with making connections, and less concerned with viewing herself as a separate *individual.* This is seen early in their play: Bruno plays in *larger* groups, while Belle plays in *smaller* groups.

Terms and Concepts

1. **Gender** refers to the biological and social characteristics by which people define *male* and *female.*

2. **Aggression** is physical or verbal behavior intended to hurt someone.

3. The **X chromosome** is the sex chromosome found in both men and women. Females inherit an X chromosome from each parent.

4. The **Y chromosome** is the sex chromosome found only in men. Males inherit an X chromosome from their mothers and a Y chromosome from their fathers.

5. **Testosterone** is the principal male sex hormone. During prenatal development, testosterone stimulates the development of the external male sex organs.

6. A **role** is a cluster of prescribed behaviors expected of those who occupy a particular social position.

7. A **gender role** is a set of expected behaviors for males and females.

8. **Gender identity** is one's sense of being male or female.

9. According to **social learning theory**, people learn social behavior (such as gender roles) by observing and imitating and by being rewarded or punished.

10. **Gender typing** is the acquisition of a traditional feminine or masculine role.

11. **Estrogens** are sex hormones secreted in greater amounts by females than by males. In mammals other than humans, estrogen levels peak during ovulation and trigger sexual receptivity.

12. The **sexual response cycle** described by Masters and Johnson consists of four stages of bodily reaction: excitement, plateau, orgasm, and resolution.

13. The **refractory period** is a resting period after orgasm, during which a male cannot be aroused to another orgasm.

14. **AIDS** (acquired immune deficiency syndrome) is the life-threatening, sexually transmitted infection caused by the human immunodeficiency virus (HIV).

15. **Sexual orientation** refers to a person's enduring attraction to members of either the same or the opposite gender.

16. **Evolutionary psychology** is the study of how our behavior and mind have changed in adaptive ways over time using the principles of natural selection.

17. **Natural selection** is the adaptive process: Among the range of inherited trait variations, those that lead to increased reproduction and survival will most likely be passed on to succeeding generations.

5

SENSATION AND PERCEPTION

Chapter 5 explores the processes by which our sense receptors and nervous system represent our external environment (sensation), as well as how we mentally organize and interpret this information (perception). The senses of vision, hearing, taste, touch, smell, and body position and movement are described, along with the ways in which we organize the stimuli reaching these senses to perceive form, depth, and constant shape, size, and lightness. To enhance your understanding of these processes, the chapter also discusses research findings from studies of subliminal stimulation, sensory restriction, recovery from blindness, adaptation to distorted environments, perceptual set, and extrasensory perception.

CHAPTER REVIEW

First, skim each text section, noting headings and boldface items. Review the section by reading the objectives and summaries provided here, then answer the questions that follow. In some cases, STUDY TIPS explain how best to learn a difficult concept and APPLICATIONS help you to know how well you understand the material. Check your understanding of the material by consulting the answers beginning on page 95. Do not continue with the next section until you understand each answer. If you need to, review or reread the section in the textbook before continuing.

Introduction

Objective 1: Contrast sensation and perception.

Sensation is the process by which we take in stimulus energy from our environment. *Perception* is the process by which our brain organizes and interprets sensory

information, enabling us to recognize meaningful objects and events.

1. The process by which we detect physical energy from the environment and encode it as neural signals is _____ .

2. The process by which sensations are organized and interpreted is _____ .

••

STUDY TIP: This chapter includes a great deal of technical information that you must memorize for each sense (vision, hearing, taste, touch, smell). An excellent way to study material such as this is to organize it into a chart. For each sense you need to know several facts, including the nature of the stimulus input, the type of receptor that transmits the stimulus energy, and how the information is processed in the brain. To help you review your understanding of sensation and perception, refer often to the summary chart below.

Sense	Stimulus Input	Receptors	Notes
Vision	Visible electromagnetic energy	Rods and cones	Wavelength = hue; intensity = brightness; rods = black and white; cones = color
Hearing	Sound waves of moving air molecules	Hair cells in the cochlea	wavelength = pitch; amplitude = loudness
Touch	Pressure, warmth, cold, pain	Specialized nerve endings	Cold + pressure = wetness; side-by-side pressure = tickle
Pain	No one type of stimulus	No special receptors	Natural endorphins relieve pain; hypnosis used for treating pain
Taste	Chemical molecules corresponding to sweet, salty, sour, bitter, and umami	Hair cells in the taste pores	Sensory interaction: smell influences; taste; smell + texture = taste = flavor
Smell	Airborne chemical molecules	Olfactory receptor cells in the nasal cavity	The brain's circuitry for smell connects with areas involved in memory storage
Body position and movement	Changes in body's position (kinesthesis)	Sensors in muscles, tendons, and joints	Millions of position and motion sensors
	Changes in head position (vestibular sense)	Hairlike receptors in the ear's semicircular canals and vestibular sacs of the inner ear	Messages sent to the brain's cerebellum

Basic Principles of Sensation and Perception

Objective 2: Identify the three steps basic to all sensory systems.

All sensory systems must receive stimulation, transform it into neural impulses (called *transduction*), and deliver the information to our brain.

1. The process of changing one form of energy into the form that your brain can use is called

   _____ .

Objective 3: Distinguish between absolute thresholds and difference thresholds, and explain Weber's law.

An *absolute threshold* is the minimum stimulation needed to detect a particular stimulus 50 percent of the time. The *priming* effect reveals that we *can* process some information (through our two-track mind) from *subliminal* stimuli, that is, stimuli below our absolute threshold.

   A *difference threshold* is the minimum difference between two stimuli that a person can detect 50 percent of the time (a *just noticeable difference [jnd]*). In humans, the stimuli must differ by a constant minimum proportion, not a constant amount. This principle is known as *Weber's law.*

2. The _____ _____ refers to the minimum stimulation necessary for a stimulus to be detected _____ percent of the time.

3. Stimuli you cannot detect 50 percent of the time are "below threshold," or _____ .

4. Under certain conditions, an invisible image or word can _____ a person's response to a later question. The _____ _____ illustrates that much of our information processing occurs _____ , outside _____ awareness. This is another illustration of our _____-_____ mind.

5. The minimum difference required to distinguish two stimuli 50 percent of the time is called the

   _____ _____ .

   Another term for this value is the

   _____ _____

   _____ .

6. The principle that the difference threshold is not a constant amount, but a constant minimum proportion, is known as _____ _____ . The proportion depends on the _____ .

APPLICATION:

7. In shopping for a new stereo, you discover that you cannot differentiate between the sounds of models X and Y. The difference between X and Y is below your

   _____ _____ .

Objective 4: Discuss whether we can detect and be affected by subliminal stimuli.

Although we can detect subliminal stimuli some of the time, advertising claims of subliminal persuasion are not true. The effect of subliminal stimuli is subtle and fleeting, with no powerful enduring influence on behavior.

8. Some marketers claim that we can _____ sense below subliminal stimuli, and that such stimuli can help us make lasting _____ _____ .

9. The effect of such stimuli is _____ , and has _____ (an enduring influence/no enduring influence) on behavior

Objective 5: Explain the function of sensory adaptation.

Sensory adaptation refers to the diminished sensitivity that is a consequence of constant stimulation. Constant, unchanging images on the eye's inner surface fade and then reappear. The phenomenon of sensory adaptation enables us to focus our attention on _____ informative changes in our environment without being distracted by the uninformative, constant stimulation of garments, odors, and street noise, for example.

10. After constant exposure to an unchanging stimulus, the receptor cells of our senses begin to fire less vigorously; this phenomenon is called

    _____ _____ .

11. This phenomenon illustrates that sensation is designed to focus on informative _____ in the environment.

APPLICATION:

12. Calvin usually runs his fingertips over a cloth's surface when trying to decide whether the texture is right for what he wants. By moving his fingers over the cloth, he prevents the occurrence of _____ _____ to the feel.

Objective 6: Explain how our assumptions, expectations, and contexts affect our perceptions.

Clear evidence that perception is influenced by our experiences—our learned assumptions and beliefs—as well as by sensory input comes from the many demonstrations of *perceptual set,* a mental predisposition to perceive one thing and not another. Perceptual set can influence what we hear, taste, feel, and see.

A given stimulus may trigger radically different perceptions because of the immediate context. For example, we discern whether a speaker said *morning* or *mourning* and *dye* or *die* from the surrounding words. Gender stereotypes and emotions also influence our perception.

13. A mental predisposition that influences perception is called a _____

_____ .

14. How a stimulus is perceived depends on our perceptual schemas and the _____ in which it is experienced.

15. Our perception is also influenced by the _____ context of our experiences.

APPLICATION:

16. Although carpenter Smith perceived a briefly viewed object as a screwdriver, police officer Wesson perceived the same object as a knife. This illustrates that perception is guided by _____

_____ .

Vision

Objective 7: Describe the characteristics of visible light.

The energies we experience as visible light are a thin slice from the broad spectrum of electromagnetic energy. Our sensory experience of light is determined largely by the light energy's **wavelength,** which determines the **hue** of a color, and its **intensity,** which influences brightness.

1. The visible spectrum of light is a small portion of the larger spectrum of _____ energy.

2. The distance from one light wave peak to the next is called _____ . This value determines the wave's color, or _____ .

3. The amount of energy in light waves, or _____ , determined by a wave's _____ , or height, influences the _____ of a light.

STUDY TIP: The stimulus energy for both vision and hearing can be described as a traveling wave that varies in wavelength

and amplitude. The wavelength of a visual or auditory stimulus is measured as the distance from the peak of one wave to the next—the shorter the distance, the greater the frequency of the waves. Short, high frequency waves produce "cool" or bluish colors for visual stimuli. They produce high-pitched sounds for auditory stimuli. Long, low frequency waves produce "warm" or reddish colors and low-pitched sounds.

The wave's amplitude is measured as the distance from the top of its peak to the bottom. High amplitude waves produce bright colors and loud sounds, while low amplitude waves produce dull colors and soft sounds.

To test your understanding, take a look at these two waves.

4. a. Assuming that these two waves were light energy, would they differ in appearance? How so?

b. Assuming that these two waves were sound energy, would they sound the same? If not, how would they differ?

Objective 8: Explain the process by which the eye converts light energy into neural messages.

After light enters the eye through the *pupil,* whose size is regulated by the *iris,* the *lens* focuses the rays by changing its curvature. The light-sensitive surface of the **retina** contains receptors that begin the processing of visual information.

The retina's **rods** and **cones** (most of which are clustered around the retina's area of central focus) transform the light energy into neural signals. These signals activate the neighboring *bipolar cells,* which in turn activate neighboring *ganglion* cells, whose axons converge to form the **optic nerve** that carries information to the brain's *thalamus,* which  distributes it to higher-level regions. Where the optic nerve leaves the eye, there are no receptor cells—creating a **blind spot.** The cones enable vision of color and fine detail. The rods enable black-and-white vision, remain sensitive in dim light, and are necessary for peripheral vision.

5. Light enters the eye through the eyeball's protective covering, the _____ , then passes through a small opening called the _____ ; the size of this opening is controlled by the colored _____ .

6. Changes in the curve and thickness of the _____ focus the image of an object onto the _____ , the light-sensitive inner surface of the eye.

7. The retina's receptor cells are the _____ (a) and _____ (b).

8. The chemical changes triggered by the light energy in the rods and cones activate neighboring _____ cells (c), which then activate neighboring _____ cells (d). The axons of these cells combine to form the _____ _____ . The visual information is carried to the _____ of the brain, which then sends it to the visual cortex.

9. Where this nerve leaves the eye, there are no receptors; thus, the area is called the _____ _____ .

10. Many cones have their own _____ cells to communicate with the visual cortex.

11. It is the _____ (rods/cones) of the eye that permit the perception of color; _____ (rods/cones) enable black-and-white vision.

12. Unlike cones, in dim light the rods are _____ (sensitive/insensitive).

APPLICATIONS:

13. Assuming that the visual systems of humans and other mammals function similarly, what would you expect the

retina of a nocturnal mammal (one active only at night) to contain? _____

14. As the football game continued into the night, LeVar noticed that he was having difficulty distinguishing the colors of the players' uniforms. This is because the _____ , which enable color vision, have a _____ absolute threshold for brightness than the available light intensity.

Objective 9: Discuss the role of feature detection and parallel processing in the brain's visual information processing.

The information from the retina's rods and cones is received and transmitted by 1 million ganglion cells whose axons make up the optic nerve. When individual ganglion cells register information, they send signals to the visual cortex. In the cortex, individual neurons (*feature detectors*) respond to specific features of a visual stimulus. These cells pass this information along to other areas of the cortex, where teams of cells respond to more complex patterns, such as recognizing faces.

Aspects of vision (color, movement, depth, and form) are processed by neural teams working separately and simultaneously, illustrating our brain's capacity for *parallel processing*. Our perceptions result from the integration of these teams working together.

15. Hubel and Wiesel discovered that certain neurons in the _____ _____ of the brain respond only to specific features of what is viewed. They called these neurons _____ _____ .

16. The brain achieves its remarkable speed in visual perception by processing several parts of a stimulus _____ (simultaneously/ sequentially). This procedure, called _____ _____ , may explain why people who have suffered a stroke may lose just one aspect of vision.

Objective 10: Describe Gestalt psychology's contribution to our understanding of perception, and identify principles of perceptual grouping in form perception.

Gestalt psychologists described principles by which we organize our sensations into perceptions. They provided many compelling demonstrations of how, given a cluster of sensations, the human perceiver organizes them into a gestalt, a German word meaning a "form" or a "whole." They further demonstrated that the whole may differ from the sum of its parts. Clearly, our brains do more than merely register information about the world. We are always filtering sensory information and constructing perceptions.

Our first task in perception is to perceive any object, called the figure, as distinct from its surroundings, called the ground. We must also organize the figure into a meaningful form. Gestalt principles for grouping that describe this process include proximity (we group nearby figures together), continuity (we perceive smooth, continuous patterns rather than discontinuous ones), and closure (we fill in gaps to create a whole object).

17. According to the _____ school of psychology, we tend to organize a cluster of sensations into a _____ , or form.

18. When we view a scene, we see the central object, or _____ , as distinct from its surroundings, or the _____ .

19. Proximity, closure, and continuity are examples of Gestalt rules of _____ .

20. The principle that we organize stimuli into smooth, continuous patterns is called _____ . The principle that we fill in gaps to create a complete, whole object is _____ . The grouping of items that are close to each other is the principle of _____ .

APPLICATION:

21. Studying the road map before her trip, Colleen had no trouble following the route of the highway she planned to travel. Colleen's ability illustrates the principle of _____ .

Objective 11: Explain the binocular and monocular cues we use to perceive depth.

Depth perception is the ability to see objects in three dimensions although the images that strike the eye are two dimensional. Depth perception enables us to judge distance. Research on the *visual cliff* (a small cliff with a drop-off covered by sturdy glass) reveals that depth perception is in part based on biological maturation. Many species perceive the world in three dimensions at, or very soon after, birth.

Binocular cues require information from both eyes. In the *retinal disparity* cue, the brain computes the relative distance of an object by comparing the slightly different images an object casts on our two retinas. The greater the difference, the greater the distance.

Monocular cues enable us to judge depth using information from only one eye. The monocular cues include *relative size* (the smaller image of two objects of the same size appears more distant), *interposition* (nearby objects partially obstruct our view of more distant objects), *relative height* (higher objects are farther away), *relative motion* (as we move, objects at different distances change their relative positions in our visual image, with those closest moving most), *linear perspective* (the converging of parallel lines indicates greater distance), and *light and shadow* (dimmer objects seem more distant).

22. The ability to see objects in three dimensions despite their two-dimensional representations on our retinas is called _____ _____ . It enables us to estimate _____ .

23. Gibson and Walk developed the _____ _____ to test depth perception in infants. They found that biological _____ prepares us to be wary of heights, and _____ amplifies that fear.

For questions 24–32, identify the depth perception cue that is defined.

24. Any cue that requires both eyes: _____ .

25. The greater the difference between the images received by the two eyes, the nearer the object: _____ _____ .

    3-D movies simulate this cue by photographing each scene with two cameras.

26. Any cue that requires either eye alone: _____ .

27. If two objects are presumed to be the same size, the one that casts a smaller retinal image is perceived as farther away: _____ _____ .

28. An object partially covered by another is seen as farther away: _____ .

29. Objects lower in the visual field are seen as nearer: _____ _____ .

30. As we move, objects at different distances appear to move at different rates: _____ _____ .

31. Parallel lines appear to converge in the distance: _____ _____ .

32. The dimmer of two objects seems farther away: _____ _____ .

••
STUDY TIP: Monocular depth cues are used by either eye alone to determine the distance of objects. They include relative height and size, interposition, linear perspective, and light and shadow.

33. Test your understanding of these cues by drawing a picture (in the box on the next page) of a tree, a person on a bus or train, a house, and trees. Use each cue at least once, and in your drawing place the objects in the following order (closest to most distant): book, person, fence, house, and tree.

```
┌─────────────────────────────────┐
│                                 │
│                                 │
│                                 │
│                                 │
│                                 │
└─────────────────────────────────┘
```

••

APPLICATIONS:

34. As her friend Milo walks toward her, Noriko perceives his size as remaining constant because his perceived distance _____ at the same time that her retinal image of him _____ .

35. Walking down the street, you see a pole that seems to partially cover a wall. You perceive the pole as _____ (farther away/nearer/larger) than the wall.

36. An artist paints a tree orchard so that the parallel rows of trees converge at the top of the canvas. The artist has used the monocular cue of _____ _____ to convey distance.

Objective 12: Explain how perceptual constancies help us to organize our sensations into meaningful perceptions.

Perceptual constancy is necessary to recognize an object. It enables us to see an object as unchanging (having consistent lightness, color, shape, and size) even as illumination and retinal images change. *Color constancy* refers to our perceiving familiar objects as having consistent color, even if changing illumination alters the wavelengths reflected by the object. We see color as a result of our brain's ability to decode the meaning of the light reflected by any object relative to its surroundings.

Shape constancy is our ability to perceive familiar objects (for example, an opening door) as unchanging in shape. *Size constancy* is perceiving objects as unchanging in size, despite the changing images they cast on our retinas.

The perceived distance of an object is a cue to the object's size. The perceived relationship between distance and size is generally valid but under special circumstances can lead us astray. For example, one reason for the Moon illusion is that cues to objects' distances at the horizon make the Moon behind them seem farther away. Thus, the Moon on the horizon seems larger.

37. Our tendency to see objects as unchanging while the stimuli from them change in size, shape, and brightness is called _____ _____ .

38. The experience of color depends on the surrounding _____ in which an object is seen. In an unvarying context, a familiar object will be perceived as having consistent color, even as the light changes. This phenomenon is called _____ _____ .

39. We see color as a result of our brains' ability to decode the meaning of the light _____ by any object relative to its _____ .

40. Due to shape and size constancy, familiar objects _____ (do/do not) appear to change shape or size despite changes in our _____ images of them.

41. Several illusions are explained by the interplay between perceived _____ and perceived _____ . When distance cues are removed, these illusions are _____ (diminished/strengthened).

Objective 13: Describe how research in restored vision, sensory deprivation, and perceptual adaptation contributes to our understanding of the nature-nurture interplay in our perceptions.

In the classic version of the nature-nurture debate, the German philosopher Immanuel Kant maintained that knowledge comes from our innate ways of organizing sensory experiences. On the other side, the British philosopher John Locke argued that we learn to perceive the world through our experiences of it. It's now clear that different aspects of perception depend more or less on both nature and nurture.

When cataracts are removed from adults who have been blind from birth, these people remain unable to perceive the world normally. Generally, they can distinguish figure from ground and sense colors, but they are unable to visually recognize objects that were familiar by touch. In controlled experiments, infant kittens and monkeys have been reared with severely restricted visual input. When their visual exposure is returned to normal, they, too, suffer enduring visual handicaps.

Human perception is remarkably *adaptable.* Given glasses that shift the world slightly to the left or right, or even turn it upside down, people manage to adapt their movements and, with practice, to move about with ease.

42. The idea that knowledge comes from inborn ways of organizing sensory experiences was proposed by the German philosopher _____ .

43. On the other side were philosophers who maintained that we learn to perceive the world by experiencing it. One British philosopher of this school was _____ .

44. Studies of cases in which vision has been restored to a person who was blind from birth show that, upon *seeing* for the first time objects familiar by touch, the person _____ (can/cannot) recognize them. Most of these people were born with clouded lenses, called _____ .

45. Studies of sensory restriction demonstrate that visual experiences during _____ are crucial for perceptual development. Such experiences suggest that there is a

_____ _____

for normal sensory and perceptual development.

46. Humans given glasses that shift or invert the visual field _____ (will/will not) adapt to the distorted perception. This is called

_____ _____ .

47. Animals such as chicks _____ (adapt/do not adapt) to distorting lenses.

The Nonvisual Senses

Objective 14: Describe the characteristics of the air pressure waves that we hear as meaningful sounds.

Audition, or hearing, is highly adaptive. The pressure waves we experience as sound vary in *amplitude* and *frequency* and correspondingly in perceived *loudness* and *pitch*. *Decibels* are the measuring unit for sound energy.

1. The stimulus for hearing, or_____ , is sound waves, created by _____ _____ being compressed and expanded.

2. The strength, or amplitude, of a sound wave determines the sound's _____ .

3. The length, or frequency, of a sound wave determines the _____ we perceive.

4. Sound energy is measured in units called _____ . The absolute threshold for hearing is arbitrarily defined as _____ such units.

Objective 15: Describe the auditory process, including the stimulus input and the structure and function of the ear and how sounds are located.

Sound waves travel through the auditory canal to the *eardrum,* a tight membrane that vibrates with the waves. Transmitted via the bones of the middle ear to the fluid-filled *cochlea* in the inner ear, these vibrations cause the *oval window* to vibrate, creating movement in the tiny

hair cells lining the cochlea's surface, triggering neural messages to be sent (via the thalamus) to the auditory cortex in the brain's temporal lobe. Damage to the hair cells accounts for most hearing loss.

Sound waves strike one ear sooner and more intensely than the other ear. We localize sounds by detecting the minute differences in the intensity and timing of the sounds received by each ear.

5. The ear is divided into three main parts: the _____ ear, the _____ ear, and the _____ ear.

6. The outer ear channels sound waves toward the _____ , a tight membrane that then vibrates.

7. The middle ear transmits the vibrations through a piston made of three tiny _____ .

8. In the inner ear, a snail-shaped, fluid-filled tube called the _____ contains the receptor cells for hearing. The incoming vibrations cause the _____ _____ to vibrate, which causes ripples in the fluid, bending the

_____ _____

lining its surface. This movement triggers impulses in nerve cells that combine to form the auditory nerve, which carries the neural messages (via the _____) to the _____ lobe's auditory cortex.

9. We locate a sound by sensing differences in the _____ and _____ with which it reaches our ears.

10. A sound that comes from directly ahead will be _____ (easier/harder) to locate than a sound that comes from off to one side.

APPLICATION:

11. Dr. Frankenstein has forgotten to give his monster an important part; as a result, the monster cannot transmit sound to the brain. Dr. Frankenstein omitted part of the ear: the _____ .

Objective 16: Describe the four basic touch sensations, noting which of them has identifiable receptors.

Our sense of touch is actually four senses—pressure, warmth, cold, and pain—that combine to produce other sensations, such as "hot." There is no simple relationship between what we feel and the type of specialized nerve ending found there. Only pressure has identifiable receptors.

12. The sense of touch is a mixture of at least four

    senses: _____ ,

    _____ , _____ ,

    and _____ . Other skin sensa-

    tions, such as tickle, itch, and wetness, are

    _____ of the basic ones. Only

    _____ has identifiable receptors.

Objective 17: Discuss the value of feelings of pain, and describe ways of treating pain.

Pain is our body's way of telling us something is wrong. Pain experiences vary greatly, depending on our physiology, our experiences and attention, and our culture. No one type of stimulus triggers pain, and there are no special receptors for pain. At low intensities, the stimuli that produce pain cause other sensations, including warmth or coolness, smoothness or roughness.

    We have some built-in pain controls, the *endorphins.* Other pain controls involve distraction, the tendency to remember only the pain we felt at the end of a procedure, and *hypnosis.*

13. The pain system _____ (is/is not)

    triggered by one specific type of physical energy.

    The body _____ (does/does not)

    have specialized receptor cells for pain.

14. Pain is a property of the _____

    as well as a product of our _____ ,

    _____ , and _____ .

15. A sensation of pain in an amputated leg is referred

    to as a _____ _____

    sensation, illustrating that pain is mostly a function

    of our brain. Our brain-pain connection is also made

    clear by our _____ of pain, which are

    based on peak and end moments of pain.

16. In response to severe pain or even vigorous exercise,

    our body produces its own natural pain-killers, the

    _____ . When combined with

    _____ , pain may go unnoticed for a

    time.

17. One technique that has proved useful in relieving

    pain is _____ . One theory of how

    this works is that it produces a split, or

_____ , between normal sensa-

tions and _____

_____ . Another theory is that it is

a form of normal _____

influences.

Objective 18: Describe the senses of taste and smell, and briefly explain the nature of sensory interaction.

Taste, a chemical sense, is a composite of sweet, sour, salty, bitter, and umami sensations and of the aromas that interact with information from the taste buds. Taste buds on the top and sides of the tongue contain taste receptor cells, which send information to an area of the temporal lobe. *Sensory interaction* refers to the principle that one sense may influence another, as when the smell of food influences its taste.

Smell is also a chemical sense, but without any basic sensations. The 5 million or more olfactory receptor cells recognize individual odor molecules, with some odors triggering a combination of receptors. The receptor cells send messages to the olfactory lobe. An odor's ability to spontaneously evoke memories is due in part to the close connections between brain areas that process smell and those involved in memory storage.

18. The basic taste sensations are _____ ,

    _____ , _____ ,

    _____ , and a meaty taste called

    _____ .

19. Taste, which is a _____ sense, is

    enabled by the 200 or more _____

    _____ on the top and sides of the

    tongue. Each contains a _____

    that has hairs projecting from it. These hairs carry

    information about food chemicals back to our taste

    _____ _____ .

20. Taste receptors reproduce themselves every

    _____ .

    As we age, the number of taste buds

    _____ (increases/decreases/remains

    unchanged) and our taste sensitivity

    _____ (increases/decreases/remains

    unchanged). Taste is also affected by

    _____ and by _____

    use.

21. When the sense of smell is blocked, as when we

    have a cold, foods do not taste the same; this illus-

    trates the principle of _____

    _____ . The _____

    effect occurs when we _____ a

speaker saying one syllable while
_____ another.

22. Like taste, smell, or _____ , is a
    _____ sense. The receptor cells
    for smell respond selectively, and they instantly
    alert the brain, bypassing the brain's sensory
    switchboard, the _____ .

APPLICATIONS:

23. Which of the following is an example of sensory interaction?
    a. finding that despite its delicious aroma, a weird-looking meal tastes awful
    b. finding that food tastes bland when you have a bad cold
    c. finding it difficult to maintain your balance when you have an ear infection
    d. All of these are examples.

24. Elderly Mrs. Martinez finds that she must spice her food heavily or she cannot taste it. Unfortunately, her son often finds her cooking inedible because it is so spicy. How might you explain their taste differences?

    _____

    _____

25. Tamiko hates the bitter taste of her cough syrup. Which of the following would she find most helpful in minimizing the syrup's bad taste?
    a. tasting something very sweet before taking the cough syrup
    b. keeping the syrup in her mouth for several seconds before swallowing it
    c. holding her nose while taking the cough syrup
    d. gulping the cough syrup so that it misses her tongue

Objective 19: Describe how our senses monitor our body's position and movement.

Kinesthesis is the system for sensing the position and movement of individual body parts. Sensors in the muscles, tendons, and joints are continually providing our brain with information. A companion **vestibular sense** monitors the head's (and thus the body's) position and movement. Controls for this sense of equilibrium are in the inner ear.

26. The system for sensing the position and movement of body parts is called _____ . The receptors for this sense are located in the

    _____ , _____ ,

    and _____ of the body.

27. The sense that monitors the position and movement of the head (and thus the body) is the

    _____ _____ .

The receptors for this sense are located in the

_____ _____

and _____ _____
of the inner ear.

ESP: Perception Without Sensation?

Objective 20: Identify the three most testable forms of ESP, and explain why most research psychologists remain skeptical of ESP claims.

Three varieties of **extrasensory perception (ESP)** are _telepathy_ (mind-to-mind communication), _clairvoyance_ (perceiving remote events), and _precognition_ (perceiving future events). Closely linked with these are claims of _psychokinesis,_ or "mind over matter."

Research psychologists remain skeptical because the acts of so-called psychics have typically turned out to be nothing more than the illusions of stage magicians, because checks of psychic visions have been no more accurate than guesses made by others, and because sheer chance guarantees that some stunning coincidences are sure to occur. An important reason for their skepticism, however, is the absence of a reproducible ESP result.

1. (Thinking Critically) Perception outside the range of normal sensation is called _____

   _____ .

2. (Thinking Critically) The form of ESP in which people claim to be capable of reading others' minds is called _____ . A person who "senses" that a friend is in danger might claim to have the ESP ability of _____ . An ability to "see" into the future is called

   _____ . A person who claims to be able to levitate and move objects is claiming the power of _____ .

3. (Thinking Critically) Analyses of psychic visions and premonitions reveal _____ (high/chance-level) accuracy.

4. (Thinking Critically) Researchers who had "senders" try to telepathically transmit one of our visual images to "receivers" deprived of sensation reported performance levels that _____ (beat/did not beat) chance levels. More recent studies _____ (failed to replicate the results/found equally high levels of performance).

PROGRESS TEST

Multiple-Choice Questions

Circle your answers to the following questions and check them with the answers beginning on page 96. If your answer is incorrect, read the explanation for why it is correct and then consult the text.

1. Which of the following is true?
   a. The absolute threshold is the same for all stimuli.
   b. The absolute threshold varies depending on the stimulus (sight, sound, or touch, for example).
   c. The absolute threshold is defined as the minimum amount of stimulation necessary for a stimulus to be detected 75 percent of the time.
   d. The absolute threshold is defined as the minimum amount of stimulation necessary for a stimulus to be detected 60 percent of the time.

2. If you can just notice the difference between 10- and 11-pound weights, which of the following weights could you differentiate from a 100-pound weight?
   a. 101-pound weight
   b. 105-pound weight
   c. 110-pound weight
   d. There is no basis for prediction.

3. A decrease in sensory responsiveness accompanying an unchanging stimulus is called
   a. sensory fatigue.
   b. feature detection.
   c. sensory adaptation.
   d. sensory interaction.

4. The size of the pupil is controlled by the
   a. lens.   c. cornea.
   b. retina.   d. iris.

5. The receptor of the eye that functions best in dim light is the
   a. ganglion cell.   c. bipolar cell.
   b. cone   d. rod.

6. Which of the following correctly lists the order of structures through which sound travels after entering the ear?
   a. auditory canal, eardrum, middle ear, cochlea
   b. eardrum, auditory canal, middle ear, cochlea
   c. eardrum, middle ear, cochlea, auditory canal
   d. cochlea, eardrum, middle ear, auditory canal

7. Frequency is to pitch as _____ is to _____ .
   a. wavelength; loudness
   b. amplitude; loudness
   c. wavelength; intensity
   d. amplitude; intensity

8. Our experience of pain when we are injured depends on
   a. our biological makeup and the type of injury we have sustained.
   b. how well medical personnel deal with our injury.
   c. our senses, expectations and attention, and culture.
   b. what our culture allows us to express in terms of feelings of pain.

9. The transduction of light energy into nerve impulses takes place in the
   a. iris.   c. lens.
   b. retina.   d. optic nerve.

10. The brain breaks vision into separate dimensions such as color, depth, movement, and form, and works on each aspect simultaneously. This is called
    a. feature detection.
    b. parallel processing.
    c. the vestibular sense.
    d. sensory adaptation.

11. Kinesthesis involves
    a. the bones of the middle ear.
    b. information from the muscles, tendons, and joints.
    c. membranes within the cochlea.
    d. the body's sense of balance.

12. One light may appear reddish and another greenish if they differ in
    a. wavelength.   c. constancy
    b. amplitude.   d. brightness.

13. Which of the following explains why a rose appears equally red in bright and dim light?
    a. sensory adaptation
    b. subliminal stimulation
    c. feature detection
    d. color constancy

14. Which of the following is an example of sensory adaptation?
    a. finding the cold water of a swimming pool warmer after you have been in it for a while
    b. developing an increased sensitivity to salt the more you use it in foods
    c. becoming very irritated at the continuing sound of a dripping faucet
    d. All of these are examples.

15. The term *gestalt* means
    a. grouping.   c. perception.
    b. sensation.   d. whole.

16. Figures tend to be perceived as whole, complete objects, even if spaces or gaps exist in the representation, thus demonstrating the principle of
    a. interposition.   c. continuity.
    b. retinal disparity. d. closure.

17. The figure-ground relationship has demonstrated that
a. perception is largely innate.
b. perception is simply a point-for-point representation of sensation.
c. the same stimulus can trigger more than one perception.
d. different people see different things when viewing a scene.

18. When we stare at an object, each eye receives a slightly different image, providing a depth cue known as
a. interposition.   c. relative motion.
b. linear perspective.   d. retinal disparity.

19. As we move, viewed objects cast changing shapes on our retinas, although we do not perceive the objects as changing. This is part of the phenomenon of
a. perceptual constancy.
b. relative motion.
c. linear perspective.
d. continuity.

20. A person claiming to be able to read another's mind is claiming to have the ESP ability of
a. psychokinesis.   c. clairvoyance.
b. precognition.   d. telepathy.

21. Which philosopher maintained that knowledge comes from inborn ways of organizing our sensory experiences?
a. Locke   c. Gibson
b. Kant   d. Walk

22. Kittens and monkeys reared seeing only diffuse, unpatterned light
a. later had difficulty distinguishing color and brightness.
b. later had difficulty perceiving color and brightness, but eventually regained normal sensitivity.
c. later had difficulty perceiving the shape of objects.
d. showed no impairment in perception, indicating that neural feature detectors develop even in the absence of normal sensory experiences.

23. Adults who are born blind but later have their vision restored
a. are almost immediately able to recognize familiar objects.
b. typically fail to recognize familiar objects.
c. are unable to follow moving objects with their eyes.
d. have excellent eye-hand coordination.

24. Which of the following is NOT a monocular depth cue?
a. light and shadow   c. retinal disparity
b. relative height   d. interposition

25. The Moon illusion occurs in part because distance cues at the horizon make the Moon seem
a. farther away and therefore larger.
b. closer and therefore larger.
c. farther away and therefore smaller.
d. closer and therefore smaller.

26. Figure is to ground as _____ is to _____ .
a. night; day   c. cloud; sky
b. top; bottom   d. sensation; perception

27. Which of the following influences perception?
a. biological maturation
b. the context in which stimuli are perceived
c. expectations
d. All of these factors influence perception.

28. Jack claims that he often has dreams that predict future events. He claims to have the power of
a. telepathy.   c. precognition.
b. clairvoyance.   d. psychokinesis.

29. Researchers who investigated telepathy found that
a. when deprived of sensation, both the "sender" and the "receiver" become much more accurate in demonstrating ESP.
b. only "senders" become much more accurate.
c. only "receivers" become much more accurate.
d. over many studies, none of these events occurred.

30. Which of the following is NOT a basic taste?
a. sweet   c. umami
b. salty   d. bland

31. Of the four distinct skin senses, the only one that has definable receptors is
a. warmth.   c. pressure.
b. cold.   d. pain.

32. The process by which sensory information is converted into neural energy is
a. sensory adaptation.   c. sensory interaction.
b. feature detection.   d. transduction.

33. The receptors for taste are located in the
a. taste buds.   c. thalamus.
b. cochlea.   d. cortex.

34. The inner ear contains receptors for
a. audition and kinesthesis.
b. kinesthesis and the vestibular sense.
c. audition and the vestibular sense.
d. audition, kinesthesis, and the vestibular sense.

35. What enables you to feel yourself wiggling your toes even with your eyes closed?
a. vestibular sense
b. sense of kinesthesis
c. the skin senses
d. sensory interaction

36. Hubel and Wiesel discovered feature detectors in the
    a. retina.
    b. optic nerve.
    c. iris.
    d. cortex.

37. Weber's law states that
    a. the absolute threshold for any stimulus is a constant.
    b. the jnd for any stimulus is a constant.
    c. the absolute threshold for any stimulus is a constant proportion.
    d. the jnd for any stimulus is a constant proportion.

38. The principle that one sense may influence another is
    a. transduction.
    b. sensory adaptation.
    c. Weber's law.
    d. sensory interaction.

39. Which of the following is the correct order of the structures through which light passes after entering the eye?
    a. lens, pupil, cornea, retina
    b. pupil, cornea, lens, retina
    c. pupil, lens, cornea, retina
    d. cornea, pupil, lens, retina

40. Wavelength is to _____ as_____ is to brightness.
    a. hue; intensity
    b. intensity; hue
    c. frequency; amplitude
    d. brightness; hue

41. Concerning the evidence for subliminal stimulation, which of the following is the best answer?
    a. The brain processes some information without our awareness.
    b. Stimuli too weak to cross our thresholds for awareness may trigger a response in our sense receptors.
    c. An unnoticed image or word can briefly prime our response to a later question.
    d. All of these statements are true.

42. Given normal sensory ability, a person standing atop a mountain on a dark, clear night can see a candle flame atop a mountain 30 miles away. This is a description of vision's
    a. difference threshold.
    b. jnd.
    c. absolute threshold.
    d. feature detection.

43. The tendency to organize stimuli into smooth, uninterrupted patterns is called
    a. closure.
    b. continuity.
    c. disparity.
    d. proximity.

44. Which of the following statements is consistent with the Gestalt theory of perception?
    a. Perception develops largely through learning.
    b. Perception is the product of heredity.
    c. The mind organizes sensations into meaningful perceptions.
    d. Perception results directly from sensation.

45. Experiments with distorted visual environments demonstrate that
    a. adaptation rarely takes place.
    b. animals adapt readily, but humans do not.
    c. humans adapt readily, while lower animals typically do not.
    d. adaptation is possible during a critical period in infancy but not thereafter.

46. The phenomenon that refers to the ways in which an individual's expectations influence perception is called:
    a. perceptual set.
    b. retinal disparity.
    c. interposition.
    d. kinesthesis.

47. According to the philosopher _____ , we learn to perceive the world.
    a. Locke
    b. Kant
    c. Gibson
    d. Walk

48. The phenomenon of size constancy is based on the close connection between an object's perceived _____ and its perceived _____ .
    a. size; shape
    b. size; distance
    c. size; brightness
    d. shape; distance

49. Which of the following statements best describes the effects of sensory restriction?
    a. It produces functional blindness when experienced for any length of time at any age.
    b. It has greater effects on humans than on animals.
    c. It has more damaging effects when experienced during infancy.
    d. It has greater effects on adults than on children.

50. The depth cue that occurs when we watch stable objects at different distances as we are moving is
    a. linear perspective.
    b. interposition.
    c. relative size.
    d. relative motion.

51. Which of the following statements concerning ESP is true?
    a. Most ESP researchers are quacks.
    b. There have been a large number of reliable demonstrations of ESP.
    c. Most research psychologists are skeptical of the claims of defenders of ESP.
    d. There have been reliable laboratory demonstrations of ESP, but the results are no different from those that would occur by chance.

52. Each time you see your car, it projects a different image on the retinas of your eyes, yet you do not perceive it as changing. This is because of
    a. perceptual set.
    b. retinal disparity.
    c. perceptual constancy.
    d. the figure-ground relationship.

53. Studies of the visual cliff have provided evidence that much of depth perception is
    a. innate.
    b. learned.
    c. innate in lower animals, learned in humans.
    d. innate in humans, learned in lower animals.

54. All of the following are laws of perceptual organization EXCEPT
    a. proximity.   c. continuity.
    b. closure.   d. retinal disparity.

43

Matching Items

Match each of the structures with its function or description.

Structures or Conditions

_____ 1. lens
_____ 2. iris
_____ 3. pupil
_____ 4. rods
_____ 5. cones
_____ 6. middle ear
_____ 7. inner ear
_____ 8. semicircular canals
_____ 9. sensors in joints

Functions or Descriptions

a. amplifies sounds
b. vestibular sense
c. controls pupil
d. changes curvature
e. admits light
f. vision in dim light
g. transduction of sound
h. kinesthesis
i. color vision

Application Essays

1. A dancer in a chorus line uses many sensory cues when performing. Discuss three senses that dancers rely on and explain why each is important. (Use the space below to list the points you want to make, and organize them. Then write the essay on a separate sheet of paper.)

2. In many movies from the 1930s, dancers performed seemingly meaningless movements which, when viewed from above, were transformed into intricate patterns and designs. Similarly, the formations of marching bands often create pictures and spell words. Using the three gestalt principles of grouping described in the text, explain the audience's perception of the images created by these types of formations. (Use the space below to list the points you want to make, and organize them. Then write the essay on a separate piece of paper.)

SUMMING UP

Use the diagrams to identify the parts of the eye and ear, then describe how each contributes to vision or hearing. Also, briefly explain the role of each structure.

The Eye

1. _____
   _____
2. _____
   _____
3. _____
   _____
4. _____
   _____
5. _____
   _____
6. _____
   _____
7. _____

The Ear

1. _____
   _____
2. _____
   _____
3. _____
   _____
4. _____
   _____
5. _____
   _____
6. _____
   _____
7. _____
   _____
8. _____
   _____

TERMS AND CONCEPTS

Using your own words, on a piece of paper write a brief definition or explanation of each of the following terms.

1. sensation
2. perception
3. transduction
4. absolute threshold
5. subliminal
6. priming
7. difference threshold
8. Weber's law
9. sensory adaptation
10. perceptual set
11. wavelength and hue
12. intensity
13. retina
14. rods and cones
15. optic nerve
16. blind spot
17. feature detectors
18. parallel processing
19. gestalt
20. figure-ground
21. grouping
22. depth perception
23. visual cliff
24. binocular cues
25. retinal disparity
26. monocular cues
27. perceptual constancy
28. color constancy
29. perceptual adaptation
30. audition
31. frequency and pitch
32. cochlea
33. hypnosis
34. sensory interaction
35. kinesthesis
36. vestibular sense
37. extrasensory perception (ESP)

ANSWERS

Chapter Review

Introduction

1. sensation
2. perception

Basic Principles of Sensation and Perception

1. transduction
2. absolute threshold; 50
3. subliminal
4. prime; priming effect; automatically; conscious; two-track
5. difference threshold; just noticeable difference
6. Weber's law; stimulus
7. absolute threshold. This is the minimum stimulation needed to detect a stimulus 50 percent of the time.
8. unconsciously; behavior changes
9. fleeting; no enduring influence
10. sensory adaptation
11. changes
12. sensory adaptation. This occurs when we remain fixed on a stimulus. Moving his fingers prevents his sense of touch from adapting.
13. perceptual set
14. context
15. emotional
16. perceptual set. The two people interpreted a briefly perceived object in terms of their perceptual sets, or mental predispositions, in this case conditioned by their work experiences.

Vision

1. electromagnetic
2. wavelength; hue
3. intensity; amplitude; brightness
4. **a.** yes. The left-hand wave has lower amplitude and the colors would be duller. The right-hand wave has similar frequency (and therefore hue) but a higher amplitude, making it brighter.

   b. yes. The sounds have similar frequency (and therefore pitch), but the right-hand sound has higher amplitude and would therefore be louder.
5. cornea; pupil; iris
6. lens; retina
7. rods; cones
8. bipolar; ganglion; optic nerve; thalamus
9. blind spot
10. bipolar
11. cones; rods
12. sensitive
13. The retina of a nocturnal animal would contain mostly rods, which are more sensitive in dim light.
14. cones; higher. If the cones' threshold was lower than the available light intensity, they would be able to function and LeVar could detect the color of the players' uniforms.
15. visual cortex; feature detectors
16. simultaneously; parallel processing
17. Gestalt; whole
18. figure; ground
19. grouping
20. continuity; closure; proximity

21. continuity. She perceives the line for the road as continuous, even though it is interrupted by lines indicating other roads.

22. depth perception; distance

23. visual cliff; maturation; experience

    Research on the visual cliff suggests that in many species the ability to perceive depth is present at, or very shortly after, birth.

24. binocular

25. retinal disparity

26. monocular

27. relative size

28. interposition

29. relative height

30. relative motion

31. linear perspective

32. light and shadow

33.

34. decreases; increases. Because we perceive the size of a familiar person (or object) as constant even as the retinal image grows larger, we perceive the person as being closer.

35. nearer. This is an example of the principle of interposition in depth perception.

36. linear perspective. With this principle, parallel lines (trees, in this case) seem to meet in the distance.

37. perceptual constancy

38. context; color constancy

39. reflected; surroundings

40. do not; retinal

41. size; distance; diminished

42. Immanuel Kant

43. John Locke

44. cannot; cataracts

45. infancy; critical period

46. will; perceptual adaptation

47. do not adapt

The Nonvisual Senses

1. audition; air molecules

2. loudness

3. pitch

4. decibels; zero

5. outer; middle; inner

6. eardrum

7. bones

8. cochlea; oval window; hair cells; thalamus; temporal

9. timing; intensity

10. harder

11. hair cells in the cochlea

12. pressure; warmth; cold; pain; variations; pressure

13. is not; does not

14. senses; culture; attention; expectations

15. phantom limb; memories

16. endorphins; distraction

17. hypnosis; dissociation; conscious awareness; social

18. sweet; sour; salty; bitter; umami

19. chemical; taste buds; pore; receptor cells

20. week or two; decreases; decreases; smoking; alcohol

21. sensory interaction; McGurk; see; hearing

22. olfaction; chemical; thalamus

23. **d.** is the answer. Each of these is an example of the interaction of two senses—vision and taste in the case of (a.), taste and smell in the case of (b.), and hearing and the vestibular sense in the case of (c.).

24. As people age they lose taste buds and their taste thresholds increase. For this reason, Mrs. Martinez needs more concentrated tastes than her son to find food palatable.

25. **c.** is the answer. Because of the powerful sensory interaction between taste and smell, eliminating the odor of the cough syrup should make its taste more pleasant.

26. kinesthesis; muscles; tendons; joints

27. vestibular sense; semicircular canals; vestibular sacs

ESP: Perception Without Sensation?

1. extrasensory perception

2. telepathy; clairvoyance; precognition; psychokinesis

3. chance-level

4. beat; failed to replicate the results

Progress Test

Multiple-Choice Questions

1. **b.** is the answer.
   a. We are very sensitive to some kinds of stimuli and not so sensitive to others. We can feel the wing of a bee on our cheek, but some sounds are above our range of hearing.
   c. & d. The absolute threshold is defined as the minimum stimulus that is detected 50 percent of the time.

2. **c.** is the answer. According to Weber's law, the difference threshold is a constant minimum proportion of the stimulus. There is a 10 percent difference between 10 and 11 pounds; because the difference threshold is a constant minimum proportion, the weight closest to 100 pounds that can be differenti-

ated from it is 110 pounds (or 100 pounds plus 10 percent).

3. **c.** is the answer.
a. "Sensory fatigue" is not a term in psychology.
b. Feature detection is the process by which neural cells in the brain respond to specific visual features.
d. Sensory interaction is the principle that one sense may influence another.

4. **d.** is the answer.
a. The lens lies behind the pupil and focuses light on the retina.
b. The retina is the inner surface of the eyeball and contains the rods and cones.
c. The cornea lies in front of the pupil and is the first structure that light passes through as it enters the eye.

5. **d.** is the answer.
a. & c. Bipolar and ganglion cells are not receptors.
b. Cones function best in bright light.

6. **a.** is the answer.

7. **b.** is the answer. Just as wave frequency determines pitch, so wave amplitude determines loudness.
a. Amplitude is the physical basis of loudness; wavelength determines frequency and thereby pitch.
c. & d. Wavelength, amplitude, and intensity are physical aspects of light and sound. Because the question is based on a relationship between a physical property (frequency) of a stimulus and its psychological attribute (pitch), these answers are incorrect.

8. **c.** is the answer. The biopsychosocial approach tells us that our experience of pain depends on biological, psychological, and social-cultural factors.

9. **b.** is the answer.
a. The iris controls the diameter of the pupil.
c. The lens changes its shape to focus images on the retina.
d. The optic nerve carries nerve impulses from the retina to the visual cortex.

10. **b.** is the answer.
a. Feature detection is the process by which nerve cells in the brain respond to specific visual features of a stimulus, such as movement or shape.
c. The vestibular sense is the sense of body position and movement.
d. Sensory adaptation refers to the decreased sensitivity that occurs with continued exposure to an unchanging stimulus.

11. **b.** is the answer. Kinesthesis, or the sense of the position and movement of body parts, is based on information from the muscles, tendons, and joints.
a. & c. The ear plays no role in kinesthesis.
d. Equilibrium, or the vestibular sense, is not involved in kinesthesis but is, rather, a companion sense.

12. **a.** is the answer. Wavelength determines hue, or color.
b. & d. The amplitude of light determines its brightness.

c. Constancy here refers to the fact that colors are not perceived as changing despite changes in illumination.

13. **d.** is the answer. Color constancy is the perception that a familiar object has consistent color, even if changing illumination alters the wavelengths reflected by that object.
a. Sensory adaptation means a diminishing sensitivity to an unchanging stimulus.
b. Subliminal stimulation refers to detecting stimuli below absolute threshold.
c. Feature detection explains how the brain recognizes visual images by analyzing their distinctive features of shape, movement, and angle.

14. **a.** is the answer. Sensory adaptation means a diminishing sensitivity to an unchanging stimulus. Only the adjustment to cold water involves a decrease in sensitivity; the other examples involve an increase.

15. **d.** is the answer. Gestalt psychology, which developed in Germany early in the twentieth century, was interested in how clusters of sensations are organized into "whole" perceptions.

16. **d.** is the answer.
a. Interposition is a monocular depth cue for judging distance.
b. Retinal disparity is a binocular depth cue for judging distance.
c. Continuity refers to the tendency to group stimuli into smooth, continuous patterns.

17. **c.** is the answer. Although we always differentiate a stimulus into figure and ground, those elements of the stimulus we perceive as figure and those as ground may change. In this way, the same stimulus can trigger more than one perception.
a. The idea of a figure-ground relationship has no bearing on the issue of whether perception is innate.
b. Perception cannot be simply a point-for-point representation of sensation, since in figure-ground relationships a single stimulus can trigger more than one perception.
d. Figure-ground relationships demonstrate the existence of general, rather than individual, principles of perceptual organization. Significantly, even the same person can see different figure-ground relationships when viewing a scene.

18. **d.** is the answer. The greater the retinal disparity, or difference between the images, the less the distance.
a. Interposition is the monocular distance cue in which an object that partially blocks another object is seen as closer.
b. Linear perspective is the monocular cue in which parallel lines appear to converge in the distance.
c. Relative motion is the monocular distance cue in which objects at different distances change their relative positions in our visual image, with those closest moving most.

19. **a.** is the answer. Perception of constant shape, like perception of constant size, is part of the phenomenon of perceptual constancy.

b. Relative motion is a monocular distance cue in which objects at different distances appear to move at different rates.

c. Linear perspective is a monocular distance cue in which lines we know to be parallel converge in the distance, thus indicating depth.

d. Continuity is the perceptual tendency to group items into continuous patterns.

20. **d.** is the answer.

   a. Psychokinesis refers to the claimed ability to perform acts of "mind over matter."

   b. Precognition refers to the claimed ability to perceive future events.

   c. Clairvoyance refers to the claimed ability to perceive remote events.

21. **b.** is the answer.

   a. Locke argued that knowledge is not inborn but comes through learning.

   c. & d. Gibson and Walk studied depth perception using the visual cliff; they made no claims about the source of knowledge.

22. **c.** is the answer.

   a. & b. The kittens had difficulty only with lines they had never experienced, and never regained normal sensitivity.

   d. Both perceptual and feature-detector impairment resulted from visual restriction.

23. **b.** is the answer. Because they have not had early visual experiences, these adults typically have difficulty learning to perceive objects.

   a. Such patients typically could not visually recognize objects with which they were familiar by touch, and in some cases this inability persisted.

   c. Being able to perceive figure-ground relationships, patients *are* able to follow moving objects with their eyes.

   d. This answer is incorrect because eye-hand coordination is an acquired skill and requires much practice.

24. **c.** is the answer. Retinal disparity is a *binocular* cue; all the other cues mentioned are monocular.

25. **a.** is the answer. The Moon appears larger at the horizon than overhead in the sky because objects at the horizon provide distance cues that make the Moon seem farther away and therefore larger. In the open sky, of course, there are no such cues.

26. **c.** is the answer. We see a cloud as a figure against the background of sky.

   a., b., & d. The figure-ground relationship refers to the organization of the visual field into objects (figures) that stand out from their surroundings (ground).

27. **d.** is the answer.

28. **c.** is the answer.

   a. This answer would be correct had Jack claimed to be able to read someone else's mind.

   b. This answer would be correct had Jack claimed to be able to sense remote events, such as a friend in distress.

d. This answer would be correct had Jack claimed to be able to levitate objects or bend spoons without applying any physical force.

29. **d.** is the answer. Subsequent studies failed to replicate the original 32 percent accuracy rate.

30. **d.** is the answer.

31. **c.** is the answer. Researchers have identified receptors for pressure but have been unable to do so for the other skin senses.

32. **d.** is the answer.

   a. Sensory adaptation refers to the diminished sensitivity that occurs with unchanging stimulation.

   b. Feature detection refers to the process by which nerve cells in the brain respond to specific aspects of visual stimuli, such as movement or shape.

   c. Sensory interaction is the principle that one sense may influence another.

33. **a.** is the answer.

   b. The cochlea contains receptors for hearing.

   c. The thalamus is the part of the brain that receives signals from the senses and distributes them to higher regions.

   d. The cortex is the outer layer of the brain, where information detected by the receptors is processed.

34. **c.** is the answer. The inner ear contains the receptors for audition (hearing) and the vestibular sense; those for kinesthesis are located in the muscles, tendons, and joints.

35. **b.** is the answer. Kinesthesis, the sense of movement of body parts, would enable you to feel your toes wiggling.

   a. The vestibular sense is concerned with movement and position, or balance, of the whole body, not of its parts.

   c. The skin, or tactile, senses are pressure, pain, warmth, and cold; they have nothing to do with movement of body parts.

   d. Sensory interaction, the principle that the senses influence each other, does not play a role in this example, which involves only the sense of kinesthesis.

36. **d.** is the answer. Feature detectors are cortical neurons and hence are located in the visual cortex.

   a. The retina is at the back of the eye. They discovered feature detectors in the brain.

   b. The optic nerve contains neurons that relay nerve impulses from the retina to higher centers in the visual system.

   c. The iris is simply a ring of muscle tissue, which controls the diameter of the pupil.

37. **d.** is the answer. Weber's law concerns difference thresholds (jnd's), not absolute thresholds, and states that these are constant proportions of the stimuli, not that they remain constant.

38. **d.** is the answer.

   a. Transduction is the process by which stimulus energy is converted into nerve impulses.

   b. Sensory adaptation is diminished sensitivity to unchanging stimulation.

c. Weber's law states that the jnd is a constant proportion of a stimulus.

39. **d.** is the answer.

40. **a.** is the answer. Wavelength determines hue, and intensity determines brightness.

41. **d.** is the answer.

42. **c.** is the answer. The absolute threshold is the minimum stimulation needed to detect a stimulus.
a. & b. The difference threshold, which is also known as the jnd, is the minimum difference between two stimuli that a person can detect. In this example, there is only one stimulus—the sight of the flame.
d. Feature detection refers to nerve cells in the brain responding to specific features of a stimulus.

43. **b.** is the answer.
a. Closure refers to the tendency to perceptually fill in gaps in recognizable objects in the visual field.
c. Disparity refers to the two different images received by the retinas of our eyes.
d. Proximity refers to the tendency to group items that are near one another.

44. **c.** is the answer.
a. & b. The Gestalt psychologists did not deal with the origins of perception; they were more concerned with its form.
d. In fact, they argued just the opposite: Perception is more than mere sensory experience.

45. **c.** is the answer. Humans are able to adjust to upside-down worlds and other visual distortions, figuring out the relationship between the perceived and the actual reality. Lower animals, such as chickens, are typically unable to adapt.
a. Humans and certain animals are able to adapt quite well to distorted visual environments (and then to readapt).
b. This answer is incorrect because humans are the most adaptable of creatures.
d. Humans are able to adapt at any age to distorted visual environments.

46. **a.** is the answer.
b. Retinal disparity is a binocular depth cue based on the fact that each eye receives a slightly different view of the world.
c. Interposition is the monocular distance cue in which an object that partially blocks another object is seen as closer.
d. Kinesthesis is the sense of the position and movement of the parts of the body.

47. **a.** is the answer.
b. Kant claimed that knowledge is inborn.
c. & d. Gibson and Walk make no claims about the origins of perception.

48. **b.** is the answer.

49. **c.** is the answer. There appears to be a critical period for perceptual development, in that sensory restriction has severe, even permanent, disruptive effects when it occurs in infancy but not when it occurs later in life.

a. & d. Sensory restriction does not have the same effects at all ages, and it is more damaging to children than to adults. This is because there is a critical period for perceptual development; whether functional blindness will result depends in part on the nature of the sensory restriction.
b. Research studies have not indicated that sensory restriction is more damaging to humans than to animals.

50. **d.** is the answer. When we move, stable objects we see also appear to move, and the distance and speed of the apparent motion cue us to the objects' relative distances.
a., b., & c. These depth cues are unrelated to movement and thus work even when we are stationary.

51. **c.** is the answer.
a. Many ESP researchers are sincere, reputable researchers.
b. & d. There have been no reliable demonstrations of ESP.

52. **c.** is the answer. Because of perceptual constancy, we see the car's shape and size as always the same.
a. Perceptual set is a mental predisposition to perceive one thing and not another.
b. Retinal disparity means that our right and left eyes each receive slightly different images.
d. Figure-ground refers to the organization of the visual field into two parts.

53. **a.** is the answer. Most infants refused to crawl out over the "cliff" even when coaxed, suggesting that much of depth perception is innate. Studies with the young of "lower" animals show the same thing.

54. **d.** is the answer.
a. Proximity is the tendency to group objects near to one another.
b. Continuity is the tendency to group stimuli into smooth, uninterrupted patterns.
c. Closure is the perceptual tendency to fill in gaps in a form.

Matching Items

1. d
2. c
3. e
4. f
5. i
6. a
7. g
8. b
9. h

Application Essays

1. The senses that are most important to dancers are vision, hearing, kinesthesis, and the vestibular sense. Your answer should refer to any three of these senses and include, at minimum, the following information.
   Dancers rely on vision to gauge their body position relative to other dancers as they perform specific choreographed movements. Vision also helps dancers assess the audience's reaction to their performance. Whenever dance is set to music, hearing is necessary so that the dancers can detect musical

cues for certain parts of their routines. Hearing also helps the dancers keep their movements in time with the music. Kinesthetic receptors in dancers' muscles, tendons, and joints provide their brains with information about the position and movement of body parts to determine if their hands, arms, legs, and heads are in the proper positions. Receptors for the vestibular sense located in the dancers' inner ears send messages to their brains that help them maintain their balance and determine the correctness of the position and movement of their bodies.

2. *Proximity*. We tend to perceive items that are near each other as belonging together. Thus, a small section of dancers or members of a marching band may separate themselves from the larger group in order to form part of a particular image.

   Continuity. Because we perceive smooth, continuous patterns rather than discontinuous ones, dancers or marching musicians moving together (as in a column, for example) are perceived as a separate unit.

   Closure. If a figure has gaps, we complete it, filling in the gaps to create a whole image. Thus, we perceptually fill in the relatively wide spacing between dancers or marching musicians in order to perceive the complete words or forms they are creating.

Summing Up

The Eye

1. Cornea. Light enters the eye through this transparent membrane, which protects the inner structures from the environment.
2. Iris. The colored part of the eye, the iris functions like the aperture of a camera, controlling the size of the pupil to optimize the amount of light that enters the eye.
3. Pupil. The adjustable opening in the iris, the pupil allows light to enter.
4. Lens. This transparent structure behind the pupil changes shape to focus images on the retina.
5. Retina. The light-sensitive inner surface of the eye, the retina contains the rods and cones, which transduce light energy into neural impulses.
6. Blind spot. The region of the retina where the optic nerve leaves the eye, the blind spot contains no rods or cones and so there is no vision here.
7. Optic nerve. This bundle of nerve fibers carries neural impulses from the retina to the brain.

The Ear

1. Outer ear. Hearing begins as sound waves enter the auditory canal of the outer ear.
2. Auditory canal. Sound waves passing through the auditory canal are brought to a point of focus at the eardrum.
3. Eardrum. Lying between the outer and middle ear, this membrane vibrates in response to sound waves.
4. Middle ear. Lying between the outer and inner ear, this air-filled chamber contains the three tiny bones: hammer, anvil, and stirrup.
5. Bones of the middle ear. These tiny bones concentrate the eardrum's vibrations on the cochlea's oval window.
6. Inner ear. This region of the ear contains the cochlea and the semicircular canals, which play an important role in balance.
7. Cochlea. This fluid-filled structure contains the hair cell receptors that transduce sound waves into neural impulses.
8. Auditory nerve. This bundle of fibers carries nerve impulses from the inner ear to the brain.

Terms and Concepts

1. **Sensation** is the process by which our sensory receptors take in stimulus energy from the environment.
2. **Perception** is the process by which our brain organizes and interprets sensory information, transforming it into meaningful objects and events.
3. **Transduction** is the process by which one form of energy is changed into another. In sensation, the transforming of stimulus energies, such as sights, sounds, and smells, into neural impulses our brains can interpret.
4. The **absolute threshold** is the minimum stimulation needed to detect a stimulus 50 percent of the time.
5. A stimulus that is **subliminal** is one that is below the absolute threshold for conscious awareness.
   Memory aid: Limen is the Latin word for "threshold." A stimulus that is **subliminal** is one that is *sub-* ("below") the *limen*, or threshold.
6. **Priming** is the activation, often unconsciously, of associations in our mind, thus setting us up to perceive or remember objects or events in certain ways.
7. The **difference threshold** (also called the *just noticeable difference*, or *jnd*) is the minimum difference between two stimuli required for detection 50 percent of the time.
8. **Weber's law** states that the just noticeable difference between two stimuli is a constant minimum proportion of the stimulus.
   Example: If a difference of 10 percent in weight is noticeable, **Weber's law** predicts that a person could discriminate 10- and 11-pound weights or 50- and 55-pound weights.
9. **Sensory adaptation** refers to the decreased sensitivity in response to constant stimulation.
10. **Perceptual set** is a mental predisposition to perceive one thing and not another.
11. **Wavelength**, which refers to the distance from the peak of one light (or sound) wave to the next, gives rise to the perceptual experiences of **hue,** or color, in vision (and **pitch** in sound).
12. The **intensity** of light and sound is determined by the amplitude of the waves and is experienced as brightness and loudness, respectively.
    Example: Sounds that exceed 85 decibels in amplitude, or **intensity**, will damage the auditory system.

13. The **retina** is the light-sensitive inner surface of the eye that contains the rods and cones as well as neurons that form the beginning of the optic nerve.

14. The **rods** and **cones** are retinal receptor cells. The rods are concentrated in the periphery of the retina, the cones in the center. The rods have poor sensitivity; detect black, white, and gray; function well in dim light; and are needed for peripheral vision. The cones have excellent sensitivity, enable color vision, and function best in daylight or bright light.

15. Made up of the axons of retinal ganglion cells, the **optic nerve** carries neural impulses from the eye to the brain.

16. The **blind spot** is the region of the retina where the optic nerve leaves the eye. Because there are no rods or cones in this area, there is no vision here.

17. **Feature detectors**, located in the visual cortex of the brain, are nerve cells that selectively respond to specific visual features, such as movement, shape, or angle. Feature detectors are evidently the basis of visual information processing.

18. **Parallel processing** is information processing in which several aspects of a stimulus, such as light or sound, are processed simultaneously.

19. **Gestalt** means "organized whole." The Gestalt psychologists emphasized our tendency to integrate pieces of information into meaningful wholes.

20. **Figure-ground** refers to the organization of the visual field into two parts: the figure, which stands out from its surroundings, and the surroundings, or background.

21. **Grouping** is the perceptual tendency to organize stimuli into meaningful groups. Gestalt psychologists identified various principles of grouping.

22. **Depth perception** is the ability to see objects in three dimensions although the images that strike the retina are two-dimensional; it allows us to judge distance.

23. The **visual cliff** is a laboratory device for testing depth perception, especially in infants and young animals. In their experiments with the visual cliff, Gibson and Walk found strong evidence that depth perception is at least in part due to biological maturation.

24. **Binocular cues** are depth cues that depend on information from both eyes.

    Memory aid: Bi- indicates "two"; *ocular* means something pertaining to the eye. **Binocular cues** are cues for the "two eyes."

25. **Retinal disparity** refers to the differences between the images received by the left eye and the right eye as a result of viewing the world from slightly different angles. It is a binocular depth cue, since the greater the difference between the two images, the nearer the object.

26. **Monocular cues** are depth cues that depend on information from either eye alone.

    Memory aid: Mono- means one; a monocle is an eyeglass for one eye. A **monocular cue** is one that is available to either the left or the right eye.

27. **Perceptual constancy** is the perception that objects have consistent brightness, color, shape, and size, even as illumination and retinal images change.

28. **Color constancy** is the perception that familiar objects have consistent color despite changes in illumination that shift the wavelengths they reflect.

29. **Perceptual adaptation** refers to our ability to adjust to an artificially displaced or even inverted visual field. Given distorting lenses, we perceive things accordingly but soon adjust by learning the relationship between our distorted perceptions and the reality.

30. **Audition** refers to the sense of hearing.

31. **Frequency** is directly related to wavelength: Longer waves produce lower pitch; shorter waves produce higher pitch. The **pitch** of a sound is determined by its frequency, that is, the number of complete wavelengths that can pass a point in a given time.

32. The **cochlea** is the coiled, bony, fluid-filled tube of the inner ear through which sound waves trigger neural impulses.

33. **Hypnosis** is a social interaction in which one person (the hypnotist) suggests to another (the subject) that certain perceptions, feelings, thoughts, or behaviors will occur without warning.

34. **Sensory interaction** is the principle that one sense may influence another.

35. **Kinesthesis** is the sense of the position and movement of the parts of the body.

36. The sense of body movement and position, including the sense of balance, is called the **vestibular sense.**

37. **Extrasensory perception (ESP)** refers to the controversial claim that perception can occur without sensory input. Supposed ESP powers include telepathy, clairvoyance, and precognition.

    Memory aid: Extra- means "beyond" or "in addition to"; **extrasensory perception** is perception outside or beyond the normal senses.

6

LEARNING

"No topic is closer to the heart of psychology than learning, a relatively permanent change in an organism's behavior due to experience." Chapter 6 covers the basic principles of three forms of learning: classical conditioning, in which we learn associations between events; operant conditioning, in which we learn to engage in behaviors that are rewarded and to avoid behaviors that are punished; and observational learning, in which we learn by observing and imitating others.

The chapter also covers several important issues, including the generality of principles of learning, the role of cognitive processes in learning, and the ways in which learning is constrained by the biological predispositions of different species.

CHAPTER REVIEW

First, skim each text section, noting headings and bold-face items. Review the section by reading the objectives and summaries provided here, then answer the questions that follow. In some cases, STUDY TIPS explain how best to learn a difficult concept and APPLICATIONS help you to know how well you understand the material. Check your understanding of the material by consulting the answers beginning on page 116. Do not continue with the next section until you understand each answer. If you need to, review or reread the section in the textbook before continuing.

How Do We Learn?

Objective 1: Define *learning,* and identify some basic forms of learning.

Learning is a relatively permanent change in an organism's behavior due to experience. We learn by *association*; our mind naturally links events that occur in sequence. The events linked may be two *stimuli* (as in classical conditioning) or a response and its consequences (as in operant conditioning). In observational learning, one form of *cognitive learning,* we learn by viewing others' experiences and examples.

1. A relatively permanent change in an organism's behavior due to experience is called

   _____ .

2. Even simple animals, such as the sea slug *Aplysia,* can learn simple _____ between stimuli. This type of learning is called _____

   _____ .

3. The type of learning in which we learn to associate two stimuli is _____ conditioning.

4. The tendency to associate a response and its consequence forms the basis of _____ conditioning.

5. We also acquire mental information that guides our behavior through _____

   _____ . In one form of this type of

learning, _____

_____ , we learn from others' experiences.

Classical Conditioning

Objective 2: Explain how classical conditioning demonstrates associative learning.

The Russian physiologist Ivan Pavlov repeatedly presented a **neutral stimulus (NS),** such as a tone, just before an **unconditioned stimulus (US),** such as food, which triggered the **unconditioned response (UR)** of salivation. After several repetitions, the tone alone (now the **conditioned stimulus [CS]**) began triggering a **conditioned response (CR),** salivation.

STUDY TIP: Students often confuse "stimulus" with "response" and "conditioned" with "unconditioned." The stimulus is the event that causes something else, the response, to happen. Unconditioned means "unlearned"; conditioned means "learned." Thus, an unconditioned response (UR) is an event that occurs naturally in response to some stimulus. An unconditioned stimulus (US) is something that naturally and automatically triggers the unlearned response. A conditioned stimulus (CS) is an originally neutral stimulus that, through learning, comes to be associated with some unlearned response. A conditioned response (CR) is the learned response to the originally neutral but now conditioned stimulus.

Stimulus (event or other trigger) → Response
Unconditioned = unlearned
Conditioned = learned
So, unconditioned stimulus + conditioned stimulus
↓   ↓
unconditioned response   conditioned response

1. In Pavlov's classic experiment, a tone, or

   _____ _____ ,

   is sounded just before food, the

   _____ _____ ,

   is placed in the animal's mouth.

2. Eventually, the dogs in Pavlov's experiment would salivate on hearing the tone, now called the

_____ _____ .

This salivation is called the

_____ _____ .

APPLICATION:

Classical conditioning is all around us. It is especially common in the realm of emotional behavior. Test your understanding of the basic elements of classical conditioning in the following example. Then, consider whether there are emotions of your own that might have developed as the product of classical conditioning.

As a child, you were playing in the yard one day when a neighbor's cat wandered over. Your mother (who has a terrible fear of animals) screamed and snatched you into her arms. Her behavior caused you to cry. You now have a fear of cats.

3. The CS is _____ .

4. The US is _____ .

5. The CR is _____ .

6. The UR is _____ .

Objective 3: Describe the processes of acquisition, extinction, spontaneous recovery, generalization, and discrimination.

Responses are *acquired* best when the CS is presented half a second before the US. They are *extinguished* when the conditioned stimulus occurs repeatedly without the unconditioned stimulus. If, after a pause, the CR reappears, *spontaneous recovery* has occurred. *Generalization* is the tendency to respond to stimuli that are similar to the conditioned stimulus. *Discrimination* is the learned ability to distinguish between a CS and other irrelevant stimuli.

• •

STUDY TIP: Some students find the terms discrimination and generalization confusing because of their negative social connotations. In the context of classical conditioning, discrimination is a healthy sign that the subject of conditioning has learned the difference between two stimuli, much as a "discriminating coffee lover" can taste subtle variations between two coffee blends. Generalization is apparent when discrimination does not occur.

• •

Use the following graph to answer 7(a), 8(b), and 9(c).

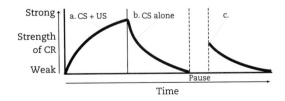

7. The initial learning of a conditioned response is called (a) _____ . For many conditioning situations, the optimal interval between a neutral stimulus and the US is

_____ _____ .

8. If a CS is repeatedly presented without the US, (b) _____ soon occurs; that is, the CR diminishes.

9. Following a pause, however, the CR reappears in response to the CS; this is called (c) _____ _____ .

10. Humans and other animals often respond to a similar stimulus as they would to the original CS. This is called _____ .

11. Humans and other animals can also be trained not to respond to _____ stimuli. This learned ability is called _____ .

APPLICATION: Bill had an American-made car that was in the shop more than it was out. Since then he will not even consider owning an American-made car.

12. Bill's attitude is an example of _____ . Bill's friend Andy also had an American-made car with similar problems. Deciding that it was just that brand, Andy decided to try another brand—rather than bunch all American-made cars together, he was a _____ buyer of cars.

Objective 4: Describe the importance of Pavlov's work to our understanding of learning, and give several examples of applications of classical conditioning.

Pavlov taught us that principles of learning apply across species and that classical conditioning is one way that virtually all organisms learn to adapt to their environment. Pavlov also demonstrated that significant psychological phenomena can be studied objectively. Finally, Pavlov taught us that conditioning principles have important applications such as how to treat fear.

Classical conditioning principles provide important insights into drug abuse and how it may be overcome. Watson's "Little Albert" study demonstrated how classical conditioning may underlie specific fears. Today, psychologists use extinction procedures to control our less adaptive emotions and condition new responses to emotion-arousing stimuli.

13. Pavlov showed that classical conditioning is one way that virtually all organisms learn to _____ to their environment.

14. Another aspect of Pavlov's legacy is that he showed how a process such as learning could be studied _____ .

15. Through classical conditioning, drug users often develop a _____ when they encounter _____ associated with previous highs.

Describe the Watson and Rayner experiment.

Operant Conditioning

Objective 5: Describe the processes of operant conditioning, including shaping.

In *operant conditioning,* we associate our own actions with their consequences. B. F. Skinner created an *operant chamber* (*Skinner box*) for his pioneering studies of operant conditioning with rats and pigeons.

In his experiments, Skinner used *shaping,* a procedure involving *reinforcers* that guide an animal's natural behavior toward a desired behavior. By rewarding responses that are ever closer to the final desired behavior (*successive approximations*) and ignoring all other responses, researchers can gradually shape complex behaviors.

1. The form of learning in which we learn to associate our behavior with its consequences is called _____ _____ .

2. B. F. Skinner designed an apparatus, called the _____ _____ , to investigate learning in animals.

3. The procedure in which a person teaches an intricate behavior by building up to it in small steps is called _____ . This method involves reinforcing successive _____ of the desired behavior.

4. An event that increases the frequency of a preceding response is a _____ .

Objective 6: Identify the basic types of reinforcers.

Reinforcers can be *positive* (presenting a pleasant stimulus after a response) or *negative* (reducing or removing an unpleasant stimulus). *Primary reinforcers,* such as food when we are hungry, are innately satisfying. *Conditioned reinforcers,* such as cash, are satisfying because we have learned to associate them with more basic rewards. Immediate reinforcers, such as the nicotine addict's cigarette, offer immediate payback. Delayed reinforcers, such as a weekly paycheck, require the ability to delay gratification.

STUDY TIP: Some students have a problem differentiating positive and negative reinforcers because they naturally think "positive" indicates a "good," or desirable, outcome, while "negative" connotes a "bad," or undesirable, outcome. Remember that from the organism's point of view, reinforcement is always a desirable outcome. You may find it useful to think of a photography analogy. A "negative" is a reverse image in which the "positive" photographic image is not present. So too, negative reinforcement involves taking away an event—in this case, one that is undesirable.

5. A pleasurable stimulus that, when presented after a response, strengthens that response is a _____ _____ .

6. A negative (unpleasant) stimulus that, when removed after a response, strengthens that response is a _____ _____ .

7. Reinforcers, such as food and shock, that are related to basic needs and so do not rely on learning are called _____ _____ . Reinforcers that gain their power through association with basic reinforcers are called _____ _____ .

8. As we mature, we learn to _____ gratification rather than opt for the immediate reward.

9. Immediate reinforcement _____ (is/is not) more effective than its alternative, _____ reinforcement. This explains in part why many people continue to use the large vehicles that use so much gas, as well as the tendency of some teens to engage in risky, _____ _____ .

APPLICATIONS:

10. Jack finally takes out the garbage in order to get his father to stop pestering him. Jack's behavior is being influenced by _____ _____ .

11. Your instructor invites you to her home as part of a select group of students to discuss possible careers in psychology. The invitation is an example of a _____ _____ .

Objective 7: Contrast the effects of continuous and partial reinforcement schedules on behavior.

When the desired response is reinforced every time it occurs, *continuous reinforcement* is involved. Learning is rapid but so is extinction if rewards cease. *Partial (intermittent) reinforcement* produces slower acquisition of the target behavior than does continuous reinforcement, but the learning is more resistant to extinction. *Reinforcement schedules* may vary according to the number of responses rewarded or the time gap between responses.

12. The procedure involving reinforcement of each and every response is called _____

_____ . Under these conditions, learning is _____ (rapid/slow). When this type of reinforcement is discontinued, extinction is _____ (rapid/slow).

13. The procedure in which responses are reinforced only part of the time is called _____ reinforcement. Under these conditions, learning is generally _____ (faster/slower) than it is with continuous reinforcement. Behavior reinforced in this manner is _____ (very/not very) resistant to extinction.

14. When behavior is reinforced after a set number of responses, a _____-

_____ schedule is in effect.

15. Three-year-old Yusef knows that if he cries when he wants a treat, his mother will sometimes give in. When, as in this case, reinforcement occurs after an unpredictable number of responses, a

_____-_____

schedule is being used.

16. Reinforcement of the first response after a set interval of time defines the

_____-_____

schedule. An example of this schedule is

_____ .

17. When the first response after varying amounts of time is reinforced, a _____-

_____ schedule is in effect.

Objective 8: Discuss how punishment affects behavior, noting how it differs from negative reinforcement, and list some of its drawbacks.

Unlike negative reinforcement, which increases the frequency of a behavior, *punishment* attempts to decrease the frequency of a behavior. Punishment administers an undesirable consequence, for example, spanking or withdrawing something desirable, such as taking away a favorite toy. Punishment can have several undesirable side effects, including suppressing rather than changing unwanted behaviors, creating fear, and teaching aggression.

18. Unlike _____ _____ , which increases the behavior that preceded it, _____ is a negative consequence that decreases the likelihood of the behavior that preceded it. Thus, taking aspirin to relieve a headache is an example of _____

_____ , and a child being sent to his room after spilling his milk is an example of

_____ .

19. Punishment can lead to _____ and a sense of helplessness, as well as to the association of the negative event with

_____ .

Also, punished behavior is _____ , not forgotten.

20. Punishment also often increases _____ and does not guide the individual toward more desirable behavior.

••

STUDY TIP/APPLICATION: To avoid the natural tendency to confuse punishment and negative reinforcement, remember that positive reinforcement and negative reinforcement both lead to an increase in behavior, while punishment decreases behavior. In punishment, something bad occurs following an undesirable behavior; in negative reinforcement, something bad is removed. Complete the chart on the next page of examples of punishment and negative reinforcement. The first example has been filled in for you.

21.

Behavior	Consequence	Which Is Taken Away, Something Good or Bad?	Is This punishment or Negative Reinforcement?
Driving while intoxicated.	Lose driver's license.	Good	Punishment
a. Forgetting to give your roommate a phone message			
b. Putting on your coat so that you are no longer cold			
c. Getting a drink when you are thirsty			
d. Using your laptop until the battery dies			
e. Your brother nagging you until you help him with his homework			

Objective 9: Explain why Skinner's ideas were controversial, ad identify some ways to apply operant conditioning principles at school, at work, and at home.

Skinner has been criticized for repeatedly insisting that external influences, not internal thoughts and feelings, shape behavior and for urging the use of operant principles to control people's behavior. Critics argue that he dehumanized people by neglecting their personal freedom and by seeking to control their actions. Skinner countered: People's behavior is already controlled by external reinforcers, so why not administer those consequences for human betterment?

Operant principles have been applied in a variety of settings. For example, in schools, Web-based learning, online testing systems, and interactive student software embody the operant ideal of individualized shaping and immediate reinforcement. In the workplace, positive reinforcement for jobs well done has boosted employee productivity. At home, parents can reward their children's desirable behaviors and not reward those that are undesirable. To reach our personal goals, we can monitor and reinforce our own desired behaviors and cut back on incentives as the behaviors become habitual.

22. Skinner's critics argued that he _____ people by neglecting their personal _____ and by seeking to _____ their actions.

23. The use of machines and textbooks was an early application of the operant conditioning procedure of _____ to education. Online _____ systems, software that is _____, and _____-based learning are newer examples of this application of operant principles.

24. In boosting productivity in the workplace, positive reinforcement is _____ (more/less) effective when applied to specific behaviors than when given to reward general merit and when the desired performance is well-defined and _____. For such behaviors, immediate reinforcement is _____ (more/no more) effective than delayed reinforcement.

Objective 10: Identify the major similarities and differences between classical and operant conditioning.

Both classical and operant conditioning are forms of associative learning. They both involve acquisition, extinction, spontaneous recovery, generalization, and discrimination. The two forms of learning differ in an important way. In classical conditioning, organisms associate different stimuli that they do not control and respond automatically (*respondent behavior*). In operant conditioning, organisms associate their own behaviors with their consequences (*operant behavior*).

25. Classical conditioning and operant conditioning are both forms of _____ _____ .

26. Both types of conditioning involve similar processes of _____ , _____ , _____ _____ , _____ , and _____ .

27. Through classical conditioning, an organism associates different _____ that it does not _____ and responds _____ .

28. The reflexive responses of classical conditioning are called _____ behavior.

29. Through operant conditioning, an organism associates its _____ _____ with their _____ .

STUDY TIP/APPLICATION: If you still find yourself confusing classical conditioning and operant conditioning, try the following. Ask yourself two questions: (1) Is the behavior voluntary (operant conditioning) or involuntary (classical conditioning)? (2) Does the learning involve an association between two stimuli (classical conditioning) or between a response and an outcome (operant conditioning)? Test your understanding with the following examples.

30.

Behavior	Is the Behavior Voluntary or Involuntary?	Type of Conditioning
a. After receiving a mild shock from the "invisible fence" surrounding his yard, a dog no longer crosses the boundary.		
b. You flinch when someone yells, "Duck!"		
c. You ask more questions in class after the professor praises you for a good question.		
d. The pupil of your eye dilates (opens wider) after you enter a darkened theater.		

Biology, Cognition, and Learning

Objective 11: Describe how biology affects conditioning.

In the middle of the twentieth century, researchers (beginning with a discovery by John Garcia and Robert Koelling) showed that there are biological constraints on learning. In line with Darwin's theory, each species is biologically prepared to learn associations that enhance its survival.

As with classical conditioning, an animal's natural predispositions constrain its capacity for operant conditioning. Biological constraints predispose organisms to learn associations that are naturally adaptive. Training that attempts to override these tendencies will probably not endure because the animals will revert to their biologically predisposed patterns.

1. Biological constraints predispose organisms to learn associations that are naturally

_____ .

2. Garcia discovered that rats would associate _____ with taste but not with other stimuli. Garcia found that taste-aversion conditioning _____ (would/would not) occur when the delay between the CS and the US was more than an hour.

3. Results such as these demonstrate that the principles of learning are constrained by the _____ predispositions of each animal species and that they help each species _____ to its environment.

Objective 12: Describe how cognitive processes influence conditioning and learning.

Pavlov and John B. Watson, who built on Pavlov's work in establishing the school of **behaviorism,** also underestimated the role of cognitive processes in learning. Research indicates that, for many animals, thoughts and perceptions are important to the conditioning process.

With operant conditioning, B. F. Skinner discounted the importance of cognitive influences. But research has shown that rats exploring a maze seem to develop a mental representation (a **cognitive map**) of the maze even in the absence of reward. Their **latent learning** becomes evident only when there is some incentive to demonstrate it.

Research indicates that people may come to see rewards, rather than intrinsic interest, as the motivation for performing a task. Again, this finding demonstrates the importance of cognitive processing in learning. By undermining *intrinsic motivation,* the desire to perform a behavior for its own sake, rewards can carry hidden costs. *Extrinsic motivation* is the desire to perform a behavior because of promised rewards or threats of punishment.

4. The view that psychology should be an objective science based on observable behavior was called

   _____ .

5. When a well-learned route in a maze is blocked, rats sometimes choose an alternative route, acting as if they were consulting a _____

   _____ .

6. Animals may learn from experience even when reinforcement is not available. When learning is not apparent until reinforcement has been provided, _____ _____ is

   said to have occurred.

7. Excessive rewards may undermine

   _____ _____ , which is

   the desire to perform a behavior for its own sake. The motivation to seek external rewards and avoid punishment is called

   _____ _____ .

Objective 13: Describe the process of observational learning, and explain how it differs from associative learning.

Among higher animals, especially humans, learning does not occur through direct experience alone (as in associative learning). *Observational learning* also plays a part. The process of observing and imitating a specific behavior is called *modeling.* Albert Bandura was a pioneering researcher of this type of learning. *Mirror neurons* demonstrate a neural basis for observational learning.

   Prosocial models can have prosocial effects. People who show nonviolent, helpful behavior prompt similar behavior in others. Models are most effective when they are attractive and when they commit seemingly justified, realistic violence that goes unpunished and causes no visible pain or harm.

   Correlational studies that link viewing violence with violent behavior do not indicate the direction of influence. Those who behave violently may enjoy watching violence on TV, or some third factor may cause observers both to behave violently and to prefer watching violent programs. To establish cause and effect, researchers have designed experiments in which some participants view violence and others do not. Later, given an opportunity to express violence, the people who viewed violence tend to be more aggressive and less sympathetic. In addition to imitating what they see, observers may become desensitized to brutality, whether on TV or in real life.

8. Learning by observing and imitating others is called

   _____ _____ ,

   or _____ when it involves a

   specific _____ .

9. Neuroscientists have found _____

   neurons in the brain that provide a neural basis for

   _____ learning.

10. The psychologist best known for research on observational learning is _____ .

11. In one experiment, the child who viewed an adult punch an inflatable doll played _____ (more/less) aggressively than the child who had not observed the adult.

12. Children will model positive, or

   _____ , behaviors.

13. Observational learning may also have

   _____ effects. These results may

   help explain why _____ parents

   might have _____ children.

   However, _____ factors may also

   be involved.

14. (Thinking Critically) Correlation does not prove

   _____ . Most researchers believe

   that watching violence on television

   _____ (does/does not) lead to

   aggressive behavior.

15. (Thinking Critically) Models are most effective when they are perceived as _____ and

   when their behavior goes _____ and

   _____ (does/does not) cause visible harm.

16. (Thinking Critically) This violence-viewing effect stems from several factors, including

   _____ of observed aggression and

   the tendency of prolonged exposure to violence to

   _____ viewers.

APPLICATION: Children—and of course, adults—learn a great deal by watching other people. Depending on the models, the behavior they learn may be good or bad.

17. During holiday breaks Lionel watches wrestling, which

   _____ his aggressive tendencies. His

   brother Michael won't watch the wrestling because he

   feels the pain of the choke hold, for example, as reflected

   in his brain's _____

   _____ . Instead, Michael spends time

   with Grandma, who cooks for the poor during the holiday

   season, helping Michael to learn _____

   behavior.

Progress Test

Multiple-Choice Questions

Circle your answers to the following questions and check them with the answers beginning on page 117. If your answer is incorrect, read the explanation for why it is incorrect and then consult the text.

1. *Learning* is best defined as
   a. any behavior produced by an organism without being provoked.
   b. a change in the behavior of an organism.
   c. a relatively permanent change in the behavior of an organism due to experience.
   d. behavior based on operant rather than respondent conditioning.

2. The type of learning associated with B. F. Skinner is
   a. classical conditioning.
   b. operant conditioning.
   c. respondent conditioning.
   d. observational learning.

3. In Pavlov's original experiment with dogs, the tone was initially a(n) _____ stimulus; after it was paired with meat, it became a(n) _____ stimulus.
   a. conditioned; neutral
   b. neutral; conditioned
   c. conditioned; unconditioned
   d. unconditioned; conditioned

4. In order to obtain a reward a monkey learns to press a lever when a 1000-Hz tone is on but not when a 1200-Hz tone is on. What kind of training is this?
   a. extinction
   b. generalization
   c. classical conditioning
   d. discrimination

5. Which of the following statements concerning reinforcement is correct?
   a. Learning is most rapid with intermittent reinforcement, but continuous reinforcement produces the greatest resistance to extinction.
   b. Learning is most rapid with continuous reinforcement, but intermittent reinforcement produces the greatest resistance to extinction.
   c. Learning is fastest and resistance to extinction is greatest after continuous reinforcement.
   d. Learning is fastest and resistance to extinction is greatest following intermittent reinforcement.

6. When a conditioned stimulus is presented without an accompanying unconditioned stimulus, _____ will soon take place.
   a. generalization
   b. discrimination
   c. extinction
   d. aversion

7. One difference between classical and operant conditioning is that
   a. in classical conditioning the responses operate on the environment to produce rewarding or punishing stimuli.
   b. in operant conditioning the responses are triggered by preceding stimuli.
   c. in classical conditioning the responses are automatically triggered by stimuli.
   d. in operant conditioning the responses are reflexive.

8. Learning by imitating others' behaviors is called _____ learning. The researcher best known for studying this type of learning is _____ .
   a. secondary; B. F. Skinner
   b. observational; Albert Bandura
   c. secondary; Ivan Pavlov
   d. observational; John B. Watson

9. Punishment is a controversial way of controlling behavior because
   a. behavior is not forgotten and may return.
   b. punishing stimuli often create fear.
   c. punishment often increases aggressiveness.
   d. of all of these reasons.

10. For the most rapid conditioning, a CS should be presented
    a. after the US.
    b. before the US.
    c. without the US.
    d. at the same time as the US.

11. During extinction, the _____ is omitted; as a result, the _____ seems to disappear.
    a. US; UR   c. US; CR
    b. CS; CR   d. CS; UR

12. In Watson and Rayner's experiment, the loud noise was the _____ and the white rat was the _____.
    a. CS; CR   c. CS; US
    b. US; CS   d. US; CR

13. In which of the following may classical conditioning play a role?
    a. emotional problems
    b. the body's reaction to an illness-producing environment
    c. helping drug addicts
    d. all of these answers

14. Shaping is a(n) _____ technique for _____ a behavior.
    a. operant; establishing
    b. operant; suppressing
    c. respondent; establishing
    d. respondent; suppressing

15. In Pavlov's studies of classical conditioning of a dog's salivary responses, spontaneous recovery occurred
    a. during acquisition, when the CS was first paired with the US.
    b. during extinction, when the CS was first presented by itself.
    c. when the CS was reintroduced following extinction of the CR and a rest period.
    d. during discrimination training, when several conditioned stimuli were introduced.

16. In distinguishing between negative reinforcers and punishment, we note that
    a. punishment, but not negative reinforcement, involves use of a negative stimulus.
    b. in contrast to punishment, negative reinforcement decreases the likelihood of a response by presenting a negative stimulus.
    c. in contrast to punishment, negative reinforcement increases the likelihood of a response by presenting a negative stimulus.
    d. in contrast to punishment, negative reinforcement increases the likelihood of a response by ending a negative stimulus.

17. In promoting observational learning, the most effective models are those we perceive as
    a. similar to ourselves.
    b. respected and admired.
    c. successful.
    d. attractive.

18. A cognitive map is a
    a. mental representation of one's environment.
    b. sequence of thought processes leading from one idea to another.
    c. set of instructions detailing the most effective means of teaching a particular concept.
    d. biological predisposition to learn a particular skill.

19. After exploring a complicated maze for several days, a rat subsequently ran the maze with very few errors when food was placed in the goal box for the first time. This performance illustrates
    a. classical conditioning.
    b. discrimination learning.
    c. observational learning.
    d. latent learning.

20. Online testing systems and interactive software are applications of the operant conditioning principles of
    a. shaping and immediate reinforcement.
    b. immediate reinforcement and punishment.
    c. shaping and primary reinforcement.
    d. continuous reinforcement and punishment.

21. Which of the following is the best example of a conditioned reinforcer?
    a. putting on a coat on a cold day
    b. relief from pain after the dentist stops drilling your teeth
    c. receiving a cool drink after washing your mother's car on a hot day
    d. receiving an approving nod from the boss for a job well done

22. Experiments on taste-aversion learning demonstrate that
    a. for the conditioning of certain stimuli the US need not immediately follow the CS.
    b. any perceivable stimulus can become a CS.
    c. all animals are biologically primed to associate illness with the taste of a tainted food.
    d. all of these findings are true.

23. Regarding the impact of watching television violence on children, most researchers believe that
    a. aggressive children simply prefer violent programs.
    b. television simply reflects, rather than contributes to, violent social trends.
    c. watching violence on television leads to aggressive behavior.
    d. there is only a weak correlation between exposure to violence and aggressive behavior.

24. You always rattle the box of dog biscuits before giving your dog a treat. As you do so, your dog salivates. Rattling the box is a _____ ; your dog's salivation is a _____ .
    a. CS; CR   c. US; CR
    b. CS; UR   d. US; UR

25. You teach your dog to fetch the paper by giving him a cookie each time he does so. This is an example of
    a. operant conditioning.
    b. classical conditioning.
    c. conditioned reinforcement.
    d. partial reinforcement.

26. A pigeon can easily be taught to flap its wings to avoid shock but not for food reinforcement. According to the text, this is most likely so because
    a. pigeons are biologically predisposed to flap their wings to escape negative events and to use their beaks to obtain food.
    b. shock is a more motivating stimulus for birds than food is.
    c. hungry animals have difficulty delaying their eating long enough to learn *any* new skill.
    d. of all of these reasons.

27. After discovering that her usual route home was closed due to road repairs, Sharetta used her knowledge of the city and sense of direction to find an alternative route. This is an example of
    a. latent learning.
    b. observational learning.
    c. shaping.
    d. using a cognitive map.

28. Cognitive processes are
   a. unimportant in classical and operant conditioning.
   b. important in both classical and operant conditioning.
   c. more important in classical than in operant conditioning.
   d. more important in operant than in classical conditioning.

29. A response that leads to the removal of an unpleasant stimulus is one being
   a. positively reinforced.
   b. negatively reinforced.
   c. punished.
   d. extinguished.

30. Which of the following is an example of reinforcement?
   a. presenting a positive stimulus after a response
   b. removing an unpleasant stimulus after a response
   c. being told that you have done a good job
   d. All of these are examples.

31. For operant conditioning to be MOST effective, when should the reinforcers be presented in relation to the desired response?
   a. immediately before
   b. immediately after
   c. at the same time as
   d. at least a half hour before

32. On an intermittent reinforcement schedule, reinforcement is given
   a. in very small amounts.
   b. randomly.
   c. for successive approximations of a desired behavior.
   d. only some of the time.

33. After watching coverage of the Olympics on television recently, Lynn and Susan have been staging their own "summer games." Which of the following best accounts for their behavior?
   a. classical conditioning
   b. observational learning
   c. latent learning
   d. shaping

34. Which of the following is an example of shaping?
   a. A dog learns to salivate at the sight of a box of dog biscuits.
   b. A new driver learns to stop at an intersection when the light changes to red.
   c. A parrot is rewarded first for making any sound, then for making a sound similar to "Laura," and then for "speaking" its owner's name.
   d. A psychology student reinforces a laboratory rat only occasionally, to make its behavior more resistant to extinction.

35. Nancy decided to take introductory psychology because she has always been interested in human behavior. Jack enrolled in the same course because he thought it would be easy. Nancy's behavior was motivated by _____ , Jack's by _____ .
   a. extrinsic motivation; intrinsic motivation
   b. intrinsic motivation; extrinsic motivation
   c. drives; incentives
   d. incentives; drives

36. The "piecework," or commission, method of payment is an example of which reinforcement schedule?
   a. fixed-interval
   b. variable-interval
   c. fixed-ratio
   d. variable-ratio

37. Leon's psychology instructor has scheduled an exam every third week of the term. Leon will probably study the most just before an exam and the least just after an exam. This is because the schedule of exams is reinforcing studying according to which schedule?
   a. fixed-ratio
   b. variable-ratio
   c. fixed-interval
   d. variable-interval

38. The highest and most consistent rate of response is produced by a _____ schedule.
   a. fixed-ratio
   b. variable-ratio
   c. fixed-interval
   d. variable-interval

Matching Items

Match each definition or description with the appropriate term.

Definitions or Descriptions

_____ **1.** presentation of a desired stimulus
_____ **2.** tendency for similar stimuli to evoke a CR
_____ **3.** removal of a negative stimulus
_____ **4.** an innately reinforcing stimulus
_____ **5.** the acquisition of mental information by watching others
_____ **6.** an acquired reinforcer
_____ **7.** the motivation to perform a behavior for its own sake
_____ **8.** reinforcers guide actions closer and closer to a desired behavior
_____ **9.** the reappearance of a weakened CR
_____ **10.** presentation of a negative stimulus
_____ **11.** learning that becomes apparent only after reinforcement is provided
_____ **12.** each and every response is reinforced
_____ **13.** a desire to perform a behavior due to promised rewards

Terms

a. shaping
b. punishment
c. spontaneous recovery
d. latent learning
e. positive reinforcement
f. negative reinforcement
g. primary reinforcer
h. generalization
i. conditioned reinforcer
j. continuous reinforcement
k. extrinsic motivation
l. intrinsic motivation
m. cognitive learning

Application Essay

Manuel is 9 years old, living in the hills of Guatemala. His school has just received 10 new computers. How might his teachers use operant conditioning to teach him computing basics? (Use the space below to list the points you want to make, and organize them. Then write the essay on a separate piece of paper.)

SUMMING UP

See pages 115–116.

Terms and Concepts

Using your own words, on a piece of paper write a brief definition or explanation of each of the following terms.

1. learning
2. associative learning
3. stimulus
4. cognitive learning
5. classical conditioning
6. neutral stimulus
7. unconditioned response (UR)
8. unconditioned stimulus (US)
9. conditioned response (CR)
10. conditioned stimulus (CS)
11. acquisition
12. extinction
13. spontaneous recovery
14. generalization
15. discrimination
16. operant conditioning
17. operant chamber
18. reinforcement
19. shaping
20. positive reinforcement
21. negative reinforcement
22. primary reinforcer
23. conditioned reinforcer
24. reinforcement schedule
25. continuous reinforcement
26. partial (intermittent) reinforcement
27. fixed-ratio schedule
28. variable-ratio schedule
29. fixed-interval schedule
30. variable-ratio schedule

31. punishment

32. respondent behavior

33. operant behavior

34. behaviorism

35. cognitive map

36. latent learning

37. intrinsic motivation

38. extrinsic motivation

39. observational learning

40. modeling

41. mirror neurons

42. prosocial behavior

SUMMING UP

To help you through this flow chart, here's a similar example.

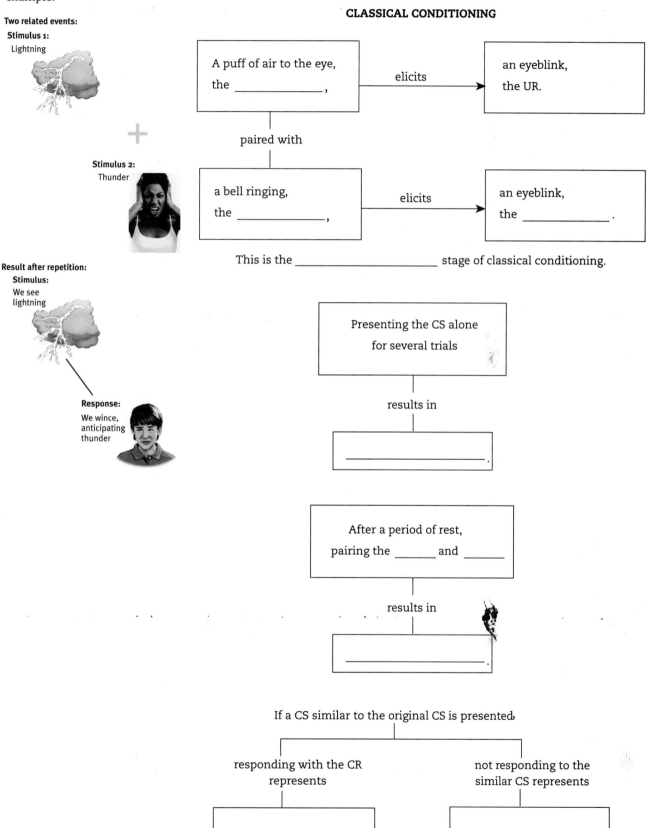

Two related events:

Stimulus 1:

Lightning

+

Stimulus 2:

Thunder

Result after repetition:

Stimulus:

We see lightning

Response:

We wince, anticipating thunder

CLASSICAL CONDITIONING

A puff of air to the eye, the _____ ,   elicits   an eyeblink, the UR.

paired with

a bell ringing, the _____ ,   elicits   an eyeblink, the _____ .

This is the _____ stage of classical conditioning.

Presenting the CS alone for several trials

results in

_____ .

After a period of rest, pairing the _____ and _____

results in

_____ .

If a CS similar to the original CS is presented,

responding with the CR represents

_____ .

not responding to the similar CS represents

_____ .

OPERANT CONDITIONING

To help you through this flow chart, here's a similar example.

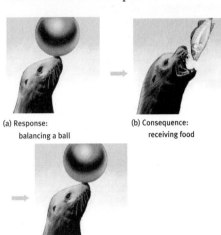

(a) Response: balancing a ball

(b) Consequence: receiving food

(c) Behavior strengthened

| A dog biscuit, a _____ reinforcer, | or | encouraging words, such as "Good dog," a _____ _____ , |

can be used to

train, or _____ , a new skill, such as sitting up.

To teach a new skill (sitting up), first use

_____ reinforcement.

To maintain the sitting behavior, use

_____ _____ .

ANSWERS

Chapter Review

How Do We Learn?

1. learning
2. associations; associative learning
3. classical
4. operant
5. cognitive learning; observational learning

Classical Conditioning

1. neutral stimulus; unconditioned stimulus
2. conditioned stimulus; conditioned response
3. Because the cat was associated with your mother's scream, it triggered a fear response, and is thus the CS.
4. Your mother's scream and evident fear, which naturally caused you to cry, was the US.
5. Your fear of cats is the CR. An acquired fear is always a conditioned response.
6. Your crying, automatically triggered by your mother's scream and fear, was the UR.
7. (a) acquisition; one-half second
8. (b) extinction
9. (c) spontaneous recovery
10. generalization
11. similar; discrimination

12. generalization; discriminating. Bill is extending (generalizing) a learned aversion to a specific American-made car to all American-made cars. Andy, on the other hand, looks at each brand of car separately (he is a discriminating buyer).
13. adapt
14. objectively
15. craving; cues

In Watson and Rayner's experiment, classical conditioning was used to condition fear of a rat in Albert, an 11-month-old infant. When Albert touched the white rat (neutral stimulus), a loud noise (unconditioned stimulus) was sounded. After several pairings of the rat with the noise, Albert began crying at the mere sight of the rat. The rat had become a conditioned stimulus, triggering a conditioned response of fear.

Operant Conditioning

1. operant conditioning
2. operant chamber (Skinner box)
3. shaping; approximations
4. reinforcer
5. positive reinforcer
6. negative reinforcer
7. primary reinforcers; conditioned (secondary) reinforcers
8. delay
9. is; delayed; unprotected sex

10. negative reinforcement. By taking out the garbage, Jack terminates a negative stimulus—his father's nagging.

11. conditioned reinforcer. Being invited to your instructor's home as part of a select group is a conditioned reinforcer in that it doesn't satisfy an innate need but has become linked with desirable consequences.

12. continuous reinforcement; rapid; rapid

13. partial (intermittent); slower; very

14. fixed-ratio

15. variable-ratio

16. fixed-interval; checking your e-mail more often as the time for an expected response approaches

17. variable-interval

18. negative reinforcement; punishment; negative reinforcement; punishment

19. fear; the person who administered it; suppressed

20. aggressiveness

21. **a.** Punishment. You lose something good—conversation with your roommate.
    b. Negative reinforcement. You are no longer cold, which means something bad has been removed.
    c. Negative reinforcement. You are no longer thirsty, so something bad has been removed.
    d. Punishment. You can't use your laptop; certainly, something good has been taken away.
    e. Negative reinforcement. Your brother stops nagging you, so something bad has been removed.

22. dehumanized; freedom; control

23. shaping; testing; interactive; Web

24. more; achievable; more

25. associative learning

26. acquisition; extinction; spontaneous recovery; generalization; discrimination

27. stimuli; control; automatically

28. respondent

29. operant behaviors; consequences

30. **a.** voluntary; operant conditioning
    b. involuntary; classical conditioning
    c. voluntary; operant conditioning
    d. involuntary; classical conditioning

Biology, Cognition, and Learning

1. adaptive

2. sickness; would

3. biological; adapt

4. behaviorism

5. cognitive map

6. latent learning

7. intrinsic motivation; extrinsic motivation

8. observational learning; modeling; behavior

9. mirror; observational

10. Albert Bandura

11. more

12. prosocial

13. antisocial; abusive; aggressive; environmental

14. causation; does

15. attractive; unpunished; does not

16. imitation; desensitize

17. increases; mirror neurons; prosocial

Progress Test

Multiple-Choice Questions

1. **c.** is the answer.
   a. This answer is incorrect because it simply describes any behavior that is automatic rather than being triggered by a specific stimulus.
   b. This answer is too general, since behaviors can change for reasons other than learning.
   d. Respondently conditioned behavior also satisfies the criteria of our definition of learning.

2. **b.** is the answer.
   a. & c. Classical conditioning is associated with Ivan Pavlov; respondent conditioning is another name for classical conditioning.
   d. Observational learning is most closely associated with Albert Bandura.

3. **b.** is the answer. Prior to its pairing with meat (the US), the tone did not trigger salivation and was therefore a neutral stimulus. Afterward, the tone triggered salivation (the CR) and was therefore a conditioned stimulus (CS).
   c. & d. Unconditioned stimuli, such as meat, innately trigger responding. Pavlov's dogs had to learn to associate the tone with the food.

4. **d.** is the answer. In learning to distinguish between the conditioned stimulus and another, similar stimulus, the monkey has received training in discrimination.
   a. In extinction training, a stimulus and/or response is allowed to go unreinforced.
   b. Generalization training involves responding to stimuli similar to the conditioned stimulus; here the monkey is being trained not to respond to a similar stimulus.
   c. This cannot be classical conditioning since the monkey is acting to obtain a reward. Thus, this is an example of operant conditioning.

5. **b.** is the answer. A continuous association will naturally be easier to learn than one that occurs on only some occasions, so learning is most rapid with continuous reinforcement. Yet, once the continuous association is no longer there, as in extinction training, extinction will occur more rapidly than it would have had the organism not always experienced reinforcement.

6. **c.** is the answer. In this situation, the CR will decline, a phenomenon known as extinction.

a. Generalization occurs when the subject makes a CR to stimuli similar to the original CS.

b. Discrimination is when the subject does not make a CR to stimuli other than the original CS.

d. An aversion is a CR to a CS that has been associated with an unpleasant US, such as shock or a nausea-producing drug.

7. **c.** is the answer.

   a. In *operant* conditioning the responses operate on the environment.

   b. In *classical* conditioning responses are triggered by preceding stimuli.

   d. In *classical* conditioning responses are reflexive.

8. **b.** is the answer.

   a. Skinner is best known for studies of *operant* learning. Moreover, there is no such thing as secondary learning.

   c. Pavlov is best known for classical conditioning.

   d. Watson is best known as an early proponent of behaviorism.

9. **d.** is the answer.

10. **b.** is the answer.

    a. Backward conditioning, in which the US precedes the CS, is ineffective.

    c. This interval is longer than is optimum for the most rapid acquisition of a CS-US association.

    d. Simultaneous presentation of CS and US is ineffective because it does not permit the subject to anticipate the US.

11. **c.** is the answer.

12. **b.** is the answer. The loud noise automatically triggered Albert's fear and therefore functioned as a US. After being associated with the US, the white rat acquired the power to trigger fear and thus became a CS. (p. 164)

13. **d.** is the answer.

14. **a.** is the answer. Shaping works on operant behaviors by reinforcing successive approximations to a desired goal.

15. **c.** is the answer.

    a., b., & d. Spontaneous recovery occurs after a CR has been extinguished, and in the absence of the US. The situations described here all involve the continued presentation of the US and, therefore, the further strengthening of the CR.

16. **d.** is the answer.

    a. Both involve a negative stimulus.

    b. All reinforcers, including negative reinforcers, increase the likelihood of a response.

    c. In negative reinforcement, a negative stimulus is withdrawn following a desirable response.

17. **d.** is the answer.

18. **a.** is the answer.

19. **d.** is the answer. The rat had learned the maze but did not display this learning until reinforcement became available.

    a. Negotiating a maze is clearly operant behavior.

b. This example does not involve learning to distinguish between stimuli.

c. This is not observational learning because the rat has no one to observe!

20. **a.** is the answer. Online testing systems apply operant principles such as reinforcement, immediate feedback, and shaping to the teaching of new skills.

    b. & d. Online testing systems provide immediate, and continuous, reinforcement for correct responses, but do not use negative control procedures such as punishment.

    c. Online testing systems are based on feedback for correct responses; this feedback constitutes conditioned, rather than primary, reinforcement.

21. **d.** is the answer. An approving nod from the boss is a conditioned reinforcer in that it doesn't satisfy an innate need but has become linked with desirable consequences. Escape from cold, relief from pain, and a drink are all primary reinforcers, which meet innate needs.

22. **a.** is the answer. Taste-aversion experiments demonstrate conditioning even with CS-US intervals as long as several hours.

    b. Despite being perceivable, a visual or auditory stimulus cannot become a CS for illness in some animals, such as rats.

    c. Some animals, such as birds, are biologically primed to associate the *appearance* of food with illness.

23. **c.** is the answer.

24. **a.** is the answer. Your dog had to learn to associate the rattling sound with the food. Rattling is therefore a conditioned, or learned, stimulus, and salivation in response to this rattling is a learned, or conditioned, response.

25. **a.** is the answer. You are teaching your dog by rewarding him when he produces the desired behavior.

    b. This is not classical conditioning because the cookie is a primary reinforcer presented after the operant behavior of the dog fetching the paper.

    c. Food is a primary reinforcer; it satisfies an innate need.

    d. Rewarding your dog each time he fetches the paper is continuous reinforcement.

26. **a.** is the answer. As in this example, conditioning must be consistent with the particular organism's biological predispositions.

    b. Some behaviors, but certainly not all, are acquired more rapidly than others when shock is used as negative reinforcement.

    c. Pigeons are able to acquire many new behaviors when food is used as reinforcement.

27. **d.** is the answer. Sharetta is guided by her mental representation of the city, or cognitive map.

    a. Latent learning, or learning in the absence of reinforcement that is demonstrated when reinforcement becomes available, has no direct relevance to the example.

b. Observational learning refers to learning from watching others.

c. Shaping is the technique of reinforcing successive approximations of a desired behavior.

28. **b.** is the answer.
c. & d. The text does not present evidence regarding the relative importance of cognitive processes in classical and operant conditioning.

29. **b.** is the answer.
a. Positive reinforcement involves presenting a favorable stimulus following a response.
c. Punishment involves presenting an unpleasant stimulus following a response.
d. In extinction, a previously reinforced response is no longer followed by reinforcement. In this situation, a response causes a stimulus to be terminated or removed.

30. **d.** is the answer. a. is an example of positive reinforcement, b. is an example of negative reinforcement, and c. is an example of conditioned reinforcement.

31. **b.** is the answer.
a., c., & d. Reinforcement that is delayed, presented before a response, or presented at the same time as a response does not always increase the response's frequency of occurrence.

32. **d.** is the answer.
a. Intermittent reinforcement refers to the ratio of responses to reinforcers, not the overall quantity of reinforcement delivered.
b. Unlike intermittent reinforcement, in which the delivery of reinforcement is contingent on responding, random reinforcement is delivered independently of the subject's behavior.
c. This defines the technique of shaping, not intermittent reinforcement.

33. **b.** is the answer. The girls are imitating behavior they have observed.
a. Because these behaviors are clearly willful rather than involuntary, classical conditioning plays no role.
c. Latent learning plays no role in this example.
d. Shaping is a procedure for teaching the acquisition of a new response by reinforcing successive approximations of the behavior.

34. **c.** is the answer. The parrot is reinforced for making successive approximations of a goal behavior. This defines shaping.
a. Shaping is an operant conditioning procedure; salivation at the sight of dog biscuits is a classically conditioned response.
b. Shaping involves the systematic reinforcement of successive approximations of a more complex behavior. In this example there is no indication that the response of stopping at the intersection involved the gradual acquisition of simpler behaviors.
d. This is an example of the partial reinforcement of an established response, rather than the shaping of a new response.

35. **b.** is the answer. Wanting to do something for its own sake is intrinsic motivation; wanting to do something for a reward (in this case, presumably, a high grade) is extrinsic motivation.
a. The opposite is true. Nancy was motivated to take the course for its own sake, whereas Jack was evidently motivated by the likelihood of a reward in the form of a good grade.
c. & d. A good grade, such as the one Jack is expecting, is an incentive. Drives, however, are aroused states that result from physical deprivation; they are not involved in this example.

36. **c.** is the answer. Payment is given after a fixed number of pieces have been completed.
a. & b. Interval schedules reinforce according to the passage of time, not the amount of work accomplished.
d. Fortunately for those working on commission, the work ratio is fixed and therefore predictable.

37. **c.** is the answer. Because reinforcement (earning a good grade on the exam) is available according to the passage of time, studying is reinforced on an interval schedule. Because the interval between exams is constant, this is an example of a fixed-interval schedule.

38. **b.** is the answer.
a. With fixed-ratio schedules, there is a pause following each reinforcement.
c. & d. Because reinforcement is not contingent on the rate of response, interval schedules, especially fixed-interval schedules, produce lower response rates than ratio schedules.

Matching Items

1.	e	**6.**	i	**11.**	d
2.	h	**7.**	l	**12.**	j
3.	f	**8.**	a	**13.**	k
4.	g	**9.**	c		
5.	m	**10.**	b		

Application Essay

Principles of operant conditioning are fundamental to all learned voluntary (operant) behaviors, especially those involved in complicated cognitive and motor behaviors such as using a computer. Teaching itself is a form of shaping, and the first step in shaping an operant response, such as teaching a child how to operate a computer, is to find an effective reinforcer. For most children, making a computer work is intrinsically rewarding. Some teachers also use gold stars, check marks, or free time on the computer (to play a game, for instance) to reward successful approximations of more complicated behaviors such as keyboarding, word processing, or spreadsheet use. These types of primary reinforcement should be accompanied by lots of praise (secondary reinforcement) whenever Manuel responds correctly. As success is achieved, the teacher should gradually require closer and closer approximations until the goal response (accurate keyboarding or software use, for example) is attained. When the new response has been established, the teacher should switch from continuous to partial reinforcement in order to strengthen the skill.

Summing Up

Classical Conditioning: A puff of air to the eye, the US, elicits an eye blink, the UR. When the puff of air is paired with a bell ringing, a CS, the CS comes to elicit an eye-blink, a CR. This is the *acquisition* stage of classical conditioning. Presenting the CS alone for several trials results in *extinction*. After a period of rest, pairing the CS and US results in *spontaneous recovery*. If a CS similar to the original CS is presented, responding with the CR represents *generalization*; not responding to the similar CS represents *discrimination*.

Operant Conditioning: A dog biscuit, a *primary* reinforcer, or encouraging words, such as "Good dog," a *conditioned reinforcer*, can be used to train, or *shape*, a new skill, such as sitting up. To teach a new skill (sitting up), first use *continuous* reinforcement. To maintain the sitting behavior, use *partial reinforcement*.

Terms and Concepts

1. **Learning** is any relatively permanent change in behavior due to experience.
2. **Associative learning** is learning that certain events occur together. Two variations of associative learning are classical conditioning and operant conditioning.
3. A **stimulus** is a situation or an event that evokes a response.
4. **Cognitive learning** is learning of mental information by observing events, other people, or via language.
5. Also known as Pavlovian conditioning, **classical conditioning** is a type of learning in which we learn to link two or more stimuli; a neutral stimulus becomes capable of triggering a conditioned response after having become associated with an unconditioned stimulus.
6. In classical conditioning, a **neutral stimulus** is one that does not elicit a response before conditioning.
7. In classical conditioning, the **unconditioned response (UR)** is the unlearned, naturally occurring response to the unconditioned stimulus.
8. In classical conditioning, the **unconditioned stimulus (US)** is the stimulus that naturally and automatically triggers the unconditioned response.
9. In classical conditioning, the **conditioned response (CR)** is the learned response to a previously neutral (but now conditioned) stimulus, which results from the acquired association between the CS and US.
10. In classical conditioning, the **conditioned stimulus (CS)** is an originally neutral stimulus that comes to trigger a CR after association with an unconditioned stimulus.

11. In a learning experiment, **acquisition** refers to the initial stage of conditioning in which the new response is established and gradually strengthened. In operant conditioning, it is the strengthening of a reinforced response.
12. **Extinction** refers to the weakening of a CR when the CS is no longer followed by the US; in operant conditioning extinction occurs when a response is no longer reinforced.
13. **Spontaneous recovery** is the reappearance of an extinguished CR after a pause.
14. **Generalization** refers to the tendency, once a response has been conditioned, to respond similarly to stimuli that resemble the original CS.
15. **Discrimination** in classical conditioning refers to the ability to distinguish the CS from similar stimuli that do not signal a US. In operant conditioning, it refers to responding differently to stimuli that signal a behavior will be reinforced or will not be reinforced.
16. **Operant conditioning** is a type of learning in which behavior is strengthened if followed by a reinforcer or diminished if followed by a punisher.

    Example: Unlike classical conditioning, which works on automatic behaviors, **operant conditioning** works on behaviors that operate on the environment.
17. An **operant chamber** (*Skinner box*) is an experimental chamber for the operant conditioning of an animal such as a pigeon or rat. The controlled environment enables the investigator to present visual or auditory stimuli, deliver reinforcement or punishment, and precisely measure simple responses such as bar presses or key pecking.
18. In operant conditioning, **reinforcement** is any event that strengthens the behavior it follows.
19. **Shaping** is the operant conditioning procedure in which reinforcers guide actions closer and closer toward a desired behavior.
20. In operant conditioning, **positive reinforcement** strengthens a response by *presenting* a typically pleasurable stimulus after that response.
21. In operant conditioning, **negative reinforcement** strengthens a response by *removing* a negative stimulus after that response.
22. The powers of **primary reinforcers** are innate and do not depend on learning.
23. **Conditioned reinforcers** are stimuli that acquire their reinforcing power through their association with primary reinforcers; also called *secondary reinforcers*.
24. A **reinforcement schedule** is a pattern that defines how often a desired response will be reinforced.
25. **Continuous reinforcement** is the operant procedure of reinforcing the desired response every time it occurs. In promoting the acquisition of a new response it is best to use continuous reinforcement.

26. **Partial (intermittent) reinforcement** is the operant procedure of reinforcing a response only part of the time. A response that has been partially reinforced is much more resistant to extinction than one that has been continuously reinforced.

27. In operant conditioning, a **fixed-ratio schedule** reinforces a response only after a specified number of responses.

28. In operant conditioning, a **variable-ratio schedule** reinforces a response after an unpredictable number of responses.

29. In operant conditioning, a **fixed-interval schedule** reinforces a response only after a specified time has elapsed.

30. In operant conditioning, a **variable-interval schedule** reinforces a response at unpredictable time intervals.

31. In operant conditioning, **punishment** is an event, such as shock, that decreases the behavior it follows.

    Memory aid: People often confuse negative reinforcement and **punishment**. The former strengthens behavior, while the latter weakens it.

32. **Respondent behavior** is that which occurs as an automatic response to some stimulus.

    Example: In classical conditioning, conditioned and unconditioned responses are examples of **respondent behavior** in that they are automatic responses triggered by specific stimuli.

33. **Operant behavior** is behavior that operates on the environment, producing consequences.

34. **Behaviorism** is the view that psychology should be an objective science that studies only observable behaviors without reference to mental processes.

    Example: Because he was an early advocate of the study of observable behavior, John Watson is often called the father of behaviorism.

35. A **cognitive map** is a mental image of the layout of your environment.

36. **Latent learning** is learning that occurs in the absence of reinforcement but only becomes apparent when there is an incentive to demonstrate it.

37. **Intrinsic motivation** is the desire to perform a behavior for its own sake, rather than for some external reason.

    Memory aid: Intrinsic means "internal": A person who is **intrinsically motivated** is motivated from within.

38. **Extrinsic motivation** is the desire to perform a behavior in order to gain a reward or avoid a punishment.

    Memory aid: Extrinsic means "external": A person who is extrinsically motivated is motivated by some outside factor.

39. **Observational learning** is learning by watching and imitating the behavior of others.

40. **Modeling** is the process of watching and then imitating a specific behavior and is thus an important means through which observational learning occurs.

41. **Mirror neurons** may be the neural basis for observational learning. These neurons fire when certain actions are performed or when another individual who performs those actions is observed.

42. The opposite of antisocial behavior, **prosocial behavior** is positive, helpful, and constructive and is subject to the same principles of observational learning as is undesirable behavior, such as aggression.

7

MEMORY

Chapter 7 explores human memory as a system that processes information in three steps: encoding, storage, and retrieval. The chapter also discusses the important role of meaning and imagery in encoding new memories, how memory is represented physically in the brain, and how forgetting may result from failure to encode or store information or to find appropriate retrieval cues. The final section of the chapter discusses the issue of memory construction. How true are our memories of events? A particularly controversial issue in this area involves suspicious claims of long-repressed memories of sexual abuse and other traumas that are "recovered" with the aid of hypnosis and other techniques. As you study this chapter, try applying some of the memory and studying tips discussed in the text.

CHAPTER REVIEW

First, skim each text section, noting headings and boldface items. Review the section by reading the objectives and summaries provided here, then answer the questions that follow. In some cases, STUDY TIPS explain how best to learn a difficult concept and APPLICATIONS help you to know how well you understand the material. Check your understanding of the material by consulting the answers beginning on page 134. Do not continue with the next section until you understand each answer. If you need to, review or reread the section in the textbook before continuing.

Studying Memory

Objective 1: Identify the three processes involved in building a memory, and describe how unconscious processing and working memory update the three-stage information-processing model of memory.

Memory is the persistence of learning over time through the storage and retrieval of information. Like a computer's information-processing system, our memory must **encode, store,** and **retrieve** information. The Atkinson-Shiffrin three-stage processing model states that we first record to-be-remembered information as a fleeting **sensory memory.** From there it is processed into a **short-term memory** bin, where we encode it through *rehearsal* for **long-term memory** and later retrieval. Sometimes we bypass the first two stages and form some memories through *unconscious* processing. Short-term memory is actually a **working memory** because it uses and actively maintains information.

1. Learning that persists over time indicates the existence of _____ for that learning.

2. Both human memory and computer memory can be viewed as _____ - _____ systems that perform three tasks: _____ , _____ , and _____ .

3. The classic model of memory has been Atkinson and Shiffrin's _____ - _____ _____ model. According to this model, we first record information as a fleeting _____ . _____ . From there it is processed into _____ - _____ memory, where the information is _____ through rehearsal into _____ - _____ memory for later retrieval.

4. The idea of short-term memory has been updated by the concept of _____ memory, which focuses more on the _____ processing of temporarily stored information.

· ·
STUDY TIP/APPLICATION: To remember the material in the first half of this chapter, you might find it helpful to use the concept of a *three-part model* as a retrieval cue. In this section, Atkinson and Shiffrin's three-stage model proposes that external events are processed through separate stages of sensory memory, working/short-term memory, and long-term memory. In the next section, the three processes of (1) getting information into the memory system (encoding), (2) retaining information over time (storage), and (3) getting information out of memory storage (retrieval) are described. Each process (encoding, storage, and retrieval) can occur at each memory stage (sensory memory, short-term memory, long-term memory). The chart on the next page applies what can happen at each stage to the example of getting the written words of a memorable poem in and out of memory. To bolster your understanding of these important concepts, you might try using this type of chart as the basis for an example you create.

Sensory Memory	Working/Short-Term Memory	Long-Term Memory
Encoding: light reflecting from printed words in the poem automatically triggers a response in the eye's receptor cells	*Encoding:* automatic processing of location of words on the page; effortful processing of meaning	*Encoding:* Memorable passage triggers deep processing of material from STM to LTM
Storage: image of each word persists in the visual system for about 1/2 sec.	*Storage:* limited capacity and duration of storing words on the page	*Storage:* relatively permanent and limitless; meaningful passage stays with you
Retrieval: visual image is attended to as it passes into STM	*Retrieval:* conscious working memory allows reader to process the meaning of the poem's words	*Retrieval:* recall, recognition, or relearning of memorized passage from the poem

Objective 2: How do automatic and effortful processing help us encode sights, sounds, and other sensations?

To some extent, encoding occurs automatically. With little or no effort, we encode an enormous amount of information about *space, time,* and *frequency.* For example, we can re-create a sequence of the day's events to guess where we might have left a coat. *Automatic processing* occurs without our awareness and without interfering with our thinking about other things. Some forms of processing, such as learning to read or drive, require attention and effort when we first perform them but with practice become automatic.

Automatic processing occurs unconsciously; *effortful processing* requires attention and conscious effort. For example, our memory of the names of researchers mentioned in this chapter will disappear unless we *rehearse* them. The *spacing effect* is our tendency to retain information more easily if we practice it repeatedly than if we practice it in one long session. The *serial position effect* is our tendency to remember the last and first items in a long list (for example, a grocery list) better than the middle items.

5. With the help of our _____-_____ mind, some encoding does not require conscious attention or effort; it is called _____ processing. Some processing requires effort at first but with _____ and _____ it becomes effortless.

6. With little or no conscious effort, you automatically process information about _____ , _____ , and _____ .

7. Encoding that requires attention and effort is called _____ processing.

8. With novel information, conscious repetition, or _____ , boosts memory.

9. A pioneering researcher in verbal memory was _____ . In one experiment, he found that the longer he studied a list of nonsense syllables, the _____ (fewer/greater) the number of repetitions he required to relearn it later.

10. Memory studies also reveal that spreading rehearsal over time is more effective for retention; this is called the _____ _____ .

11. The tendency to remember the first and last items in a list best is called the _____ _____ _____ .

APPLICATION:

12. The first thing Karen did when she discovered that she had misplaced her keys was to re-create in her mind the day's events. That she had little difficulty in doing so illustrates _____ _____ .

Objective 3: Distinguish between implicit and explicit memory, and identify the main brain structure associated with each.

Studies of brain-damaged patients who cannot form new memories confirm our two-track mind by revealing two types of memory. *Implicit* (unconscious) *memory* is retention of learned skills or conditioning. *Explicit* (conscious) *memory* is the memory of facts and experiences that one can consciously retrieve.

Scans of the brain in action and autopsies of people who had memory loss reveal that the *hippocampus,* a limbic system structure, plays a vital role in the gradual processing of our explicit memories into long-term memory. The hippocampus is not the permanent storehouse, but a loading dock that feeds new information to other brain circuits for permanent storage. Implicit memories are formed and stored by the *cerebellum.*

13. Studies of people who have lost their memory suggest that there _____ (is/is not) a single unified system of memory.

14. Although memory-loss victims typical _____ (have/have not) lost their capacity for learning, which is called _____ memory, they _____ (are/are not) aware of their memory, suggesting a deficit in their _____ memory systems.

15. Memory-loss patients typically have suffered damage to the _____ of their limbic system. This brain structure is important in registering and _____ (temporarily/permanently) storing the elements of a memory. However, memories _____ (do/ do not) migrate for storage elsewhere.

16. The cerebellum is important in forming and storing _____ memories created by classical conditioning. Humans with a damaged cerebellum are unable to develop certain conditioned _____ .

APPLICATIONS:

17. Elderly Mr. Flanagan, a retired electrician, can easily remember how to wire a light switch, but he cannot remember the name of the president of the United States. Evidently, Mr. Flanagan's _____ memory is better than his _____ memory.

18. After suffering damage to the hippocampus, a person would probably
    a. lose memory for skills such as bicycle riding.
    b. be incapable of being classically conditioned.
    c. lose the ability to store new facts.
    d. experience all of these changes.

Building Memories

Objective 4: Explain the most common and effective ways of encoding information.

When processing verbal information for storage, we usually encode its meaning. For example, we associate it with what we already know or imagine. We also more easily remember things that we process using visual *imagery*. For example, we remember words that lend themselves to picture images better than we remember low-imagery words. We can associate both an image and a meaning with *fire* but only a meaning with *process*.

1. Research has shown that you will more easily remember what you read and hear if you translate it into information that is personally _____ .

2. Memory that consists of mental pictures is based on the use of _____ .

3. High-imagery words tend to be remembered _____ (better/less well) than abstract, low-imagery words.

APPLICATION:

4. Although you can't recall the answer to a question on your psychology midterm, you have a clear mental image of the textbook page on which it appears. Evidently, your _____ encoding of the answer was _____ .

Objective 5: Describe the duration and working capacity of sensory, short-term, and long-term memory.

Sensory memory is truly fleeting. Unless our working memory rehearses or meaningfully encodes sensory information, it quickly disappears. Our short-term memory span for information just presented is very limited—a seconds-long retention of about seven items, give or take two. We know that our capacity for storing information permanently has no real limit.

5. If something you experienced is to be recalled, it must first enter your fleeting _____ memory.

6. George Sperling found that when people were briefly shown three rows of letters, they could recall _____ (virtually all/about half) of them. When Sperling sounded a tone immediately after a row of letters was flashed to indicate which letters were to be recalled, the subjects were much _____ (more/less) accurate. This suggests that information _____ (is/is not) briefly available for recall.

7. Researchers found that when _____ was prevented by asking people to count backward, memory for letters was gone after 12 seconds. Without _____ processing, short-term memories have a limited life.

8. Our short-term memory capacity is about _____ bits of information. This capacity was discovered by _____ .

9. In contrast to short-term memory—and contrary to popular belief—the capacity of permanent memory has no real _____ .

APPLICATION:

10. Brenda has trouble remembering her new seven-digit phone number plus three-digit area code. What is the most likely explanation for the difficulty Brenda is having?

_____

Objective 6: Discuss the biological changes that may underlie memory formation and storage.

The search for the physical basis of memory has recently focused on the synapses and their neurotransmitters and on the **long-term potentiation (LTP)** of brain circuits. In response to increased activity in neural pathways, neural interconnections form or strengthen. Studies of the sea slug indicate that when learning occurs, the slug releases more of the neurotransmitter *serotonin* at certain synapses, and these synapses become more sensitive and more efficient at transmitting signals. LTP appears to be a neural basis for learning and remembering.

The naturally stimulating hormones that we produce when excited or stressed make more glucose energy available to fuel brain activity, signaling the brain that something important has happened. Emotion-processing clusters in the brain boost activity in memory-forming areas. These emotion-triggered hormonal changes help explain our *flashbulb memories* of surprising, significant events.

11. Researchers believe that the physical basis of memory involves a strengthening of certain neural connections, which occurs at the _____ between neurons.

12. Kandel and Schwartz have found that when learning occurs in the sea slug *Aplysia*, the neurotransmitter _____ is released in greater amounts, making synapses more efficient.

13. As synapses become more efficient, so do _____ _____ . Sending neurons now release neurotransmitters _____ (more/less) easily, and the number of _____ _____ they stimulate may increase. This process, called _____-_____ _____ , may be the neural basis for learning and memory. Causing the absence of an _____ interferes with learning. Rats given a drug that enhances _____ will learn a maze _____ (faster/more slowly).

14. After LTP has occurred, an electric current passed through the brain _____ (will/will not) disrupt old memories and _____ (will/will not) wipe out recent experiences.

15. Hormones released when we are excited or under stress often _____ (enable/prevent) learning and memory.

16. Memories for surprising, significant moments that are especially clear are called _____ memories. Like other memories, these memories _____ (can/cannot) err.

APPLICATION:

17. Which of the following is the best example of a flashbulb memory?
    a. suddenly remembering to buy bread while standing in the checkout line at the grocery store
    b. recalling the name of someone from high school while looking at his or her yearbook snapshot
    c. remembering to make an important phone call
    d. remembering what you were doing on September 11, 2001, when terrorists crashed planes into the World Trade Center towers.

Objective 7: Contrast the recall, recognition, and relearning measures of memory.

Recall is memory demonstrated by retrieving information learned earlier, as on a fill-in-the-blank test. *Recognition* is memory demonstrated by identifying items previously learned, as on a multiple-choice test. *Relearning* is memory demonstrated by time saved when relearning previously learned information. Tests of recognition and relearning reveal that we remember more than we recall.

18. The ability to draw information out of storage and into conscious awareness is called _____ .

19. Researchers found that 25 years after graduation, people were not able to _____ (recall/recognize) the names of their classmates but were able to _____ (recall/recognize) 90 percent of their names and their yearbook pictures.

20. If you have learned something and then forgot it, you will probably be able to _____ it _____ (more/less) quickly than you did originally.

APPLICATION:

21. Complete this analogy: Fill-in-the-blank test questions are to multiple-choice questions as _____ is to _____ .

Objective 8: Explain how retrieval cues can help us access stored memories, and describe the impact of environmental contexts and internal emotional states on retrieval.

We can think of a memory as held in storage by a web of associations. *Retrieval cues* are bits of related information we encode while encoding a target piece of information. They become part of the web. To retrieve a specific memory, we need to identify one of the strands that leads to it. Activating retrieval cues within our web of associations aids memory.

Memory is sometimes *primed* (activated) by returning to the original context in which we experienced an event or encoded a thought. It can flood our memories with retrieval cues that lead to the target memory. Sometimes, being in a context similar to one we've been in before may trick us into subconsciously retrieving the target memory. The result is the eerie sense that we are reliving something that we have experienced before—a phenomenon known as *déjà vu.*

Memories are somewhat *mood-congruent*. While in a good or bad mood, we often retrieve memories consistent with that mood. Moods also prime us to interpret others' behavior in ways consistent with our emotions. Mood-congruent memory is part of a larger concept, called *state-dependent memory,* the tendency to recall information best in the same state as when the information was learned.

22. The best _____ cues come from the associations formed at the time we _____ a memory.

23. Studies have shown that retention is best when learning and testing are done in _____ (the same/different) contexts. Doing this can activate, or _____ , your memory of an experience.

Summarize the text explanation of the déjà vu experience.

24. Our tendency to recall experiences that are consistent with our current emotional state is called _____-_____ memory.

Describe the effects of mood on memory.

25. People who are currently depressed may recall their parents as _____ _____. People who have recovered from depression typically recall their parents about the same as do people who _____ _____ .

26. This type of emotion-related memory is part of a larger concept called _____-_____ memory: What we learn in one state is more easily recalled in that state.

APPLICATIONS:

27. In an effort to remember the name of the classmate who sat behind her in fifth grade, Martina mentally recited the names of other classmates who sat near her. Martina's effort to refresh her memory by activating related associations is an example of the use of _____ _____ .

28. Walking through the halls of his high school 10 years after graduation, Tom experienced a flood of old memories. Tom's experience showed the role of _____ _____ .

29. Being in a bad mood after a hard day of work, Susan could think of nothing positive in her life. This is best explained as an example of _____-_____ _____ .

30.

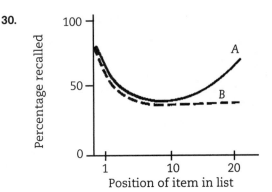

The above figure depicts the recall of a list of words under two conditions. Which of the following best describes the difference between the conditions?
a. In A, the words were studied and retrieved in the same context; in B, the contexts were different.
b. In B, the words were studied and retrieved in the same context; in A, the contexts were different.
c. The delay between presentation of the last word and the test of recall was longer for A than for B.
d. The delay between presentation of the last word and the test of recall was longer for B than for A.

Forgetting

Objective 9: Explain why we should value our ability to forget, and discuss the roles of encoding failure and storage decay in the process of forgetting.

The capacity to forget is helpful. Because of his inability to forget, the Russian memory whiz S found it more difficult than others to think abstractly—to generalize, to organize, to evaluate. Without an ability to forget we would be overwhelmed by out-of-date and unimportant information. Our memories fail us through forgetting (absent-mindedness, transience, and blocking), through distortion (misattribution, suggestibility, and bias), and through intrusion (persistence of unwanted memories).

One explanation for forgetting is that we fail to encode information for entry into our memory system. Without effortful processing, much of what we sense we never notice or process. For example, although most people in the United States have looked at a phone countless times, they may not be able to recall the letters associated with a specific number. Another explanation, based on Ebbinghaus' *forgetting curve,* is a gradual fading of the physical *memory trace.*

1. Without the ability to _____ , we would constantly be overwhelmed by information.

2. Memory researcher Daniel Schacter has identified the seven sins of memory, divided into three categories that identify the ways in which our memory can fail: the three sins of _____ , the three sins of _____ , and the one sin of _____ .

3. The first type of forgetting is caused by _____ failure.

4. This type of forgetting occurs because some of the information that we sense never actually

_____ .

5. One reason for age-related memory decline is that the brain areas that jump into action when a young person _____ new information are _____ (more/less) responsive in older adults.

6. Studies by Ebbinghaus and others indicate that most forgetting occurs _____ (soon/a long time) after the material is learned, as noted on Ebbinghaus' famous _____

_____ .

7. This type of forgetting is known as

_____ ,

which may be caused by a gradual fading of the physical _____ .

8. When he was 8 years old, Frank was questioned by the police about a summer camp counselor suspected of molesting children. Even though he was not, in fact, molested by the counselor, today 19-year-old Frank "remembers" the counselor touching him inappropriately. Frank's false memory is an example of the "sin" of memory called _____ .

Objective 10: Explain why retrieval failure, and in particular interference, might cause forgetting, and discuss whether Freud's concept of repression is supported by current research.

Retrieval failure can occur if we have too few cues to summon information from long-term memory. It may also happen when old and new information compete for retrieval. In some cases, something we learned in the past *interferes* with our ability to recall information we have recently learned. In other cases, something we have recently learned interferes with information we learned in the past.

With his concept of *repression,* Sigmund Freud proposed that our memories are self-censoring. To protect our self-concepts and to minimize anxiety, we may block from consciousness anxiety-arousing thoughts, feelings, and memories. In Freud's view, this motivated forgetting submerges memories but leaves them available for later retrieval under the right conditions. Increasing numbers of memory researchers think repression rarely, if ever, occurs. More typically, we have trouble forgetting traumatic experiences.

9. When information that is stored in memory temporarily cannot be found, _____ failure has occurred.

10. Research suggests that memories are also lost as a result of _____ , which is

especially possible if we simultaneously learn similar, new material.

11. Researchers found that if people went to sleep after learning, their memory for a list of nonsense syllables was _____ (better/worse) than it was if they stayed awake.

12. Freud proposed that motivated forgetting, or _____ , may protect a person from painful memories.

13. Increasing numbers of memory researchers think that motivated forgetting is _____ (less/more) common than Freud believed.

APPLICATIONS:

14. At your high school reunion you cannot remember the last name of your homeroom teacher. Your failure to remember is most likely the result of _____ failure.

15. Which of the following sequences would be best to follow if you wanted to minimize interference-induced forgetting in order to improve your recall on the psychology midterm?
a. study, eat, test
b. study, sleep, test
c. study, listen to music, test
d. study, exercise, test

16. When Carlos was promoted, he moved into a new office with a new phone extension. Every time he is asked for his phone number, Carlos first thinks of his old extension, illustrating the effects of _____ .

17. Lewis cannot remember the details of the torture he experienced as a prisoner of war. According to Freud, Lewis' failure to remember these painful memories is an example of _____ .

Memory Construction

Objective 11: Explain how misinformation, imagination, and source amnesia can distort our memory of an event.

Memories are not stored as exact copies, and they certainly are not retrieved as such. Rather, we construct our memories, using both stored and new information. In many experiments, people have witnessed an event, received or not received misleading information about it, and then taken a memory test. The  repeated result is a *misinformation effect:* After exposure to subtle misinformation, many people misremember. Asking leading questions can plant false memories. As people recount an experience, they fill in their memory gaps with plausible guesses. Other vivid retellings may also implant false memories. Even *imagining* nonexistent actions and events can create false memories.

Our memory for the source of an event is particularly frail. In *source amnesia,* we link the wrong source with an event that we have experienced, heard about, read about, or imagined. Thus, we may recognize someone but have no idea where we have seen the person. Or we imagine or dream an event and later are uncertain whether it actually happened.

1. Research has shown that recall of an event is often influenced by our experiences and assumptions. The workings of these influences illustrate the process of memory _____ .

2. When witnesses to an event receive misleading information about it, they may experience a _____ _____ and misremember the event. A number of experiments have demonstrated that false memories _____ (can/cannot) be created when people are encouraged to imagine nonexistent events. This is because visualizing something and actually perceiving it activate similar _____ areas.

Describe what Loftus' studies have shown about the effects of misleading postevent information on eyewitness reports.

3. At the heart of many false memories is _____ _____ , which occurs when we retain the memory of an event but not the _____ in which we acquired it.

APPLICATION:

4. Which of the following illustrates the constructive nature of memory?
a. Janice keeps calling her new boyfriend by her old boyfriend's name.
b. After studying all afternoon and then getting drunk in the evening, Don can't remember the material he studied.
c. After getting some good news, elated Kareem has a flood of good memories from his younger years.
d. Although elderly Mrs. Harvey, who has Alzheimer's disease, has many gaps in her memory, she invents sensible accounts of her activities so that her family will not worry.

Objective 12: Discuss whether young children's eye-witness reports are reliable and the controversy over reports of repressed and recovered memories.

Because memory is often reconstructive, we can't be sure a memory is real by how real it feels. Preschool children are particularly sensitive to suggestion, and their memory of sexual abuse may be prone to error. Researchers who have used suggestive interviewing techniques have found that most preschoolers and many older children can be led to report false events. But, even young children can accurately recall events if a neutral person talks to them in words they can understand and uses less suggestive, more effective techniques.

Innocent people have been falsely convicted of abuse that never happened, and true abusers have used the controversy over recovered memories to avoid punishment. Forgetting of isolated past events, both negative and positive, is an ordinary part of life. Cued by a remark or an experience, we may later recover a memory. Controversy, however, focuses on whether the unconscious mind forcibly represses painful experiences and whether they can be retrieved by therapist-aided techniques. Memories "recovered" under hypnosis or drugs are especially unreliable, as are memories of things happening before age 3. Traumatic experiences are usually vividly remembered, not banished into an active but inaccessible unconscious.

5. Because memory is reconstruction as well as reproduction, we _____ (can/cannot) be sure whether a memory is real by how real it feels.

6. Research studies of children's eyewitness recall reveal that preschoolers and many older children _____ (are/are not) suggestible. For this reason, whether a child produces an accurate eyewitness memory depends heavily on how he or she is _____ .

7. Children are most accurate when it is a first interview with a _____ person who asks _____ questions.

8. Researchers increasingly agree that memories obtained under the influence of hypnosis or drugs _____ (are/are not) reliable.

9. Memories of events that happened before age _____ are unrelaible. This phenomenon is called _____ _____ .

Improving Memory

Objective 13: Explain how an understanding of memory can contribute to effective study techniques.

The psychology of memory suggests several effective study strategies. These include overlearning; using spaced practice; active rehearsal; making new material personally meaningful by relating it to what is already known; mentally re-creating the contexts and moods in which the original learning occurred in order to activate retrieval cues; minimizing interference, for example, by studying just before sleeping; and testing one's knowledge both to rehearse it and to determine what must still be learned.

Discuss several specific strategies for improving memory.

PROGRESS TEST

Multiple-Choice Questions

Circle your answers to the following questions and check them with the answers beginning on page 135. If your answer is incorrect, read the explanation for why it is incorrect and then consult the text.

1. The steps in memory information processing are
   a. input, processing, output.
   b. input, storage, output.
   c. input, storage, retrieval.
   d. encoding, storage, retrieval.

2. Which of the following is NOT a measure of retention?
   a. recall   c. relearning
   b. recognition   d. retrieval

3. Our short-term memory span is approximately _____ items.
   a. 2   c. 7
   b. 5   d. 10

4. Researchers have found that when learning occurs, more of the neurotransmitter _____ is released into synapses.
   a. ACh   c. serotonin
   b. dopamine   d. noradrenaline

5. Research on memory construction reveals that memories
   a. are stored as exact copies of experience.
   b. reflect a person's biases and assumptions.
   c. may be chemically transferred from one organism to another.
   d. even if long term, usually decay within about five years.

6. In a study on context cues, people learned words while on land or when they were underwater. In a later test of recall, those with the best retention had
   a. learned the words on land, that is, in the more familiar context.
   b. learned the words underwater, that is, in the more exotic context.
   c. learned the words and been tested on them in different contexts.
   d. learned the words and been tested on them in the same context.

7. The spacing effect means that
   a. study spread over time results in better retention than cramming.
   b. retention is improved when encoding and retrieval are separated by no more than one hour.
   c. learning causes a decrease in the size of the synaptic gap between certain neurons.
   d. delaying retrieval until memory has been coded improves recall.

8. Studies demonstrate that learning causes permanent neural changes in the _____ of animals' neurons.
   a. myelin
   b. cell bodies
   c. synapses
   d. all of these answers

9. In Sperling's memory experiment, research participants were shown three rows of three letters, followed immediately by a low, medium, or high tone, which indicated the row to remember. The participants were able to report
   a. all three rows with perfect accuracy.
   b. only the top row of letters.
   c. only the middle row of letters.
   d. any one of the three rows of letters.

10. Studies of memory-loss victims suggest that
   a. memory is a single, unified system.
   b. there are two distinct types of memory.
   c. there are three distinct types of memory.
   d. memory losses following brain trauma are unpredictable.

11. Memory for skills is called
   a. explicit memory.
   b. conscious memory.
   c. prime memory.
   d. implicit memory.

12. The eerie feeling of having been somewhere before is an example of
   a. state dependency.
   b. encoding failure.
   c. priming.
   d. déjà vu.

13. The three-stage processing model of memory was proposed by
   a. Richard Atkinson and Richard Shiffrin.
   b. Hermann Ebbinghaus.
   c. Elizabeth Loftus.
   d. George Sperling.

14. Memories produced under hypnosis may prove inaccurate—especially if the hypnotist asks leading questions—because of
   a. encoding failure.
   b. state-dependent memory.
   c. interference.
   d. memory construction.

15. Which area of the brain is most important in the processing of implicit memories?
   a. hippocampus   c. hypothalamus
   b. cerebellum   d. cortex

16. Which of the following terms does NOT belong with the others?
   a. misattribution   c. suggestibility
   b. blocking   d. bias

17. Which of the following best describes the typical forgetting curve?
   a. a steady, slow decline in retention over time
   b. a steady, rapid decline in retention over time
   c. a rapid initial decline in retention becoming stable thereafter
   d. a slow initial decline in retention becoming rapid thereafter

18. Psychologists found that memory was better in research participants who were
   a. awake during the retention period, presumably because decay was reduced.
   b. asleep during the retention period, presumably because decay was reduced.
   c. awake during the retention period, presumably because interference was reduced.
   d. asleep during the retention period, presumably because interference was reduced.

19. Which of the following is LEAST effective in triggering retrieval?
   a. recall   c. relearning
   b. recognition   d. They are equally sensitive.

20. Memory-loss victims typically have experienced damage to the _____ of the brain.
   a. frontal lobes   c. thalamus
   b. cerebellum   d. hippocampus

21. According to the serial position effect, when recalling a list of words you should have the greatest difficulty with those
   a. at the beginning of the list.
   b. at the end of the list.
   c. at the end and in the middle of the list.
   d. in the middle of the list.

22. If experimenters gave people a list of words to be recalled, the participants, who were tested after a delay, would recall best those words
   a. at the beginning of the list.
   b. in the middle of the list.
   c. at the end of the list.
   d. at the beginning and the end of the list.

23. *Long-term potentiation* refers to
   a. old memories interfering with the formation of new memories.
   b. recent memories interfering with the retrieval of old memories.
   c. our tendency to recall experiences that are consistent with our current mood.
   (d.) the increased efficiency of a synapse's firing potential following learning.

24. Repression is an example of
   a. encoding failure.   **(c.)** motivated forgetting.
   b. memory decay.   **d.** all of these events.

25. Research by Elizabeth Loftus, in which people were quizzed about a film of an accident, indicates that
   a. when quizzed immediately, people can recall very little, due to the stress of witnessing an accident.
   b. when questioned as little as one day later, their memory was very inaccurate.
   c. most people had very accurate memories as much as 6 months later.
   (d.) people's recall may easily be affected by misleading information.

26. Which of the following was NOT recommended as a strategy for improving memory?
   a. active rehearsal
   b. study spread over time
   (c.) speed reading
   d. encoding meaningful associations

27. The process of getting information out of memory storage is called
   a. encoding.   **c.** rehearsal.
   (b.) retrieval.   **d.** storage.

28. Memory-loss patients typically experience problems with
   a. implicit memories.   **c.** working memories.
   (b.) explicit memories.   **d.** flashbulb memories.

29. Information is maintained in working/short-term memory only briefly unless it is
   a. encoded.   **c.** suggestible.
   (b.) rehearsed.   **d.** retrieved.

30. Memory researchers are suspicious of long-repressed memories of traumatic events that are "recovered" with the aid of drugs or hypnosis because
   a. such experiences usually are vividly remembered.
   b. such memories are unreliable and easily influenced by misinformation.
   c. memories of events happening before about age 3 are especially unreliable.
   (d.) of all of these reasons.

31. The misinformation effect provides evidence that memory
   a. is constructed during encoding.
   b. is unchanging once established.
   (c.) may be reconstructed during recall according to how questions are framed.
   d. is highly resistant to misleading information.

32. According to memory researcher Daniel Schacter, blocking occurs when
   a. our inattention to details produces encoding failure.
   b. we confuse the source of information.
   c. our beliefs influence our recollections.
   (d.) information is on the tip of our tongue, but we can't get it out.

Matching Items

Match each definition or description with the appropriate term.

Definitions or Descriptions

_____ **1.** the process by which information gets into the memory system
_____ **2.** mental pictures that aid memory
_____ **3.** the blocking of painful memories
_____ **4.** the phenomenon in which one's mood can influence retrieval
_____ **5.** memory for a list of words is affected by word order
_____ **6.** memory demonstrated by time saved when learning material a second time
_____ **7.** old knowledge disrupts the recall of new learning
_____ **8.** misattributing the origin of an event
_____ **9.** the fading of unused information over time
_____ **10.** the lingering effects of misinformation
_____ **11.** a memory sin of intrusion

Terms

a. repression
b. relearning
c. serial position effect
d. persistence
e. interference
f. transience
g. source amnesia
h. suggestibility
i. imagery
j. mood-congruent memory
k. encoding

Application Essay

Discuss the points of agreement among experts as to whether recovered memories of child abuse are real or can be considered scientific evidence. (Use the space below to list the points you want to make, and organize them. Then write the essay on a separate piece of paper.)

SUMMING UP

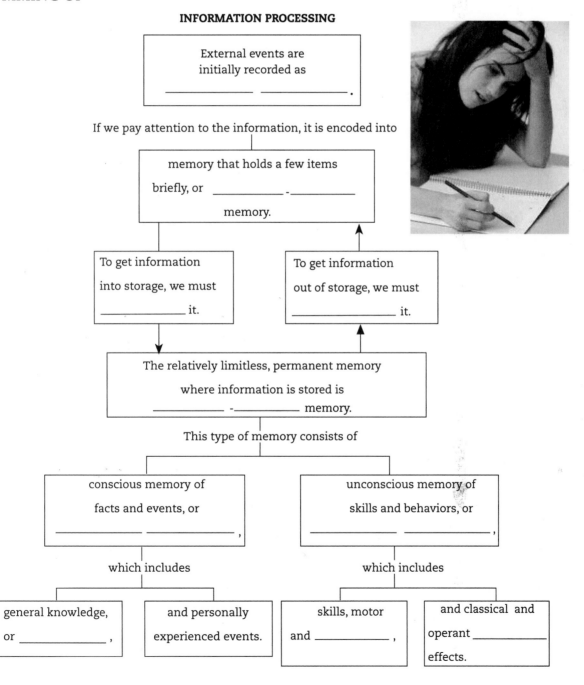

INFORMATION PROCESSING

External events are initially recorded as

_____ _____ .

If we pay attention to the information, it is encoded into

memory that holds a few items briefly, or _____ -_____ memory.

To get information into storage, we must _____ it.

To get information out of storage, we must _____ it.

The relatively limitless, permanent memory where information is stored is _____ -_____ memory.

This type of memory consists of

conscious memory of facts and events, or _____ _____ ,

unconscious memory of skills and behaviors, or _____ _____ ,

which includes

which includes

general knowledge, or _____ ,

and personally experienced events.

skills, motor and _____ ,

and classical and operant _____ effects.

TERMS AND CONCEPTS

Using your own words, on a separate piece of paper write a brief definition or explanation of each of the following terms.

1. memory
2. encoding
3. storage
4. retrieval
5. sensory memory
6. short-term memory
7. long-term memory
8. working memory
9. automatic processing
10. effortful processing
11. rehearsal
12. spacing effect
13. serial position effect
14. implicit memory
15. explicit memory
16. imagery
17. long-term potentiation (LTP)
18. flashbulb memory
19. recall
20. recognition
21. relearning
22. retrieval cue
23. déjà vu
24. mood-congruent memory
25. memory trace
26. interference
27. repression
28. misinformation effect
29. source amnesia

ANSWERS
Chapter Review

Studying Memory

1. memory
2. information-processing; encoding; storage; retrieval
3. three-stage processing; sensory memory; short-term; encoded; long-term
4. working; active
5. two-track; automatic; practice; experience
6. space; time; frequency
7. effortful
8. rehearsal
9. Hermann Ebbinghaus; fewer
10. spacing effect
11. serial position effect
12. automatic processing. Time and space—and therefore sequences of events—are often automatically processed.
13. is not
14. have not; implicit; are not; explicit
15. hippocampus; temporarily; do
16. implicit; reflexes
17. implicit; explicit. Mr. Flanagan has retained his memory of skills. However, he has lost his explicit memory, his awareness of what he knows.
18. c. is the answer. The hippocampus is involved in processing new facts for storage.

Building Memories

1. meaningful
2. imagery
3. better
4. visual; automatic. We may struggle to remember facts, but visual images occur automatically and stay with us.
5. sensory
6. about half; more; is
7. rehearsal; active
8. 7; George Miller
9. limit
10. Short-term memory capacity is about seven digits, so the ten-digit phone number may be above Brenda's short-term memory capacity.
11. synapses
12. serotonin
13. neural circuits; more; receptor sites; long-term potentiation; enzyme; LTP; faster
14. will not; will
15. enable
16. flashbulb; can
17. d. is the answer. Flashbulb memories are unusually clear memories of emotionally significant moments in life.
18. recall
19. recall; recognize
20. relearn; more
21. recall; recognition. Fill-in-the-blank questions provide no clues to the correct answer; multiple-choice questions allow you to recognize an answer that you might have seen before.
22. retrieval; encode

23. the same; prime

The déjà vu experience is most likely the result of being in a context similar to one that we have actually been in before. If we have previously been in a similar situation, though we cannot recall what it was, the current situation may present cues that unconsciously help us to retrieve the earlier experience.

24. mood-congruent

When happy, for example, we perceive things in a positive light and recall happy events; these perceptions and memories, in turn, prolong our good mood.

25. rejecting and punishing; have never suffered depression

26. state-dependent

27. retrieval cues. The names of nearby classmates provide retrieval cues for her memory of the forgotten classmate.

28. context effects. Being back in the context in which the original experiences occurred triggered memories of those experiences.

29. mood-congruent memory

30. **d.** is the answer. When recall is delayed, only the first items in a list are recalled more accurately than the others.

Forgetting

1. forget

2. forgetting; distortion; intrusion

3. encoding

4. enters the memory system

5. encodes; less

6. soon; forgetting curve

7. storage decay; memory trace

8. suggestibility. In this example, the questions Frank was asked to answer created misinformation that later became part of his memory.

9. retrieval

10. interference

11. better

12. repression

13. less

14. retrieval. The name of your homeroom teacher, which you probably heard at least once a day, was surely encoded and stored there for some time, so the problem had to be retrieval.

15. **b.** is the answer. Performing other activities, even just eating or listening to music, is more likely to disrupt memory than sleep is.

16. interference. In this case, old information made it difficult to recall new information.

17. repression. Although most researchers today believe that traumatic events are remembered vividly, Freud believed that we repressed painful memories.

Memory Construction

1. construction

2. misinformation effect; can; brain

When people viewed a film of a traffic accident and were quizzed a week later, phrasing of questions affected answers; the word "smashed," for instance, made viewers mistakenly think they had seen broken glass.

3. source amnesia; context

4. **d.** is the answer.

5. cannot

6. are; questioned

7. neutral; nonleading

8. are not

9. 3; infantile amnesia

Improving Memory

Suggestions for improving memory include rehearsing material over many separate and distributed study sessions with the objective of overlearning material. Studying should also involve active rehearsal, rather than mindless repetition of information. Organizing information, relating material to what is already known, developing numerous retrieval cues, and making the material meaningful are helpful, too. Frequent activation of retrieval cues, such as the context and mood in which the original learning occurred, can also help strengthen memory, as can recalling events while they are fresh, before possible misinformation is encountered. Studying should also be arranged to minimize potential sources of interference. Finally, self-tests in the same format (recall or recognition) that will later be used on the actual test are useful.

Progress Test

Multiple-Choice Questions

1. **d.** is the answer. Information must be encoded, or put into appropriate form; stored, or retained over time; and retrieved, or located and gotten out when needed.

2. **d.** is the answer. Retrieval refers to the *process* of remembering.

3. **c.** is the answer.

4. **c.** is the answer. Kandel and Schwartz found that when learning occurred in the sea slug *Aplysia*, serotonin was released at certain synapses, which then became more efficient at signal transmission.

5. **b.** is the answer. In essence, we construct our memories, bringing them into line with our biases and assumptions, as well as with our subsequent experiences.

a. If this were true, it would mean that memory construction does not occur. Through memory construction, memories may deviate significantly from the original experiences.

c. There is no evidence that such chemical transfers occur.

d. Many long-term memories are apparently unlimited in duration.

6. **d.** is the answer. In general, being in a context similar to that in which you experienced something will tend to help you recall the experience.
    a. & b. The learning environment per se—and its familiarity or exoticness—did not affect retention.

7. **a.** is the answer.
    b. & d. The text does not suggest that there is an optimal interval between encoding and retrieval.
    c. Learning increases the efficiency of synaptic transmission in certain neurons, but not by altering the size of the synapse.

8. **c.** is the answer.

9. **d.** is the answer. When asked to recall all the letters, participants could recall only about half; however, if immediately after the presentation they were signaled to recall a particular row, their recall was near perfect. This showed that they had a brief photographic memory—so brief that it faded in less time than it would have taken to say all nine letters.

10. **b.** is the answer. Because memory-loss victims lose their fact (explicit) memories but not their skill (implicit) memories or their capacity to learn, it appears that human memory can be divided into two distinct types.
    d. As studies of memory-loss victims show, memory losses following damage to the hippocampus are quite predictable.

11. **d.** is the answer.
    a. & b. Explicit (conscious) memory is memory of facts and experiences that one can consciously know.
    c. There is no such thing as prime memory.

12. **d.** is the answer.
    a. With state-dependent memory, information is best retrieved when the person is in the same emotional or physiological state he or she was in when the material was learned.
    b. Encoding failure occurs when a person has not processed information sufficiently for it to enter the memory system.
    c. Priming is the process by which a memory is activated through retrieval of an associated memory.

13. **a.** is the answer.
    b. Herman Ebbinghaus conducted pioneering studies of verbal learning and memory.
    c. Loftus and Palmer conducted influential research studies of eyewitness memory.
    d. George Sperling is known for his research studies of iconic memory.

14. **d.** is the answer. It is in both encoding and retrieval that we construct our memories, and as Loftus'

studies showed, leading questions affect people's memory construction.
    a. The memory encoding occurred at the time of the event in question, not during questioning by the hypnotist.
    b. State-dependent memory refers to the influence of one's own emotional or physiological state on encoding and retrieval, and would not apply here.
    c. Proactive interference is the interfering effect of prior learning on the recall of new information.

15. **b.** is the answer.
    a. The hippocampus is a temporary processing site for *explicit memories.*
    c. & d. These areas of the brain are not directly involved in the memory system.

16. **b.** is the answer. Blocking is an example of retrieval failure. Each of the others is an example of a "sin of distortion," in which memories, although inaccurate, are retrieved.

17. **c.** is the answer. As Ebbinghaus and others showed, most of the forgetting that is going to occur happens soon after learning.

18. **d.** is the answer.
    a. & b. This study did not find evidence that memories fade (decay) with time.
    c. When one is awake, there are many *more* potential sources of memory interference than when one is asleep.

19. **a.** is the answer. A test of recall presents the fewest retrieval cues and usually produces the most limited retrieval.

20. **d.** is the answer.

21. **d.** is the answer. According to the serial position effect, items at the beginning and end of a list tend to be remembered best.

22. **a.** is the answer.
    b. In the serial position effect, the items in the middle of the list always show the *poorest* retention.
    c. & d. Delayed recall erases the memory for items at the end of the list.

23. **d.** is the answer.

24. **c.** is the answer. According to Freud, we repress painful memories to preserve our self-concepts.
    a. & b. The fact that repressed memories can sometimes be retrieved suggests that they were encoded and have not decayed with time.

25. **d.** is the answer. When misled by the phrasings of questions, subjects incorrectly recalled details of the film and even "remembered" objects that weren't there.

26. **c.** is the answer. Speed reading, which entails little active rehearsal, yields poor retention.

27. **b.** is the answer.
    a. Encoding is the process of getting information *into* memory.
    c. Rehearsal is the conscious repetition of information in order to maintain it in memory.
    d. Storage is the maintenance of encoded material over time.

28. **b.** is the answer. Memory-loss patients typically have suffered damage to the hippocampus, a brain structure involved in processing explicit memories for facts.
    a. Memory-loss patients do retain implicit memories for how to do things; these are processed in the cerebellum.
    c. & d. Memory-loss patients generally do not experience impairment in their working or flashbulb memories.

29. **b.** is the answer.
    a. Information in short-term memory has *already* been encoded.
    c. Suggestibility is one of Schacter's "sins" of memory.
    d. Retrieval is the process of getting material out of storage and into conscious, short-term memory. Thus, all material in short-term memory has either already been retrieved or is about to be placed in storage.

30. **d.** is the answer.

31. **c.** is the answer. Loftus and Palmer found that eyewitness testimony could easily be altered when questions were phrased to imply misleading information.
    a. Although memories *are* constructed during encoding, the misinformation effect is a retrieval, rather than an encoding, phenomenon.
    b. & d. In fact, just the opposite is true.

32. **d.** is the answer.
    a. This defines absent-mindedness.
    b. This is misattribution.
    c. This is bias.

Matching Items

1.	k	6.	b	11.	d
2.	i	7.	e		
3.	a	8.	g		
4.	j	9.	f		
5.	c	10.	h		

Application Essay

Experts agree that child abuse is a real problem that can have long-term adverse effects on individuals. They also acknowledge that forgetting of isolated events, both good and bad, is an ordinary part of life. Although experts all accept the fact that recovered memories are commonplace, they warn that memories "recovered" under hypnosis or with the use of drugs are unreliable, as are memories of events before age 3. Finally, they agree that memories can be traumatic, whether real or false.

Summing Up

Information Processing

External events are initially recorded as *sensory memory*. If we pay attention to the information, it is encoded into memory that holds a few items briefly, or *short-term* memory. To get information into storage, we must *encode* it. To get information out of storage, we must *retrieve* it. The relatively limitless, permanent memory where information is stored is *long-term* memory. This type of memory consists of conscious memory of facts and events, or *explicit memory*, which includes general knowledge, or *facts,* and personally experienced events; and unconscious memory of skills and behaviors, *or implicit memory,* which includes skills, motor and *cognitive,* and classical and operant *conditioning* effects.

Key Terms and Concepts

1. **Memory** is the persistence of learning over time through the storage and retrieval of information.
2. **Encoding** is the first step in memory; information is translated into some form that enables it to enter our memory system.
3. **Storage** is the process by which encoded information is maintained over time.
4. **Retrieval** is the process of bringing to consciousness information from memory storage.
5. **Sensory memory** is the immediate, very brief recording of sensory information in the memory system.
6. **Short-term memory** is activated memory, which can hold about seven items for a short time.
7. **Long-term memory** is the relatively permanent and unlimited capacity memory system into which information from short-term memory may pass. It includes knowledge, skills, and experiences.
8. **Working memory** is the newer understanding of short-term memory as a work site for the active processing of incoming information, and of information retrieved from long-term memory.
9. **Automatic processing** refers to our unconscious encoding of incidental information such as space, time, and frequency and of well-learned information.
10. **Effortful processing** is encoding that requires attention and conscious effort.
11. **Rehearsal** is the conscious, effortful repetition of information that you are trying either to maintain in consciousness or to encode for storage.
12. The **spacing effect** is the tendency for study or practice spread over time to yield better long-term retention than cramming.
13. The **serial position effect** is the tendency for items at the beginning and end of a list to be more easily retained than those in the middle.
14. **Implicit memories** are memories of learned skills or conditioning, often without conscious awareness of this learning. These memories are evidently processed, not by the hippocampus, but by a more primitive part of the brain, the cerebellum.
15. **Explicit memories** are conscious memories of facts and personal events that you can consciously retrieve.

16. **Imagery** refers to mental pictures and can be an important aid to effortful processing.

17. **Long-term potentiation (LTP)** is an increase in a synapse's firing potential. LTP is believed to be the neural basis for learning and memory.

18. A **flashbulb memory** is an unusually vivid memory of an emotionally important moment or event.

19. **Recall** is memory demonstrated by retrieving information learned earlier.

20. **Recognition** is memory demonstrated by identifying previously learned information.

21. **Relearning** is memory demonstrated by time saved when learning material a second time.

22. A **retrieval cue** is any stimulus (event, feeling, place, and so on) linked to a specific memory.

23. **Déjà vu** is the eerie sense that you have already experienced a current situation.

24. **Mood-congruent memory** is the tendency to recall experiences that are consistent with our current mood.

25. A **memory trace** is an enduring physical change in the brain as a memory forms.

26. **Interference** is the blocking of recall as old or new learning disrupts the recall of other memories.

27. **Repression** is an example of motivated forgetting in that painful and unacceptable memories are prevented from entering consciousness. In psychoanalytic theory, it is the basic defense mechanism.

28. The **misinformation effect** is the tendency of eyewitnesses to an event to incorporate misleading information about the event into their memories.

29. At the heart of many false memories, **source amnesia** refers to attributing an event to the wrong source.

8 THINKING, LANGUAGE, AND INTELLIGENCE

The section on thinking emphasizes how people logically—or at times illogically—use tools such as algorithms and heuristics when making decisions and solving problems. Also discussed are several common obstacles to problem solving. The section concludes with discussions of the power and perils of intuition. The next section is concerned with language, including its structure, development in children, relationship to thinking, and use by animals. The rest of the chapter discusses intelligence, including whether intelligence is a single general ability or several specific ones. It describes the historical origins of intelligence tests and discusses several important issues concerning their use. The chapter also explores the extent of genetic and environmental influences on intelligence.

CHAPTER REVIEW

First, skim each text section, noting headings and bold-face items. Review the section by reading the objectives and summaries provided here, then answer the questions that follow. In some cases, STUDY TIPS explain how best to learn a difficult concept and APPLICATIONS help you to know how well you understand the material. Check your understanding of the material by consulting the answers beginning on page 153. Do not continue with the next section until you understand each answer. If you need to, review or reread the section in the textbook before continuing.

Thinking

Objective 1: Define *cognition*, and compare algorithms, heuristics, and insight as problem-solving strategies.

Cognition refers to the mental activities associated with thinking, knowing, remembering, and communicating. Problem solving is one of our most impressive cognitive skills. We approach some problems through trial and error, attempting various solutions until stumbling on one that works. For other problems we may follow a methodical rule or step-by-step procedure called an **algorithm**. Because algorithms can be laborious, we often rely instead on simple thinking strategies called **heuristics**. Speedier than algorithms, heuristics are also more error-prone. Sometimes, however, we are unaware of using any problem-solving strategy; the answer just comes to us as a sudden flash of **insight**.

1. Cognition can be defined as _____ _____ .

   Humans are especially capable of using their reasoning powers for coping with new situations, and thus for _____ _____ .

2. When we try each possible solution to a problem, we are using _____ _____ _____ .

3. Logical, methodical, step-by-step procedures for solving problems are called _____ .

4. Simple thinking strategies that allow us to solve problems efficiently are referred to as _____ .

5. When you suddenly realize a problem's solution, _____ has occurred.

STUDY TIP/APPLICATION: We all use any of four techniques for solving problems: trial and error, algorithms, heuristics, and insight. To test your understanding of these approaches, apply them to a problem you might actually face, such as finding a misplaced set of car keys. Using the chart below, see if you can come up with an example of how you could find your keys using each of the four problem-solving approaches.

6. Problem-Solving Approach	How You Would Find Car Keys Using Each Method
a. Trial and error	
b. Algorithm	
c. Heuristics	
d. Insight	

APPLICATIONS:

7. A dessert recipe that gives you the ingredients, their amounts, and the steps to follow is an example of a(n)

   _____ .

8. Boris the chess master selects his next move by considering moves that would threaten his opponent's queen. His opponent, a chess-playing computer, selects its next move by considering all possible moves. Boris is using a(n) _____ and the computer is using a(n) _____ .

Objective 2: Describe the obstacles that can hinder smart thinking.

A major obstacle to problem solving is the **availability heuristic**, which operates when we base our judgments on the availability of information in our memories. If instances of an event come to mind readily, we presume such events are common. Heuristics enable us to make snap judgments. However, these quick decisions sometimes lead us to ignore important information or to underestimate the chances of something happening.

Another obstacle to problem solving is **fixation**—the inability to see a problem from a fresh perspective. It may interfere with our taking a fresh approach when faced with problems that demand an entirely new solution.

Another obstacle is our eagerness to search for information that confirms our ideas, a phenomenon known as **confirmation bias.** This can mean that once we form a wrong idea, we will not budge from our illogic.

Overconfidence, the tendency to overestimate the accuracy of our knowledge and judgments, can have adaptive value. People who err on the side of overconfidence live more happily, find it easier to make tough decisions, and seem more believable than others.

The same issue presented in two different but logically equivalent ways can elicit quite different answers. This **framing** effect suggests that our judgments and decisions may not be well reasoned and that those who understand the power of framing can use it to influence important decisions—for example, by wording survey questions to support or reject a particular viewpoint.

We exhibit **belief perseverance,** clinging to our ideas in the face of contrary evidence, because the explanation we accepted as valid lingers in our minds. Once beliefs are formed and justified, it takes more compelling evidence to change them than it did to create them. The best remedy for this form of bias is to make a deliberate effort to consider evidence supporting the opposite position.

9. When we judge the likelihood of something occurring in terms of how readily it comes to mind, we are using the _____

   _____ .

10. Not being able to take a new perspective when attempting to solve a problem is referred to as

    _____ .

11. The tendency of people to look for information that supports their preconceptions is called

    _____ _____ .

12. The tendency of people to overestimate the accuracy of their knowledge results in _____ .

13. Overconfidence has _____ value because self-confident people tend to live _____ (more/less) happily, find it _____ (easier/harder) to make tough decisions, and seem _____ (more/less) believable than others.

14. When research participants are given prompt and clear feedback on the accuracy of their judgments, such feedback generally _____ (does/does not) help them become more realistic about how much they know.

15. The way an issue is posed is called _____ . This effect _____ (does/does not) influence our decisions about what to buy or who to vote for, for example.

16. Research has shown that once we form a belief, it may take more convincing evidence for us to change the belief than it did to create it; this is because of

    _____ _____ .

17. A cure for this is to _____

    _____ _____ .

APPLICATIONS:

18. During a televised political debate, the Republican and Democratic candidates each argued that the results of a recent public opinion poll supported their party's platform regarding sexual harassment. Because both candidates saw the information as supporting their belief, it is clear that both were victims of _____

    _____ .

19. Dominic is certain that he will be able to finish reading the assigned text chapter over the weekend even though he also has to write a five-page essay on the U.S. political process and will be going to a party on Saturday night. If he's like most people, Dominic
    a. is accurate in knowing how much he can do over the weekend.
    b. underestimates how much he'll get done over the weekend.
    c. overestimates how much he can get done over the weekend.

20. In relation to ground beef, consumers respond more positively to an ad describing it as "75 percent lean" than to one referring to its "25 percent fat" content. This is an example of the _____ effect.

21. Which of the following illustrates belief perseverance?
    a. Your belief remains intact even in the face of evidence to the contrary.
    b. You refuse to listen to arguments counter to your beliefs.
    c. You tend to become flustered and angered when your beliefs are refuted.
    d. You tend to search for information that supports your beliefs.

Objective 3: Discuss why we tend to fear the wrong things, noting how we can improve our risk assessment.

Our intuition about risk can be wrong because of four forces that feed our fears. First, we fear what our ancestral history has prepared us to fear. Also, we fear what we cannot control, what is immediate, and what is most readily available in memory.

22. Many people fear terrorism more than accidents, despite the fact that these fears are not supported by death and injury statistics. This type of faulty thinking occurs because we fear
    a. _____
    b. _____
    c. _____
    d. _____

APPLICATION:

23. Airline reservations typically decline after a highly publicized airplane crash because people overestimate the incidence of such disasters. In such instances, their decisions are being influenced by the _____
_____ .

Objective 4: Describe the usefulness of intuition in our judgments and decision making.

Although human intuition is sometimes perilous, it can be remarkably efficient and adaptive. Moreover, it feeds our creativity, our love, and our spirituality. Intuition is born of experience. As we gain expertise in a field, we become better at making quick, adept judgments. Experienced nurses, firefighters, art critics, and hockey players learn to size up a situation in an eyeblink. Smart thinkers recognize that their gut reactions are terrific at some things, for example, reading emotions in others' faces, but not so good at other things, such as assessing risks.

24. Intuitive reactions allow us to react
_____ and in ways that are
usually _____ .

Language

Objective 5: Trace the course of language development from the babbling stage through the two-word stage.

Children's *language* development moves from simplicity to complexity. Their *receptive language* abilities mature before their *productive language*. Beginning at about 4 months, infants enter a **babbling stage** in which they spontaneously utter various sounds at first unrelated to the household language. By about age 10 months, a trained ear can identify the language of the household by listening to an infant's babbling. Around the first birthday, most children enter the **one-word stage,** and by their second birthday, they are uttering two-word sentences. This **two-word stage** is characterized by **telegraphic speech.** This soon leads to their uttering longer phrases, and by early elementary school, they understand complex sentences.

1. Language is defined as _____
_____ .

   The correct way to string words together to form sentences is the language's _____

2. By _____ months of age, babies can read lips and sort out speech sounds. This marks the beginning of their _____
_____ , their ability to understand what is said to them. This ability begins to mature before their _____ _____ ,
or ability to produce words.

3. The first stage of language development, in which children spontaneously utter different sounds, is the _____ stage. This stage typically begins at about _____
months of age. The sounds children make during this stage _____ (do/do not) include only the sounds of the language they hear.

4. Deaf infants who observe their Deaf parents _____ begin to babble more with their hands.

5. As infant babbling begins to resemble the household language, the ability to perceive speech sounds outside the infant's native language is _____ (lost/acquired).

6. During the second stage, called the
_____-_____
stage, children convey complete thoughts using single words. This stage begins at about _____ year(s) of age.

7. During the _____-_____ stage, children speak in sentences containing mostly nouns and verbs. This type of speech is called _____ speech.

8. After this stage, children quickly begin to utter longer phrases that _____ (do/do not) follow the rules of syntax.

APPLICATIONS:

9. A listener hearing a recording of Japanese, Spanish, and North American 6-month-old infants babbling would

  a. not be able to tell them apart.

  b. be able to tell them apart if they were older than 6 months.

  c. be able to tell them apart if they were older than 10 months.

  d. be able to tell them apart at any age.

10. The child who says "Milk gone" is engaging in _____ _____ . This type of utterance demonstrates that children are actively experimenting with the rules of _____ .

Objective 6: Discuss how children acquire grammar, and explain why critical periods are an important concept in children's language learning.

Noam Chomsky notes that children are born with a built-in readiness to learn grammar rules. He argues that children acquire untaught words and grammar so well that it can't be explained solely by training. Moreover, there is a *universal grammar* that underlies all human language.

Childhood does seem to represent a *critical period* for certain aspects of learning. Research indicates that children who have not been exposed to either a spoken or signed language by about age 7 gradually lose their ability to master any language. Learning a second language also becomes more difficult after the window of opportunity closes.

11. The theorist who believes that humans are born with a built-in readiness to learn grammar rules is _____ . This theorist argues that all human languages have the same grammatical building blocks, which suggests that there is a

_____ _____ .

12. Childhood seems to represent a _____ _____ for mastering certain aspects of language. Those who learn a second language as adults _____ (do/do not) understand English grammar as well as native speakers do.

13. The window for learning language gradually begins to close after age _____ . When a young brain doesn't learn any language, its language-learning capacity _____ (never/may still) fully develop(s).

Objective 7: Describe the value of thinking in images.

We often think in images. In remembering how we do things, for example, turning on the water in the bathroom, we use a mental picture of how we do it. Imagining a physical activity triggers action in the same brain areas that are triggered when actually performing that activity. Researchers have found that thinking in images is especially useful for mentally practicing upcoming events (*process simulation*) and can actually increase our skills.

14. It appears that thinking _____ (can/cannot) occur without the use of language.

15. Athletes often supplement physical practice with _____ practice.

16. Research studies have shown that imagining an event can activate _____ _____ in the brain.

17. In one study of psychology students preparing for a midterm exam, the greatest benefits were achieved by those who visualized themselves _____ (receiving a high grade/studying effectively).

APPLICATION:

18. Luke is the backup quarterback for his high school football team. The starting quarterback has been injured, so Luke will play on Saturday. In addition to physical practice, Luke should visualize throwing the ball, a process called _____ _____ , rather than seeing a touchdown noted on the scoreboard, called _____ _____ .

Objective 8: List the cognitive skills shared by the humans and other animals, and outline the arguments for and against the idea that animals and humans share the capacity for language.

Animals show remarkable capacities for thinking. Like humans, they can (1) form concepts, (2) comprehend numbers, (3) display insight, (4) use tools, and (5) transmit cultural patterns. They have other cognitive skills as well, including the ability to read intent and self-awareness.

Animals obviously communicate. Vervet monkeys have different alarm cries for different predators. Several teams of psychologists have taught various species of apes, including a number of chimpanzees, to communicate with humans by signing or by pushing buttons. Apes have developed considerable vocabularies. They string words together to express meaning and have taught their skills to younger animals. Skeptics point out important differences between apes' and humans' facilities with language, especially in their respective abilities to master the verbal or signed expression of complex rules of grammar. Nevertheless, studies reveal that apes have considerable ability to think and communicate.

19. Animals are capable of forming

   _____ . Wolfgang Köhler demonstrated that chimpanzees also exhibit the "Aha!" reaction that characterizes reasoning by

   _____ .

20. Forest-dwelling chimpanzees learn to use branches, stones, and other objects as _____ . These behaviors, along with behaviors related to grooming and courtship, _____ (vary/ do not vary) from one group to another, suggesting the transmission of _____ customs.

21. Animals definitely _____ .

22. The Gardners attempted to communicate with the chimpanzee Washoe by teaching her

   _____ _____ .

23. Skeptics believe that interpreting chimpanzees' signs may be little more than the trainers' wishful thinking, an example of _____

   _____ .

24. Most now agree that humans _____ (alone/along with primates) possess language that involves complex grammar.

Summarize some of the arguments of skeptics of animal language research and some responses of believers.

Intelligence

Objective 9: Discuss the difficulty of defining *intelligence*, and present arguments as to whether intelligence should be considered one general ability or many specific abilities.

Intelligence varies from context to context. Thus, most psychologists now define intelligence as the ability to learn from experience, solve problems, and use knowledge to adapt to new situations.

Charles Spearman granted that people have specific abilities, such as verbal and mathematical aptitudes, but he believed that a *general intelligence (g)* factor runs through all our intelligent behavior. Spearman's position stemmed in part from *factor analysis*, a statistical tool that searches for clusters of related items.

Howard Gardner disagrees. Evidence that brain damage may diminish one ability but not others, as well as studies of *savant syndrome,* led Gardner to propose his theory of multiple intelligences. These include linguistic, logical-mathematical, musical, spatial, bodily-kinesthetic, intrapersonal, interpersonal, and naturalist.

Recent research has confirmed that there is a general intelligence factor. But intelligence alone doesn't predict success. Grit (your motivation and drive) is also important.

1. In any context, intelligence can be defined as

   _____

   _____ .

2. One controversy regarding the nature of intelligence centers on whether intelligence is one _____ ability or several _____ abilities.

3. Charles Spearman, based in part on his work with the statistical tool _____

   _____ , believed that a factor called *g*, or _____

   _____ , runs through the more specific aspects of intelligence.

4. People with _____ _____ score at the low end of intelligence tests but possess exceptional specific skills. Many such people also have the developmental disorder

   _____ .

5. Howard Gardner proposes that there are

   _____ _____ , each independent of the others. However, critics point out that the world is not so just: People with mental disadvantages often have lesser _____ abilities as well. General intelligence scores _____ (do/do not) predict performance on complex tasks and in various jobs. But equally important for success is a person's _____ , his or her motivation and drive.

APPLICATION:

6. Melvin is limited in mental ability but has an exceptional ability to play complex music on the piano after hearing it only once. He has been diagnosed as having

_____ _____ .

Objective 10: Identify the factors associated with creativity, and explain what psychologists mean by emotional intelligence.

Creativity requires a certain level of aptitude, but beyond a score of about 120 on a standard intelligence test, the correlation between intelligence scores and creativity disappears. Robert Sternberg views creativity as a separate form of intelligence, with five necessary parts: expertise, imaginative thinking skills, a venturesome personality, intrinsic motivation, and a creative environment.

The four components of *emotional intelligence,* a critical part of *social intelligence,* are (1) the ability to perceive emotions (to recognize them in faces, music, and stories), (2) to understand emotions (to predict them and how they change and blend), (3) to manage emotions (to know how to express them in varied situations), and (4) to use emotions to enable adaptive or creative thinking. Those who are emotionally smart often succeed in careers, marriages, and parenting where other academically smarter (but emotionally less intelligent) people fail.

7. The ability to produce ideas that are both novel and valuable is called _____ . The relationship between intelligence and creativity holds only up to a certain point—an intelligence score of about _____ .

Describe five components of creativity other than intelligence.

8. Social intelligence is defined as _____

_____ .

9. A critical part of social intelligence is

_____ _____—

the ability to _____ ,

_____ , _____ ,

and _____ emotions.

Briefly describe emotionally intelligent people.

APPLICATIONS:

10. Vanessa is a very creative sculptress. We would expect that Vanessa also
    a. has an exceptionally high intelligence score.
    b. tries to solve problems in ways that worked before.
    c. has a venturesome personality and is intrinsically motivated.
    d. lacks expertise in most other skills.

11. Gerardeen has superb social skills, manages conflicts well, and has great empathy for her friends and co-workers. Researchers would probably say that Gerardeen possesses a high degree of

_____ _____ .

Objective 11: Discuss the history of intelligence testing, and describe modern tests of mental abilities such as the WAIS.

Psychologists define an **intelligence test** as a method for assessing an individual's mental aptitudes and comparing them with those of others, using numerical scores. Barely a century ago, psychologists undertook to assess people's **aptitude** (ability) to learn as well as their **achievement.** The modern intelligence-testing movement started when French psychologist Alfred Binet began assessing intellectual abilities. Together with Théodore Simon, Binet developed an intelligence test containing questions that assessed **mental age** and helped predict children's future progress in the Paris school system. The test sought to identify French schoolchildren needing special attention.

Lewis Terman of Stanford University adapted Binet's test as the **Stanford-Binet;** he had found that the Paris-developed age norms did not work well with California schoolchildren. William Stern derived the **intelligence quotient,** or **IQ,** for Terman's test. The IQ was simply a person's mental age divided by chronological age multiplied by 100. Today, we refer to intelligence test scores, which represent the test-taker's performance relative to the average performance (assigned a score of 100) of others the same age.

The **Wechsler Adult Intelligence Test (WAIS),** created by David Wechsler, is the most widely used intelligence test. It consists of 11 subtests and yields not only an overall intelligence score but also separate verbal comprehension, perceptual organization, working memory, and processing speed scores. Striking differences among these scores can provide clues to cognitive strengths or weaknesses that teachers or therapists might build upon.

12. Tests that assess a person's mental capacities and compare them to those of others, using numerical scores, are called _____ tests. Tests designed to predict your ability to learn something new are called _____ tests. Tests designed to measure what you have already learned are called _____ tests.

13. The French psychologist who devised a test to predict the success of children in school was _____ . Predictions were made by comparing children's chronological age with their _____ age, which was determined by the test.

14. Lewis Terman's revision of Binet's test is referred to as the _____-_____ . William Stern developed the formula for computing a test-taker's performance. The term for the person's score was _____ _____ .

Give the original formula for computing IQ, and explain any items used in the formula.

15. Today's tests _____ (do/do not) compute an IQ score. They represent the test-taker's performance relative to the average performance of others of _____ (the same/different) age(s). These tests are designed so that a score of _____ is considered average.

16. The most widely used intelligence test is the

_____ _____

_____ _____ .

Consisting of 11 subtests, it provides not only a general intelligence score but also separate scores for

_____ _____ ,

_____ _____ ,

_____ _____ ,

and _____ _____ .

17. Before becoming attorneys, law students must pass a special licensing exam, which is an _____ test. Before entering college, high school students must take the SAT, which is an _____ test.

18. Benito was born in 1937. In 1947, he scored 130 on an intelligence test. Benito's mental age when he took the test was _____ .

19. If asked to guess the intelligence score of a stranger, your best guess would be _____ .

Objective 12: Discuss the criteria for judging intelligence tests, including standardization, reliability, and validity.

Because scores become meaningful only when they can be compared with others' performance, they must be defined relative to a pretested group, a process called *standardization*. Obviously, the group on which a test is standardized must be representative of those who will be taking the test in the future. Standardized test results typically form a bell-shaped pattern of scores that forms the *normal curve*. Most scores cluster around average, and increasingly fewer are distributed at the extremes.

Reliability refers to the extent to which a test yields consistent scores. Consistency may be assessed by comparing scores on two halves of the test or on retesting. A test can be reliable but not valid.

Validity refers to the extent to which a test measures or predicts what it is supposed to. Intelligence tests do have *predictive validity:* They can predict future performance.

20. One requirement of a good test is the process of defining meaningful scores by comparison with the performance of a pretested group, which is called

_____ .

21. When scores on a test are compiled, they generally result in a bell-shaped pattern, or

_____ _____ .

Describe this bell-shaped pattern, and explain its significance in the standardization process.

22. If a test yields consistent results, it is said to be

_____ .

23. To determine a test's reliability, researchers may retest people using _____ (the same/a different) test or they may _____

_____ .

24. The degree to which a test measures or predicts what it is supposed to is referred to as the test's

_____ .

25. The degree to which a test predicts future performance of a particular behavior is referred to as the test's _____ _____ .

APPLICATIONS:

26. If you wanted to develop a test of musical aptitude in North American children, which would be the appropriate standardization group?
   a. children all over the world
   b. North American children
   c. children of musical parents
   d. children with known musical ability

27. Jack takes the same test of mechanical reasoning on several different days and gets virtually identical scores. This suggests that the test has high _____ .

28. You would not use a test of hearing ability as an intelligence test because it would lack _____ .

Objective 13: Discuss the evidence for genetic and environmental contributions to individual intelligence, and explain what psychologists mean by the heritability of intelligence.

Studies of twins, family members, and adopted children together point to a significant genetic contribution to intelligence scores. For example, even when identical twins are reared separately, their test scores are similar. Furthermore, the most genetically similar people have the most similar scores. However, shared environment also matters. *Heritability* refers to the extent to which differences among people are attributable to genes. To say that the heritability of intelligence is 50 percent does not mean that half of an individual's intelligence is inherited. Rather, it means that we can attribute to heredity 50 percent of the variation of intelligence among those studied.

Studies of children reared in extremely neglectful or enriched environments also indicate that life experiences significantly influence intelligence test scores. However, although extreme deprivation can retard normal brain development, there is no environmental recipe for creating a genius out of a normal infant.

29. The intelligence scores of identical twins reared together are _____ (more/no more) similar than those of fraternal twins.

30. The intelligence test scores of fraternal twins are _____ (more alike/no more alike) than the intelligence test scores of other siblings. This provides evidence of a(n) _____ (genetic/environmental) effect because fraternal twins, being the same _____ , are treated more alike.

31. Studies of adopted children and their adoptive and biological families demonstrate that with age, genetic influences on intelligence become _____ (more/less) apparent. Thus, children's intelligence scores are more like those of their _____ (biological/adoptive) parents than those of their _____ (biological/adoptive) parents.

32. The amount of variation in a trait within a group that is attributed to genetic factors is called its _____ . For intelligence, this has been estimated as _____ percent.

33. If we know a trait has perfect heritability, this knowledge _____ (does/does not) enable us to rule out environmental factors in explaining differences between groups.

34. Studies indicate that neglected children _____ (do/do not) show signs of recovery in intelligence and behavior when placed in more nurturing environments. Although normal brain development can be retarded by _____ , _____ deprivation, and _____ , there is no sure environment that will produce a "superbaby."

STUDY TIP: Heritability is a difficult concept to grasp in part because it is often confused with genetic determination, which refers to what causes a characteristic to develop. The number of toes on your feet is genetically determined because your genes cause five toes to develop on each foot. Heritability, on the other hand, is what causes differences in a characteristic. As explained in the text, to say that the heritability of intelligence is 50 percent does not mean that half of an individual's intelligence is inherited. Rather, it means that we can attribute to heredity 50 percent of the variation of intelligence among those studied. A good way to keep the two concepts straight is to remember that while the concept of genetic determination makes sense in the case of a single person, heritability does not. Genetic determination is biological; heritability is a statistical measure. Heritability only makes sense relative to differences among groups of people. It doesn't make sense to ask, "What's the heritability of my intelligence?"

APPLICATION:

35. Raoul and Fidel are identical twins separated at birth. Because they have similar heredity and different environments, heritability for their intelligence is likely to be _____ (high/low). Ramona was adopted by Francesa's parents when she was 2 months old. The heritability for their intelligence is likely to be _____ (high/low).

Objective 14: Describe ethnic group differences in intelligence test scores, and discuss some genetic and environmental factors that might explain them.

Black Americans average about 10 points lower than White Americans on intelligence tests. European New Zealanders outscore native Maori New Zealanders, Israeli Jews outscore Israeli Arabs, and most Japanese outscore the stigmatized Japanese minority. Research suggests that environmental differences are largely responsible for these group differences. Consider: (1) Genetics research indicates that the races are remarkably alike under the skin; (2) race is not a neatly defined biological category; (3) intelligence test performance of today's better-fed, better-educated, and more test-prepared population exceeds that of the 1930s population by the same margin that the score of the average White today exceeds that of the average Black; (4) White and Black infants tend to score equally well on tests measuring preferences for looking at novel stimuli—a predictor of future intelligence; (5) Asian students outperform North American students on math achievement and aptitude tests; and (6) in different eras, different ethnic groups have experienced periods of remarkable achievement.

36. Research evidence suggests that group differences in intelligence are mainly _____ (genetic/environmental).

37. Group differences in intelligence scores _____ (do/do not) provide an accurate basis for judging individuals. Individual differences within a race are _____ (greater than/less than) between-race differences. Furthermore, race _____ (is/is not) a neatly defined biological category.

38. The test scores of today's better-educated population are _____ (higher/lower) than those of earlier populations, and in different eras, different _____ groups have experienced golden ages.

39. On an infant intelligence measure (preference for looking at novel stimuli), Black infants score _____ (lower than/higher than/as well as) White infants.

40. Although Asian students on the average score _____ (higher/lower) than North American students on math tests, this difference may be due to the fact that _____ _____ .

APPLICATION:

41. Hiroko, who goes to school in Osaka, Japan, has a math achievement score that is considerably higher than that of most American students her age. Explain this difference between Asian and North American students.

_____

_____

Objective 15: Describe gender differences in cognitive abilities.

Although gender similarities far outnumber gender differences, we find the differences in abilities more interesting. Research indicates that, compared to boys, girls are better spellers, are more verbally fluent, are better at locating objects, and are more sensitive to touch, taste, and color. Boys are more likely than girls to be underachievers and to outperform girls at math problem solving but underperform them in math computation. Women detect emotions more easily than do men.

42. Females tend to outscore males on _____ tests and are more _____ fluent. They also have an edge in locating objects; are more sensitive to odor, _____ , and _____ ; and are better _____ detectors.

43. The gender gap in math achievement _____ (varies/does not vary) across countries. The stronger a culture's _____-_____ stereotype, the greater the gender difference. Males tend to outscore females on tests of _____ _____ .

44. Working from an _____ perspective, some theorists speculate that these gender differences in spatial manipulation helped our ancestors survive.

Objective 16: Discuss whether intelligence tests are biased, and describe the stereotype threat phenomenon.

Intelligence tests are "biased" in the sense that they are sensitive to performance differences caused by cultural experience. However, tests are not biased in that they predict as accurately for one group as they do for another. For example, the predictive validity is roughly the same for women and men, for Blacks and Whites, and for rich and poor. *Stereotype threat* is a self-confirming concern that one will be evaluated based on a negative stereotype. The phenomenon sometimes appears in intelligence testing among Blacks and among women.

45. In the sense that they detect differences caused by cultural experiences, intelligence tests probably _____ (are/are not) biased.

46. Most psychologists agree that, in terms of predictive validity, the major aptitude tests _____ (are/are not) biased in the scientific meaning of the term.

47. When women and members of ethnic minorities are led to expect that they won't do well on a test, a

_____ _____

may result, and their scores may actually be lower.

PROGRESS TEST

Multiple-Choice Questions

Circle your answers to the following questions and check them with the answers beginning on page 155. If your answer is incorrect, read the explanation for why it is incorrect and then consult the text.

1. The text defines *cognition* as
   a. silent speech.
   b. all mental activity.
   c. mental activity associated with thinking, knowing, remembering, and communicating information.
   d. logical reasoning.

2. Confirmation bias refers to the tendency to
   a. overestimate the accuracy of your beliefs and judgments.
   b. cling to your initial conceptions after the basis on which they were formed has been discredited.
   c. search randomly through alternative solutions when problem solving.
   d. look for information that is consistent with your beliefs.

3. Which of the following is NOT true of babbling?
   a. It is imitation of adult speech.
   b. It is the same in all cultures.
   c. It typically occurs from about age 4 months to 1 year.
   d. Babbling increasingly comes to resemble a particular language.

4. Which of the following has been argued by critics of ape language research?
   a. Ape language is merely imitation of the trainer's behavior.
   b. There is little evidence that apes can equal even a 3-year-old's ability to order words with proper syntax.
   c. Interpreting chimpanzee signs as language may be little more than the trainers' wishful thinking.
   d. All of these points have been argued.

5. Which of the following BEST describes Chomsky's view of language development?
   a. Humans are born with a built-in specific language.
   b. Language is an innate ability.
   c. Humans have a biological predisposition to acquire language.
   d. There are no social influences on the development of language.

6. Which of the following is an example of the use of heuristics?
   a. trying every possible letter ordering when unscrambling a word
   b. considering each possible move when playing chess
   c. using the formula "area = length x width" to find the area of a rectangle
   d. playing chess using a defensive strategy that has often been successful for you

7. The chimpanzee Sultan used a short stick to pull a longer stick that was out of reach into his cage. He then used the longer stick to reach a piece of fruit. Researchers hypothesized that Sultan's discovery of the solution to his problem was the result of
   a. trial and error.   **c.** fixation.
   b. heuristics.   **d.** insight.

8. Researchers who are convinced that animals can think point to evidence that
   a. monkeys can learn to classify dogs and cats.
   b. chimpanzees regularly use branches, stones, and other objects as tools in their natural habitats.
   c. chimps invent grooming and courtship customs and pass them on to their peers.
   d. all of these are true.

9. Deaf children who are NOT exposed to sign language until they are teenagers
   a. are unable to master the basic words of sign language.
   b. learn the basic words but not how to order them.
   c. are unable to master either the basic words or syntax of sign language.
   d. never become as fluent as those who learned to sign at a younger age.

10. A 6-year-old child has a mental age of 9. Using the original formula, the child's IQ would be
   a. 96.   **c.** 125.
   b. 100.   **d.** 150.

11. Which of the following is NOT true?
   a. In spatial ability, males have an edge over females.
   b. In science and math achievement, males always surpass females.
   c. Women are better than men at detecting emotions.

d. Males score higher than females on tests of spatial abilities.

12. One reason psychologists give for their belief that racial gaps in test scores are environmental is that
    a. the differences are too large to be explained biologically.
    b. the heritability of intelligence is increasing.
    c. race is primarily a social category, not a neatly defined biological category.
    d. the gap is increasing as environment changes.

13. Standardization refers to the process of
    a. determining the portion of test-score variation that can be assigned to genes.
    b. defining meaningful scores relative to a representative pretested group.
    c. determining the consistency of test scores obtained by retesting people.
    d. measuring the success with which a test predicts the behavior it is designed to predict.

14. Which of the following is NOT a requirement of a good test?
    a. reliability   **c.** fixation
    b. standardization   **d.** validity

15. First-time parents Geena and Brad want to give their baby's intellectual abilities a jump start by providing a super-enriched learning environment. Experts would suggest that the new parents should
    a. pipe stimulating classical music into the baby's room.
    b. hang colorful mobiles and artwork over the baby's crib.
    c. take the child to one of the new "superbaby" preschools that specialize in infant enrichment.
    d. relax, since there is no surefire environmental recipe for giving a child a superior intellect.

16. Which of the following statements is true?
    a. The predictive validity of intelligence tests is not as high as their reliability.
    b. The reliability of intelligence tests is not as high as their predictive validity.
    c. Modern intelligence tests have extremely high predictive validity and reliability.
    d. The predictive validity and reliability of most intelligence tests is very low.

17. Which of the following best describes the relationship between creativity and intelligence?
    a. Creativity appears to depend on the ability to think imaginatively and has little if any relationship to intelligence.
    b. Creativity is best understood as a certain kind of intelligence.
    c. The more intelligent a person is, the greater his or her creativity.
    d. A certain level of intelligence is necessary but not sufficient for creativity.

18. The existence of _____ reinforces the generally accepted notion that intelligence is a multidimensional quality.
    a. adaptive skills   **c.** general intelligence
    b. stereotype threat   **d.** savant syndrome

19. Current estimates are that _____ percent of the total variation among intelligence scores can be attributed to genetic factors.
    a. less than 10   **c.** 50
    b. 25   **d.** 75

20. Reported racial gaps in average intelligence scores are most likely due to
    a. the use of biased tests of intelligence.
    b. the use of unreliable tests of intelligence.
    c. genetic factors.
    d. environmental factors.

21. The bell-shaped pattern of intelligence scores in the general population is called a
    a. *g* distribution.
    b. standardization curve.
    c. intelligence quotient.
    d. normal curve.

22. A common problem in everyday reasoning is our tendency to
    a. cling to our beliefs in the face of contrary evidence.
    b. accept as logical those conclusions that disagree with our own opinions.
    c. underestimate the accuracy of our knowledge.
    d. accept as logical conclusions that involve unfamiliar concepts.

23. Many psychologists are skeptical of claims that chimpanzees can acquire language because the chimps have not shown the ability to
    a. use symbols meaningfully.
    b. acquire speech.
    c. acquire even a limited vocabulary.
    d. use syntax in communicating.

24. Assume that Congress is considering revising its approach to welfare and to this end is hearing a range of testimony. A member of Congress who uses the availability heuristic would be most likely to
    a. want to experiment with numerous possible approaches to see which of these seems to work best.
    b. want to find the best solution by systematically examining every possibility.
    c. refuse to be budged from his or her beliefs despite persuasive testimony to the contrary.
    d. base his or her ideas on the most memorable testimony given, even though many of the statistics presented run counter to this testimony.

25. If you want to be absolutely certain that you will find the solution to a problem you know *is* solvable, you should use
    - **a.** a heuristic.
    - **b.** an algorithm.
    - **c.** insight.
    - **d.** trial and error.

26. Telegraphic speech is typical of the _____ stage.
    - **a.** babbling
    - **b.** one-word
    - **c.** two-word
    - **d.** three-word

27. Children first demonstrate a rudimentary understanding of syntax during the _____ stage.
    - **a.** babbling
    - **b.** one-word
    - **c.** two-word
    - **d.** three-word

28. The study in which people who immigrated to the United States at various ages were compared in terms of their ability to understand English grammar found that
    - **a.** age of arrival had no effect on mastery of grammar.
    - **b.** those who immigrated as children understood grammar as well as native speakers.
    - **c.** those who immigrated as adults understood grammar as well as native speakers.
    - **d.** whether or not English was spoken in the home was the most important factor in mastering the rules of grammar.

29. Researchers taught the chimpanzee Washoe to communicate by using
    - **a.** various sounds.
    - **b.** plastic symbols of various shapes and colors.
    - **c.** sign language.
    - **d.** all of these things.

30. The test created by Alfred Binet was designed specifically to
    - **a.** measure inborn intelligence in adults.
    - **b.** measure inborn intelligence in children.
    - **c.** predict school performance in children.
    - **d.** identify children who are mentally slow so that they could be institutionalized.

31. Which of the following provides the strongest evidence of environment's role in intelligence?
    - **a.** Adopted children's intelligence scores are more like their adoptive parents' scores than their biological parents'.
    - **b.** Children's intelligence scores are more strongly related to their mothers' scores than to their fathers'.
    - **c.** Children moved from a deprived environment into an intellectually enriched one show gains in intellectual development.
    - **d.** The intelligence scores of identical twins raised separately are no more alike than those of siblings.

32. If a test designed to indicate which applicants are likely to perform the best on the job fails to do so, the test has
    - **a.** low reliability.
    - **b.** low validity.
    - **c.** low predictive validity.
    - **d.** not been standardized.

33. The formula for the intelligence quotient was devised by
    - **a.** Sternberg.
    - **b.** Binet.
    - **c.** Terman.
    - **d.** Stern.

34. Current intelligence tests compute an individual's intelligence score as
    - **a.** the ratio of mental age to chronological age multiplied by 100.
    - **b.** the ratio of chronological age to mental age multiplied by 100.
    - **c.** the test-taker's performance relative to the average performance of others the same age.
    - **d.** the ratio of the test-taker's verbal intelligence score to his or her nonverbal intelligence score.

35. The concept of a *g* factor implies that intelligence
    - **a.** is a single overall ability.
    - **b.** is several specific abilities.
    - **c.** cannot be defined.
    - **d.** cannot be measured.

36. Most experts view intelligence as a person's
    - **a.** ability to perform well on intelligence tests.
    - **b.** innate mental capacity.
    - **c.** ability to learn from experience, solve problems, and adapt to new situations.
    - **d.** diverse skills acquired throughout life.

37. Originally, IQ was defined as
    - **a.** mental age divided by chronological age and multiplied by 100.
    - **b.** chronological age divided by mental age and multiplied by 100.
    - **c.** mental age subtracted from chronological age and multiplied by 100.
    - **d.** chronological age subtracted from mental age and multiplied by 100.

38. Which of the following statements most accurately reflects the text's position regarding the relative contribution of genes and environment in determining intelligence?
    - **a.** Except in cases of a neglectful early environment, each individual's basic intelligence is largely the product of heredity.
    - **b.** Intelligence is primarily the product of environmental experiences.
    - **c.** Both genes and life experiences significantly influence performance on intelligence tests.
    - **d.** Because intelligence tests have such low predictive validity, the question cannot be addressed until psychologists agree on a more valid test of intelligence.

39. The contribution of environmental factors to racial gaps in intelligence scores is indicated by
   a. evidence that individual differences within a race are much greater than differences between races.
   b. evidence that White and Black infants score equally well on certain measures of infant intelligence.
   c. the fact that Asian students outperform North American students on math achievement and aptitude tests.
   d. all of these facts.

40. Tests of _____ measure what an individual can do now, whereas tests of _____ predict what an individual will be able to do later.
   a. aptitude; achievement
   b. achievement; aptitude
   c. reliability; validity
   d. validity; reliability

Matching Items

Match each definition or description with the appropriate term.

Definitions or Descriptions

_____ **1.** the consistency with which a test measures performance
_____ **2.** the way an issue or question is posed
_____ **3.** the process of defining meaningful scores relative to a pretested group
_____ **4.** the degree to which a test measures what it is designed to measure
_____ **5.** presuming that something is likely if it comes readily to mind
_____ **6.** the tendency to overestimate the accuracy of one's judgments
_____ **7.** being unable to see a problem from a different angle
_____ **8.** haphazard problem solving by trying one solution after another
_____ **9.** the sudden realization of the solution to a problem
_____ **10.** Terman's revision of Binet's original intelligence test
_____ **11.** an underlying, general intelligence factor
_____ **12.** the proportion of variation among individuals that we can attribute to genes
_____ **13.** a very low intelligence score accompanied by one extraordinary skill

Terms

   a. standardization
   b. heritability
   c. *g*
   d. trial and error
   e. availability heuristic
   f. savant syndrome
   g. insight
   h. framing
   i. overconfidence
   j. fixation
   k. Stanford-Binet
   l. predictive validity
   m. reliability

Application Essay

You have been asked to devise a Psychology Achievement Test (PAT) that will be administered to freshmen who declare psychology as their major. What steps will you take to ensure that the PAT is a good intelligence test? (Use the space below to list the points you want to make, and organize them. Then write the essay on a separate sheet of paper.)

SUMMING UP

You can solve problems in many ways. To test your understanding of the various techniques and obstacles to making them work, suppose you are creating recipes for pasta sauce.

At first, you try mixing different ingredients. This hit-and-miss method is referred to as _____ and _____ .

After tossing out several recipes, you learn more about which herbs mix well together and in what order,

and so you write out a recipe, a step-by-step procedure, or _____ , for your pasta sauce.

After a while, you have a good sense of what works. So, you use a simple thinking strategy, or _____ , to create many more recipes.

Occasionally, you create a recipe that comes to you in a flash of inspiration, or _____ .

right temporal lobe activity

Sometimes, your efforts are not so successful. For example, you can't get past what you've always thought belongs in a pasta sauce. That is, you can't look at the problem from a fresh perspective—you're _____ on the traditional ingredients.

Other times, you try combinations that readily come to mind rather than thinking outside the box about other possibilities; that is, you are hindered by the _____ _____ .

TERMS AND CONCEPTS

Using your own words, on a piece of paper write a brief definition or explanation of each of the following terms.

1. cognition
2. algorithm
3. heuristic
4. insight
5. availability heuristic
6. fixation
7. confirmation bias
8. overconfidence
9. framing
10. belief perseverance
11. language
12. babbling stage
13. one-word stage
14. two-word stage
15. telegraphic speech
16. intelligence
17. general intelligence (g)
18. savant syndrome
19. creativity
20. emotional intelligence
21. intelligence test
22. aptitude test
23. achievement test
24. mental age
25. Stanford-Binet
26. intelligence quotient (IQ)
27. Wechsler Adult Intelligence Scale (WAIS)
28. standardization
29. normal curve
30. reliability
31. validity
32. heritability
33. stereotype threat

ANSWERS

Chapter Review

Thinking

1. the mental activity associated with thinking, knowing, remembering, and communicating; problem solving

2. trial and error
3. algorithms
4. heuristics
5. insight
6. a. Trial and error: randomly looking everywhere in the house
   b. Algorithm: Methodically checking every possible location in the house as well as all the pockets in your clothes
   c. Heuristics: Thinking about the most logical place for you to have left your keys
   d. Insight: Suddenly realizing that you left your keys in the car when you took the groceries out
7. algorithm. Follow the recipe precisely and you can't miss!
8. heuristic; algorithm. Boris is using a simple, more efficient thinking strategy. The computer is programmed to check every possible move.
9. availability heuristic
10. fixation
11. confirmation bias
12. overconfidence
13. adaptive; more; easier; more
14. does
15. framing; does
16. belief perseverance
17. consider the opposite
18. confirmation bias. The confirmation bias is the tendency to search for information that confirms your preconceptions. In this example, the politicians' preconceptions are biasing their interpretations of the survey results.
19. c. is the answer. Most people are more confident than correct in estimating their knowledge and the amount of time a task will take.
20. framing. How a question or statement is worded can have a major effect on how people respond.
21. a. is the answer. Although b. and c. may be true, they do not describe belief perseverance. The d. answer is the confirmation bias.
22. a. what our ancestral history has prepared us to fear.
    b. what we cannot control.
    c. what is immediate.
    b. what is most readily available in memory.
23. availability heuristic. The publicity surrounding disasters makes such events vivid and seemingly more probable than they actually are.
24. quickly; adaptive

Language

1. our spoken, written, or signed words and the ways we combine them as we think and communicate; syntax
2. 4; receptive language; productive language
3. babbling; 4; do not

4. signing

5. lost

6. one-word; 1

7. two-word; telegraphic

8. do

9. **c.** is the answer. Before 10 months of age, infants babble sounds from all languages.

10. telegraphic speech; syntax. These "sentences," characteristic of a child of about 2 years, are like telegrams, in that they consist mainly of nouns and verbs and show use of syntax.

11. Noam Chomsky; universal grammar

12. critical period; do not

13. 7; never

14. can

15. mental

16. neural networks

17. studying effectively

18. process simulation; outcome simulation. Imagining the procedure activates the brain areas involved in actually performing the activity, so process simulation produces better results than outcome simulation.

19. concepts; insight

20. tools; vary; cultural

21. communicate

22. sign language

23. perceptual set

24. alone

Chimps have gained only limited vocabularies and—in contrast to children—have gained these vocabularies only with great difficulty. Also in contrast to children, it's unclear that chimps can use syntax to express meaning. The signing of chimps is often nothing more than imitation of the trainer's actions. People tend to interpret such unclear behavior in terms of what they want to see. Believers argue that although animals do not have our facility for language, they have the abilities to communicate. For example, Washoe and Loulis sign spontaneously. Also, bonobos can learn to understand English syntax.

Intelligence

1. the ability to learn from experience, solve problems, and use knowledge to adapt to new situations

2. general; specific

3. factor analysis; general intelligence

4. savant syndrome; autism

5. multiple intelligences; physical; do; grit

6. savant syndrome. People with savant syndrome tend to score low on intelligence tests but have one exceptional ability.

7. creativity; 120

Creative people tend to have expertise, or a well-developed base of knowledge; imaginative thinking skills, which allow them to see things in new ways, to recognize patterns, and to make connections; intrinsic motivation, or the tendency to focus on the pleasure and challenge of their work; and a venturesome personality that tolerates gray areas and seeks new experiences. Creative people also have generally benefited from living in creative environments.

8. the know-how involved in understanding social situations and managing yourself successfully

9. emotional intelligence; perceive; understand; manage; use

Emotionally intelligent people are self-aware. They enjoy higher-quality interaction with friends. They can manage their emotions and they can delay gratification. They handle others' emotions skillfully.

10. **c.** is the answer. Beyond an intelligence test score of 120, intelligence is not a necessary part of creativity. Most creative people have imaginative thinking skills and see things in novel ways.

11. emotional intelligence. Emotionally intelligent people are able to perceive, manage, understand, and use emotions.

12. intelligence; aptitude; achievement

13. Alfred Binet; mental

14. Stanford-Binet; intelligence quotient

In the original formula for IQ, measured mental age is divided by chronological age and multiplied by 100. "Mental age" refers to the chronological age that most typically corresponds to a given level of performance. Multiplying by 100 gets rid of the decimal point.

15. do not; the same; 100

16. Wechsler Adult Intelligence Scale; verbal comprehension; perceptual organization; working memory; processing speed

17. achievement; aptitude. An exam for a professional license is intended to measure whether you have gained the overall knowledge and skill to practice the profession. The SAT is designed to predict ability, or aptitude, for learning a new skill.

18. 13. At the time he took the test, Benito's chronological age (CA) was 10. Knowing that IQ = 130 and CA = 10, solving the equation for mental age yields a value of 13.

19. 100. Standard intelligence tests today set 100 as the average score for a given age.

20. standardization

21. normal curve

The normal curve describes the pattern of scores for many physical and psychological attributes (including mental aptitudes), with most scores falling near the average and fewer near the extremes. When a test is standardized on a normal curve, individual scores are assigned according to how far they are above or below the average.

22. reliable

23. the same; split the test in half

24. validity

25. predictive validity

26. **b.** is the answer. A standardization group provides a representative comparison for the trait being measured by a test. Because this test will measure musical aptitude in North American children, the standardization group should be limited to North American children but should include children of all degrees of musical aptitude.

27. reliability. Reliability is the extent to which a test produces the same results each time.

28. validity. A test is not valid if it does not measure what it is designed to measure. Obviously, a hearing test would not measure intelligence.

29. more

30. more alike; environmental; age

31. more; biological; adoptive

32. heritability; 50

33. does not

34. do; malnutrition; sensory; social isolation

35. low; high. When people are genetically similar, heritability is low (in this case, 0, because they are identical twins) when environments are similar but not necessarily identical (as in the case of Ramona and Francesca), heritability is high (closer to 100 percent).

36. environmental

37. do not; greater than; is not

38. higher; ethnic

39. as well as

40. higher; Asian students have a longer school year and spend more time studying math

41. Asian students have a longer school year, and they spend more time at home and in school studying math

42. spelling; verbally; touch; taste; emotion

43. varies; male-science; mental rotation

44. evolutionary

45. are

46. are not

47. stereotype threat

Progress Test

Multiple-Choice Questions

1. **c.** is the answer.

2. **d.** is the answer. It is a major obstacle to problem solving.
   a. & b. These refer to overconfidence and belief perseverance, respectively.
   c. This is trial-and-error problem solving.

3. **a.** is the answer. Babbling is not the imitation of adult speech since babbling infants produce sounds from languages they have not heard and could not be imitating.

4. **d.** is the answer.

5. **c.** is the answer.
   a. Chomsky did not believe this.
   b. According to Chomsky, although we are born with a readiness to learn language, we only acquire language in association with others.
   d. Social influences are an important example of the influence of learning on language development.

6. **d.** is the answer. Heuristics are simple thinking strategies—such as playing chess defensively—that are based on past successes in similar situations.
   a., b., & c. These are all algorithms.

7. **d.** is the answer. Sultan suddenly arrived at a novel solution to his problem, thus displaying apparent insight.
   a. Sultan did not randomly try various strategies of reaching the fruit; he demonstrated the "light bulb" reaction that is the hallmark of insight.
   b. Heuristics are simple thinking strategies.
   c. Fixation hinders problem solving. Sultan obviously solved his problem.

8. **d.** is the answer.

9. **d.** is the answer. Compared with Deaf children exposed to sign language from birth, those who learn to sign as teens have the same grammatical difficulties as do hearing adults trying to learn a second spoken language.

10. **d.** is the answer. If we divide 9, the measured mental age, by 6, the chronological age, and multiply the result by 100, we obtain 150.

11. **b.** is the answer. The stronger a culture's male-science stereotype, the greater its gender difference in math and science achievement. So, in some countries, females may achieve more in these fields.

12. **c.** is the answer.
    a. On the contrary, many *group* differences are highly significant, even though they tell us nothing about specific *individuals*.
    b. Although heredity contributes to individual differences in intelligence, it does not necessarily contribute to group differences.
    d. In fact, the difference has weakened somewhat in recent years.

13. **b.** is the answer.
    a. This answer refers to heritability.
    c. This answer refers to test-retest reliability.
    d. This answer refers to predictive validity.

14. **c.** is the answer. Fixation is an obstacle to problem solving.

15. **d.** is the answer.

16. **a.** is the answer.
    c. & d. Most modern tests have very high reliabilities; their predictive validity is not as high.

17. **d.** is the answer. Up to an intelligence score of about 120, there is a positive relationship between intelligence and creativity. But beyond this point the link disappears, indicating that factors other than intelligence are also involved.
    a. The ability to think imaginatively and intelligence are *both* components of creativity.

b. Creativity, the capacity to produce ideas that are novel and valuable, is related to and depends in part on intelligence but cannot be considered simply a kind of intelligence.

c. Beyond an intelligence score of about 120 there is no link between intelligence scores and creativity.

18. **d.** is the answer. That people with savant syndrome excel in one area but are intellectually slow in others suggests that there are multiple intelligences.
    a. The ability to adapt defines the capacity we call intelligence.
    b. Stereotype threat is the concept that the fear of being evaluated negatively may result in a poorer performance.
    c. A general intelligence factor was hypothesized by Spearman to underlie each specific factor of intelligent behavior, but its existence is controversial and remains to be proved.

19. **c.** is the answer.

20. **d.** is the answer. Findings from a range of studies have led experts to focus on the influence of environmental factors.
    a. Most experts believe that in terms of predictive validity, the major tests are not racially biased.
    b. The reliability of the major tests is actually very high.
    c. The bulk of the evidence on which experts base their findings points to the influence of environmental factors.

21. **d.** is the answer.
    a. *g* is Spearman's term for "general intelligence"; there is no such thing as a "*g* distribution."
    b. There is no such thing.
    c. IQ is Terman's original term for an individual's score on the Stanford-Binet.

22. **a.** is the answer. Reasoning in daily life is often distorted by our beliefs, which may lead us, for example, to accept conclusions that haven't been arrived at logically.
    b., c., & d. These are just the opposite of what we tend to do.

23. **d.** is the answer. Syntax is one of the fundamental aspects of language, and chimps seem unable, for example, to use word order to convey differences in meaning.
    a. & c. Chimps' use of sign language demonstrates that they can use symbols and can have fairly large vocabularies.
    b. No psychologist would require the use of speech as evidence of language; significantly, all the research and arguments focus on what chimps are and are not able to do in learning other aspects of language.

24. **d.** is the answer. If we use the availability heuristic, we base judgments on the availability of information in our memories, and more vivid information is often the most readily available.
    a. This would be an example of the use of the trial-and-error approach to problem solving.

b. This would be an example of the use of an algorithm.
c. This would be an example of belief perseverance.

25. **b.** is the answer. Because they involve the systematic examination of all possible solutions to a problem, algorithms guarantee that a solution will be found.
    a., c., & d. None of these methods guarantees that a problem's solution will be found.

26. **c.** is the answer.

27. **c.** is the answer. Although the child says only two words as a sentence, the words are placed in a sensible order. In English, for example, adjectives are placed before nouns.
    a. & b. Syntax specifies rules for *combining* two or more units in speech.
    d. There is no three-word stage.

28. **b.** is the answer.

29. **c.** is the answer.

30. **c.** is the answer. A new French law brought more children into the school system, and the government didn't want to rely on teachers' biases to determine which children would require special help.
    a. & b. Binet's test was intended for children; there is nothing in the text to indicate that Binet's test was intended to measure inborn intelligence.
    d. This was not a purpose of the test, which dealt with children in the school system.

31. **c.** is the answer.
    a., b., & d. None of these is true.

32. **c.** is the answer. Predictive validity is the extent to which tests predict future performance.
    a. Reliability is the consistency with which a test samples the particular behavior of interest.
    b. This is too general a term.
    d. Standardization is the process of defining meaningful test scores based on the performance of a representative group.

33. **d.** is the answer.

34. **c.** is the answer.
    a. This is William Stern's original formula for the intelligence quotient.
    b. & d. Neither of these formulas is used to compute the score on current intelligence tests.

35. **a.** is the answer.

36. **c.** is the answer.
    a. Performance ability and intellectual ability are separate traits.
    b. This has been argued by some, but certainly not most, experts.
    d. Although many experts believe that there are multiple intelligences, this would not be the same thing as diverse acquired skills.

37. **a.** is the answer.

38. **c.** is the answer.
    a. & b. Studies of twins, family members, and adopted children point to a significant hereditary

contribution to intelligence scores. These same studies, plus others comparing children reared in neglectful or enriched environments, indicate that life experiences also significantly influence test performance.

d. Although the issue of how intelligence should be defined is controversial, intelligence tests generally have predictive validity, especially in the early years.

39. d. is the answer.

40. b. is the answer.

c. & d. Reliability and validity are characteristics of good tests.

Matching Items

1. m	**6.** i	**11.** c
2. h	**7.** j	**12.** b
3. a	**8.** d	**13.** f
4. l	**9.** g	
5. e	**10.** k	

Application Essay

The first step in constructing the test is to create a valid set of questions that measure psychological knowledge and therefore give the test overall validity. If your objective is to predict students' future achievement in psychology courses, the test questions should be selected to measure, for example, information faculty members expect all psychology majors to master before they graduate.

To enable meaningful comparisons, the test must be standardized. That is, the test should be administered to a representative sample of incoming freshmen at the time they declare psychology to be their major. From the scores of your pretested sample you will then be able to assign an average score and evaluate any individual score according to how much it deviates above or below the average.

To check your test's reliability you might retest a sample of people using the same test or another version of it. If the two scores are correlated, your test is reliable. Alternatively, you might split the test in half and determine whether scores on the two halves are correlated.

Summing Up

You can solve problems in many ways. To test your understanding of the various techniques and obstacles to making them work, suppose you are creating recipes for pasta sauces. At first, you try mixing different ingredients. This hit-and-miss method is referred to as *trial and error*. After tossing out several recipes, you learn more about which herbs mix well together and in what order, and so you write out a recipe, a step-by-step procedure, or *algorithm*, for your pasta sauce. After awhile, you have a good sense of what works. So, you use a simple thinking strategy, or *heuristic*, to create many more recipes. Occasionally, you create a recipe that comes to you in a flash of inspiration, or *insight*.

Sometimes, your efforts are not so successful. For example, you can't get past what you've always thought belongs in a pasta sauce. That is, you can't look at the problem from a fresh perspective—you're *fixated* on the traditional ingredients. Other times, you try combinations that readily come to mind rather than thinking outside the box about other possibilities. That is, you are hindered by the *availability heuristic*.

Terms and Concepts

1. **Cognition** refers to the mental activity associated with thinking, knowing, remembering, and communicating information.

2. An **algorithm** is a methodical, logical procedure that, while sometimes slow, guarantees success.

3. A **heuristic** is a simple thinking strategy that often allows us to make judgments and solve problems efficiently. Although heuristics are more efficient than algorithms, they do not guarantee success and are more error-prone.

4. **Insight** is a sudden and often novel realization of the solution to a problem.

5. The **availability heuristic** is based on estimating the likelihood of certain events based on how readily they come to mind.

6. **Fixation** is an inability to approach a problem in a new way.

7. The **confirmation bias** is an obstacle to problem solving in which people tend to search for information that confirms their preconceptions.

8. Another obstacle to problem solving, **overconfidence** refers to the tendency to overestimate the accuracy of your beliefs and judgments.

9. **Framing** refers to the way an issue or question is posed. It can affect people's perception of the issue or answer to the question.

10. **Belief perseverance** is the tendency for people to cling to a particular belief even after the information that led to the formation of the belief is proven wrong.

11. **Language** refers to spoken, written, or signed words and how we combine them to communicate meaning.

12. The **babbling stage** of speech development, which begins around 4 months, is the stage in which the infant spontaneously utters various sounds at first unrelated to the household language. During the babbling stage, children the world over sound alike.

13. Between 1 and 2 years of age children speak mostly in single words; they are therefore in the **one-word stage** of speech development.

14. Beginning about age 2, children are in the **two-word stage** and speak mostly in two-word sentences.

15. **Telegraphic speech** is the telegramlike speech of children in the two-word stage. Speech consists mostly of nouns and verbs; however, words occur in

the correct order, showing that the child has learned some of the language's syntactic rules.

16. Most experts define **intelligence** as the ability to learn from experience, solve problems, and use knowledge to adapt to new situations.

17. **General intelligence (g)**, according to Spearman and others, is a general factor that underlies specific mental abilities and is therefore measured by every task on an intelligence test.

18. A person with **savant syndrome** has a very low intelligence score, yet possesses one exceptional ability, for example, in music or drawing.

19. Most experts agree that **creativity** refers to an ability to produce novel and valuable ideas. People with high IQs may or may not be creative, which indicates that intelligence is only one component of creativity.

20. **Emotional intelligence** is the ability to perceive, manage, understand, and use emotions.

21. **Intelligence tests** measure people's mental aptitudes and compare them with those of others through numerical scores.

22. **Aptitude tests** are designed to predict future performance. They measure your capacity to learn new information, rather than measuring what you already know.

23. **Achievement tests** measure a person's current knowledge.

24. A concept introduced by Binet, **mental age** is the chronological age that most typically corresponds to a given level of performance.

25. The **Stanford-Binet** is Lewis Terman's widely used revision of Binet's original intelligence test.

26. The **intelligence quotient (IQ)** was defined originally as the ratio of mental age to chronological age multiplied by 100. Contemporary intelligence tests assign a score of 100 to the average performance for a given age.

27. The **Wechsler Adult Intelligence Scale (WAIS)** is the most widely used intelligence test. It is individually administered and contains 11 subtests broken into verbal and performance areas.

28. **Standardization** is the process of defining meaningful scores by comparison with the performance of a pretested standardization group.

29. The **normal curve** is a symmetrical bell-shaped curve that represents the distribution (frequency of occurrence) of many physical and psychological attributes. The curve is symmetrical, with most scores near the average and fewer near the extremes.

30. **Reliability** is the extent to which a test produces consistent results.

31. **Validity** is the degree to which a test measures or predicts what it is supposed to.

32. **Heritability** is the proportion of variation in a trait among individuals that we can attribute to genes.

33. **Stereotype threat** is a self-confirming concern that we will be evaluated based on a negative stereotype (as on an aptitude test, for example).

9

MOTIVATION AND EMOTION

Motivation is the forces that energize and direct our behavior. Chapter 9 discusses various motivational concepts and looks closely at two motives: hunger and the need to belong. Research on hunger points to the fact that our biological drive to eat is strongly influenced by psychological and social-cultural factors. The need to affiliate with others had survival value for our ancestors, and societies everywhere control the behavior of individuals with the threat of social isolation.

Chapter 9 also discusses emotion, beginning with several theoretical controversies concerning the relationship and sequence of the components of emotion. After describing the physiology of emotion and emotional expressiveness, it examines the components of emotion in detail, particularly as they relate to the emotions of anger and happiness.

CHAPTER REVIEW

First, skim each text section, noting headings and bold-face items. Review the section by reading the objectives and summaries provided here, then answer the questions that follow. In some cases, STUDY TIPS explain how best to learn a difficult concept and APPLICATIONS help you to know how well you understand the material. Check your understanding of the material by consulting the answers beginning on page 177. Do not continue with the next section until you understand each answer. If you need to, review or reread the section in the textbook before continuing.

Introduction and Motivational Concepts

Objective 1: Define *motivation* as psychologists use the term today, and describe three key perspectives on motivation.

Motivation is a need or desire that energizes behavior and directs it toward a goal. The perspectives useful for studying motivated behavior include (1) drive-reduction theory, (2) arousal theory, and (3) Abraham Maslow's hierarchy of needs.

Drive-reduction theory proposes that unmet *physiological needs* create aroused states that translate into a psychological drive to reduce those needs. We are also pulled by **incentives**. Whether the incentive is toasted bread or toasted ants depends on your culture and experience.

Arousal theory states that rather than reducing our feelings of arousal, some motivated behaviors increase arousal. Curiosity-driven behaviors, for example, suggest that too little or too much stimulation can motivate people to seek just the right level of arousal.

Abraham Maslow's **hierarchy of needs** expresses the idea that, until satisfied, some motives are more compelling than others. At the base of the hierarchy are our physiological needs, such as for food and water. Only if these are met are we prompted to meet our need for safety, and then to meet the uniquely human needs to give and receive love and to enjoy self-esteem. Beyond this, said Maslow, lies the highest human needs. At the *self-actualization* level, people seek to realize their own potential. At the *self-transcendence* level, people strive for "transpersonal" meaning, purpose, and identity that is beyond (*trans*) the self.

1. Motivation is defined as _____ _____ _____ .

2. Three perspectives on motivation are _____-_____ theory, _____ theory, and the _____ of needs proposed by _____ .

3. According to one view of motivation, an unmet physiological _____ creates a state of arousal. This physical arousal translates into a psychological _____ to reduce the need.

4. Behavior is often not so much pushed by our drives as it is pulled by _____ in the environment.

5. Rather than reduce a physiological need, some motivated behaviors actually _____ arousal. This demonstrates that human motives _____ (do/do not) always satisfy some biological need. Too much stimulation, however, brings _____ .

6. Starting from the idea that some needs are more important than others, Maslow constructed a _____ of needs.

7. According to Maslow, the _____ needs are the most pressing. The highest-order needs relate to the need to live up to your full potential, or _____ , followed by the need for meaning and purpose beyond the self, called _____ .

8. Surveys reveal that _____ , and the food and shelter it buys, more strongly predicts feelings of well-being in poorer nations; _____-_____ satisfaction matters more in wealthy nations.

APPLICATIONS:

9. Mary loves hang-gliding. It would be most difficult to explain Mary's behavior according to _____-_____ theory.

10. For two weeks, Orlando has been on a hunger strike to protest his country's involvement in what he perceives as an immoral war. Orlando's willingness to starve himself to make a political statement conflicts with the theory of motivation advanced by _____ .

Hunger

Objective 2: Describe the physiological factors that cause us to feel hungry.

Although the stomach's pangs contribute to hunger, variations in body chemistry are more important. A major source of energy in your body is the blood sugar *glucose,* which is controlled by *insulin,* a hormone secreted by the pancreas. We do not consciously feel changes in blood chemistry. Rather, our body's internal state is monitored by the hypothalamus, which regulates the body's weight as it influences our feelings of hunger and fullness. Other hormones monitored by the hypothalamus include *ghrelin* (which is secreted by an empty stomach), *leptin* (secreted by fat cells), and PYY (a digestive tract hormone). *Orexin* is a hunger-triggering hormone secreted by the hypothalamus. One neural arc (called the *arcuate nucleus*) has a center that secretes appetite-stimulating hromones and another center that secretes appetite-suppressing hormones. Some researchers have abandoned the idea that the body has a precise **set point**—the stable weight at which our body's "weight thermostat" is set—preferring the term *settling point* to indicate an environmentally and biologically influenced level at which weight settles in response to caloric input and expenditure. Human bodies regulate weight through the control of food intake,

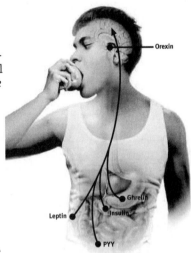

energy output, and **basal metabolic rate**—a measure of the body's resting rate of energy expenditure.

1. Ancel Keys observed that men became preoccupied with thoughts of food when they underwent _____ .

2. Cannon and Washburn's experiment using a balloon indicated that there is an association between hunger and _____ _____ .

3. When an animal has had its stomach removed, hunger _____ (does/does not) continue.

4. A major source of energy in the body is the blood sugar _____ . Decreases in the level of this sugar cause hunger to _____ (increase/decrease).

5. The brain area that plays a role in hunger and other bodily maintenance functions is the _____ . Animals will begin eating when a center of the neural arc called the _____ _____ is electrically stimulated. When a different center in this neural arc is electrically stimulated, hunger _____ (increases/ decreases).

6. The hunger-arousing hormone secreted by an empty stomach is _____

7. When a portion of an obese person's stomach is surgically sealed off, the remaining stomach produces _____ (more/less) of this hormone.

For questions 8–12, identify the appetite hormone that is described (see Figure 9.6):

8. Hunger-triggering hormone: _____ .

9. Hormone secreted by empty stomach: _____ .

10. Hormone secreted by pancreas: _____ .

11. Protein secreted by fat cells: _____ .

12. Digestive tract hormone that signals fullness: _____ .

13. The weight level at which an individual's body is programmed to stay is referred to as the body's _____ _____ . A person whose weight goes beyond this level will tend to feel _____ (more/less) hungry than usual and expend _____ (more/less) energy.

14. The rate of energy expenditure in maintaining basic functions when the body is at rest is the

_____ _____

rate. When food intake is reduced, the body compensates by _____ (raising/ lowering) this rate.

15. The concept of a precise body set point that drives hunger _____ (is accepted/is not accepted) by all researchers. Some researchers believe that set point is too rigid to explain some things. Support for this idea comes from evidence that set point can be altered by

_____

_____ .

Also, when people and other animals are given unlimited access to tasty foods, they tend to

_____ and _____

_____ . For these reasons, some researchers prefer to use the term

_____ _____

as an alternative to the idea that there is a fixed set point.

STUDY TIP: Mnemonics are memory devices that can help you learn hard-to-remember material by associating it with easy-to-remember ideas that are personally meaningful. Medical students often use mnemonics to memorize details of anatomy, chemistry, and physiology. For instance, to remember the colors of the rainbow in order, the first letters in the made-up name Roy G Biv or the sentence "Richard Of York Gave Battle in Vain" will trigger the answer: Red, Orange, Yellow, Green, Blue, Indigo, and Violet. You might find mnemonics helpful in learning some of the physiological terms in this chapter. See if you can create a memorable mnemonic device for the five appetite hormones: Insulin, Leptin, Orexin, Ghrelin, and PYY.* You might want to think of other ways to use mnemonics to learn important terms in psychology and other subjects—for example, HOMES will help you to learn the names of the Great Lakes (Huron, Ontario, Michigan, Erie, and Superior).

APPLICATIONS:

*One possibility is GLOP, which is a very visual image of food going through the digestive process.

16. A lab technician needs your help in explaining why one well-fed rat begins to eat while a starving rat has no interest in food. You explain that the the appetite-enhancing center of the well-fed rat's _____

_____ has been electrically stimulated, while the appetite-supressing area of that same

_____ arc has been stimulated in the starving rat.

17. Kenny and his brother have nearly identical eating and exercise habits, yet Kenny is obese and his brother is very thin. The most likely explanation for the difference in their body weights is that they differ in their _____

_____ .

18. Lucille has been sticking to a strict diet but can't seem to lose weight. What is the most likely explanation for her difficulty?

  a. Her body has a very low set point.

  b. Her prediet weight was near her body's set point.

  c. Her weight problem is actually caused by an underlying eating disorder.

  d. Lucille is influenced primarily by external factors.

Objective 3: Discuss psychological and cultural influences on hunger, and explain how anorexia nervosa and bulimia nervosa demonstrate the power of psychological influences to overwhelm biological factors.

Part of knowing when to eat is our memory of our last meal. As time passes, we anticipate eating again and feel hungry.

Although some taste preferences are genetic, learning and culture also affect taste. For example, Bedouins enjoy eating the eye of a camel, which most North Americans would find repulsive. Most North Americans and Europeans also shun dog, rat, and horse meat, all of which are prized elsewhere. We avoid unfamiliar foods, especially those that are animal-based.
We may learn to prefer some tastes because they are adaptive.

Anorexia nervosa is an eating disorder in which a normal-weight person (usually an adolescent female) diets to become significantly (15 percent or more) underweight, yet feels fat and is obsessed with losing weight.

Bulimia nervosa is an eating disorder characterized by a binge-purge cycle of overeating, followed by vomiting, laxative use, fasting, or excessive exercise.

With *binge-eating disorder,* significant binge eating is followed by remorse but not by attempts to get rid of the excess food.

People with anorexia often come from competitive, high-achieving families. They tend to have low self-esteem, set impossible standards, and fret about falling short of expectations. Although twin studies suggest that eating disorders may also have a genetic component, environment plays a bigger role, especially in weight-obsessed cultures.

19. Research with patients who do not remember events occurring more than a minute ago indicates that part of knowing when to eat is our

_____ of our last meal.

20. (Close-Up) The disorder in which a person becomes significantly underweight and yet feels fat is known as _____ _____ .

21. (Close-Up) A more common disorder is

_____ _____ ,

which is characterized by repeated

_____-_____

episodes and by feelings of depression or anxiety.
The disorder in which binge eating is followed by
remorse but without the purging or fasting is known

as _____-_____

_____ .

22. (Close-Up) The families of anorexia patients tend to

be _____ and

_____-_____ .

The patients tend to have low

_____ , set impossible

_____ , and fret about falling

short of expectations.

23. (Close-Up) Heredity _____

(may/does not) influence susceptibility to eating

disorders. _____ twins share the

disorder somewhat more than _____

twins do.

24. (Close-Up) Women students in _____

rate their actual shape as closer to the cultural ideal.
In impoverished areas of the world, plump means

_____ . In _____

cultures, however, the rise in eating disorders has
coincided with an increasing number of women

having a poor _____

_____ .

25. (Close-Up) Researchers found that when young
women were shown pictures of unnaturally thin

models, they often felt more _____ ,

_____ , and

_____ with their own bodies.

26. Carbohydrates boost levels of the neurotransmitter

_____ , which

_____ (calms/arouses) the

body.

27. Taste preferences for sweet and salty are

_____ (genetic/learned) and

universal. Other influences on taste include

_____ and _____ .

We have a natural dislike of many foods that are

_____ ; this was probably adap-

tive for our ancestors and protected them from toxic

substances.

28. (Close-Up) Kathy has been undergoing treatment for
bulimia. Kathy is in her late teens or early twenties, is preoccupied with food (craves sweet and high-fat foods),

and is _____

_____ .

29. (Close-Up) Of the following individuals, who might be
most prone to developing an eating disorder?
    a. Jason, an adolescent boy who is somewhat over-
weight and is unpopular with his peers
    b. Jennifer, a teenage girl who has a poor self-image
and a fear of not being able to live up to her parents'
high standards
    c. Susan, a 35-year-old woman who is a "workaholic"
and devotes most of her energies to her high-
pressured career
    d. Bill, a 40-year-old man who has had problems with
alcohol dependence and is seriously depressed after
losing his job of 20 years

30. Ali's parents have tried hard to minimize their son's exposure to sweet, fattening foods. If Ali has the occasion to
taste sweet foods in the future, which of the following is
likely?
    a. He will have a strong aversion to such foods.
    b. He will have a neutral reaction to sweet foods.
    c. He will display a preference for sweet tastes.
    d. It is impossible to predict Ali's reaction.

Objective 4: Describe research findings on obesity and
weight control.

Fat is an ideal form of stored energy. It is a fuel reserve
that can carry the body through periods of famine. In
fact, where people face famine, obesity signals wealth
and social status. However, the tendency to eat energy-
rich fat or sugar works against us in a world where food
and sweets are abundant. Significant obesity can shorten
your life and greatly reduce your quality of life. It
increases the risk of diabetes and heart disease, for
example.

Obesity affects both how you are treated and how
you feel about yourself. Obese people, especially obese
women, experience weight discrimination in job hiring,
placement, promotion, compensation, and discharge.
Similarly, they are less likely to be married.

Our body fat depends on the size and number of our
fat cells. In an obese person, the
original fat cells are two to three
times their original size. People also
differ in their resting metabolic
rates, and once someone gains fat
tissue, less energy is needed to
maintain that tissue than is needed
to maintain other tissue.
Unquestionably, environmental fac-
tors such as often eating high-calorie foods and living an
inactive life-style also matter. Genes have a lot to do
with our weight.

Research indicates that most people who succeed on a weight-loss program eventually regain most of the weight. Those who wish to diet should set realistic goals, minimize exposure to food cues, boost energy expenditure through exercise, eat healthy foods spaced throughout the day, be aware of social influences, and beware of the binge.

31. Being slightly overweight _____ (poses/does not pose) serious health risks. Significant obesity increases the risk of _____ _____ .

32. The risks of obesity are greater for people who carry their weight in pot bellies, that is, who are _____-shaped.

33. Obese people are often unfairly stereotyped as _____ , _____ , and _____ .

34. One study found that obese women earned _____ than a control group of nonobese women and were less likely to be _____ .

35. In one experiment, job applicants were rated as less worthy of hiring when they were made to appear _____ .

36. The energy equivalent of a pound of fat is _____ calories.

37. Body fat is most immediately determined by the size and number of _____ _____ we have. This number is, in turn, determined by several factors, including our _____ and _____ _____ .

38. The size of fat cells _____ (can/cannot) be decreased by dieting; the number of fat cells _____ (can/cannot) be decreased by dieting.

39. Fat tissue takes _____ (more/less) food energy to maintain. The body weight "thermostat" of obese people _____ (is/is not) set to maintain a higher-than-average weight. When weight drops below this setting, _____ increases and _____ decreases.

40. Studies of adoptees and twins _____ (do/do not) provide evidence of a genetic influence on obesity.

41. Obesity is _____ (more/less) common among those who sit still and watch TV and _____ (more/less) common among people living in communities where walking is common.

42. Most obese persons who lose weight _____ (gain/do not gain) it back.

(Close-Up) State several pieces of advice for those who want to lose weight.

APPLICATIONS:

43. Owen is on a diet. After an initial _____ (slow/rapid) weight loss, he loses weight _____ (more slowly/more rapidly). This slowdown occurs because his metabolism rate has _____ (increased/decreased).

44. (Close-Up) Which of the following would be the worst piece of advice to offer to someone trying to lose weight?
    a. "To treat yourself to one 'normal' meal each day, eat very little until the evening meal."
    b. "Reduce your consumption of saturated fats."
    c. "Boost your metabolism by exercising regularly."
    d. "Without increasing total caloric intake, increase the relative proportion of carbohydrates in your diet."

The Need to Belong

Objective 5: Describe the benefits of belonging, and discuss the consequences of our need to belong, especially as related to the practice of social networking.

Social bonds boosted our ancestors' chances of survival. Adults who formed attachments were more likely to come together to reproduce and to stay together to nurture their offspring to maturity. Cooperation in groups also enhanced survival. When relationships form, we feel included, accepted, and loved. Even our self-esteem is a measure of how valued and accepted we feel.

When something threatens our social ties, negative emotions overwhelm us. When *ostracized,* people may engage in self-defeating or mean or aggressive behaviors.

The growth of the Internet has in many ways changed the way we connect with people. The Internet is diversifying our social networks and enhancing our existing real-world friendships. Electronic communication makes us less self-conscious and less inhibited, resulting in increased self-disclosure, which deepens friendships. In general, social networks reveal people's real personalities. It is important that we find a healthy balance between our real-world time with people and our online sharing.

1. The philosopher _____ referred to humans as the _____ animal. From an evolutionary standpoint, social bonds in humans boosted our ancestors' _____ rates. Those who felt this need to _____ survived and reproduced more successfully, and so their _____ now rule.

2. Feeling included, accepted, and loved by others boosts our _____ .

3. Much of our _____ behavior aims to increase our belonging. For most people, familiarity leads to _____ (liking/disliking).

4. After years of placing individual refugee and immigrant families in _____ communities, U.S. policies today encourage _____ _____ .

5. _____ (Throughout the world/Only in certain cultures do) people use social exclusion, or _____ , to control social behavior.

6. Researchers have found that people who are rejected are more likely to engage in _____ behaviors and may act in more _____ ways.

7. In the Internet's early years, adolescents and adults who spent more time on the Internet spent _____ (more/less) time with friends. Today, social networking is mostly _____ (strengthening/

weakening) our connections with people we already know.

8. When communicating electronically rather than face to face, we often are less focused on others' reactions, less _____ , and thus less _____ . The result is increased _____ , which serves to deepen friendships.

9. Generally, social networks _____ (do/do not) reveal people's real personalties.

10. Those who score high on items reflecting self-importance and self-promotion, or _____ , are more active on social networking sites.

List some suggestions proposed by experts for maintaining a healthy balance of online connecting with friends and meeting your real-world responsibilities.

APPLICATION:

11. Summarizing her report on the need to belong, Rolanda states that
    a. "Cooperation amongst our ancestors was uncommon."
    b. "Social bonding is not in our nature; it is a learned human trait."
    c. "Because bonding with others increased our ancestors' success at reproduction and survival, it became part of our biological nature."
    d. "Some cultures encourage people to separate from their families."

12. Right after dinner, Dennis goes to his room, turns on his computer, and begins chatting with friends on Facebook. Which of the following is true, according to the most recent research?
    a. His connections with friends have been strengthened.
    b. He is more willing to disclose personal thoughts and feelings, which deepens his friendships.
    c. He reveals his true personality to friends and others online.
    d. All of these statements are true.

Theories of Emotion

Objective 6: Identify the three components of emotion, and contrast the James-Lange, Cannon-Bard, and two-factor theories of emotion.

An *emotion* is a response of the whole organism that involves an interplay among (1) bodily arousal, (2) expressive behaviors, and (3) conscious experience.

The *James-Lange theory* states that our experience of an emotion is a consequence of our physiological responses to emotion-arousing stimuli; we are afraid because our heart pounds (say, in response to an approaching stranger). The *Cannon-Bard theory,* on the other hand, proposes that the physiological response and subjective experience of emotion occur simultaneously. Heart pounding and fear occur at the same time—one does not cause the other. In the Schachter and Singer *two-factor theory* of emotion, to experience emotion, one must (1) be physically aroused and (2) cognitively label the arousal.

1. Emotions have three components: _____
   _____ , _____
   _____ , and _____
   _____ .

2. According to the James-Lange theory, emotional
   states _____ (come before/
   follow) body arousal.

Describe two problems that Walter Cannon identified with the James-Lange theory.

3. Cannon proposed that emotional stimuli in the environment travel at the same time to the
   _____ , which results in awareness of the emotion, and to the
   _____ nervous system, which causes the body's arousal. Because another scientist proposed similar ideas, this theory has come to be known as the _____-
   _____ theory.

4. The two-factor theory of emotion proposes that emotion has two components:
   _____ arousal and
   _____ appraisal. This theory was proposed by _____ and
   _____ .

••

STUDY TIP/APPLICATION: The three theories of emotion discussed in this chapter seem so similar that it's often hard to tell them apart. As you think about the theories, remember: The theories differ in the order of importance they assign to the three components of emotions: physical arousal (increased heart rate, for example), the expression of the emotion (feeling angry, for example), and the importance of cognitive appraisal of the situation in which the emotion has occurred. To help ensure your understanding of the theories, see if you can fill in the missing information in the chart below for a common emotional experience: Hearing the screeching of a car's tires. For example, the first response might be a physical reaction such as increased heart beat or an emotional expression of fear, or it might be the opposite.

5. Theory	Stimulus Event	First Response	Second Response	Third Response
James-Lange	Screeching tires			
Cannon-Bard	Screeching tires			
Two-factor	Screeching tires			

APPLICATIONS:

6. You are on your way to school to take a big exam. Suddenly, you feel nervous and you notice that your pulse is racing and you are sweating. This fits with the

   _____-_____

   theory of emotion.

7. Two years ago, Maria was in an automobile accident in which her spinal cord was severed, leaving her paralyzed from the neck down. Today, Maria finds that she experiences emotions less intensely than she did before her accident. This tends to support the

   _____-_____

   theory of emotion.

8. After hitting a grand-slam home run, Mike noticed that his heart was pounding. Later that evening, after nearly having a collision while driving on the freeway, Mike again noticed that his heart was pounding. That he interpreted this reaction as fear, rather than as ecstasy, can best be explained by the _____-

   _____ theory of emotion.

Embodied Emotion

Objective 7: Describe the bodily changes that accompany emotions.

The *autonomic nervous system (ANS)* controls arousal. In an emergency, the sympathetic nervous system automatically mobilizes the body to fight or flee. Your adrenal glands release stress hormones, your liver pours extra sugar into your bloodstream, your muscles tense. Other physical changes include dilated pupils, slowed digestion, and increased sweating. The parasympathetic nervous system calms the body after a crisis has passed, although arousal diminishes gradually.

1. Describe the major physiological changes that each of the following undergoes during emotional arousal.

   a. heart: _____

   b. muscles: _____

   c. liver: _____

   d. breathing: _____

   e. digestion: _____

   f. pupils: _____

   g. blood: _____

   h. skin: _____

   i. immune system: _____

2. The responses of arousal are activated by the _____ nervous system. The _____ division arouses; the _____ division calms.

Objective 8: Describe the relationship between physiological states and specific emotions, and discuss the effectiveness of the polygraph in detecting lies.

Similar physiological arousal occurs during fear, anger, and sexual arousal. Nonetheless, these emotions feel different. And, despite similar arousal, sometimes our facial expressions differ during these three states. For example, people may appear "paralyzed" with fear or "ready to explode" with anger.

Fear and rage are sometimes accompanied by differing finger temperatures and hormone secretions. Emotions may also stimulate different facial muscles. During fear, brow muscles tense. During joy, muscles in the cheek and under your eyes pull into a smile. Emotions differ in the brain circuits they use. For example, the right frontal cortex becomes more active as people experience negative emotions, such as disgust. The left frontal lobe shows more activity with positive moods.

The *polygraph* measures several physiological responses accompanying emotion—for example, changes in breathing, heart rate, and perspiration. Research suggests it errs about one-third of the time, too often to justify its widespread use in business and government. A more effective approach is the *guilty knowledge test.*

3. The various emotions are associated with _____ (similar/different) responses. In particular, the emotions of

   _____ , _____ , and _____ _____ are difficult to spot by measuring perspiration, breathing, and heart rate.

4. The emotions _____ and _____ are accompanied by differing _____ temperatures and _____ secretions.

5. The emotions _____ and _____ stimulate different facial muscles.

6. The brain circuits underlying different emotions _____ (are/are not) different. For example, when you experience negative emotions, your _____ _____ cortex is more active. People who have generally negative personalities, and those who are prone to _____ , show more activity in this area.

7. When people experience positive moods, brain scans reveal more activity in the

   _____ _____

   lobe.

8. Individuals with more active

   _____ (right/left)

   _____ lobes tend to be more cheerful than those in whom this pattern of brain activity is reversed.

9. (Thinking Critically) The technical name for the "lie detector" is the _____ .

(Thinking Critically) Explain how lie detectors supposedly indicate whether a person is lying.

10. (Thinking Critically) How well the lie detector works depends on whether a person becomes

    _____ while lying.

11. (Thinking Critically) Those who criticize lie detectors feel that the tests are particularly likely to err in the case of the _____ (innocent/ guilty) because different _____ all register as _____ .

12. (Thinking Critically) By and large, experts _____ (agree/do not agree) that lie detector tests are highly accurate.

13. (Thinking Critically) A test that assesses a suspect's knowledge of details of a crime that only the guilty person should know is the

    _____ _____

    _____ .

APPLICATIONS:

14. A student participating in an experiment concerned with physical responses that indicate emotions reports that her mouth is dry, her heart is racing, and she feels flushed. Can the emotion she is experiencing be determined?
    a. Yes, it is anger.
    b. Yes, it is fear.
    c. Yes, it is ecstasy.
    d. No, it cannot be determined from the information given.

15. As part of her job interview, Jan is asked to take a lie-detector test. Jan politely refuses and points out the problems with the text, which are that
    a. _____
    b. _____
    c. _____

16. Nine-month-old Nicole's left frontal cortex is generally more active than her right frontal cortex. This would indicate that she probably has a _____ (positive/negative) personality.

17. Julio was extremely angry when he came in for a routine EEG of his brain activity. When he later told this to the doctor, she was no longer concerned about the _____ electrical activity in Julio's

    _____ _____

    lobe.

Objective 9: Explain the role of cognition in emotion, and describe how our two-track brain processes emotions.

The *spillover effect* occurs when arousal from one event affects our response to other events. Dozens of experiments show that a stirred-up state can be experienced as different emotions, depending on how we interpret and label it. Arousal fuels emotion and cognition channels it.

Because of our two-track mind, some emotion-provoking stimuli can follow a pathway that leads via the thalamus to the amygdala, bypassing the cortex and triggering a rapid reaction that is outside our conscious awareness. Other, more complex emotions, including hatred and love, require interpretation and are routed along the slower route to the cortex for analysis.

18. The spillover effect refers to occasions when our _____ response to one event carries over into our response to another event.

19. Schachter and Singer found that physically aroused college men told that an injection would cause arousal _____ (did/did not) become emotional in response to an accomplice's aroused behavior. Physically aroused volunteers not expecting arousal _____ (did/did not) become emotional in response to an accomplice's behavior.

20. Arousal _____ emotion; cognition _____ emotion.

21. Robert Zajonc believes that the feeling of emotion _____ (can/cannot) precede our cognitive labeling of that emotion.

Cite two pieces of evidence that support Zajonc's position.

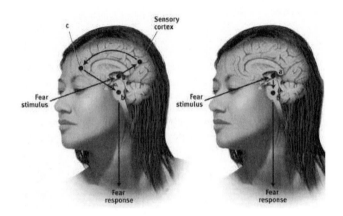

22. A stimulus may travel a pathway from the senses via the _____ (a) to the _____ (b), enabling us to experience emotion before _____ . For more complex emotions, sensory input is routed through the _____ (c) for interpretation.

23. The researcher who argues that although some emotions do not require conscious thinking, most emotions require some kind of cognitive processing is _____ . According to this view, emotions arise when we _____ an event as beneficial or harmful to our well-being.

24. Complex emotions are affected by our _____ , _____ , and _____ .

APPLICATION:

25. Who will probably be angrier after getting a parking ticket?
    a. Bob, who has just awakened from a nap
    b. Veronica, who has just finished eating a big lunch
    c. Dan, who has just completed a tennis match
    d. Alicia, who has been reading a romantic novel

Expressed Emotion

Objective 10: Describe our ability to communicate nonverbally, and discuss gender differences in this capacity.

All of us communicate nonverbally as well as verbally. For example, a firm handshake immediately conveys an outgoing, expressive personality. A glance or a stare can communicate intimacy, submission, or dominance. Most people can detect nonverbal cues, and we are especially sensitive to nonverbal threats.

Women generally surpass men at reading people's emotional cues. Women's skill at decoding others' emotions may also contribute to their greater emotional responsiveness in both positive and negative situations. When surveyed, women are far more likely than men to describe themselves as *empathic*. Women also tend to experience emotional events more deeply with greater brain activation in areas sensitive to emotion.

1. Most people are especially good at interpreting nonverbal _____ .

2. Women are generally _____ (better/worse) than men at detecting nonverbal signs of emotion and in spotting _____ . Women's skill at _____ emotions may contribute to their greater emotional _____ .

3. Although women are _____ (more/less) likely than men to describe themselves as empathic, physiological measures reveal a much _____ (smaller/larger) gender difference. Women are _____ (more/less) likely than men to express empathy.

APPLICATION:

4. Pat is very accurate at reading others' nonverbal behavior and is more likely to express empathy. Based on body responses, Alex seems to feel almost as much empathy. Pat is _____ (male/female); Alex is _____ (male/female).

Objective 11: Discuss the culture-specific and culturally universal aspects of emotional expression, and describe the effects of facial expressions on emotional experience.

Although the meaning of gestures varies with culture, facial expressions, such as those of happiness and anger, are common the world over. Cultures and languages also tend to categorize emotions as anger, fear, and so on in similar ways. Charles Darwin suggested that before our ancestors communicated in words, their ability to convey threats, greetings, and submissions with facial expressions helped them survive. Emotional expressions may also enhance our survival in other ways. For example, surprise widens the eyes, enabling us to take in more information. Disgust wrinkles the nose, closing it from foul odors.

The *facial feedback effect* indicates that facial muscle states tend to trigger corresponding feelings, such as fear or anger. For example, students induced to make a frowning expression reported feeling a little angry. Students induced to smile felt happier and found cartoons funnier. Similarly, the *behavior feedback effect* shows that if we move our body as we would when experiencing some emotion (shuffling along with downcast eyes, as when sad), we are likely to feel that emotion to some degree.

5. Gestures have _____ (the same/different) meanings in different cultures.

6. Studies of adults indicate that in different cultures facial expressions have _____ (the same/different) meanings.

7. According to _____ , human emotional expressions evolved because they helped our ancestors communicate before language developed. They also may enhance our _____ in other ways, such as by widening our eyes in surprise so we can take in more information.

8. William James believed we can control our emotions by going through outward movements of any emotion we want to experience. In one study, students who were induced to smile _____ (found/did not find) cartoons funnier.

9. When facial muscles trigger corresponding feelings, it is called the _____ _____ effect.

10. Studies have found that imitating another person's facial expressions _____ (leads/does not lead) to greater empathy with that person's feelings.

11. Similarly, moving our body as we would when experiencing a particular emotion causes us to feel that emotion. This is the _____ _____ effect.

APPLICATIONS:

12. The candidate stepped before the hostile audience, panic written all over his face. It is likely that the candidate's facial expression caused his fear to _____ (lessen/intensify).

13. Children in New York, Nigeria, and New Zealand smile when they are happy and frown when they are sad. This

suggests that facial expressions of emotion are _____ and are part of our shared _____ .

Experienced Emotion

Objective 12: Name several basic emotions, and discuss anger in terms of causes and consequences.

Carroll Izard's investigations identified 10 basic emotions: joy, interest-excitement, surprise, sadness, anger, disgust, contempt, fear, shame, and guilt.

People report that anger is often a response to friends' or loved ones' perceived misdeeds and is especially common when those acts seem willful, unjustified, and avoidable. Anger can harm us by fueling physically or verbally aggressive acts we later regret. Anger also primes prejudice. Also, chronic anger is linked to heart disease.

Although venting your anger may temporarily calm an angry person, it may also magnify anger and turn a minor conflict into a major confrontation. The *catharsis* hypothesis refers to the idea that "releasing" aggressive energy through action or fantasy reduces anger. Research has not supported the catharsis hypothesis. Angry outbursts may be reinforcing and therefore habit forming. In contrast, anger expressed as a nonaccusing statement of feeling can benefit relationships by helping to end the conflict that caused the anger. When the conflict can't be resolved, forgiveness can reduce one's anger and its physical symptoms.

1. Izard believes that there are _____ basic emotions, most of which _____ (are/are not) present in infancy.

2. Most people become angry several times per week and especially when another person's act seemed _____ , _____ , and _____ .

3. The belief that expressing pent-up emotion is adaptive is the _____ hypothesis.

4. Some potential problems with expressing anger are that it may fuel physical or _____ acts we later regret. It can also prime _____ . Chronic anger is linked to _____ disease. Anger can breed more anger, and it can _____ anger.

5. Psychologists have found that when anger has been provoked, retaliation may have a calming effect under certain circumstances. List the circumstances.

   a. _____
   b. _____
   c. _____

6. Researchers have found that students who mentally rehearsed the times they _____ someone who had hurt them had lower bodily arousal than when they thought of times when they did not.

APPLICATION:

7. Jane was so mad at her brother that she exploded at him when he entered her room. That she felt less angry afterward is best explained by the principle of

_____ .

Objective 13: Identify some causes and consequences of happiness, and describe two psychological phenomena that help explain the relatively short duration of emotions.

A good mood boosts people's perceptions of the world and their willingness to help others (the *feel-good, do-good phenomenon*). Mood-boosting experiences make us more likely to give money, pick up someone's dropped papers, volunteer time, and do other good deeds. After decades of focusing on negative emotions, psychologists are now actively exploring the causes and consequences of *subjective well-being* (self-perceived happiness or satisfaction with life).

Positive emotion rises over the early to middle part of most days. Although stressful events trigger bad moods, the gloom nearly always lifts by the next day. Times of elation are similarly hard to sustain and, over the long run, our emotional ups and downs tend to balance. Even significant bad events, such as a serious illness, seldom destroy happiness for long. The surprising reality is that we overestimate the duration of emotions and underestimate our resilience.

At a basic level, money helps us to avoid misery, but having it is no guarantee of happiness. Sudden increases in wealth such as winning a state lottery only increase happiness in the short term. In the long run, increased wealth hardly affects happiness. For example, during the last four decades, the average U.S. citizen's buying power almost tripled, yet the average American is no happier. More generally, research indicates that economic growth in wealthy countries has not boosted morale or social well-being. What matters more is how we feel about what we have.

The *adaptation-level phenomenon* describes our tendency to judge events relative to a neutral level defined by our previous experience. If our income or social prestige increases, we may feel initial pleasure. However, we then adapt to this new level of achievement, come to see it as normal, and require something better to give us another surge of happiness.

Relative deprivation is the perception that we are worse off relative to those with whom we compare ourself. As people climb the ladder of success, they mostly compare themselves with those who are at or above

their current level. This explains why increases in income may do little to increase happiness.

High self-esteem, close friendships or a satisfying marriage, and meaningful religious faith are among the predictors of happiness. Age, gender, educational level, and parenthood are among the factors unrelated to happiness.

8. Happy people tend to perceive the world as _____ and live _____ and more energized and satisfied lives.

9. Happy people are also _____ (more/less) willing to help others. This is called the _____-_____ , _____-_____ phenomenon.

10. An individual's self-perceived happiness or satisfaction with life is called his or her

_____ _____ .

11. Positive emotions _____ (rise/fall) early in the day and _____ (rise/fall) during the later hours. The gloom of stressful events usually _____ (is gone by/continues into) the next day.

12. After experiencing tragedy or dramatically positive events, people generally _____ (regain/do not regain) their previous degree of happiness.

13. Most people tend to _____ (underestimate/overestimate) the duration of emotions and _____ (underestimate/overestimate) their resilience.

14. Researchers have found that levels of happiness _____ (do/do not) mirror differences in standards of living.

15. During the last four decades, spendable income in the United States has almost tripled; personal happiness has _____ (increased/decreased/remained almost unchanged).

16. The idea that happiness is relative to our recent experience is stated by the _____-_____ phenomenon.

Explain how this principle accounts for the fact that, for some people, material desires can never be satisfied.

17. The principle that one feels worse off than others is known as _____

_____ . This helps to explain why comparing ourselves with those who are less well off _____ (does/does not) boost our contentment.

18. List six factors that have been shown to be positively correlated with feelings of happiness.

_____
_____
_____
_____
_____
_____

19. List five factors that are evidently unrelated to happiness.

_____
_____
_____
_____
_____

20. Research studies of identical and fraternal twins have led to the estimate that about

_____ percent of the variation in people's happiness ratings is heritable.

(Close-Up) State several research-based suggestions for increasing your satisfaction with life.

APPLICATIONS:

21. As elderly Mr. Hooper crosses the busy intersection, he stumbles and drops the packages he is carrying. Which passerby is most likely to help Mr. Hooper?

a. Drew, who has been laid off from work for three months
b. Leon, who is on his way to work
c. Bonnie, who graduated from college the day before
d. Nancy, whose father recently passed away

22. Cindy was happy with her promotion until she found out that Janice, who has the same amount of experience, receives a higher salary. Cindy's feelings are best explained by which principle? _____

_____

23. When Professor Simon acquired a spacious new office, he was overjoyed. Six months later, however, he was taking the office for granted. His behavior illustrates which principle? _____

_____ _____

PROGRESS TEST

Multiple-Choice Questions

Circle your answers to the following questions and check them with the answers beginning on page 173. If your answer is incorrect, read the explanation for why it is incorrect and then consult the text.

1. Motivation is best understood as a state that
a. reduces a drive.
b. aims at satisfying a biological need.
c. energizes an organism to act.
d. energizes and directs behavior.

2. Which of the following is a difference between a drive and a need?
a. Needs are learned; drives are inherited.
b. Needs are physiological states; drives are psychological states.
c. Drives are generally stronger than needs.
d. Needs are generally stronger than drives.

3. One problem with the idea of motivation as drive reduction is that
a. because some motivated behaviors do not seem to be based on physiological needs, they cannot be explained in terms of drive reduction.
b. it fails to explain any human motivation.
c. it cannot account for metabolic rates.
d. it does not explain the hunger drive.

4. Electrical stimulation of the arcuate nucleus of the hypothalamus will cause an animal to
a. begin eating.
b. lose weight.
c. become obese.
d. begin copulating.

5. The text suggests that the tendency to avoid unfamiliar tastes
a. is more common in children than in adults.
b. protected our ancestors from potentially toxic substances.
c. may be an early warning sign of an eating disorder.
d. only grows stronger with repeated exposure to those tastes.

ARCUATE nucleus (handwritten margin note)

6. I am a protein hormone produced by fat cells and monitored by the hypothalamus. When in abundance, I cause the brain to increase metabolism. What am I?
   a. PYY
   b. ghrelin
   c. orexin
   d. leptin

7. Drive-reduction theory emphasizes _____ factors in motivation.
   a. environmental
   b. cognitive
   c. psychological
   d. biological

8. In his study of men on a semistarvation diet, Keys found that
   a. the metabolic rate of the men increased.
   b. the men eventually lost interest in food.
   c. the men became obsessed with food.
   d. the men's behavior directly contradicted predictions made by Maslow's hierarchy of needs.

9. As the Greek philosopher Aristotle noted, we all
   a. behave in ways that allow us to maintain good health.
   b. need challenging work.
   c. are social animals.
   d. want to serve others.

10. (Close-Up) Which of the following is true of bulimia nervosa?
    a. It involves bingeing and purging.
    b. Bulimia patients starve themselves.
    c. Bulimia patients show a dramatic weight loss.
    d. Bulimia is unrelated to a concern with appearance.

11. Research on genetic influences on obesity reveals that
    a. the body weights of adoptees most closely resemble those of their biological parents.
    b. the body weights of adoptees most closely resemble those of their adoptive parents.
    c. identical twins usually have very different body weights.
    d. the body weights of identical twin women are more similar than those of identical twin men.

12. Research on obesity indicates that
    a. pound for pound, fat tissue requires more calories to maintain than lean tissue.
    b. once fat cells are acquired they are never lost, no matter how rigorously you diet.
    c. one pound of weight is lost for every 3500-calorie reduction in diet.
    d. when weight drops below the set point, hunger and metabolism also decrease.

13. The number of fat cells a person has is influenced by
    a. heredity.
    b. childhood eating patterns.
    c. adulthood eating patterns.
    d. all of these factors.

14. Which of the following influences on hunger motivation does NOT belong with the others?
    a. set/settling point
    b. attraction to sweet and salty tastes
    c. reduced production of ghrelin after stomach bypass surgery
    d. memory of time elapsed since your last meal

15. The tendency to overeat when food is plentiful
    a. is a recent occurrence that is related to the luxury of having ample food.
    b. emerged in our prehistoric ancestors as an adaptive response to alternating periods of feast and famine.
    c. is greater in developed, than in developing, societies.
    d. is stronger in women than in men.

16. (Close-Up) Although the cause of eating disorders is still unknown, proposed explanations focus on all of the following *except*
    a. metabolic factors.
    b. genetic factors.
    c. family background factors.
    d. cultural factors.

17. The brain area that when stimulated secretes appetite-suppressing hormones is the
    a. hippocampus.
    b. arcuate nucleus.
    c. thalamus.
    d. amygdala.

18. (Close-Up) Women students in _____ rate their body ideals closest to their actual shape.
    a. Western cultures
    b. countries in Africa, where thinness can signal poverty and AIDS,
    c. countries such as India
    d. Australia, New Zealand, and England

19. According to Maslow's theory
    a. the most basic motives are based on physiological needs.
    b. needs are satisfied in a specified order.
    c. the highest motives relate to self-transcendence.
    d. all of these are true.

20. (Close-Up) Which of the following is true concerning eating disorders?
    a. Genetic factors may influence susceptibility.
    b. Cultural pressures for thinness strongly influence teenage girls.
    c. Family background is a significant factor.
    d. All of these facts are true.

21. The digestive tract hormone that sends "I'm not hungry" signals to the brain is.
    a. leptin.
    b. PYY.
    c. insulin.
    d. glucose.

22. Which of the following is NOT necessarily a reason that obese people have trouble losing weight?
    a. Fat tissue has a lower metabolic rate than lean tissue.
    b. Once a person has lost weight, it takes fewer calories to maintain his or her current weight.
    c. The tendency toward obesity may be genetically based.
    d. Obese people tend to lack willpower.

23. Beginning with the most basic needs, which of the following represents the correct sequence of needs in the hierarchy described by Maslow?
    a. safety; physiological; esteem; belongingness and love; self-fulfillment; self-transcendence
    b. safety; physiological; belongingness and love; self-transcendence; esteem; self-fulfillment
    c. physiological; safety; esteem; belongingness and love; self-transcendence; self-fulfillment
    d. physiological; safety; belongingness and love; esteem; self-fulfillment; self-transcendence

24. Which division of the nervous system is especially involved in bringing about emotional arousal?
    a. somatic nervous system
    b. peripheral nervous system
    c. sympathetic nervous system
    d. parasympathetic nervous system

25. Concerning emotions and their accompanying body responses, which of the following appears to be true?
    a. Each emotion has its own body response and underlying brain circuit.
    b. All emotions involve the same body response as a result of the same underlying brain circuit.
    c. Many emotions involve similar body responses but have different underlying brain circuits.
    d. All emotions have the same underlying brain circuits but different body responses.

26. The Cannon-Bard theory of emotion states that
    a. emotions have two ingredients: physical arousal and a cognitive label.
    b. the conscious experience of an emotion occurs at the same time as the body's physical reaction.
    c. emotional experiences are based on an awareness of the body's responses to an emotion-arousing stimulus.
    d. emotional ups and downs tend to balance in the long run.

27. Which of the following was NOT raised as a criticism of the James-Lange theory of emotion?
    a. The body's responses are too similar to trigger the various emotions.
    b. Emotional reactions occur before the body's responses can take place.
    c. The cognitive activity of the cortex plays a role in the emotions we experience.
    d. People with spinal cord injuries at the neck typically experience less emotion.

28. (Thinking Critically) Current estimates are that the polygraph is inaccurate approximately _____ of the time.
    a. three-fourths
    b. one-half
    c. one-third
    d. one-fourth

29. In one experiment, college men were injected with the hormone epinephrine. Which participants reported feeling an emotional change in the presence of the experimenter's highly emotional confederate?
    a. those receiving epinephrine and expecting to feel physical arousal
    b. those receiving a placebo and expecting to feel physical arousal
    c. those receiving epinephrine and not expecting to feel physical arousal
    d. those receiving a placebo and not expecting to feel physical arousal

30. Which of the following is true regarding happiness?
    a. People with more education tend to be happier.
    b. Beautiful people tend to be happier than plain people.
    c. Women tend to be happier than men.
    d. People who are socially outgoing or who exercise regularly tend to be happier.

31. Catharsis will be most effective in reducing anger toward another person if
    a. you wait until you are no longer angry before confronting the person.
    b. the target of your anger is someone you feel has power over you.
    c. your anger is directed specifically toward the person who angered you.
    d. the other person is able to confront you by also expressing anger.

32. Emotions consist of which of the following components?
    a. physiological reactions
    b. behavioral expressions
    c. conscious feelings
    d. all of these components

33. Law enforcement officials sometimes use a lie detector to assess a suspect's responses to details of the crime believed to be known only to the perpetrator. This is known as the
    a. inductive approach.
    b. deductive approach.
    c. guilty knowledge test.
    d. screening examination.

34. In laboratory experiments, fear and joy
    a. result in an increase in heart rate.
    b. stimulate different facial muscles.
    c. increase heart rate and stimulate different facial muscles.
    d. result in a decrease in heart rate.

35. Research indicates that a person is most likely to be helpful to others if he or she
    a. is feeling guilty about something.
    b. is happy.
    c. recently received help from another person.
    d. recently offered help to another person.

36. With regard to emotions, Darwin believed that
    a. the expression of emotions helped our ancestors to survive.
    b. our ancestors communicated threats, greetings, and submission with facial expressions.
    c. human facial expressions of emotion retain elements of animals' emotional displays.
    d. all of these are true.

37. A graph depicting the course of positive emotions over the hours of the day since waking would:
    a. start low and rise steadily until bedtime.
    b. start high and decrease steadily until bedtime.
    c. remain at a stable, moderate level throughout the day.
    d. rise over the early hours and dissipate during the day's last several hours.

38. The Schachter and Singer two-factor theory emphasizes that emotion involves both
    a. the sympathetic and parasympathetic divisions of the nervous system.
    b. verbal and nonverbal expression.
    c. physical arousal and cognitive appraisal.
    d. universal and culture-specific aspects.

39. When students studied others who were worse off than themselves, they felt greater satisfaction with their own lives. This is an example of the principle of
    a. relative deprivation.
    b. adaptation level.
    c. behavioral contrast.
    d. opponent processes.

40. Which theory of emotion emphasizes the simultaneous experience of body response and emotional feeling?
    a. James-Lange
    b. Cannon-Bard
    c. two-factor
    d. catharsis

41. Izard believes that there are _____ basic emotions.
    a. 3   c. 7
    b. 5   d. 10

42. (Thinking Critically) The polygraph measures
    a. lying.
    b. brain rhythms.
    c. chemical changes in the body.
    d. physiological responses accompanying emotion.

43. People who are exuberant and persistently cheerful show increased activity in the brain's
    a. right frontal lobe.
    b. left frontal lobe.
    c. amygdala.
    d. thalamus.

44. Which of the following is true regarding gestures and facial expressions?
    a. Gestures are universal; facial expressions, culture-specific.
    b. Facial expressions are universal; gestures, culture-specific.
    c. Both gestures and facial expressions are universal.
    d. Both gestures and facial expressions are culture-specific.

45. Which theory of emotion implies that every emotion is associated with a unique physiological reaction?
    a. James-Lange
    b. Cannon-Bard
    c. two-factor
    d. catharsis

46. Concerning catharsis, which of the following is true?
    a. Expressing anger can be temporarily calming if it does not leave one feeling guilty or anxious.
    b. The arousal that accompanies unexpressed anger never lessens.
    c. Expressing your anger always calms you down.
    d. Psychologists agree that under no circumstances is catharsis beneficial.

47. In an emergency situation, emotional arousal will result in
    a. increased rate of respiration.
    b. increased blood sugar.
    c. a slowing of digestion.
    d. all of these actions.

48. (Thinking Critically) Many psychologists are opposed to the use of lie detectors because
    a. they represent an invasion of a person's privacy and could easily be used for unethical purposes.
    b. there are often serious discrepancies among the various indicators such as perspiration and heart rate.
    c. polygraphs cannot distinguish the various possible causes of arousal.
    d. they are accurate only about 50 percent of the time.

49. In studying what makes people angry, researchers have found that most people become angry
    a. once a day.
    b. once a week.
    c. several times a week.
    d. several times a month.

50. Which of these factors have researchers NOT found to relate to happiness?

40
50

a. a satisfying marriage or close friendship
b. high self-esteem
c. religious faith
d. education

Matching Items

Match each term with its definition or description.

Terms

_____ **1.** anorexia nervosa
_____ **2.** set point
_____ **3.** relative deprivation
_____ **4.** drive
_____ **5.** feel-good, do-good phenomenon
_____ **6.** physiological needs
_____ **7.** incentive
_____ **8.** bulimia nervosa
_____ **9.** adaptation-level phenomenon
_____ **10.** catharsis
_____ **11.** subjective well-being
_____ **12.** binge-eating disorder

Definitions or Descriptions

a. environmental stimulus that motivates behavior
b. an eating disorder characterized by repeated episodes of overeating following by vomiting, fasting, or laxative use
c. our basic bodily requirements
d. the body's weight-maintenance setting
e. the tendency to react to changes on the basis of recent experience
f. an individual's self-perceived happiness
g. emotional release
h. an eating disorder characterized by significantly below normal weight
i. the perception that we are worse off than those with whom we compare ourselves
j. the tendency of people to be helpful when they are in a good mood
k. an aroused state arising from some physiological need
l. an eating disorder characterized by eating binges followed by remorse.

Application Essay

Explain how the three major theories of motivation differ and why each one separately cannot fully account for human behavior. (Use the space below to list the points you want to make, and organize them. Then write the essay on a separate sheet of paper.)

SUMMING UP

Walking home from school after the basketball game, Jesse takes a shortcut through an area with no street lights. He sees a shadow of a person with something glistening in his hand, which causes him to experience the three parts of a distinct emotion.

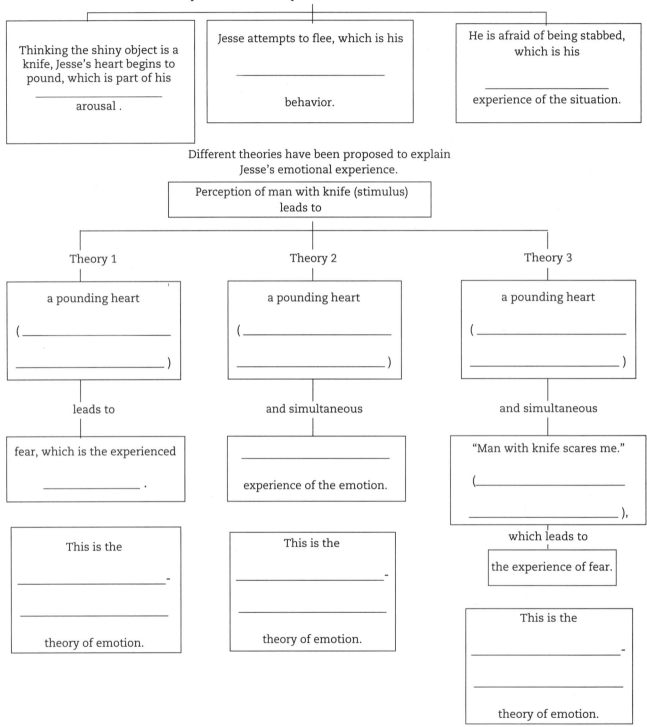

Thinking the shiny object is a knife, Jesse's heart begins to pound, which is part of his

_____ arousal .

Jesse attempts to flee, which is his

_____

behavior.

He is afraid of being stabbed, which is his

_____

experience of the situation.

Different theories have been proposed to explain Jesse's emotional experience.

Perception of man with knife (stimulus) leads to

Theory 1

a pounding heart

(_____

_____)

leads to

fear, which is the experienced

_____ .

This is the

_____ -

_____

theory of emotion.

Theory 2

a pounding heart

(_____

_____)

and simultaneous

_____

experience of the emotion.

This is the

_____ -

_____

theory of emotion.

Theory 3

a pounding heart

(_____

_____)

and simultaneous

"Man with knife scares me."

(_____

_____),

which leads to

the experience of fear.

This is the

_____ -

_____

theory of emotion.

TERMS AND CONCEPTS

Using your own words, write on a separate piece of paper a brief definition or explanation of each of the following terms.

1. motivation
2. drive-reduction theory
3. physiological needs
4. drive
5. incentive
6. hierarchy of needs
7. glucose
8. set point
9. basal metabolic rate
10. anorexia nervosa
11. bulimia nervosa
12. binge-eating disorder
13. emotion
14. James-Lange theory
15. Cannon-Bard theory
16. two-factor theory
17. polygraph
18. facial feedback effect
19. catharsis
20. feel-good, do-good phenomenon
21. subjective well-being
22. adaptation-level phenomenon
23. relative deprivation

ANSWERS
Chapter Review

Motivational Concepts

1. a need or desire that energizes behavior and directs it toward a goal
2. drive-reduction; arousal; hierarchy; Abraham Maslow
3. need; drive
4. incentives
5. increase; do not; stress
6. hierarchy
7. physiological; self-actualization; self-transcendence
8. money; home-life
9. drive-reduction. Drive-reduction theory maintains that behavior is motivated when a biological need creates an aroused state, driving the individual to satisfy the need. It's unlikely that Mary's hang-gliding is satisfying a biological need.
10. Maslow. According to Maslow's theory, physiological needs, such as the need to satisfy hunger, must be satisfied before a person pursues loftier needs, such as making political statements.

Hunger

1. semistarvation
2. stomach contractions
3. does
4. glucose; increase
5. hypothalamus; arcuate nucleus; decreases
6. ghrelin
7. less
8. orexin
9. ghrelin
10. insulin
11. leptin
12. PYY
13. set point; less; more
14. basal metabolic; lowering
15. is not accepted; slow, steady changes in body weight; overeat; gain weight; settling point
16. arcuate nucleus; neural. The arcuate nucleus in the hypothalamus includes centers that either enhance or suppress eating behavior.
17. metabolic rates. Individual differences in metabolism and set point explain why it is possible for two people to have very different weights despite similar patterns of eating and exercise.
18. b. is the answer. The body acts to defend its set point, or the weight to which it is predisposed. If Lucille was already near her set point, weight loss would prove difficult.
19. memory
20. anorexia nervosa
21. bulimia nervosa; binge-purge; binge-eating disorder
22. competitive; high-achieving; self-esteem; standards
23. may; Identical; fraternal
24. India; prosperous; Western; body image
25. ashamed; depressed; dissatisfied
26. serotonin; calms
27. genetic; learning; culture; unfamiliar
28. obsessed with her weight and appearance. She also experiences bouts of depression and anxiety.
29. b. is the answer. Adolescent females with low self-esteem and high-achieving families seem especially prone to eating disorders such as anorexia nervosa.
30. c. is the answer. Our preferences for sweet and salty tastes are genetic and universal.
31. does not pose; diabetes, high blood pressure, heart disease, gallstones, joint pain, arthritis, and certain types of cancer
32. apple
33. slow; lazy; sloppy
34. less; married

35. obese

36. 3500

37. fat cells; heredity; personal history

38. can; cannot

39. less; is; hunger; metabolism

40. do

41. more; less

42. gain

Begin only if you are motivated and self-disciplined. Minimize exposure to tempting food cues. Eat healthy foods. Don't starve all day and eat one big meal at night. Beware of binge eating. Be realistic and moderate. Boost your metabolism through exercise.

43. rapid; more slowly; decreased. When a diet forces weight to drop below the person's settling point, as it did with Owen, the dieter's hunger increases and metabolism decreases.

44. **a.** is the answer. Dieting, including fasting, lowers the body's metabolic rate and reduces the amount of food energy needed to maintain body weight.

The Need to Belong

1. Aristotle; social; survival; belong; genes

2. self-esteem

3. social; liking

4. isolated; cluster migration

5. Throughout the world; ostracism

6. self-defeating; aggressive

7. less; strengthening

8. self-conscious; inhibited; self-disclosure

9. do

10. narcissism

Experts suggest that you monitor your time, noting whether your time online is interfering with school or work performance; monitor your feelings; "hide" your more distracting online friends, try turning off your handheld devices or leaving them elsewhere; and try a Facebook fast or a time-controlled Facebook diet.

11. **c.** is the answer.

12. **d.** is the answer.

Theories of Emotion

1. physiological arousal; expressive behaviors; conscious experience

2. follow

Cannon argued that the body's responses were not distinct enough to trigger the different emotions. Also, physiological changes occur too slowly to trigger sudden emotion.

3. cortex; sympathetic; Cannon-Bard

4. physical; cognitive; Stanley Schachter; Jerome Singer

5. Answers are given in order: first response, second response, third response.

James-Lange theory: physical arousal, expressed emotion, cognitive appraisal is unimportant
Cannon-Bard theory: physical arousal and cognitive appraisal occur simultaneously, expressed emotion
Two-factor theory: physical arousal, cognitive appraisal, expressed emotion

6. Cannon-Bard

7. James-Lange

8. two-factor

Embodied Emotion

1. **a.** Heart rate increases.
   b. Muscles receive more blood sugar, making running, for example, easier.
   c. The liver pours extra sugar into the bloodstream.
   d. Breathing increases.
   e. Digestion slows.
   f. Pupils dilate.
   g. Blood tends to clot more rapidly.
   h. Skin perspires.
   i. Immune system functioning is reduced.

2. autonomic; sympathetic; parasympathetic

3. similar; fear; anger; sexual arousal

4. fear; rage; finger; hormone

5. fear; joy

6. are; right frontal; depression

7. left frontal

8. left; frontal

9. polygraph

The polygraph measures several of the physiological responses that accompany emotion, such as changes in breathing, heart rate, and perspiration. The underlying idea is that lying is stressful, so a person who is lying will become physiologically aroused.

10. nervous

11. innocent; emotions; arousal

12. do not agree

13. guilty knowledge test

14. **d.** is the answer.

15. **a.** A guilty person can be found innocent.
   b. An innocent person can be found guilty.
   c. These tests err about one-third of the time.

16. positive. Individuals with more active right frontal lobes tend to be less cheerful.

17. increased; right frontal. As people experience negative emotions, such as anger, the right hemisphere becomes more electrically active.

18. arousal

19. did not; did

20. fuels; channels

21. can

First, an experiment involving subliminally presented fearful eyes indicated that although the eyes were flashed too quickly for people to perceive them, they did trigger increased amygdala activity. Second, there is some separation of the neural pathways involved in emotion and cognition.

22. thalamus; amygdala; cognition; cortex

23. Richard Lazarus; appraise

24. interpretations; expectations; memories

25. **c.** is the answer. Because physical arousal tends to intensify emotions, Dan (who is likely to be physically aroused after playing tennis) will probably be angrier than Bob or Veronica, who are in more relaxed states.

Expressed Emotion

1. threats
2. better; decoding; responsiveness
3. more; smaller; more
4. female; male
5. different
6. the same
7. Charles Darwin; survival
8. found
9. facial feedback
10. leads
11. behavior feedback
12. intensify. Expressions may amplify the associated emotions.
13. universal; heritage

Experienced Emotion

1. 10; are
2. willful; unjustified; avoidable
3. catharsis
4. verbal; prejudice; heart; magnify
5. **a.** Retaliation must be directed against the person who provoked the anger.
   b. Retaliation must be justifiable.
   c. The target of the retaliation must not be someone who is intimidating.
6. forgave
7. catharsis. In keeping with the catharsis hypothesis, Jane feels less angry after releasing her aggression.
8. safer; healthier
9. more; feel-good, do-good
10. subjective well-being
11. rise; fall; is gone by
12. regain
13. overestimate; underestimate
14. do not
15. remained almost unchanged
16. adaptation-level

If we acquire new possessions, we feel an initial surge of pleasure. But we then adapt to having these new possessions, come to see them as normal, and require other things to give us another surge of happiness.

17. relative deprivation; does

18. high self-esteem; satisfying marriage or close friendships; meaningful religious faith; optimistic outgoing personality; good sleeping habits and regular exercise; having work and leisure that engage our skills

19. age; gender; education; parenthood; physical attractiveness

20. 50

Realize that happiness doesn't come from financial success. Take control of your time. Act happy. Seek work and leisure that engage your skills. Engage in regular aerobic exercise. Get plenty of sleep. Give priority to close relationships. Focus beyond self. Be grateful. Nurture your spiritual self.

21. **c.** is the answer. People who are in a good mood are more likely to help others. Bonnie, who is probably pleased with herself following her graduation from college, is likely to be in a better mood than Drew, Leon, or Nancy.

22. relative deprivation. Cindy is unhappy with her promotion because she feels deprived relative to Janice.

23. adaptation-level phenomenon. Professor Simon's judgment of his office is affected by his recent experience: When that experience was of a smaller office, his new office seemed terrific; now, however, it is commonplace.

Progress Test

Multiple-Choice Questions

1. **d.** is the answer.
   a. & b. Although motivation is often aimed at reducing drives and satisfying biological needs, this is by no means always the case.
   c. Motivated behavior not only is energized but also is directed at a goal.

2. **b.** is the answer. A drive is the psychological consequence of a physiological need.
   a. Needs are unlearned states of deprivation.
   c. & d. Because needs are physical and drives psychological, their strengths cannot be compared directly.

3. **a.** is the answer. The curiosity of a child or a scientist is an example of behavior apparently motivated by something other than a physiological need.
   b. & d. Some behaviors, such as thirst and hunger, are partially explained by drive reduction.
   c. Metabolic rate is unrelated to drive reduction.

4. **a.** is the answer. This area of the hypothalamus seems to elevate hunger.
   b. If the animal begins eating, it will most likely gain weight.
   c. Obesity may be a long-term effect but is not the first result of such stimulation.
   d. The hypothalamus is involved in sexual motivation, but not in this way.

5. **b.** is the answer.
   a. The tendency to avoid food based on taste is typical of all age groups.

c. The tendency to avoid food based on taste is *not* an indicator of an eating disorder.
d. With repeated exposure, our appreciation for a new taste typically *increases*.

6. **d.** is the answer.
   a. PYY signals fullness, which is associated with decreased metabolism.
   b. Ghrelin is a hormone secreted by the empty stomach that sends hunger signals.
   c. Orexin is a hormone secreted by the hypothalamus.

7. **d.** is the answer.

8. **c.** is the answer. The deprived men focused on food almost to the exclusion of anything else. (p. 238)
   a. To conserve energy, the men's metabolic rate actually *decreased*.
   b. & d. Far from losing interest in food, the men came to care only about food—a finding consistent with Maslow's hierarchy, in which physiological needs are at the base.

9. **c.** is the answer.

10. **a.** is the answer.

11. **a.** is the answer.

12. **b.** is the answer.

13. **d.** is the answer. Personal history clearly includes both childhood and adult eating patterns.

14. **d.** is the answer. Memory of the time of the last meal is an example of a psychological influence on hunger motivation.
    a., b., & c. Each of these is a biological influence on hunger motivation.

15. **b.** is the answer.
    c. If anything, just the opposite is true.
    d. Men and women do not differ in the tendency to overeat.

16. **a.** is the answer. The text does not indicate whether their metabolism is higher or lower than most.
    b., c., & d. Genes, family background, and cultural influence have all been proposed as factors in eating disorders.

17. **b.** is the answer.
    a. The hippocampus is involved in memory.
    c. The thalamus is a sensory relay station; stimulation of it has no effect on eating.
    d. The amygdala is involved in emotions, especially fear and rage.

18. **c.** is the answer.

19. **d.** is the answer.

20. **d.** is the answer.

21. **b.** is the answer.
    a. Leptin is secreted by fat cells.
    c. & d. Insulin is secreted by the pancreas and regulates the amount of glucose in the bloodstream.

22. **d.** is the answer. Most researchers today discount the idea that people are obese because they lack willpower.

23. **d.** is the answer.

24. **c.** is the answer.
    a. The somatic division of the peripheral nervous system carries sensory and motor signals to and from the central nervous system.
    b. The peripheral nervous system is too general an answer, since it includes the sympathetic and parasympathetic divisions, as well as the somatic division.
    d. The parasympathetic nervous system restores the body to its unaroused state.

25. **c.** is the answer. Although many emotions have the same general body arousal, resulting from activation of the sympathetic nervous system, they appear to be associated with different brain circuits.

26. **b.** is the answer.
    a. This expresses the two-factor theory.
    c. This expresses the James-Lange theory.
    d. This theory was not discussed.

27. **d.** is the answer. The finding that people whose brains can't sense the body's responses experience considerably less emotion in fact supports the James-Lange theory, which claims that experienced emotion follows from body responses.
    a., b., & c. All these statements go counter to the theory's claim that experienced emotion is essentially just an awareness of the body's response.

28. **c.** is the answer.

29. **c.** is the answer. As proof of the spillover effect, the men who received epinephrine without an explanation felt arousal and experienced this arousal as whatever emotion the experimental confederate in the room with them was displaying.
    a. Epinephrine recipients who expected arousal attributed their arousal to the drug and reported no emotional change in reaction to the confederate's behavior.
    b. & d. In addition to the two groups discussed in the text, the experiment involved placebo recipients; these men were not physically aroused and did not experience an emotional change.

30. **d.** is the answer. Education level, parenthood, gender, and physical attractiveness seem unrelated to happiness.

31. **c.** is the answer.
    a. This would not be an example of catharsis because catharsis involves releasing, rather than suppressing, aggressive energy.
    b. Expressions of anger in such a situation tend to cause the person anxiety and thus tend not to be effective.
    d. One danger of expressing anger is that it will lead to a major confrontation.

32. **d.** is the answer. These are the three components of emotions identified in the text.

33. **c.** is the answer. If the suspect becomes physically aroused while answering questions about details only the guilty person could know, the test-giver can assume that he or she committed the crime.

34. **c.** is the answer. Both fear and joy increase heart rate but stimulate different facial muscles.

35. b. is the answer.
a., c., & d. Research studies have not found these factors to be related to helpful behavior.

36. d. is the answer.

37. d. is the answer.

38. c. is the answer. According to Schachter and Singer, the two factors in emotion are (1) physical arousal and (2) conscious interpretation of the arousal.

39. a. is the answer. The principle of relative deprivation states that happiness is relative to others' attainments. This helps explain why those who are relatively well off tend to be slightly more satisfied than the relatively poor, with whom the better-off can compare themselves.
b. Adaptation level is the tendency for our judgments to be relative to our prior experience.
c. This phenomenon has nothing to do with the interpretation of emotion.
d. Opponent processes are not discussed in the text in relation to emotion.

40. b. is the answer.
a. The James-Lange theory states that the experience of an emotion is an awareness of one's physical response to an emotion-arousing stimulus.
c. The two-factor theory states that to experience emotion one must be physically aroused and cognitively label the arousal.
d. There is no such theory; catharsis refers to the release of emotion.

41. d. is the answer.

42. d. is the answer. No device can literally measure lying. The polygraph measures breathing, blood pressure, and perspiration for changes indicative of physiological arousal.

43. b. is the answer.

44. b. is the answer. The meanings of gestures vary from culture to culture; facial expressions seem to have the same meanings around the world.

45. a. is the answer. If, as the theory claims, emotions are triggered by physiological reactions, then each emotion must be associated with a unique physiological reaction.
b. According to the Cannon-Bard theory, the same general body response accompanies many emotions.
c. The two-factor theory states that the cognitive interpretation of a general state of physical arousal determines different emotions.
d. There is no such theory; catharsis refers to the release of emotion.

46. a. is the answer.
b. The opposite is true. Any emotional arousal will simmer down if you wait long enough.
c. Catharsis often magnifies anger and leads to confrontation.
d. When counterattack is justified and can be directed at the offender, catharsis may be helpful.

47. d. is the answer.

48. c. is the answer. As heightened arousal may reflect feelings of anxiety or irritation rather than of guilt, the polygraph, which simply measures arousal, may easily err.
a. Misuse and invasion of privacy are valid issues, but researchers primarily object to the use of lie detectors because of their inaccuracy.
b. Although there are discrepancies among the various measures of arousal, this was not what researchers objected to.
d. The lie detector errs about one-third of the time.

49. c. is the answer.

50. d. is the answer.

Matching Items

1. h	**6.** c	**11.** f
2. d	**7.** a	**12.** l
3. i	**8.** b	
4. k	**9.** e	
5. j	**10.** g	

Application Essay

Drive-reduction is the idea that biological needs create aroused drive states that motivate the individual to satisfy these needs. Drive-reduction theory failed as a complete account of human motivation because many human motives do not satisfy any obvious biological need. Instead, such behaviors are motivated by environmental incentives.

Arousal theory emerged in response to evidence that some motivated behaviors *increase*, rather than decrease, arousal.

Maslow's hierarchy of needs suggests that we are motivated to satisfy basic needs, such as the need for food and water, first. We then look to satisfy needs for self-esteem, love and belongingness, and so on until we reach the highest-level needs of self-actualization and self-transcendence. The problem with Maslow's hierarchy is that some people will sacrifice their need for food, for example, to make a philosophical statement.

Summing Up

Walking home from school after the basketball game, Jesse takes a shortcut through an area with no street lights. He sees a shadow of a person with something glistening in his hand, which causes him to experience the three parts of a distinct emotion. Thinking the shiny object is a knife, Jesse's heart begins to pound, which is part of his *physical* arousal. Jesse attempts to flee, which is his *expressive* behavior. He is afraid of being stabbed, which is his *conscious* experience of the situation.

Different theories have been proposed to explain Jesse's emotional experience. Perception of man with knife (stimulus) leads to Theory 1: a pounding heart (*physical arousal*) leads to fear, which is the experienced *emotion*. This is the *James-Lange* theory of emotion. Theory 2: a pounding heart (*physical arousal*) and simultaneous *subjective* experience of the emotion. This is the *Cannon-Bard* theory of emotion. Theory 3: a pounding heart (*physical arousal*) and simultaneous "Man with knife scares me" (*cognitive appraisal*), which leads to the experience of fear. This is the *two-factor* theory of emotion.

Terms and Concepts

1. **Motivation** is a need or desire that energizes and directs behavior.

2. **Drive-reduction theory** attempts to explain behavior as arising from a physiological need that creates an aroused tension state (drive) that motivates an organism to satisfy the need.

3. **Physiological needs** include our basic bodily requirements such as thirst and hunger.

4. **Drives** are motivated states that result from deprivation of a needed substance such as water.

5. **Incentives** are positive or negative environmental stimuli that motivate behavior.

6. Maslow's **hierarchy of needs** proposes that human motives may be ranked from the basic, physiological level through higher-level needs for safety, love, esteem, self-actualization, and self-transcendence; until they are satisfied, the more basic needs are more compelling than the higher-level ones.

7. **Glucose**, or blood sugar, is the major source of energy for the body's tissues. Elevating the level of glucose in the body will reduce hunger.

8. **Set point** is an individual's regulated weight level, which is maintained by adjusting food intake and energy output.

9. **Basal metabolic rate** is the body's base rate of energy expenditure when resting.

10. **Anorexia nervosa** is an eating disorder, most common in adolescent females, in which a person restricts food intake to become significantly underweight and yet still feels fat.

11. **Bulimia nervosa** is an eating disorder characterized by episodes of overeating followed by vomiting, laxative use, fasting, or excessive exercise.

12. **Binge-eating disorder** is an eating disorder characterized by significant binge-eating, followed by distress, disgust, or guilt, but without the purging, fasting, or excessive exercise that marks bulimia nervosa.

13. **Emotion** is a response of the whole organism involving three components: (1) physical arousal, (2) expressive behaviors, and (3) conscious experience.

14. The **James-Lange theory** states that emotional experiences are based on an awareness of the body's responses to emotion-arousing stimuli. A stimulus triggers the body's responses that in turn trigger the experienced emotion.

15. The **Cannon-Bard theory** states that the subjective experience of an emotion occurs at the same time as the body's physical reaction.

16. The **two-factor theory** of emotion proposes that emotions have two ingredients: physical arousal and cognitive appraisal. Thus, physical arousal is a necessary, but not a sufficient, component of emotional change. For an emotion to be experienced, arousal must be attributed to an emotional cause.

17. The **polygraph**, or lie detector, is a device that measures several of the physiological responses accompanying emotion.

18. The **facial feedback effect** occurs when making an emotional facial expression (such as smiling) triggers the corresponding emotional feeling (happiness).

19. **Catharsis** is emotional release; according to the catharsis hypothesis, by expressing our anger, we can reduce it.

20. The **feel-good, do-good phenomenon** is our tendency to be helpful when we are in a good mood.

21. **Subjective well-being** refers to a our sense of satisfaction with our life.

22. The **adaptation-level phenomenon** refers to our tendency to judge things relative to a neutral level defined by our prior experience.

23. **Relative deprivation** is the perception that we are worse off relative to those with whom we compare ourselves.

10

STRESS, HEALTH, AND HUMAN FLOURISHING

Behavioral factors play a major role in maintaining health and causing illness. The effort to understand this role more fully focuses on questions such as How do our perceptions of a situation determine the stress we feel? How do our emotions and personality influence our risk of disease? How can psychology contribute to the prevention of illness? Chapter 10 addresses key topics in this area. First and foremost is stress—its nature, its effects on the body, psychological factors that determine how it affects us, and how stress contributes to heart disease, infectious diseases, and cancer. The chapter concludes by looking at physical and psychological factors that promote good health, including exercise and social support.

CHAPTER REVIEW

First, skim each text section, noting headings and boldface items. Review the section by reading the objectives and summaries provided here, then answer the questions that follow. In some cases, STUDY TIPS explain how best to learn a difficult concept and APPLICATIONS help you to know how well you understand the material. Check your understanding of the material by consulting the answers on page 192. Do not continue with the next section until you understand each answer. If you need to, review or reread the section in the textbook before continuing.

Stress: Some Basic Concepts

Objective 1: Discuss the role of appraisal in the way we respond to stressful events, and identify the three main types of stressors.

Stress is the process by which we appraise and cope with environmental events. When perceived as challenges, *stressors* can arouse and motivate us to conquer problems. When perceived as threats, stressors can lead to severe stress. Three main types of stressors are catastrophes, significant life changes, and daily hassles.

1. Stress is the _____ by which we perceive and respond to environmental threats and challenges.

2. This definition highlights the fact that stressful events, or _____ , can have _____ (only negative/both positive and negative) effects, depending on how they are perceived. Three categories of stressors are

   _____ , _____

   _____ _____ ,

   and _____ _____ .

3. Long-term studies have found that people who have recently been widowed, fired, or divorced are _____ (more/no more) vulnerable to illness.

Objective 2: Describe the biology of the fight-or-flight response as well as the physical characteristics and stages of the general adaptation syndrome.

Walter Cannon observed that, in response to stress, the sympathetic nervous system activates the secretion of stress hormones, triggers increased heart rate and respiration, diverts blood to skeletal muscles, dulls your feelings of pain, and releases sugar and fat from the body's stores, all to prepare the body for the *fight-or-flight response.*

In Hans Selye's *general adaptation syndrome (GAS),* the body's adaptive response to stress is a three-stage process. In Stage 1, we experience an *alarm reaction* due to the sudden activation of our sympathetic nervous system. Heart rate increases and blood flows to our skeletal muscles. With our resources mobilized, we then fight the challenge  during Stage 2, *resistance.* Temperature, blood pressure, and respiration remain high, and stress hormones pour out from our adrenal glands. If the stress is persistent, it may eventually deplete our body's reserves during Stage 3, *exhaustion.* With exhaustion, we are more vulnerable to illness or even, in extreme cases, collapse and death.

There are other options for dealing with stress. One is to withdraw, pull back, and so conserve energy. Another option, found especially among women, is to *tend and befriend,* that is, to provide or seek support from others.

4. In the 1920s, physiologist Walter _____ began studying the effect of stress on the body. He discovered that stress _____ are released into the bloodstream in response to stress. This and the response of your _____ nervous system prepare your body for the _____-_____-_____ .

5. In studying animals' reactions to stressors, Hans Selye referred to the body's adaptive response to stress as the _____ _____ _____ .

6. During the first stage of the GAS—the _____ reaction—the person is in a state of shock due to the sudden arousal of the _____ nervous system.

7. This is followed by the stage of _____ , in which the body's resources are mobilized to cope with the stressor.

8. If stress continues, the person enters the stage of _____ . During this stage, a person is _____ (more/less) vulnerable to disease.

9. Another common response to stress among women has been called _____ _____ _____ ,

which refers to the increased tendency to

_____ .

•••

STUDY TIP/APPLICATION: The words *stress* and *stressor* are so similar it's easy to think that they mean the same thing. To understand the difference, remember that *stress* is the process by which we appraise and cope with challenging environmental events (the *stressors*). But they are different concepts describing different aspects of a behavior. It may help you to see the difference between these concepts if you realize that stressors can be external events, such as having your flight cancelled, or internal events, such as worrying about an upcoming term paper assignment, and that stress includes those events plus your response to them. To make sure you understand the differences between stress and stressors, see if you can come up with examples of each as you complete the following chart. The first example has already been filled in.

10. Stressor (Stressful Event)	Appraisal		Response	
	Threat	Challenge	Threat	Challenge
Getting cut off by a driver on the freeway	"I'm going to be in an accident"	"I need to watch more carefully"	Heart races; hit the brakes hard	Heart races; swerve out of the way

APPLICATIONS:

11. Cristina complains to the campus psychologist that she has too much stress in her life. The psychologist tells her that the level of stress people experience depends primarily on
   a. how many activities they are trying to do at the same time.
   b. how they appraise the events of life.
   c. their physical hardiness.
   d. how predictable stressful events are.

12. Each semester, Jin does not start studying until just before midterms. Then he is forced to work around the clock until after final exams, which makes him sick, probably because he is in the _____ stage of the _____ _____ _____ .

Stress Effects and Health

Objective 3: Describe the effect of stress on immune system functioning.

Our understanding of the impact of stress on resistance to disease has fostered the development of the field of *psychoneuroimmunology,* which studies how psychological, neural, and endocrine processes together affect our immune system and health.

The immune system has two types of white blood cells, called **lymphocytes.** *B lymphocytes* are important in fighting bacterial infections, and *T lymphocytes* fight cancer cells, viruses, and foreign substances. Other agents of the immune system are the *macrophage,* which ingests harmful invaders and worn-out cells, and *natural killer cells* (NK cells), which pursue diseased cells. When animals are physically restrained, given unavoidable electric shocks, or subjected to noise, crowding, cold water, social defeat, or maternal separation, they become more susceptible to disease. Studies suggest that stress similarly depresses the human immune system, making us more vulnerable to illness.

Stress and negative emotions speed the progression of HIV infection to AIDS and predict a faster decline in those infected. Efforts to reduce stress also help somewhat to control the disease. Educational programs, grief

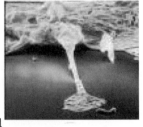

support groups, talk therapy, and exercise programs that reduce distress have all had good results for HIV-positive individuals.

Although stress does not produce cancer cells, some researchers have reported that people are at risk for cancer a year or so after experiencing depression, helplessness, or grief. A large study found that people with a history of workplace stress had a 5.5 times greater risk of colon cancer than those who reported no such problems. Although a relaxed, hopeful attitude may enhance the body's natural defenses against a few growing cancer cells, merely maintaining a determined attitude is not likely to derail the powerful biological forces at work in advanced cancer or AIDS.

1. The relatively new field of _____ studies how psychological, neural, and endocrine processes together affect the immune system and health.

2. The body's system of fighting disease is the _____ system. This system includes two types of white blood cells, called _____ : the _____ _____ , which fight bacterial infections, and the _____ _____ , which attack viruses, cancer cells, and foreign substances.

3. Two other immune agents are the _____ , which identifies, pursues, and ingests foreign substances and worn-out cells, and _____ _____ cells, which pursue diseased cells.

4. Responding too strongly, the immune system may attack the body's tissues and cause _____ or an _____ reaction. Or it may _____ , allowing a dormant herpes virus to erupt or _____ cells to multiply.

5. Stress responses draw energy away from the disease-fighting _____ _____ and send it to the _____ and _____ , mobilizing the body for action.

6. Stress suppresses immune functioning. People with AIDS already have a damaged immune system, as indicated by the name of the virus that causes it, the _____ _____ _____ .

7. Stressful events _____ (have/have not) been shown to speed the transition from infection to full-blown AIDS.

8. Educational initiatives, support groups, and other efforts to control stress _____ (have/have not) been shown to have positive consequences on HIV-positive individuals.

9. Stress _____ (does/does not) create cancer cells.

10. When rodents were inoculated with _____ cells or given _____ , tumors developed sooner in those that were also exposed to _____ stress.

11. In some studies, workplace stress and experiencing depression, _____ , or grief _____ (have/have not) been linked to increased risk for cancer. Other studies _____ (have/have not) found elevated cancer rates in former prisoners of war.

APPLICATIONS:

12. A white blood cell that attacks cancer cells is a _____ _____ .

13. When would you expect that your immune responses would be weakest?
    a. during summer vacation
    b. during exam weeks
    c. just after receiving good news
    d. Immune activity would probably remain constant during these times.

Objective 4: Discuss why stress may increase our vulnerability to coronary heart disease, and contrast Type A and Type B personalities.

Stress can increase the risk of *coronary heart disease,* the leading cause of death in North America today. It has been linked with the competitive, hard-driving, and impatient *Type A* personality. The toxic core of Type A is negative emotions, especially the anger associated with an aggressively reactive temperament. Under stress, the sympathetic nervous system of the Type A person redistributes bloodflow to the muscles and away from internal organs such as the liver, which removes cholesterol and fat from the blood. The resulting excess cholesterol later gets deposited around the heart. The more easygoing *Type B* personality is less likely to suffer coronary heart disease. Depression also can be lethal.

14. The leading cause of death in North America is _____ _____ _____ . List several risk factors for developing this condition: _____ _____ _____ _____ .

15. Friedman and Rosenman discovered that tax accountants experience an increase in blood _____ level and blood-_____ speed during tax season. This showed there was a link between heart attack risk and _____ .

Friedman and Rosenman, in a nine-year study, grouped people into Type A and Type B personality types. Characterize these types, and indicate how they differed over the course of this study.

16. The Type A characteristic that is most strongly linked with coronary heart disease is

_____ _____ ,

especially _____ .

17. When a _____ (Type A/Type B) person is angered, bloodflow is pulled away from the internal organs, including the liver, which normally removes _____ and fat from the blood. Thus, such people have high levels of these substances in the blood.

18. Depression _____ (increases/has no effect on) one's risk of having a heart attack or developing other heart problems.

APPLICATION:

19. Jill is an easygoing, noncompetitive person who is happy in her job and enjoys her leisure time. She would probably be classified as _____ _____ .

Human Flourishing

Objective 5: Identify two ways people cope with stress.

Through *problem-focused coping* we attempt to alleviate stress by changing the stressor or the way we interact with that stressor. We tend to use problem-focused strategies when we think we can change the situation, or at least change ourselves to more capably deal with the situation. We tend to use *emotion-focused coping* when we believe we cannot change a situation. For example, we may confide in friends when we cannot get along with a family member.

1. When we cope directly with a stressor, we are using

_____-_____ coping.

2. When we attempt to alleviate stress by avoiding it and attending to emotional needs, we are using

_____-_____ coping.

3. People tend to use _____-_____ coping when they feel a sense of _____ over a situation. They turn to _____-_____ coping when they cannot or believe they cannot _____ a situation.

Objective 6: Discuss the effects of people's sense of control and outlook on life on stress and health.

Both animal and human studies show that loss of perceived *personal control* can trigger physical symptoms. Facing an ongoing series of events beyond our control can lead to feelings of hopelessness and passive resignation, which is called *learned helplessness.*

As compared to those with an *external locus of control,* those with an *internal locus of control* cope better with stressful events. In comparison to *pessimists, optimists* enjoy better health and better moods, and they respond to stress with smaller increases in blood pressure. Optimists also tend to outlive pessimists. Excessive optimism can blind us to real risks, however.

4. Personal control refers to our sense of either controlling our _____ or feeling _____ by it.

5. The state of passive resignation called

_____ _____

occurs when we experience no control over repeated negative events.

6. In animals and humans, sudden lack of control is followed by a drop in immune responses, a(n) _____ (increase/decrease) in blood pressure, and a rise in the levels of

_____ _____ .

7. The perception that outside forces beyond our control determine our fate is called

_____ _____

_____ _____ .

The perception that we control our own fate is called _____ _____

_____ _____ .

State several behavioral and health differences between people with an internal locus of control and those with an external locus of control.

9. Excessive or _____ optimism often blinds students to risky behaviors such as

_____

_____ .

•••

STUDY TIP/APPLICATION: Two basic strategies for coping with stressors are problem-focused coping and emotion-focused coping. *Problem-focused coping* is an action-oriented strategy in which we attempt to reduce stress by changing the stressor or the way we interact with that stressor. In contrast, with *emotion-focused coping* we focus on our feelings and try to change how we think about stressors. Think about how you typically cope with stress. Do you more often rely on problem-focused coping or emotion-focused coping? Now complete the chart below. For each stressor, write down one example of a problem-focused strategy and one example of an emotion-focused strategy.

8. People who expect the best and therefore are _____ are less likely than those who are _____ to suffer ill health.

10. Stressor	Emotion-Focused Strategy	Problem-Focused Strategy
You are worried about the amount of reading needed to prepare for an exam.	To take your mind off things, you go to a movie.	You divide the reading into manageable, daily sessions, and get started!
a. You get into an argument with your roommate.		
b. Your car muffler falls off.		
c. You develop a cold sore on your lip the day of an important dance.		

APPLICATIONS:

11. Ricardo has been unable to resolve a stressful relationship with a family member. To cope, he turns to a close friend for social support. Ricardo's strategy is an example of _____-_____ coping.

12. To help him deal with a stressful schedule of classes, work, and studying, Randy turns to a regular program of exercise and relaxation training. Randy's strategy is an example of _____-_____ coping.

Objective 7: Describe the influence of social support and meaning in life on health.

Feeling liked and encouraged by intimate friends and family promotes both happiness and health. Compared to those with few social ties, people supported by close relationships are less likely to die prematurely. Social support strengthens immune functioning and calms the cardiovascular system, lowering blood pressure and stress hormones. A strong sense of meaning can have positive health consequences.

13. Besides control and optimism, another buffer against the effects of stress is _____ support. This helps fight illness by calming our _____ system and strengthening _____ functioning.

14. Longitudinal research reveals that a

_____ _____

at age 50 predicts healthy aging better than

_____ _____

at the same age.

15. For many people, an important part of coping with stress is having a strong sense of

_____ , giving them a purpose for which to live.

16. Close relationships provide a chance to

_____ painful feelings.

17. Another way to reduce stress is to talk or write about it. In one study, researchers contacted surviving spouses of people who had committed suicide or died in car accidents. If they bore their grief alone, they were _____ (more/less) likely to have health problems.

APPLICATIONS:

18. Genji is in love with Chen but wants to wait until they are married to have sex with him. Genji's ability to delay gratification suggests an _____ locus of control.

19. Pilar says that she hasn't been promoted at work because her boss doesn't think women should be in management. Pilar's reasoning indicates a _____ locus of control.

Objective 8: Discuss the advantages of aerobic exercise as a technique for managing stress and improving well-being.

Many studies suggest that *aerobic exercise,* sustained activity that increases heart and lung fitness, can reduce stress, depression, and anxiety. It strengthens the heart, increases bloodflow, keeps blood vessels open, and lowers both blood pressure and the blood pressure reaction to stress. Research has linked aerobic exercise to increased arousal and increases in serotonin activity in the brain.

20. Sustained exercise that increases heart and lung fitness is known as

_____ exercise.

21. Experiments _____ (have/have not) been able to demonstrate conclusively that such exercise reduces anxiety, depression, and stress.

State two ways aerobic exercise reduces depression and anxiety.

Objective 9: Discuss the ways in which relaxation and spiritual engagement might influence stress and health.

Research indicates that relaxation procedures can help lower blood pressure, heart rate, and oxygen consumption and raise fingertip temperature. It also provides relief from headaches, high blood pressure, anxiety, and insomnia. Those experienced in meditation assume a comfortable position, breathe slowly, relax their muscles, close their eyes, and focus on a simple repeated phrase. Meditation is associated with increased left hemisphere activity and improved immune functioning.

Investigators who attempt to explain the *faith factor* have isolated three intervening variables. (1) Religiously active people have healthier life-styles; for example, they smoke and drink less. (2) Faith communities provide social support networks and often encourage marriage, which, when happy, is linked with better health and a longer life span. (3) Religious attendance is often accompanied by a stable worldview, sense of hope for the long-term future, feelings of ultimate acceptance, and a relaxed meditative state.

22. Lowered blood pressure, heart rate, and oxygen consumption have been found to be characteristic of people who regularly practice

_____ . The _____ response accompanies sitting quietly, with closed eyes, while breathing deeply.

23. Brain scans of experienced meditators show a high level of activity in the _____ (right/left) hemisphere, which is associated with _____ emotions.

24. Several recent studies demonstrate that religious involvement _____ (predicts/does not predict) health and longevity.

State two possible reasons for the "faith factor" in health.

APPLICATIONS:

25. You have just transferred to a new campus and find yourself in a potentially stressful environment. According to the text, which of the following would help you cope with the stress?
    a. believing that you have some control over your environment
    b. having a friend to confide in
    c. feeling optimistic that you will eventually adjust to your new surroundings
    d. All of these behaviors would help.

26. Concluding her presentation on spirituality and health, Maja notes that
    a. historically, religion and medicine joined hands in caring for the sick.
    b. religious involvement predicts health and longevity.
    c. people who attend religious services weekly have healthier life-styles.
    d. all of these statements are true.

PROGRESS TEST

Multiple-Choice Questions

Circle your answers to the following questions and check them with the answers on page 193. If your answer is incorrect, read the explanation for why it is incorrect and then consult the text.

1. Researchers Friedman and Rosenman refer to individuals who are very time-conscious, supermotivated, verbally aggressive, and easily angered as
    a. ulcer-prone personalities.
    b. cancer-prone personalities.
    c. Type A.
    d. Type B.

2. During which stage of the general adaptation syndrome is a person especially vulnerable to disease?
    a. alarm reaction   c. stage of exhaustion
    b. stage of resistance   d. stage of adaptation

3. The leading cause of death in North America is
    a. lung cancer.
    b. AIDS.
    c. coronary heart disease.
    d. alcohol-related accidents.

4. Stress has been demonstrated to place a person at increased risk of
    a. cancer.
    b. progressing from HIV infection to AIDS.
    c. bacterial infections.
    d. all of these problems.

5. *Stress* is defined as
    a. unpleasant or aversive events that cannot be controlled.
    b. situations that threaten health.
    c. the process by which we perceive and respond to challenging or threatening events.
    d. anything that decreases immune responses.

6. Attempting to reduce stress directly by changing a stressor or how we interact with it is an example of
    a. problem-focused coping.
    b. emotion-focused coping.
    c. managing rather than coping with stress.
    d. meditation.

7. Researchers have found that social support helps us fight illness by fostering stronger immune functioning and by
    a. increasing our ability to control muscle tension.
    b. controlling the activity of our autonomic nervous system.
    c. calming our cardiovascular system.
    d. promoting the relaxation response.

8. Which of the following was NOT mentioned in the text as a potential health benefit of exercise?
    a. Exercise can increase ability to cope with stress.
    b. Exercise can lower blood pressure.
    c. Exercise can reduce stress, depression, and anxiety.
    d. Exercise improves immune system functioning.

9. Social support _____ our ability to cope with stressful events.
    a. has no effect on
    b. usually increases
    c. usually decreases
    d. has an unpredictable effect on

10. Research has demonstrated that as a predictor of health and longevity, religious involvement
    a. has a small, insignificant effect.
    b. is more accurate for women than men.
    c. is more accurate for men than women.
    d. rivals nonsmoking and exercise.

11. In order, the sequence of stages in the general adaptation syndrome is
    a. alarm reaction, stage of resistance, stage of exhaustion.
    b. stage of resistance, alarm reaction, stage of exhaustion.
    c. stage of exhaustion, stage of resistance, alarm reaction.
    d. alarm reaction, stage of exhaustion, stage of resistance.

12. AIDS is a disorder that causes a breakdown in the body's
    a. endocrine system.
    b. circulatory system.
    c. immune system.
    d. respiratory system.

13. Tend and befriend refers to
    a. the final stage of the general adaptation syndrome.
    b. the health-promoting impact of having a strong system of social support.
    c. an alternative to the fight-or-flight response that may be more common in women.
    d. the fact that spiritual people typically are not socially isolated.

14. Which of the following statements concerning Type A and B persons is true?
    a. Even when relaxed, Type A persons have higher blood pressure than Type B persons.
    b. When stressed, Type A persons redistribute bloodflow to the muscles and away from internal organs.
    c. Type B persons tend to suppress anger more than Type A persons.
    d. Type A persons tend to be more outgoing than Type B persons.

15. The disease- and infection-fighting cells of the immune system include
    a. B lymphocytes.
    b. T lymphocytes.
    c. NK cells.
    d. all of these types of cells.

16. One effect of stress on the body is to
    a. weaken the immune system.
    b. facilitate the immune system response.
    c. increase disease resistance.
    d. increase the growth of B and T lymphocytes.

17. Allergic reactions and arthritis are caused by
    a. an overreactive immune system.
    b. an underreactive immune system.
    c. the presence of B lymphocytes.
    d. the presence of T lymphocytes.

18. Some research on cancer patients reveals that
    a. stress affects the growth of cancer cells by weakening the body's natural resources.
    b. avoiding stress is not likely to derail the biological processes of advanced cancer.
    c. cancer occurs slightly more often than usual among those experiencing depression, helplessness, or grief.
    d. all of these facts are true.

19. The toxic core of Type A behavior that is the most predictive of coronary disease is
    a. time urgency.
    b. competitiveness.
    c. high motivation.
    d. anger.

20. Which of the following was NOT suggested as a possible explanation of the faith factor in health?
    a. Having a stable worldview is a buffer against stress.
    b. Religious people tend to have healthier lifestyles.
    c. Those who are religious have stronger networks of social support.
    d. Because they are more affluent, religiously active people receive better health care.

Application Essay

Discuss several factors that enhance a person's ability to cope with stress. (Use the space below to list the points you want to make, and organize them. Then write the essay on a separate sheet of paper.)

SUMMING UP

Consider your first year at college. The courses are tough. You are away from home and away from your steady girl/boyfriend, who has suddenly found a new love.

To handle the stress of schoolwork, you write out a detailed schedule that enables you to keep up with your studies. This behavior is called _____-_____ coping.

However, dealing with the breakup is not so easy: Because you feel you had no say in the decision, that is, you had no _____ over the situation, you use _____-_____ coping.

You have several things going for you that will help alleviate the stress:

You have an _____ outlook on life,

you express mostly _____ emotions, and

you have a large group of close friends, who provide good _____ _____ .

For you to manage the stress, you count on

your daily run with your professor, a major source of _____ _____ ,

plus

your regular practice of yoga, which is a form of meditative _____ .

TERMS AND CONCEPTS

Using your own words, on a separate piece of paper write a brief definition or explanation of each of the following terms.

1. stress
2. fight-or-flight response
3. general adaptation syndrome (GAS)
4. tend and befriend
5. psychoneuroimmunology
6. lymphocytes
7. coronary heart disease
8. Type A
9. Type B
10. problem-focused coping
11. emotion-focused coping
12. personal control
13. learned helplessness
14. external locus of control
15. internal locus of control
16. optimism
17. pessimism
18. aerobic exercise

ANSWERS

Chapter Review

Stress: Some Basic Concepts

1. process
2. stressors; both positive and negative; catastrophes; significant life changes; daily hassles
3. more
4. Cannon; hormones; sympathetic; fight-or-flight response
5. general adaptation syndrome
6. alarm; sympathetic
7. resistance
8. exhaustion; more
9. tend and befriend; seek and give support
10. Many answers will complete the table. Just think about stressful events in your life—an upcoming exam, a first date, a job interview. For each one, consider how you would appraise it (as a subject beyond your ability or as a task to be completed with extra work), then ask yourself how you would respond (if beyond your ability, you might go out with friends the night before the exam; as a challenge, you would stay home and study hard).
11. **b.** is the answer. How an event is *perceived* is important in deciding whether it is stressful.
12. exhaustion; general adaptation syndrome. According to Selye's GAS, diseases are most likely to occur during this final stage.

Stress Effects and Health

1. psychoneuroimmunology
2. immune; lymphocytes; B lymphocytes; T lymphocytes
3. macrophage; natural killer (NK)
4. arthritis; allergic; underreact; cancer
5. immune system; brain; muscles
6. human immunodeficiency virus (HIV)
7. have
8. have
9. does not
10. tumor; carcinogens; uncontrollable
11. helplessness; have; have not
12. T lymphocyte
13. **b.** is the answer. Stressful situations, such as exam weeks, decrease immune responses.
14. coronary heart disease; smoking, obesity, high-fat diet, physical inactivity, high cholesterol level
15. cholesterol; clotting; stress

Type A people were competitive, hard-driving, supermotivated, impatient, time-conscious, verbally aggressive, and easily angered. Type B people were more relaxed and easygoing. Heart attack victims over the course of the study came overwhelmingly from the Type A group.

16. negative emotions; anger
17. Type A; cholesterol
18. increases
19. Type B

Human Flourishing

1. problem-focused
2. emotion-focused
3. problem-focused; control; emotion-focused; change
4. environment; controlled
5. learned helplessness
6. increase; stress hormones
7. external locus of control; internal locus of control

"Internals" expect to have more control and to cope better with stressful events, and they enjoy better health than "externals." They are also better able to delay gratification.

8. optimists; pessimists
9. unrealistic; excess drinking, smoking, engaging in unprotected sex
10. **a.** Emotion-focused: You go next door to be comforted by another close friend.

    Problem-focused: You talk with your roommate about resolving your disagreement.

    b. Emotion-focused: You call a friend but keep driving, leaving the muffler where it is and listening to the loud noises of the car.

    Problem-focused: You immediately drive to the nearest muffler shop to have a new muffler put on.

    c. Emotion-focused: You start crying, saying you can't possibly go to the dance.

    Problem-focused: You go to the local drug store to find out what kind of cream you can buy to get rid of the cold sore.
11. emotion-focused
12. problem-focused
13. social; cardiovascular; immune
14. good marriage; low cholesterol
15. meaning
16. confide
17. more
18. internal
19. external
20. aerobic
21. have

Aerobic exercise reduces depression and anxiety by increasing arousal and by doing naturally what some prescription drugs do chemically—increasing serotonin activity in the brain.

22. meditation (relaxation); relaxation
23. left; positive
24. predicts

Religiously active people have healthier life-styles. They also tend to have stronger networks of social support and are more likely to be married.

25. **d.** is the answer.
26. **d.** is the answer.

Progress Test

Multiple-Choice Questions

1. **c.** is the answer.
a. & b. Researchers have not identified such personality types.
d. Individuals who are more easygoing are labeled Type B.

2. **c.** is the answer.
a. & b. During these stages, the body's defensive mechanisms are at peak function.
d. This is not a stage of the GAS.

3. **c.** is the answer.

4. **d.** is the answer. Because stress depresses the immune system, stressed individuals are prone to all of these conditions.

5. **c.** is the answer.
a., b., & d. Whether an event is stressful or not depends on how it is appraised.

6. **a.** is the answer.
b. In emotion-focused coping, we attempt to alleviate stress by avoiding or ignoring it.
c. This is an example of coping rather than managing stress because it involves an attempt to actually alleviate a stressor.
d. Meditation is a way of managing stress by sitting quietly and focusing on a word, phrase, or prayer.

7. **c.** is the answer. In calming our cardiovascular system, social support lowers blood pressure and stress hormones.
a. & b. The autonomic nervous system has no effect on immune responses.
d. Social support may help us relax, but research has not found this effect specifically.

8. **d.** is the answer. Regular aerobic exercise has been shown to increase the ability to cope with stress, lower blood pressure, and reduce depression and anxiety. The text does not cite evidence that exercise enhances immune function.

9. **b.** is the answer.

10. **d.** is the answer.
b. & c. The text does not indicate that a gender difference exists in the faith factor in health.

11. **a.** is the answer.

12. **c.** is the answer.

13. **c.** is the answer.
a. The final stage of the general adaptation syndrome is exhaustion.
b. & d. Although both of these are true, neither has anything to do with tend and befriend.

14. **b.** is the answer. The result is that their blood may contain excess cholesterol and fat.
a. Under relaxed situations, there is no difference in blood pressure.
c. Anger, both expressed and suppressed, is more characteristic of Type A people.
d. The text doesn't indicate that Type A persons are more outgoing than Type B persons.

15. **d.** is the answer. B lymphocytes fight bacterial infections; T lymphocytes attack cancer cells, viruses, and foreign substances; and NK cells pursue diseased cells.

16. **a.** is the answer. A variety of studies have shown that stress depresses the immune system, increasing the risk and potential severity of many diseases.

17. **a.** is the answer.
b. An *underreactive* immune system would make an individual more susceptible to infectious diseases or the growth of cancer cells.
c. & d. Lymphocytes are disease- and infection-fighting white blood cells in the immune system.

18. **d.** is the answer.

19. **d.** is the answer. The crucial characteristic of Type A behavior seems to be a tendency to react with negative emotions, especially anger. Other aspects of Type A behavior appear not to predict heart disease, and some appear to be helpful to the individual.

20. **d.** is the answer. As a group, religiously active people are no more affluent than other people.

Application Essay

When potentially stressful events occur, a person's appraisal is a major factor in determining their impact. Catastrophes, significant life events, and daily hassles are especially stressful when appraised as negative and uncontrollable and when the person has a pessimistic outlook on life. Under these circumstances, stressful events may suppress immune responses and make the person more vulnerable to disease. If stressors cannot be eliminated, aerobic exercise, relaxation, and spirituality can help the person cope. Aerobic exercise can reduce stress, depression, and anxiety, perhaps by increasing production of mood-boosting serotonin. Research demonstrates that people who regularly practice relaxation techniques enjoy a diminished sense of self, space, and time, and their brain's frontal lobe, which is associated with positive emotions, is more active. People with strong social ties have lower blood pressure and stronger immune functioning. Religiously active people enjoy a better life-style, smoking and drinking less.

Summing Up

Consider your first year at college. The courses are tough. You are away from home and away from your steady girl/boyfriend, who has suddenly found a new love. To handle the stress of schoolwork, you write out a detailed schedule that enables you to keep up with your studies. This behavior is called *problem-focused* coping. However, dealing with the breakup is not so easy: Because you feel you had no say in the decision, that is, you had no *control* over the situation, you use *emotion-focused* coping.

You have several things going for you that will help alleviate the stress: You have an *optimistic* outlook on life, you express mostly *positive* emotions, and you have a large group of close friends, who provide good *social support*. For you to manage the stress, you count on your daily run with your professor, a major source of *aerobic exercise,* plus your regular practice of Yoga, which is a form of meditative *relaxation.*

Terms and Concepts

1. **Stress** refers to the process by which people perceive and react to events, called stressors, that they perceive as threatening or challenging.

2. The **fight-or-flight response** refers to the body's response to an emergency, including activity of the sympathetic nervous system to mobilize energy for attacking or escaping a threat.

3. The **general adaptation syndrome (GAS)** is the three-stage sequence of bodily reaction to stress outlined by Hans Selye.

4. **Tend and befriend** is the stress response in which people (especially women) offer support (tend) and seek support from others (befriend).

5. **Psychoneuroimmunology (PNI)** is the study of how psychological, neural, and endocrine processes affect the immune system and resulting health.

6. **Lymphocytes** are the two types of white blood cells of the immune system that fight bacterial infections (B lymphocytes) and viruses, cancer cells, and foreign substances in the body (T lymphocytes).

7. The leading cause of death in North America today, **coronary heart disease** results from the clogging of the vessels that nourish the heart muscle.

8. **Type A** personality is Friedman and Rosenman's term for the coronary-prone behavior pattern of competitive, hard-driving, impatient, verbally aggressive, and anger-prone people.

9. **Type B** personality is Friedman and Rosenman's term for the coronary-resistant behavior pattern of easygoing, relaxed people.

10. **Problem-focused coping** is the strategy of attempting to alleviate stress directly by changing the stressor itself or the way we interact with it.

11. **Emotion-focused coping** is the strategy of attempting to alleviate stress indirectly by attending to emotional needs.

12. **Personal control** is our sense of controlling our environment rather than feeling helpless.

13. **Learned helplessness** is the state of passive resignation that often results when a person or animal is exposed to unavoidable and repeated negative events.

14. **External locus of control** is the perception that chance or another outside force determines our fate.

15. **Internal locus of control** is the perception that we control our own fate.

16. **Optimism** is the tendency to expect positive outcomes.

17. **Pessimism** is the tendency to expect negative outcomes.

18. **Aerobic exercise** is any sustained activity such as running, swimming, or cycling that promotes heart and lung fitness and may help alleviate depression and anxiety.

11

PERSONALITY

Personality refers to each individual's characteristic pattern of thinking, feeling, and acting. Chapter 11 examines four perspectives on personality. Psychoanalytic theory emphasizes the unconscious and irrational aspects of personality. Humanistic theory draws attention to the concept of self and to the human potential for healthy growth. Trait theory led to advances in techniques for evaluating and describing personality. The social-cognitive perspective emphasizes the effects of our interactions with the environment. The text first describes and then evaluates the contributions, shortcomings, and historical significance of the psychoanalytic and humanistic perspectives. Next, the text turns to contemporary research on personality, looking at how the trait and social-cognitive perspectives explore and assess traits and at how many of today's researchers focus on the concept of self.

CHAPTER REVIEW

First, skim each text section, noting headings and boldface items. Review the section by reading the objectives and summaries provided here, then answer the questions that follow. In some cases, STUDY TIPS explain how best to learn a difficult concept and APPLICATIONS help you to know how well you understand the material. Check your understanding of the material by consulting the answers beginning on page 207. Do not continue with the next section until you understand each answer. If you need to, review or reread the section in the textbook before continuing.

Introduction and The Psychoanalytic Perspective

Objective 1: Define *personality,* and explain how Freud's treatment of psychological disorders led to his study of the unconscious mind.

Psychologists consider **personality** to be an individual's characteristic pattern of thinking, feeling, and acting.

In his private practice, Freud found that nervous disorders often made no medical sense. Piecing together his patients' accounts of their lives, he concluded that their disorders had psychological causes. His effort to understand these causes led to his "discovery" of the **unconscious.**

At first, Freud thought hypnosis might unlock the door to the unconscious. However, hypnosis did not do the job, so Freud turned to *free association,* which he believed produced a chain of thoughts in the patient's unconscious.

Freud believed the mind is mostly hidden. Below the surface is this large unconscious region, which contains unacceptable passions and thoughts. Freud believed we *repress* these unconscious thoughts and feelings.

1. Personality is defined as an individual's characteristic pattern of _____ , _____ , and _____ .

2. The two grand theories are the psychoanalytic perspective on personality, which was proposed by _____ , and the _____ perspective, which

focused on our inner capacities for _____ and _____ .

3. Today's approach is more _____ than the two grand theories. Personality theorists also note that our personality is organized around the concept of _____ .

4. Sigmund Freud was a medical doctor who specialized in _____ disorders.

5. Freud developed his theory in response to his observation that many patients had disorders that did not make _____ sense.

6. At first, Freud thought _____ would unlock the door to the unconscious. The technique later used by Freud, in which the patient relaxes and says whatever comes to mind, is called

   _____ _____ .

7. According to Freud's theory, many of a person's thoughts, wishes, and feelings are hidden in a large _____ region. Many of the memories of this region are blocked, or _____ , from consciousness.

APPLICATION:

8. Suppose a child frequently calls her teacher "Mom." How would Freud's psychoanalytic perspective explain these slips?

Objective 2: Describe Freud's view of personality structure in terms of the id, ego, and superego.

Freud called his treatment and the underlying theory of personality *psychoanalysis.* He believed that personality arises from our efforts to resolve the conflict between our biological impulses and the social restraints against them. He theorized that the conflict centers on three interacting systems: the *id*, which operates on the *pleasure principle*; the *ego*, which functions on the *reality principle*; and the *superego*, an internalized set of ideals. The superego's demands often oppose the id's, and the ego, as the "executive" part of personality, seeks to reconcile the two. Although the modern iceberg image is useful, it is a simplification and doesn't show the interactive nature of the three systems.

9. Freud called his theory and treatment, in which painful unconscious memories are exposed, _____ .

10. Freud believed that all facets of personality arise from conflict between our _____ impulses and the _____ restraints against them.

11. According to Freud, personality consists of three interacting structures: the _____ , the _____ , and the _____ .

12. The id stores energy that is _____ (conscious/unconscious) and operates according to the _____ principle.

13. The ego is the _____ (conscious/unconscious) part of personality that tries to satisfy the id's impulses according to the _____ principle.

Explain why the ego is considered the "executive" of personality.

14. The personality structure that reflects moral values is the _____ , which Freud believed began emerging at about age _____ .

STUDY TIP/APPLICATION: Each of Freud's three interacting systems—the id, the ego, and the superego—has a different role in our conscious and unconscious thought processes. To help you understand the systems and how they differ, try completing the following table. It includes three real-life conflicts and asks you to explain how each system would respond in each situation.

15. Conflict	The Id's Response	The Ego's Response	The Superego's Response
a. The driver ahead of you is driving 10 miles/hour below the speed limit.			
b. You have pledged a charitable donation but now need money to buy a new sweater.			
c. You've procrastinated about completing a term paper and a friend suggests buying one online.			

Objective 3: Identify Freud's psychosexual stages of development, and describe the effects of fixation on behavior.

Freud maintained that children pass through a series of *psychosexual stages* during which the id's pleasure-seeking energies focus on distinct pleasure-sensitive areas of the body called *erogenous zones*. During the *oral stage* (0–18 months) pleasure centers on the mouth, and during the *anal stage* (18–36 months) the focus is on bowel/bladder elimination.

During the critical *phallic stage* (3–6 years), pleasure centers on the genitals. Boys experience the *Oedipus complex*, with unconscious sexual desires toward their mother and hatred of their father. They cope with these threatening feelings through *identification* with their father, thereby incorporating many of his values and developing a sense of what psychologists now call *gender identity*. The *latency stage* (6 years to puberty), in which sexuality is dormant, gives way to the genital stage (from puberty on) as sexual interests mature.

In Freud's view, conflicts unresolved during the oral, anal, and phallic stages may cause trouble in adulthood. At any point, conflict can lock, or *fixate,* the person's pleasure-seeking energies in that stage.

16. According to Freud, personality is formed as the child passes through a series of _____ stages, each of which is focused on a distinct body area called an _____ _____ .

17. (Table 11.1) The first stage is the _____ stage. During this stage, the id's energies are focused on behaviors such as _____ .

18. (Table 11.1) The second stage is the _____ stage, where energies are focused on bowel and bladder elimination.

19. (text and Table 11.1) The third stage is the _____ stage. During this stage, the id's energies are focused on the _____ . Freud also believed that during this stage children develop sexual desires for the _____ (same/opposite)-sex parent. Freud referred to these feelings as the _____ _____ in boys.

20. Freud believed that _____ with the same-sex parent is the basis for what psychologists now call _____ _____ .

Explain how this conflict is resolved through the process of identification.

21. (Table 11.1) During the next stage, sexual feelings are repressed. This phase is called the _____ stage and lasts until puberty.

22. (Table 11.1) The final stage of development is called the _____ stage.

23. According to Freud, it is possible for a person's development to become blocked in any of the stages; in such an instance, the person is said to be _____ .

APPLICATION:

24. Song Yi works in a smoke-free office. So, she frequently has to leave work and go outside to smoke a cigarette. Freud would probably say that Song Yi is _____ at the _____ stage of development.

Objective 4: Discuss how defense mechanisms serve to protect the individual from anxiety.

Defense mechanisms reduce or redirect anxiety in various ways, but always by unconsciously distorting reality. *Repression,* which underlies the other defense mechanisms, banishes anxiety-arousing thoughts from consciousness; *regression* involves retreat to an earlier stage of development; and *reaction formation* makes unacceptable impulses look like their opposites. *Projection* attributes our own threatening impulses to others, *rationalization* offers self-justifying explanations for behavior, *displacement* shifts sexual or aggressive impulses to a more acceptable object or person, and *denial* involves refusal to believe or even perceive painful realities.

25. The ego attempts to protect itself against anxiety through the use of _____ . The process underlying each of these mechanisms is _____ .

26. Dealing with anxiety by returning to an earlier stage of development is called _____ .

27. When we transform our true feelings into their opposites, _____ is said to have occurred.

28. When we assign our own feelings to another person, _____ has occurred.

29. When we explain our actions in ways that make us look good, _____ has occurred.

30. When impulses are directed toward a target that is more acceptable than the one that caused arousal, _____ has occurred.

APPLICATION:

31. Match each defense mechanism in the following list with the proper example of how it could show itself.

Defense Mechanisms

_____ 1. displacement
_____ 2. projection
_____ 3. reaction formation
_____ 4. rationalization
_____ 5. regression
_____ 6. denial

Example

a. nail biting or thumb sucking in an anxiety-producing situation
b. overzealous crusaders against "immoral behaviors" who don't want to admit to their own sexual desires
c. saying you drink "just to be sociable" when in reality you have a drinking problem
d. a parent will not admit that his child could cheat on a test
e. thinking someone hates you when in reality you hate that person
f. a child who is angry at his parents and vents this anger on the family pet, a less threatening target

32. Defense mechanisms are _____ (conscious/unconscious) processes.

Objective 5: Contrast the views of the neo-Freudians and psychodynamic theorists with Freud's original theory.

Neo-Freudians such as Alfred Adler, Karen Horney, and Carl Jung accepted Freud's basic ideas regarding personality structures, the importance of the unconscious, the shaping of personality in children, and the use of defense mechanisms to ward off anxiety. However, in contrast to Freud, the neo-Freudians generally placed more emphasis on the conscious mind, and they emphasized loftier motives and social interactions over sex and aggression. Contemporary *psychodynamic theorists* and clinicians reject the notion that sex is the basis of personality but agree with Freud that much of our mental life is unconscious, that we struggle with inner conflicts, and that childhood shapes our personalities and attachment styles.

33. The theorists who established their own, modified versions of psychoanalytic theory are called

_____-_____ .

These theorists typically place _____ (more/less) emphasis on the conscious mind than Freud did and _____ (more/less) emphasis on sex and aggression. Included in this group were Karen _____ , Alfred _____ , and Carl _____ .

34. More recently, some of Freud's ideas have been incorporated into _____ theory. Unlike Freud, the theorists who study personality from this perspective do not believe that _____ is the basis of

personality. They do agree, however, that much of mental life is _____ , that _____ shapes personality, and that we often struggle with _____

_____ .

Objective 6: Describe how projective tests are used to assess personality, and discuss some criticisms of them.

Projective tests provide unclear images designed to trigger projection of the test-taker's unconscious thoughts or feelings. The *Rorschach inkblot test* seeks to identify people's inner feelings and conflicts by analyzing their interpretations of 10 inkblots. Rorschach has neither much reliability nor great validity.

35. Tests that ask people to describe an unclear image or tell a story about it are called

_____ tests.

36. The most widely used projective test is the

_____ , in which test-takers are shown a series of _____ . Generally, this test appears to have _____ (little/significant) validity and reliability. This is because different scoring systems show _____ (little/a great deal of) agreement, and it _____ (is/is not) successful at predicting behaviors.

APPLICATION:

37. Teresa is taking a personality test that asks her to describe random patterns of dots. This is a _____ test.

Objective 7: Summarize psychology's current assessment of Freud's theory of psychoanalysis.

Critics contend that new research has made many of Freud's specific ideas out of date and that his theory offers only after-the-fact explanations. Developmental psychologists question the overriding importance of childhood experiences, the degree of parental influence, the timing of gender-identity formation, the significance of childhood sexuality, and the existence of hidden content in dreams. Many researchers now believe that repression rarely, if ever, occurs. Nevertheless, Freud drew psychology's attention to the unconscious and the irrational. Although the current view of the unconscious differs from Freud's view, research does confirm the reality of unconscious information processing. Recent research provides some support for his idea of defense mechanisms. For example, his idea of projection is what researchers now call the *false consensus effect.* Freud also focused attention on the importance of human sexuality and the tension between biological impulses and social restraints. Unquestionably, his cultural impact has been enormous.

38. Criticism of psychoanalysis as a scientific theory centers on the fact that it provides

_____-_____ _____ explanations and does not offer _____ _____ .

39. Psychoanalytic theory rests on the assumption that the human mind often _____ painful experiences. Many of today's researchers think that this process is much _____ (more common/rarer) than Freud believed. They also believe that when it does occur, it is a reaction to terrible _____ .

40. Contrary to Freud's theory, research indicates that human development is _____ (fixed in childhood/lifelong), that children gain their gender identity at a(n) _____ (earlier/later) age, and that the presence of a same-sex parent _____ (is/is not) necessary for the child to become strongly masculine or feminine.

41. Research also disputes Freud's belief that dreams disguise unfulfilled _____ .

42. Today's psychologists agree with Freud that we have limited access to all that goes on in our minds. Research confirms the reality of the _____ . However, they disagree with his view that it is a place to store anxiety-causing thoughts. Instead, they see it as a place for routine _____ _____ .

43. An example of the defense mechanism that Freud called _____ is what researchers today call the _____ _____ effect. This refers to our tendency to _____ the extent to which others share our beliefs and behaviors.

State several of Freud's ideas that have endured.

The Humanistic Perspective

Objective 8: Describe the humanistic perspective on personality in terms of Maslow's focus on self-actualization and Rogers' emphasis on people's potential for growth.

According to Maslow, human motivations form a *hierarchy of needs.* At the top are *self-actualization* and *self-transcendence,* the ultimate psychological needs that arise after basic physical and psychological needs are met and self-esteem is achieved. A humanistic psychologist, Maslow focused on healthy, creative people.

Carl Rogers agreed with Maslow that people have self-actualizing tendencies. He believed that people are basically good. To nurture growth in others, Rogers advised being *genuine, empathic,* and *accepting* (offering **unconditional positive regard**). In such a climate, people can develop a deeper self-awareness and a more realistic and positive *self-concept.*

1. Two influential theories of humanistic psychology were proposed by _____ and _____ . These theorists focused on the ways people strive for self-determination and _____ .

2. According to Maslow, humans are motivated by needs that are organized into a _____ . Maslow refers to the process of fulfilling our potential as _____ and the striving for meaning beyond the self as _____ . Many people who fulfill their potential have been moved by _____ _____ that surpass ordinary consciousness.

List some of the characteristics Maslow associated with those who fulfilled their potential.

3. According to Rogers, a person nurtures growth in a relationship by being _____ , _____ , and _____ .

4. People who are accepting of others offer them _____ _____ _____ . By so doing, they enable others to be _____ without fearing what others will think.

5. For both Maslow and Rogers, an important feature of personality is how an individual perceives himself or herself; this is the person's _____ .

APPLICATIONS:

6. Professor Choi believes that people are basically good and are endowed with self-actualizing tendencies. Evidently, Professor Choi is a proponent of _____ hierarchy of needs.

7. Javier's grandfather, who has lived a rich and productive life, is a spontaneous, loving, and self-accepting person. Maslow might say that he is a _____ person.

8. The school psychologist works within the humanistic perspective. She believes that having a positive _____ is necessary before students can achieve their potential.

9. Wanda wishes to instill in her children an accepting attitude toward other people. Maslow and Rogers would probably recommend that she
   a. teach her children first to accept themselves.
   b. use discipline sparingly.
   c. be affectionate with her children only when they behave as she wishes.
   d. do all of these things.

Objective 9: Discuss the major criticisms of the humanistic perspective on personality.

Critics complain that the humanistic perspective's concepts are vague and based on the theorists' personal opinions. For example, the description of self-actualizing people seems more a reflection of Maslow's personal values than a scientific description. Critics also argue that the individualism promoted by humanistic psychology may promote self-indulgence, selfishness, and a lack of moral restraints. A final complaint is that humanistic psychology fails to appreciate the reality of our human capacity for evil.

10. Humanistic psychologists have influenced such diverse areas as _____ , _____ , _____ , and _____ . They have also had a major impact on today's _____ psychology.

State three criticisms of humanistic psychology.

The Trait Perspective

Objective 10: Describe research efforts to identify fundamental personality traits.

Trait theorists attempt to describe personality in terms of stable and enduring behavior patterns, or tendencies to feel and act.

One strategy that psychologists have used to identify a person's personality has been to identify *factors*, clusters of behavior tendencies that occur together. For example, using this approach Hans and Sybil Eysenck reduced normal variations to two or three genetically influenced dimensions, including extraversion–introversion and emotional stability–instability. Brain-activity scans suggest that extraverts and introverts differ in their level of arousal, with extraverts seeking stimulation because their normal brain arousal level is relatively low. Jerome Kagan maintains that heredity, by influencing autonomic nervous system arousal, also affects our temperament and behavioral style, which help define our personality.

UNSTABLE
Moody — Touchy
Anxious — Restless
Rigid — Aggressive
Sober — Excitable
Pessimistic — Changeable
Reserved — Impulsive
Unsociable — Optimistic
Quiet — Active
INTROVERTED —— EXTRAVERTED
Passive — Sociable
Careful — Outgoing
Thoughtful — Talkative
Peaceful — Responsive
Controlled — Easygoing
Reliable — Lively
Even-tempered — Carefree
Calm — Leadership
STABLE

1. Trait theory defines personality in terms of people's characteristic _____ and conscious _____ . Unlike Freud, researchers testing this theory are generally less interested in _____ individual traits than in _____ them.

2. To reduce the number of traits to a few basic ones, psychologists attempt to identify clusters of behavior tendencies called _____ . The Eysencks think that two or three genetically influenced personality dimensions are sufficient; these include _____–_____ and emotional _____–_____ .

3. Some researchers believe that extraverts seek stimulation because their level of _____ _____ is relatively low. PET scans reveal an area of the brain's _____ lobe that is less active in _____ (extraverts/introverts) than in _____ (extraverts/introverts).

4. Research increasingly reveals that our _____ play an important role in defining our _____ and _____ style.

5. Jerome Kagan attributes differences in children's _____ to autonomic nervous system reactivity.

APPLICATIONS:

6. Dr. Gonzalez observes that Lili is outgoing and likes excitement and practical jokes. He believes that this cluster of behaviors, or _____ , reflects what the Eysencks referred to as _____ .

7. Because you have a relatively low level of brain arousal, a trait theorist would suggest that you are a(n) _____ who would naturally seek _____ .

8. Nadine has a relatively high level of brain arousal. Trait theorists would probably predict that she is an _____ .

9. The personality inventory that was originally developed to identify emotional disorders is the _____ _____ _____ _____ , which also assesses people's personality _____ .

10. Researchers have arrived at a cluster of five factors that seem to describe the major features of personality. List the Big Five, which cover a range of traits between two extremes. (Hint: Remember that the first letters of these traits spell CANOE.)

   a. _____
   b. _____
   c. _____
   d. _____
   e. _____

11. While some traits wane a bit after college, others increase. For example, as young adults mature and learn to manage their commitments, _____ increases. From the thirties through the sixties, _____ increases.

12. In adulthood, the Big Five are quite _____ (stable/variable), with our genes being credited for roughly _____ percent or more for each dimension. Moreover, these traits _____ (describe/do not describe) personality in other cultures.

(Thinking Critically) Explain several techniques used by astrologers to persuade people to accept their advice.

Objective 11: Identify the Big Five trait dimensions.

The *Minnesota Multiphasic Personality Inventory (MMPI),* originally developed to identify emotional disorders, also assesses people's personality traits. Researchers have isolated five distinct personality dimensions, called the *Big Five:* conscientiousness, agreeableness, neuroticism (emotional stability versus instability), openness, and extraversion. These traits appear to be stable in adulthood, about 50 percent heritable, and common to all cultures. Locating an individual on these five dimensions provides a comprehensive picture of personality.

APPLICATION:

13. For his class presentation, Bruce plans to discuss the Big Five personality factors used by people throughout the world to describe others or themselves. Which of the following is not a factor that Bruce will discuss?

   a. extraversion   c. independence
   b. openness   d. conscientiousness

The Social-Cognitive Perspective

Objective 12: Describe the social-cognitive perspective.

The *social-cognitive perspective* views behavior as influenced by the interaction between persons (and their thinking) and their social context. Although our specific behaviors may vary from one situation to the next, our average personality traits are predictable. *Reciprocal determinism* is Albert Bandura's term for the interacting influences of behavior, internal personal factors, and environment. Differences occur because different people choose different environments, people's personalities shape how they interpret and react to events, and their personalities help create situations to which they react.

1. Social-cognitive theory focuses on how the individual and the _____ interact.

2. To be useful indicators of personality, traits would have to persist over time. Researchers have found that trait scores over a seven-year period were _____ correlated. The correlations were strongest for comparisons done in _____ (childhood/adulthood).

3. Although traits _____ (are/are not) stable, behavior _____ (is/is not) consistent from one situation to the next.

4. Social-cognitive theorists propose that personality is shaped by the mutual influence of our _____ , internal _____ factors, and _____ influences. This is the principle of _____ _____ , a concept described by Albert _____ .

Describe three different ways in which the environment and personality interact.

APPLICATIONS:

5. Ramona identifies with her politically conservative parents. At college, most of her friends also held conservative views. After four years in this environment Ramona's politics have become even more conservative. According to the social-cognitive perspective, in this case Ramona's parents (_____ factor) helped shape her political beliefs (_____ factor), which influenced her choice of college (also a _____ factor) and created an

_____ that fostered her already formed political attitudes.

6. In high school, Chella and Nari were best friends. They thought they were a lot alike, as did everyone else who knew them. After high school, they went on to very different colleges, careers, and life courses. Now, at their twenty-fifth reunion, they are shocked at how little they have in common. Bandura would suggest that their differences reflect the interactive effects of environment, personality, and behavior, which he refers to as

_____ _____ .

Exploring the Self

Objective 13: Explain how psychologists define the *self*, and discuss the importance of self-esteem to human well-being.

The *self* is organizer of our thoughts, feelings, and actions, and as such is the center of personality. The concept of *possible selves* includes people's visions of the self they dream of becoming. Such possible selves motivate us by laying out specific goals and calling forth the energy to work toward them. Carried too far, a self-focused perspective can lead to a *spotlight effect,* which is our tendency to overestimate others' noticing and evaluating our appearance, performance, and blunders.

People who have high *self-esteem* have fewer sleepless nights, are less conforming, are more persistent at difficult tasks, are less shy and lonely, and are just plain happier. Some research shows a destructive effect of low self-esteem. For example, temporarily deflating people's self-esteem can lead them to insult others and express greater racial prejudice. Some researchers have separated self-esteem into two categories. *Defensive self-esteem* is fragile and correlates with aggressive and antisocial behaviors. *Secure self-esteem* relies less on other people's evaluations and leads to greater quality of life. Feeling accepted for who we are enables us to lose ourselves in relationships and purposes larger than self.

Members of groups who experience discrimination maintain their self-esteem by (1) valuing the things at which they excel, (2) attributing problems to prejudice, and (3) comparing themselves to those in their own group.

1. The organizer of our thoughts, feelings, and actions—the center of our personality—is the

_____ .

2. Psychologists introduced the concept of an individual's _____ _____ to emphasize how our vision of ourself motivates us toward specific goals.

3. Our tendency to overestimate the extent to which others are noticing and evaluating us is called the

_____ _____ .

4. According to self theorists, personality development hinges on our feelings of self-worth, or

_____ . People who feel good about themselves feel _____ (more/less) pressure to conform.

5. In a series of experiments, researchers found that people whose self-images were deflated were _____ (more/less) likely to insult other persons or tended to express

_____ _____ .

6. Some researchers distinguish _____ self-esteem, which is fragile and sensitive to _____ , from _____ self-esteem, which is less focused on _____ evaluations.

7. Research studies demonstrate that ethnic minorities, people with disabilities, and women generally _____ (have/do not have) lower self-esteem.

8. Members of stigmatized groups maintain self-esteem in three ways:

a. _____

b. _____

c. _____

APPLICATION:

9. The behavior of many people has been described in terms of a spotlight effect. This means that they
   a. tend to see themselves as being above average in ability.
   b. perceive that their fate is determined by forces not under their personal control.
   c. overestimate the extent to which other people are noticing them.
   d. do all of these things.

Objective 14: Discuss some evidence for self-serving bias.

Self-serving bias is our readiness to perceive ourselves favorably. This bias is evident in our tendency to accept more responsibility for good deeds than for bad and for successes than for failures. Most people also see themselves as better than average. Self-serving bias underlies conflicts. It is very common, even though people tend to put themselves down. There are three reasons for these put-downs: People are prompting positive feedback, they are preparing themselves for possible failure, and they are really criticizing past selves.

10. The tendency of people to judge themselves favorably is called the _____ bias.

11. Responsibility for success is generally accepted _____ (more/less) readily than responsibility for failure.

12. Most people perceive their own behavior and traits as being _____ (above/below) average.

APPLICATION:

13. James attributes his failing grade in chemistry to an unfair final exam. His attitude is an example of the

_____ .

Objective 15: Explain how the self is viewed by individualist and collectivist cultures.

Individualists give priority to personal goals. They define their identity mostly in terms of personal traits, and they strive for personal control and individual achievement. *Collectivists* give priority to group identity, which provides a sense of belonging and a set of values. Preserving group spirit and avoiding social embarrassment are important goals. People in individualist cultures have more personal freedom but at the cost of more loneliness, divorce, homicide, and stress-related disease.

14. Cultures and people who give higher priority to personal goals are called _____ .
People in such cultures have more personal _____ , but they also suffer more often from _____ _____ .

15. Cultures and people who give higher priority to group goals are called _____ .

PROGRESS TEST

20/34

Multiple-Choice Questions

Circle your answers to the following questions and check them with the answers beginning on page 211. If your answer is incorrect, read the explanation for why it is incorrect and then consult the text.

1. The text defines *personality* as
   a. the set of personal attitudes that characterizes a person.
   b. an individual's characteristic pattern of thinking, feeling, and acting.
   c. a predictable set of responses to environmental situations.
   d. an unpredictable set of responses to environmental situations.

2. Which of the following places the greatest emphasis on the unconscious mind?
   a. the humanistic perspective
   b. the social-cognitive perspective
   c. the trait perspective
   d. the psychoanalytic perspective

3. Which of the following is the correct order of psychosexual stages proposed by Freud?
   a. oral, anal, phallic, latency, genital
   b. anal, oral, phallic, latency, genital
   c. oral, anal, genital, latency, phallic
   d. anal, oral, genital, latency, phallic

4. According to Freud, defense mechanisms are methods of reducing
   a. anger.
   b. fear.
   c. anxiety.
   d. lust.

5. Neo-Freudians such as Alfred Adler and Karen Horney believed that
   a. Freud placed too great an emphasis on the conscious mind.
   b. Freud placed too great an emphasis on sexual and aggressive instincts.
   c. the years of childhood were more important in the formation of personality than Freud had indicated.
   d. Freud's ideas about the id, ego, and superego as personality structures were incorrect.

6. Which two dimensions of personality have the Eysencks emphasized?
   a. extraversion–introversion and emotional stability–instability
   b. ego–superego and extraversion–introversion
   c. ego–superego and emotional stability–instability
   d. identification–fixation and individualism–collectivism

7. With regard to personality, it appears that
   a. there is little consistency of behavior from one situation to the next and little consistency of traits over the life span.
   b. there is little consistency of behavior from one situation to the next but significant consistency of traits over the life span.
   c. there is significant consistency of behavior from one situation to the next but little consistency of traits over the life span.
   d. there is significant consistency of behavior from one situation to the next and significant consistency of traits over the life span.

8. The humanistic perspective on personality
   a. emphasizes unconscious motivations in personality.
   b. emphasizes the growth potential of "healthy" individuals.
   c. emphasizes the importance of interaction with the environment in shaping personality.
   d. describes rather than explains personality traits.

9. According to Carl Rogers, three conditions are necessary to promote growth in personality. These are
   a. honesty, sincerity, and empathy.
   b. high self-esteem, honesty, and empathy.
   c. high self-esteem, genuineness, and acceptance.
   d. genuineness, acceptance, and empathy.

10. Regarding the self-serving bias, psychologists who study the self have found that self-love, or pride,
   a. is generally not good for the individual because it distorts reality by overinflating self-esteem.
   b. is generally adaptive to the individual because it maintains self-confidence and minimizes depression.
   c. tends to prevent the individual from viewing others with compassion and understanding.
   d. tends not to characterize people who have experienced unconditional positive regard.

11. Which of Freud's ideas would NOT be accepted by most contemporary psychologists?
   a. Development is essentially fixed in childhood.
   b. Sexuality is a potent drive in humans.
   c. Many of our thoughts and feelings are unconscious.
   d. Repression can be the cause of forgetting.

12. Projective tests such as the Rorschach inkblot test have been criticized because
   a. their scoring system is too rigid and leads to unfair labeling.
   b. they were standardized with unrepresentative samples.
   c. they have low reliability and low validity.
   d. it is easy for people to fake answers in order to appear healthy.

13. For humanistic psychologists, many of our behaviors and perceptions are ultimately shaped by whether our _____ is _____ or _____ .
   a. ego; strong; weak
   b. self-esteem; internal; external
   c. personality structure; introverted; extraverted
   d. self-concept; positive; negative

14. In studying personality, a trait theorist would MOST LIKELY
   a. use a projective test.
   b. observe a person in a variety of situations.
   c. use a personality inventory.
   d. use the method of free association.

15. Id is to ego as _____ is to _____ .
   a. reality principle; pleasure principle
   b. pleasure principle; reality principle
   c. conscious forces; unconscious forces
   d. conscience; "personality executive"

16. Research has provided more support for defense mechanisms such as _____ than for defense mechanisms such as _____ .
    a. projection; reaction formation
    b. reaction formation; projection
    c. displacement; regression
    d. displacement; projection

17. Many of today's personality researchers focus their work on
    a. the basic goodness of people.
    b. the interaction of persons and environments.
    c. grand theories of behavior.
    d. unconscious conflicts.

18. Which perspective on personality emphasizes the interaction between the individual and the environment in shaping personality?
    a. psychoanalytic
    b. trait
    c. humanistic
    d. social-cognitive

19. According to Freud's theory, personality arises in response to conflicts between
    a. our unacceptable urges and our tendency to become self-actualized.
    b. the process of identification and the ego's defense mechanisms.
    c. our projections and our individual desires.
    d. our biological impulses and the social restraints against them.

20. Research has shown that individuals who are made to feel insecure are subsequently
    a. more likely to insult others.
    b. less likely to insult others.
    c. more likely to display a self-serving bias.
    d. less likely to display a self-serving bias.

21. An example of the self-serving bias described in the text is the tendency of people to
    a. see themselves as better than average on nearly any desirable dimension.
    b. accept less responsibility for successes than failures.
    c. be overly critical of other people.
    d. conform to what most people expect of them.

22. The Minnesota Multiphasic Personality Inventory (MMPI) is a
    a. projective personality test.
    b. personality test that covers a wide range of feelings and behaviors.
    c. personality test developed mainly to assess job applicants.
    d. personality test used primarily to assess unconscious beliefs.

23. Trait theory attempts to
    a. show how personality development is lifelong.
    b. describe and classify people in terms of their tendency to behave in certain ways.
    c. determine which traits are most likely to lead to individual self-actualization.

    d. explain how behavior is shaped by the interaction between traits, behavior, and the environment.

24. Which of the following statements about self-esteem is NOT correct?
    a. People with low self-esteem tend to be negative about others.
    b. People with high self-esteem are more persistent at difficult tasks.
    c. People with low self-esteem tend to be nonconformists.
    d. People with high self-esteem suffer less from insomnia.

25. The Oedipus complex has its roots in the
    a. anal stage.
    b. oral stage.
    c. latency stage.
    d. phallic stage.

26. Which of the following is a common criticism of the humanistic perspective?
    a. Its concepts are vague and subjective.
    b. The emphasis on the self encourages selfishness in individuals.
    c. The humanistic perspective fails to appreciate the reality of evil in human behavior.
    d. All of these are common criticisms.

27. In studying personality, a social-cognitive theorist would MOST likely make use of
    a. personality inventories.
    b. projective tests.
    c. observing behavior in different situations.
    d. the Rorschach inkblot test.

28. A major difference between the psychoanalytic and trait perspectives is that
    a. trait theory defines personality in terms of behavior; psychoanalytic theory, in terms of its underlying dynamics.
    b. trait theory describes behavior but does not attempt to explain it.
    c. psychoanalytic theory emphasizes the origins of personality in childhood sexuality.
    d. all of these answers give differences.

29. The Big Five personality factors are
    a. emotional stability, openness, introversion, sociability, projection.
    b. neuroticism, extraversion, openness, emotional stability, sensitivity.
    c. neuroticism, displacement, extraversion, impulsiveness, conscientiousness.
    d. neuroticism, extraversion, openness, agreeableness, conscientiousness.

30. Which of the following was NOT mentioned in the text as a criticism of Freud's theory?
    a. The theory rests on few objective observations.
    b. It offers few testable hypotheses.
    c. There is no evidence of anything like an unconscious.
    d. The theory ignores the fact that human development is lifelong.

31. According to Freud, _____ is the process by which children incorporate their parents' values into their _____ .
    a. reaction formation; superegos
    b. reaction formation; egos
    c. identification; superegos
    d. identification; egos

32. Which of the following groups tend to suffer from relatively low self-esteem?
    a. women
    b. ethnic minorities
    c. disabled persons
    d. None of these groups suffer from low self-esteem.

33. In promoting personality growth, the person-centered perspective emphasizes all but
    a. empathy.   c. genuineness.
    b. acceptance.   d. altruism.

34. Recent research on the Big Five personality factors provides evidence that
    a. some tendencies decrease during adulthood, while others increase.
    b. these traits only describe personality in Western, individualist cultures.
    c. the genetic contribution to individual differences in these traits generally runs about 25 percent or less.
    d. all of these facts are true.

Matching Items

Match each term with the appropriate definition or description.

Terms

_____ 1. projective test
_____ 2. identification
_____ 3. reality principle
_____ 4. psychosexual stages
_____ 5. pleasure principle
_____ 6. reciprocal determinism
_____ 7. personality inventory
_____ 8. Oedipus complex

Definitions or Descriptions

a. the id's demand for immediate gratification
b. a boy's sexual desires toward the opposite-sex parent
c. stages of development proposed by Freud
d. questionnaire used to assess personality traits
e. the two-way interactions of behavior with personal and environmental factors
f. personality test that provides unclear images
g. the process by which children incorporate their parents' values into their developing superegos
h. the process by which the ego seeks to gratify impulses of the id in nondestructive ways

Application Essay

You are an honest, open, and responsible person. Discuss how these characteristics would be explained according to the major perspectives on personality. (Use the space below to list points you want to make, and organize them. Then write the essay on a separate piece of paper.)

SUMMING UP

See pages 208 and 209.

TERMS AND CONCEPTS

Using your own words, on a separate piece of paper write a brief definition or explanation of each of the following terms.

1. personality

2. unconscious

3. free association

4. psychoanalysis

5. id

6. ego

7. superego

8. psychosexual stages

9. Oedipus complex

10. identification

11. fixation

12. defense mechanisms

13. repression

14. psychodynamic theory

15. projective test

16. Rorschach inkblot test

17. hierarchy of needs

18. self-actualization

19. self-transcendence

20. unconditional positive regard

21. self-concept

22. trait

23. factor

24. social-cognitive perspective

25. reciprocal determinism

26. self

27. spotlight effect

28. self-esteem

29. self-serving bias

30. individualism

31. collectivism

ANSWERS

Chapter Review

Introducing Personality and *The Psychoanalytic Perspective*

1. thinking; feeling; acting
2. Sigmund Freud; humanistic; growth; self-fulfillment
3. scientific; self
4. nervous
5. medical
6. hypnosis; free association

7. unconscious; repressed

8. The child probably has some unresolved conflicts with her mother. Freud did not believe anything was accidental. Unconscious conflicts seeped out through slips of the tongue and pen, for example.

9. psychoanalysis

10. biological; social

11. id; ego; superego

12. unconscious; pleasure

13. conscious; reality

The ego is considered the executive of personality because it directs our actions as it reconciles the impulsive demands of the id, the reality of the external world, and the restraining demands of the superego.

14. superego; 4 or 5

15. There are no right or wrong answers. Here's a sample answer to a. Complete b. and c. on your own.

   a. The id's response: "I'm so angry; the driver is extremely thoughtless. So, I think I'll speed up and tailgate."

   The ego's response: "I'll relieve my frustration by mentioning the other driver to my friend in the car, then wait for a safe opportunity to pass."

   The superego's response: "The driver may be going way below the speed limit because he or she is an elderly person or is sick or having car trouble."

16. psychosexual; erogenous zone

17. oral; sucking (also biting, chewing)

18. anal

19. phallic; genitals; opposite; Oedipus complex

20. identification; gender identity

Children cope with their feelings for the opposite-sex parent by repressing them and by identifying with the rival (same-sex) parent. Through this process children take on many of their parents' values, thereby strengthening the superego.

21. latency

22. genital

23. fixated

24. fixated; oral. Song Yi was probably orally deprived (weaned too early) as an infant, so she is fixated at the oral stage. Smoking satisfies her id's needs.

25. defense mechanisms; repression

26. regression

27. reaction formation

28. projection

29. rationalization

30. displacement

31. *Matching Items*

1. f	4. c
2. e	5. a
3. b	6. d

32. unconscious

SUMMING UP

1. Klaus is 18 years old and, like all adolescents, is trying to figure out who he is.

He wants to know why he thinks, feels, and acts the way he does;

that is, he wants to define his _____ .

Klaus decides to read about the various personality theorists, beginning with

Sigmund _____ , who believed that most

of the mind is hidden from view, and is therefore

_____ ,

and that

personalty is a product of the _____

between our basic sexual and aggressive impulses,

directed by the _____ , and the social restraints

derived from the _____ .

After reading about psychoanalytic theory, Klaus decided that his long-standing aggressive behavior toward his younger brother

could have been the result of

_____ his anger with his

parents for being so strict,

and that this

protects him from the

_____ he might feel if he

were to express that anger.

Perhaps

the part of his personality called the _____

redirects his anger, and so the hitting of his brother is

a _____ mechanism called

_____ .

Klaus also thought that perhaps he had

_____ his behavior by saying

that his brother needed the discipline.

SUMMING UP

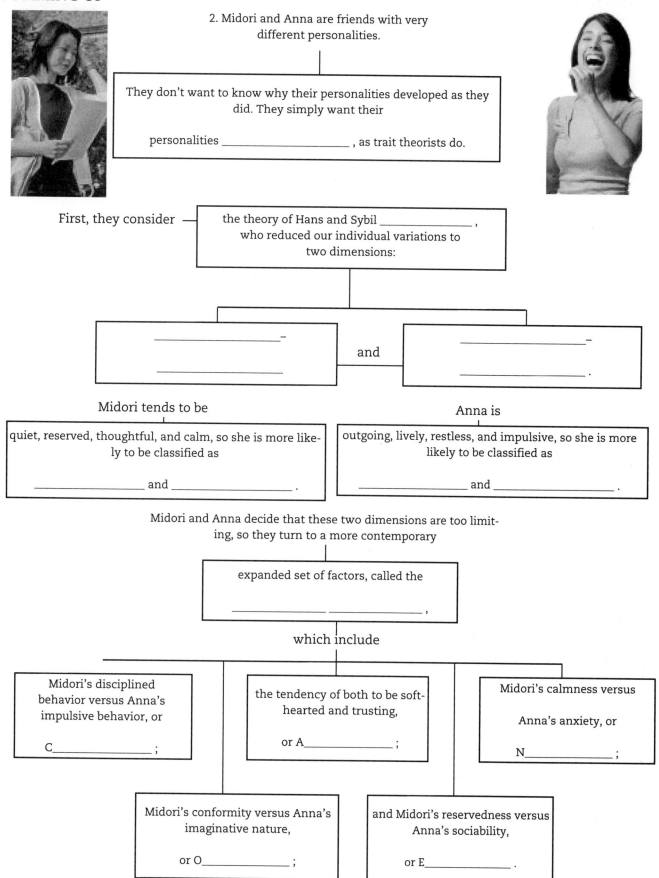

2. Midori and Anna are friends with very different personalities.

They don't want to know why their personalities developed as they did. They simply want their

personalities _____ , as trait theorists do.

First, they consider — the theory of Hans and Sybil _____ , who reduced our individual variations to two dimensions:

_____ -
_____

and

_____ -
_____ .

Midori tends to be

quiet, reserved, thoughtful, and calm, so she is more likely to be classified as

_____ and _____ .

Anna is

outgoing, lively, restless, and impulsive, so she is more likely to be classified as

_____ and _____ .

Midori and Anna decide that these two dimensions are too limiting, so they turn to a more contemporary

expanded set of factors, called the

_____ _____ ,

which include

Midori's disciplined behavior versus Anna's impulsive behavior, or

C_____ ;

the tendency of both to be soft-hearted and trusting,

or A_____ ;

Midori's calmness versus

Anna's anxiety, or

N_____ ;

Midori's conformity versus Anna's imaginative nature,

or O_____ ;

and Midori's reservedness versus Anna's sociability,

or E_____ .

33. neo-Freudians; more; less; Horney; Adler; Jung
34. psychodynamic; sex; unconscious; childhood; inner conflicts
35. projective
36. Rorschach; inkblots; little; little; is not
37. projective. Projective tests provide unclear images, such as random dot patterns, in an attempt to trigger in the test-taker projection of his or her personality.
38. after-the-fact; testable predictions
39. represses; rarer; trauma
40. lifelong; earlier; is not
41. wishes
42. unconscious; information processing
43. projection; false consensus; overestimate

Freud drew attention to the unconscious and the irrational, to human defenses against anxiety, to the importance of human sexuality, to the tension between our biological impulses and our social well-being, and to our potential for evil.

The Humanistic Perspective

1. Abraham Maslow; Carl Rogers; self-realization
2. hierarchy; self-actualization; self-transcendence; peak experiences

For Maslow, such people were self-aware, open, self-accepting, spontaneous, loving, caring, not paralyzed by others' opinions, and problem-centered rather than self-centered.

3. genuine; accepting; empathic
4. unconditional positive regard; themselves
5. self-concept
6. Maslow's. As a humanistic theorist, Maslow believed that people are basically good and that at their best they strive for self-actualization and self-transcendence.
7. self-actualizing. Maslow studied healthy people and found that they had all the characteristics of Javier's grandfather, as well as being self-aware and unconcerned about other people's opinions.
8. self-concept. Humanistic psychologists believed that the self-concept is central to our personality. A positive self-concept allows us to act and perceive the world positively.
9. a. is the answer. Humanistic psychologists believe that to love and accept others, we must first love and accept ourselves.
10. counseling; education; child-rearing; management; popular

Three criticisms of humanistic psychology are that its concepts are vague and subjective; that the attitudes it encourages can lead to self-indulgence, selfishness, and a lack of moral restraints; and that it fails to appreciate the human capacity for evil.

The Trait Perspective

1. behaviors; motives; explaining; describing
2. factors; extraversion–introversion; stability–instability
3. brain arousal; frontal; extraverts; introverts
4. genes; temperament; behavioral
5. shyness
6. factor; extraversion. Factors are clusters of behavior tendencies that occur together. Lili's characteristic behaviors indicate she is an extravert.
7. extravert; stimulation. The relatively low level of brain arousal causes extraverts to seek stimulation.
8. introvert. This situation is the reverse of that described in 7.
9. Minnesota Multiphasic Personality Inventory; traits
10. a. **C**onscientiousness
    b. **A**greeableness
    c. **N**euroticism (emotional instability)
    d. **O**penness
    e. **E**xtraversion
11. conscientiousness; agreeableness
12. stable; 50; describe

Astrologers use a "stock spiel" that includes information that is generally true of almost everyone. A second technique used by astrologers is to "read" a person's clothing, features, reactions, etc., and build their advice from these observations.

13. c. is the answer.

The Social-Cognitive Perspective

1. environment
2. positively; adulthood
3. are; is not
4. behaviors; personal; environmental; reciprocal determinism; Bandura

Different people choose different environments partly on the basis of their personalities. Our personality shapes how we interpret and react to events. It also helps create the situations to which we react.

5. situational; internal; situational; environment. This shows the interaction of internal and situational factors, using the social-cognitive view of how personality develops.
6. reciprocal determinism. This shows how the interaction of behavior, internal personal factors, and environment can change behavior.

Exploring the Self

1. self
2. possible selves
3. spotlight effect
4. self-esteem; less
5. more; racial prejudice
6. defensive; criticism; secure; external
7. do not have

8. a. They value the things at which they excel.
    b. They attribute problems to prejudice.
    c. They compare themselves to those in their own group.

9. **c.** is the answer.

10. self-serving

11. more

12. above

13. self-serving bias

14. individualists; freedom; loneliness, divorce, homicide, and stress-related disease

15. collectivists

Progress Test

Multiple-Choice Questions

1. **b.** is the answer. Personality is defined as patterns of response—of thinking, feeling, and acting—that are relatively consistent across a variety of situations.

2. **d.** is the answer.
    a. & b. Conscious processes are the focus of these perspectives.
    c. The trait perspective focuses on the description of behaviors.

3. **a.** is the answer.

4. **c.** is the answer. According to Freud, defense mechanisms reduce anxiety unconsciously, by disguising our threatening impulses.
    a., b., & d. Unlike these specific emotions, anxiety need not be focused. Defense mechanisms help us cope when we are unsettled but are not sure why.

5. **b.** is the answer.
    a. According to most neo-Freudians, Freud placed too great an emphasis on the *unconscious* mind.
    c. Freud placed great emphasis on early childhood, and the neo-Freudians basically agreed with him.
    d. The neo-Freudians accepted Freud's ideas about the basic personality structures.

6. **a.** is the answer.
    b. & c. Ego and superego are Freudian concepts.
    d. Identification and fixation are also Freudian concepts.

7. **b.** is the answer. Studies have shown that people do not act with predictable consistency from one situation to the next. But, over a number of situations, consistent patterns emerge, and this basic consistency of traits persists over the life span.

8. **b.** is the answer.
    a. This is true of the psychoanalytic perspective.
    c. This is true of the social-cognitive perspective.
    d. This is true of the trait perspective.

9. **d.** is the answer.

10. **b.** is the answer. Psychologists who study the self emphasize that for the individual, self-affirming thinking is generally adaptive (therefore, not a.); that such thinking maintains self-confidence, minimizes depression, and enables us to view others with compassion and understanding (therefore, not c.); and that unconditional positive regard tends to promote self-esteem and thus self-affirming thinking (therefore, not d.).

11. **a.** is the answer. Developmental research indicates that development is lifelong.
    b., c., & d. To varying degrees, research has partially supported these Freudian ideas. The modern view of the unconscious is that routine information processing occurs there.

12. **c.** is the answer. As scoring is largely subjective and the tests have not been very successful in predicting behavior, their reliability and validity have been called into question.
    a. This is untrue.
    b. Unlike empirically derived personality tests, projective tests are not standardized.
    d. Although this may be true, it was not mentioned as a criticism of projective tests.

13. **d.** is the answer.
    a. & c. Personality structure is a concern of the psychoanalytic perspective.
    b. Self-esteem is a major focus of research on the self.

14. **c.** is the answer.
    a. & d. A psychoanalytic theorist would be most likely to use a projective test or free association.
    b. This would most likely be the approach taken by a social-cognitive theorist.

15. **b.** is the answer. In Freud's theory, the id operates according to the pleasure principle; the ego operates according to the reality principle.
    c. The id is presumed to be unconscious.
    d. The superego is, according to Freud, the equivalent of a conscience; the ego is the "personality executive."

16. **b.** is the answer. Today's researchers call it the false consensus effect.
    a., c., & d. The evidence supports defenses that defend self-esteem, rather than those that are tied to instinctual energy.

17. **b.** is the answer.

18. **d.** is the answer.
    a. This perspective emphasizes unconscious dynamics in personality.
    b. This perspective is more concerned with *describing* than *explaining* personality.
    c. This perspective emphasizes the healthy, self-actualizing tendencies of personality.

19. **d.** is the answer.
    a. Self-actualization is a concept of the humanistic perspective.
    b. Through identification, children *reduce* conflicting feelings as they incorporate their parents' values.
    c. Projection is a defense mechanism.

20. **a.** is the answer. Feelings of insecurity reduce self-esteem, and those who feel negative about themselves tend to feel negative about others as well.

21. **a.** is the answer.
    b., c., & d. Just the opposite is true.

22. **b.** is the answer. The MMPI was originally developed to identify emotional disorders; it is now used as a personality inventory.

    a. & d. Projective tests present unclear images for people to interpret. These tests are designed to detect unconscious conflicts. Personality inventories assess personality traits.

    c. As part of its function as a personality inventory, the MMPI may be used to assess job applicants, but that is not its only purpose.

23. **b.** is the answer. Trait theory attempts to describe behavior and not to develop explanations or applications. The emphasis is more on consistency than on change.

24. **c.** is the answer. In actuality, people with *high* self-esteem are generally more independent of pressures to conform.

25. **d.** is the answer.

26. **d.** is the answer.

27. **c.** is the answer. In keeping with their emphasis on interactions between people and situations, social-cognitive theorists would most likely make use of observations of behavior in relevant situations.

    a. Personality inventories would more likely be used by a trait theorist.

    b. Projective tests would more likely be used by a psychologist working within the psychoanalytic perspective.

    d. The Rorschach would be used by a psychoanalyst.

28. **d.** is the answer. Trait theory defines personality in terms of behavior and is therefore interested in describing behavior; psychoanalytic theory defines personality as dynamics underlying behavior and therefore is interested in explaining behavior in terms of these dynamics.

29. **d.** is the answer.

30. **c.** is the answer. Although many researchers think of the unconscious as information processing without awareness rather than as a home for repressed information, they agree with Freud that we do indeed have limited access to all that goes on in our minds.

31. **c.** is the answer.

    a. & b. Reaction formation is the defense mechanism by which people transform unacceptable impulses into their opposites.

    d. It is the superego, rather than the ego, that represents parental values.

32. **d.** is the answer.

33. **d.** is the answer.

34. **a.** is the answer. Neuroticism, extraversion, and openness tend to decrease, while agreeableness and conscientiousness tend to increase.

    b. The Big Five dimensions describe personality in various cultures reasonably well.

    c. The genetic contribution generally runs 50 percent or more for each dimension.

Matching Items

1. f   5. a
2. g   6. e
3. h   7. d
4. c   8. b

Application Essay

Because you are apparently in good psychological health, according to the psychoanalytic perspective you must have experienced a healthy childhood and successfully passed through Freud's stages of psychosexual development. Freud would also say that your ego is functioning well in balancing the demands of your id with the restraining demands of your superego and reality. Freud might also say that your honest nature reflects a well-developed superego.

According to the humanistic perspective, your open and honest nature indicates that your basic needs have been met and that you are in the process of self-actualization (Maslow). Furthermore, your openness indicates that you have a healthy self-concept and were likely nurtured by genuine, accepting, and empathic caregivers (Rogers). More recently, researchers who emphasize the self would also focus on the importance of a high self-esteem.

Trait theorists would be less concerned with explaining these specific characteristics than with describing them. Some trait theorists, such as Hans Eysenck and Jerome Kagan, attribute certain trait differences to biological factors such as autonomic reactivity and heredity.

According to the social-cognitive perspective, your internal personal factors, behavior, and environmental influences interacted in shaping your personality and behaviors.

Summing Up

1. Klaus is 18 years old and, like all adolescents, is trying to figure out who he is. He wants to know why he thinks, feels, and acts the way he does; that is, he wants to define his *personality*. Klaus decides to read about the various personality theorists, beginning with Sigmund *Freud*, who believed that most of the mind is hidden from view, and is therefore *unconscious*, and that personality is a product of the *conflict* between our basic sexual and aggressive impulses, directed by the *id*, and the social restraints derived from the *superego*. After reading about psychoanalytic theory, Klaus decided that his long-standing aggressive behavior toward his younger brother could have been the result of *repressing* his anger with his parents for being so strict, and that this protects him from the *anxiety* he might feel if he were to express that anger. Perhaps the part of his personality called the *ego* redirects his anger, and so the hitting of his brother is a *defense* mechanism called *displacement*. Klaus also thought that perhaps he had *rationalized* his behavior by saying that his brother needed the discipline.

2. Midori and Anna are friends with very different personalities. They don't want to know why their personalities developed as they did. They simply want their personalities *described*, as trait theorists do. First, they consider the theory of Hans and Sybil *Eysenck*, who reduced our individual variations to two dimensions: *extraversion–introversion* and *emotional stability–instability*. Midori tends to be quiet, reserved, thoughtful, and calm, so she is more likely to be classified as *introverted* and *stable*. Anna is outgoing, lively, restless, and impulsive, so she is more likely to be classified as *extraverted* and *unstable*. Midori and Anna decide that these two dimensions are too limiting, so they turn to a more contemporary expanded set of factors, called the *Big Five*, which include Midori's disciplined behavior versus Aanna's impulsive behavior, or *Conscientiousness*; the tendency of both to be soft-hearted and trusting, or *Agreeableness*; Midori's calmness versus Anna's anxiety, or *Neuroticism*; Midori's conformity versus Anna's imaginative nature, or *Openness*; and Midori's reservedness versus Anna's sociability, or *Extraversion*.

Terms and Concepts

1. **Personality** is an individual's characteristic pattern of thinking, feeling, and acting.

2. In Freud's theory, the **unconscious** is the repository of mostly unacceptable thoughts, wishes, feelings, and memories. According to contemporary psychologists, it is a level of information processing of which we are unaware.

3. **Free association** is the Freudian technique in which the person is encouraged to say whatever comes to mind as a means of exploring the unconscious.

4. **Psychoanalysis** is Freud's theory of personality that attributes thoughts and actions to unconscious motives and conflicts; also, the techniques used in treating psychological disorders by seeking to expose and interpret the tensions within a patient's unconscious.

5. In Freud's theory, the **id** is the unconscious system of personality, consisting of basic sexual and aggressive drives, that supplies psychic energy to personality. It operates on the *pleasure principle*.

6. In psychoanalytic theory, the **ego** is the conscious division of personality that attempts to mediate between the demands of the id, the superego, and reality. It operates on the *reality principle*.

7. In Freud's theory, the **superego** is the division of personality that contains the conscience and develops by incorporating the perceived moral standards of society.

8. Freud's **psychosexual stages** are developmental periods children pass through during which the id's pleasure-seeking energies are focused on different erogenous zones.

9. According to Freud, boys in the phallic stage develop a collection of feelings, known as the **Oedipus complex,** that center on sexual attraction to the mother and resentment of the father.

10. In Freud's theory, **identification** is the process by which the child's superego develops and incorporates the parents' values. Freud saw identification as crucial, not only to resolution of the Oedipus complex but also to the development of *gender identity*.

11. In Freud's theory, **fixation** occurs when development becomes arrested, due to unresolved conflicts, in an immature psychosexual stage.

12. In Freud's theory, **defense mechanisms** are the ego's methods of unconsciously protecting itself against anxiety by distorting reality.

13. The basis of all defense mechanisms, **repression** is the unconscious exclusion of anxiety-arousing thoughts, feelings, and memories from the conscious mind. Repression is an example of motivated forgetting: We "forget" what we really do not wish to remember.

14. **Psychodynamic theory** is a Freud-influenced perspective that emphasizes the importance of unconscious motives in mental life while downplaying the importance of sex as the basis of personality.

15. **Projective tests**, such as the Rorschach, present unclear images onto which people supposedly *project* their own inner feelings.

16. The **Rorschach inkblot test,** the most widely used projective test, consists of 10 inkblots that people are asked to interpret; it seeks to identify people's inner feelings by analyzing their interpretations of the blots.

17. In Maslow's theory, physiological needs, safety needs, and psychological needs are organized into a **hierarchy of needs** that must be met in that order.

18. In Maslow's theory, **self-actualization** describes the process of fulfilling our potential and becoming spontaneous, loving, creative, and self-accepting. Self-actualization is at the very top of Maslow's need hierarchy and therefore becomes active only after the more basic physical and psychological needs have been met.

19. In Maslow's theory, **self-transcendence** describes the process of striving for meaning and identity beyond the self.

20. **Unconditional positive regard** is, according to Rogers, an attitude of total acceptance toward another person.

21. **Self-concept** refers to all our thoughts and feelings about ourselves, in answer to the question, "Who am I?" In the humanistic perspective, the self-concept is a central feature of personality; life happiness is significantly affected by whether the self-concept is positive or negative.

22. **Traits** are people's characteristic patterns of behavior.

23. A **factor** is a cluster of traits that occur together.

24. According to the **social-cognitive perspective,** behavior is the result of interactions between people (and their thinking) and their social context.

25. According to the social-cognitive perspective, personality is shaped through **reciprocal determinism,** or the interaction between personality and environmental factors.

26. The **self** refers to your understanding of who you are.

27. The **spotlight effect** is the tendency of people to overestimate the extent to which other people are noticing and evaluating them.

28. **Self-esteem** refers to an individual's sense of self-worth.

29. The **self-serving bias** is the tendency to perceive oneself favorably.

30. **Individualism** is the cultural value that gives priority to personal goals over group goals.

31. **Collectivism** is the cultural value that gives priority to group goals over personal goals.

12

PSYCHOLOGICAL DISORDERS

Although there is no clear-cut line between normal and abnormal behavior, we can characterize as abnormal those behaviors that are deviant, distressful, and dysfunctional. Chapter 12 discusses types of anxiety disorders, dissociative and personality disorders, substance-related disorders, mood disorders, and schizophrenia, as classified by the Diagnostic and Statistical Manual of Mental Disorders (DSM-IV-TR). Although this classification system follows a medical model, in which disorders are viewed as illnesses, the chapter discusses psychological as well as physiological factors, as advocated by the current biopsychosocial approach.

CHAPTER REVIEW

First, skim each text section, noting headings and bold-face items. Review the section by reading the objectives and summaries provided here, then answer the questions that follow. In some cases, STUDY TIPS explain how best to learn a difficult concept and APPLICATIONS help you to know how well you understand the material. Check your understanding of the material by consulting the answers beginning on page 231. Do not continue with the next section until you understand each answer. If you need to, review or reread the section in the textbook before continuing.

What Is a Psychological Disorder?

Objective 1: Identify the criteria for judging whether behavior is psychologically disordered.

Psychological disorders consist of *deviant, distressful,* and *dysfunctional* thoughts, feelings, or behaviors. Standards of deviant behavior vary by culture, the situation, and even time. For example, high-energy children once regarded as normal children running wild are now being diagnosed with *attention-deficit hyperactivity disorder (ADHD)*.

1. Psychological disorders are ongoing

   _____ , _____ ,

   and _____ that are

   _____ , _____ ,

   and _____ .

2. This definition emphasizes that standards for determining whether behavior is considered disordered are _____ (constant/variable).

3. These standards depend on the situation, the _____ , and time.

• •

STUDY TIP: To be considered evidence of a psychological disorder, a behavior pattern must be deviant, distressful, *and* dysfunctional. Most people sometimes behave in ways that fit one or two of these criteria yet fall short of being clinically significant. For example, a deviant behavior is simply one that does not occur in most other people in a specific culture. The

remarkable skills of a professional rodeo athlete, for example, while deviant from most of us, are not distressful or dysfunctional. Think about your own behavior patterns and see if you can think of examples that fit one or two of the three criteria that characterize psychological disorders.

• •

APPLICATION:

4. Kitty has agreed to appear on the TV show *Fear Factor*. Her test involves eating roaches, a practice that disgusts most North Americans. Although Kitty's task is

   _____ and possibly briefly

   _____ , it is not

   _____ and so is not disordered.

Objective 2: Contrast the medical model of psychological disorders with the biopsychosocial approach to disordered behavior.

Resulting in part from Philippe Pinel's work to improve the treatment of the mentally ill, the **medical model** assumes that psychological disorders are mental illnesses that need to be diagnosed on the basis of their symptoms and cured through therapy. Psychologists who reject the "sickness" idea typically note that all behavior arises from the interaction of our biology, our psychology, and our social-cultural environment. The biopsychosocial approach recognizes that disorders are influenced by genes, physiology, inner psychological dynamics, and social and cultural circumstances, that is, that mind and body are inseparable.

5. The view that psychological disorders are sicknesses is the basis of the _____ model. According to this view, psychological disorders are viewed as mental _____ , diagnosed on the basis of _____ , treated, and, in most cases, cured through

   _____ .

6. To call psychological disorders "sicknesses" tilts research heavily toward the influence of _____ . However, behavior also is influenced by our _____ histories and _____ and _____ surroundings.

7. Psychological disorders such as _____ and _____ are universal; others, such as _____ _____ and _____ _____ , are culture-bound. These culture-bound disorders may share an underlying _____ , such as _____ , yet differ in their _____ .

••

STUDY TIP: Think about the implications of the medical model and biopsychosocial models of psychological disorders. If a behavior pattern that is deviant, distressful, and dysfunctional is caused by a brain abnormality, for example, how would you answer the following questions?

1. How should this behavior be diagnosed?
2. How should this behavior be treated in efforts to cure it?
3. How will people view people who are diagnosed with this disorder? For example, are they to blame for their plight?

Now think about a disordered behavior that is caused by a person's environment, thinking patterns, and habits. Would your answers to these questions change for this type of behavior? Why or why not?

••

APPLICATION:

8. Haya, who suffers from taijin-kyofusho, is afraid of direct eye contact with another person. A therapist who believes in the medical model would say that her problem has a _____ basis. A biopsychosocial therapist would want to look into the interaction of her

_____ , _____ , and _____-_____ environment.

Objective 3: Describe the goals and content of the DSM-IV-TR, and discuss the potential dangers and benefits of using diagnostic labels.

The American Psychiatric Association's *Diagnostic and Statistical Manual of Mental Disorders* (Fourth, Text Revision), nicknamed *DSM-IV-TR,* is the current best scheme for describing psychological disorders and estimating how often they occur. Referred to as the "text revision," it assumes the medical model. DSM-V is expected in 2013. A first draft was released in 2010, showing that some diagnostic labels are changing and that others are being added. The DSM-IV-TR is fairly reliable. Two clinicians working independently applying the guidelines are likely to reach the same diagnosis.

Some critics believe the DSM casts too wide a net, including "almost any kind of behavior" that might be considered disordered. Other critics point out that labels are just society's value judgments and can cause us to prejudge people. Labels can also be self-fulfilling. Despite their risks, diagnostic labels help not only to describe a psychological disorder but also to enable mental health professionals to communicate about their cases, to pinpoint the underlying causes, and to share information about effective treatments.

9. The current best scheme for classifying psychological disorders is the American Psychiatric Association manual, commonly known by its abbreviation, _____ . This manual _____ (does/does not) explain the cause of a disorder; rather, it _____ the disorder and estimates how often it occurs.

10. Independent diagnoses made with the current manual generally _____ (show/do not show) agreement, so it is considered fairly _____ .

11. One criticism of DSM-IV-TR is that as the number of disorder categories has _____ (increased/decreased), the number of adults who meet the criteria for at least one disorder has _____ (increased/decreased).

12. Studies have shown that labeling has _____ (little/a significant) effect on our interpretation of individuals and their behavior.

Outline the pros and cons of labeling psychological disorders.

Anxiety Disorders

Objective 4: Describe the symptoms of generalized anxiety disorder, panic disorder, phobias, obsessive-compulsive disorder, and post-traumatic stress disorder.

Many everyday experiences—public speaking, preparing to play in a big game, looking down from a high ledge—may elicit anxiety. In contrast, *anxiety disorders* are characterized by distressing, persistent anxiety or maladaptive behaviors that reduce anxiety.

Generalized anxiety disorder is an anxiety disorder in which a person is continually tense, fearful, and in a state of autonomic nervous system arousal. *Panic disorder* is an anxiety disorder in which the anxiety may at times suddenly escalate into a terrifying panic attack, a minutes-long feeling of intense fear in which a person experiences terror and accompanying chest pain, choking, or other frightening sensations.

A *phobia* is an anxiety disorder marked by a persistent, irrational fear of a specific object or situation. In contrast to the normal fears we all experience, phobias can be so severe that they consume the person. For example, *social phobia*, an intense fear of being scrutinized by others, is shyness taken to an extreme. The anxious person may avoid speaking up, eating out, or going to parties. If the fear is intense enough, it can lead to agoraphobia. Others suffer *specific phobias*, avoiding specific animals, insects, heights, blood, or tunnels.

An *obsessive-compulsive disorder (OCD)* is an anxiety disorder characterized by unwanted repetitive thoughts (*obsessions*) and/or actions (*compulsions*). The repetitive thoughts and behaviors become so haunting and senselessly time-consuming that they interfere with everyday living.

Post-traumatic stress disorder (PTSD) is characterized by haunting memories, nightmares, social withdrawal, jumpy anxiety, and/or insomnia that last for four weeks or more after a traumatic experience. Many combat veterans, accident and disaster survivors, and violent and sexual assault victims have experienced the symptoms of PTSD. Most of us, however, display an impressive *survivor resiliency*. About half of adults experience at least one traumatic experience in their lifetime but only about 1 in 10 women and 1 in 20 men develop PTSD symptoms. For some, suffering can lead to "post-traumatic growth."

1. Anxiety disorders are psychological disorders characterized by _____

   _____ .

   Anxiety disorders differ from normal anxiety in the _____ and
   _____ of the uneasiness.

2. When a person is continually tense, fearful, and physiologically aroused for no apparent reason, he or she is diagnosed as suffering from a

   _____ _____

   disorder. In Freud's term, the anxiety is

   _____-_____ .

3. Generalized anxiety disorder can lead to physical problems, such as _____

   _____ _____ .

   In some instances, anxiety may intensify dramatically and unpredictably and be accompanied by chest pain or choking, for example; people with these symptoms are said to have _____
   _____ . This anxiety may escalate into a minutes-long episode of intense fear, or a

   _____ _____ .

4. People who smoke have at least a doubled risk of a first-time _____ _____
   because _____ is a stimulant.

5. When a person has an irrational fear of a specific object or situation, the diagnosis is a
   _____ . Although in many situations, the person can live with the problem, some

   _____ _____ ,

   such as a fear of thunderstorms, are incapacitating.

6. When a person has an intense fear of being scrutinized by others, the diagnosis is a

   _____ _____ .

   People who fear situations in which escape or help might not be possible when panic strikes suffer from

   _____ .

7. When a person cannot control repetitive thoughts and actions, an _____-
   _____ disorder is diagnosed.

8. Traumatic stress, such as that associated with witnessing atrocities or combat, can produce

   _____-_____

   _____ disorder. The symptoms of this disorder include _____

   _____

   _____ .

   People who have a sensitive emotion-producing

   _____ _____

   are more vulnerable to this disorder.

9. After stress, most people display an impressive

   _____ _____ .

   Also, researchers have pointed out that suffering can lead to _____-

   _____ .

   Some researchers believe that this disorder has been overdiagnosed, due partly to a broader definition of

   _____ .

APPLICATIONS:

10. Han has an intense, irrational fear of snakes. He is suffering from a _____ .

11. Isabela is continually tense, jittery, and fearful for no specific reason. She would probably be diagnosed as suffering from _____ _____
    disorder.

12. Jason is so preoccupied with staying clean that he showers as many as 10 times a day. Jason would be diagnosed as suffering from _____-
    _____ disorder.

13. Although she escaped from war-torn Bosnia two years ago, Zheina still has haunting memories and nightmares. Because she is also severely depressed, her therapist diagnoses her condition as _____-_____ _____ disorder.

14. Song Yi occasionally experiences unpredictable episodes of intense dread accompanied by chest pains and a sensation of smothering. Since her symptoms have no apparent cause, they would probably be classified as indicative of _____ _____ .

Objective 5: Discuss the contributions of the learning and biological perspectives to understanding the development of anxiety disorders.

The learning perspective views anxiety disorders as a product of fear conditioning, stimulus generalization, reinforcement of fearful behaviors, and observational learning of others' fear. The biological perspective helps explain why we learn some fears more readily and why some individuals are more vulnerable. It emphasizes genetic, physiological, and evolutionary influences.

15. Freud proposed that anxiety disorders are symptoms of submerged mental energy that occurs because impulses that were _____ during childhood leak out in odd ways.

16. Learning theorists, drawing on research in which rats are given unpredictable shocks, link general anxiety with _____ conditioning of _____ .

17. Some fears arise from _____ _____ , such as when a person who fears heights after a fall also comes to fear airplanes.

18. Phobias and compulsive behaviors reduce anxiety and thereby are _____ . Through _____ learning, someone might also learn fear by seeing others display their own fears.

19. The anxiety response probably _____ (is/is not) genetically influenced.

20. PET scans of persons with obsessive-compulsive disorder reveal higher-than-normal activity in brain areas involved in _____ control and _____ behaviors.

21. Humans probably _____ (are/are not) biologically prepared to develop certain fears. Compulsive acts typically are exaggerations of behaviors that contributed to our species' _____ .

APPLICATIONS:

22. Julia's psychologist believes that Julia's fear of heights can be traced to a conditioned fear she developed after falling from a ladder. This explanation reflects a _____ perspective.

23. After falling from a ladder, Joseph is afraid of airplanes, although he has never flown. This demonstrates that some fears arise from _____ _____ .

24. Before he can study, Rashid must arrange his books, pencils, paper, and other items on his desk so that they are "just so." The campus counselor suggests that Rashid's compulsive behavior may result from higher-than-normal activity in the brain area that control habitual behavior. This explanation of obsessive-compulsive behavior is most consistent with the _____ perspective.

25. To which of the following is a person most likely to acquire a phobia?
    a. heights
    b. being in public
    c. being dirty
    d. All of these are equally likely to become phobias.

Dissociative and Personality Disorders

Objective 6: Describe the symptoms of dissociative disorders and the controversy regarding the diagnosis of dissociative identity disorder.

In *dissociative disorders,* the person appears to experience a sudden loss of memory or change in identity. **Dissociative identity disorder** is a rare disorder in which a person exhibits two or more distinct and alternating personalities, with the original personality typically unaware of the other(s).

Psychoanalysts see these dissociative disorders as defenses against the anxiety caused by unacceptable impulses. Learning theorists see them as behaviors reinforced by anxiety reduction. Still others view dissociative disorders as post-traumatic disorders—a natural protective response to traumatic childhood experiences. Some research suggests that those diagnosed with dissociative identity disorder have suffered physical, sexual, or emotional abuse as children. Skeptics find it suspicious that the disorder became so popular in the late twentieth century and that it is not found in many countries and is very rare in others.

Some argue that the condition is either role-playing by fantasy-prone people or constructed out of the therapist-patient interaction.

1. In _____ disorders, a person experiences a sudden loss of _____ or change in _____ .

2. A person who develops two or more distinct personalities is suffering from _____ _____ disorder.

3. Those who accept this as a genuine disorder point to evidence that differing personalities may be associated with distinct _____ and _____ states.

Identify two pieces of evidence cited by those who do not accept dissociative identity disorder as a genuine disorder.

4. The psychoanalytic and learning perspectives view dissociative disorders as ways of dealing with _____ . Others view them as a protective response to histories of _____ _____ . Skeptics claim these disorders are sometimes created by _____-_____ people and are sometimes constructed out of the _____-_____ interaction.

APPLICATION:

5. Multiple personalities have long been a popular subject of films and novels. For example, Dr. Jekyll, whose second personality was Mr. Hyde, had _____ _____ disorder.

Objective 7: Identify the characteristics that are typical of personality disorders, and describe the behaviors, genetic tendencies, and brain activity associated with the antisocial personality disorder.

Personality disorders are psychological disorders characterized by inflexible and enduring behavior patterns that impair social functioning. The most troubling of these disorders is the *antisocial personality disorder,* in which a person (usually a man) exhibits a lack of conscience for wrongdoing, even toward friends and family members. This person may be aggressive and ruthless or a clever con artist. Those with antisocial personality have a genetic tendency toward an uninhibited approach to life

and low levels of arousal, which may interact with environmental influences to produce this disorder. Brain scans of murderers with this disorder have revealed reduced activity in the frontal lobes, an area of the cortex that helps control impulses. Violent repeat offenders also have less frontal lobe tissue, which may help explain why people with antisocial personality disorder show impaired planning, organization, and inhibition.

6. Personality disorders exist when an individual has character traits that are enduring and impair _____ _____ .

7. An individual who seems to have no conscience, lies, steals, is generally irresponsible, and may be criminal is said to have an _____ personality. Previously, this person was labeled a _____ .

8. Studies of biological relatives of those with antisocial and unemotional tendencies suggest that there _____ (is/is not) a biological predisposition to such traits.

9. Some studies have detected early signs of antisocial behavior in children, including low levels of _____ and lower levels of _____ hormones.

10. PET scans of murderers' brains reveal reduced activity in the _____ _____ , an area of the brain that helps control _____ .

11. As in other disorders, in antisocial personality, genetics _____ (is/is not) the whole story. Genetic influences, in combination with _____ _____ , help wire the brain.

APPLICATION:

12. Ming has never been able to keep a job. He's been in and out of jail for charges such as theft, sexual assault, and spousal abuse. Ming would most likely be diagnosed as having _____ _____ disorder.

Substance-Related Disorders

Objective 8: Discuss the nature of substance-related disorders, and explain how drug tolerance, addiction, and dependence contribute to these problems.

Substance-related disorders are maladaptive patterns of substance use leading to clinically significant impairment or distress. Drugs that can lead to abuse, *psychoactive drugs,* are chemicals that change perceptions and moods. Continued use of a psychoactive drug produces *tolerance.* The ever-increasing doses required as a result of tolerance may lead to *addiction,* a compulsive craving for a substance despite negative consequences. Discontinuing use may produce the undesirable side effects of *withdrawal.* The pain of withdrawal and intense craving for a drug indicates a *physical dependence.* People can also develop *psychological dependence,* particularly for drugs used to relieve stress.

A drug's overall effect depends not only on its *biological* effects but also on the *psychology* of the user's expectations, which vary with *cultures.*

Psychoactive drugs operate at the brain's synapses by stimulating, inhibiting, or mimicking the activity of neurotransmitters, the brain's chemical messengers. Our expectations also play a role in the effects of drugs.

1. Drugs that alter moods and perceptions are called _____ drugs. The overall effect of a drug depends on its _____ effects and the user's _____ , which vary from one _____ to another.

2. The diminishing effect that occurs with regular use of the same dose of a drug is called _____ . This may lead to compulsive craving of the drug, or _____ .

3. After ceasing to use a drug, a person who experiences _____ symptoms has developed a physical _____ . Regular use of a drug to relieve stress is an example of a _____ dependence.

4. The three broad categories of drugs discussed in the text include _____ , which tend to slow body functions; _____ , which speed body functions; and _____ , which alter perception. These drugs all work by mimicking, stimulating, or inhibiting the activity of the brain's _____ .

APPLICATION:

5. Dan has recently begun using an addictive, euphoria-producing drug. Which of the following will probably occur if he repeatedly uses this drug?
    a. As tolerance to the drug develops, Dan will experience increasingly pleasurable "highs."
    b. The dosage needed to produce the desired effect will increase.
    c. After each use, he will become more and more elated.
    d. Dependence will become less of a problem.

Objective 9: Explain how depressants, such as alcohol, influence neural activity and behavior

Depressants such as alcohol, the barbiturates, and the opiates act by calming neural activity and slowing body functions. Each offers its own pleasures, but at the cost of impaired memory and self-awareness or other physical consequences. Alcohol is a *disinhibitor* and thus increases the likelihood that we will act on both helpful and harmful impulses. It also impairs judgment, lowers inhibitions, and disrupts memory processes by suppressing REM sleep. In those with *alcohol dependence,* prolonged and excessive drinking can shrink the brain. Research indicates that when people believe that alcohol affects social behavior in specific ways, and believe that they have been drinking alcohol, they will behave accordingly.

Scan of woman with alcohol dependence

Scan of woman without alcohol dependence

The *barbiturates,* or tranquilizers, may be prescribed to induce sleep or reduce anxiety. They can impair memory and judgment.

When the brain is repeatedly flooded with artificial *opiates,* it stops producing its own opiates, the *endorphins.*

6. Depressants _____ neural activity and _____ body function. Alcohol, which acts as a _____ , slows brain activity that controls _____ and _____ .

7. Low doses relax the drinker by slowing _____ nervous system activity. With larger doses, speech slurs, _____ slow, and skilled performance declines.

8. Cognitively, alcohol disrupts the processing of recent experiences into _____-_____ memories. Prolonged and excessive drinking may cause the brain to actually _____ . There is a strong correlation between early drinking and _____ _____ .

Describe how a person's expectations can influence the behavioral effects of alcohol.

9. Tranquilizers, which are also known as

_____, have effects

similar to those of alcohol.

10. Opium, morphine, and heroin all

_____ (excite/depress) neural func-

tioning. Together, these drugs are called the

_____ . When they are present, the

brain eventually stops producing

_____ .

Objective 10: Explain how the major stimulants can affect neural activity and behavior.

Stimulants, such as caffeine, *nicotine,* and the *amphetamines* and the even more powerful cocaine, Ecstasy, and *methamphetamine,* excite neural activity and speed up body functions. As with nearly all psychoactive drugs, they act at the synapses by influencing the brain's neurotransmitters, and their effects depend on dosage and the user's personality and expectations. Methamphetamine is highly addictive; over time, it appears to reduce the brain's normal output of dopamine. Nicotine triggers the release of epinephrine and norepinephrine, which in turn diminish appetite and boost alertness and mental efficiency. Cocaine produces a euphoric rush that lasts 15 to 30 minutes and depletes the brain's supply of the neurotransmitters dopamine, serotonin, and norepinephrine. A crash of agitated depression follows as the drug's effects wear off. Regular users become addicted. *Ecstasy (MDMA)* is both a stimulant and a mild hallucinogen. By releasing serotonin and blocking its reuptake, it produces euphoria and feelings of intimacy. Its repeated use may suppress the immune system, destroy serotonin-producing neurons, and permanently damage mood and memory.

11. Types of stimulants include _____

_____

_____ .

Stimulants _____ (can be/cannot

be) addictive.

12. Cigarette smokers _____ (do/do not)

become dependent on the drug

_____ . This drug quickly stimu-

lates the _____ _____

system to release _____

and _____ , two neurotransmitters

that diminish _____

and boost _____ and

_____ _____ .

Nicotine also stimulates the release of

_____ and _____ ,

neurotransmitters that calm _____

and reduce sensitivity to _____ .

13. Cocaine and crack deplete the brain's supply of the

neurotransmitters _____ ,

_____ , and

and result in depression as the drugs' effects wear

off. The powerfully addictive stimulant

_____ triggers the release of the

neurotransmitter _____ , which

stimulates brain cells that enhance

_____ and _____ .

14. The drug_____ , or MDMA, is both

a _____ and a mild

_____ . This drug triggers the

release of the neurotransmitter

_____ . It also releases stored

_____ and blocks its reuptake, thus

interfering with its regulation of body

_____ (including sleep), our

disease-fighting _____

_____ , and our memory and other

_____ functions.

Objective 11: Describe the physiological and psychological effects of LSD and marijuana.

Hallucinogens distort perceptions and evoke sensory images in the absence of sensory input. *LSD* and other powerful hallucinogens are chemically similar to (and therefore block the actions of) one type of the neurotransmitter serotonin. An LSD "trip" may include hallucinations and emotions ranging from euphoria to panic. People who have had a *near-death experience* have reported sensations that resemble an LSD experience, possibly reflecting a brain under stress. Marijuana's main active ingredient, *THC,* produces a variety of effects, including disinhibition, a euphoric high, feelings of relaxation, relief from pain, and intense sensitivity to colors, sounds, tastes, and smells. It may also increase anxiety or depression, impair motor coordination and reaction time, and disrupt memory formation. Because THC lingers in the body for a month or more, regular users may achieve a high with smaller amounts of the drug than do occasional users.

15. Hallucinogens are also referred to as

_____ . The best-known synthetic

hallucinogens are _____ and LSD,

which is chemically similar to a subtype of the neu-

rotransmitter _____ . LSD works by

_____ the actions of this neuro-

transmitter.

16. The reports of LSD users are very similar to the

_____-_____

experiences reported by some people who survive a

brush with death. These experiences may be the

result of _____ deprivation or other

insults to the brain.

17. The active ingredient in marijuana is abbreviated
_____ . This drug, which lingers in
the body _____ (about as long
as/much longer than) alcohol, stimulates receptors
in the brain's _____ lobes,
_____ system, and
_____ cortex.

Describe some of the physical and psychological effects
of marijuana.

APPLICATIONS:

18. Roberto is moderately intoxicated by alcohol. Which of
the following changes in his behavior is likely to occur?
  a. If angered, he is more likely to become aggressive
    than when he is sober.
  b. He will be less self-conscious about his
    behavior.
  c. If sexually aroused, he will be less inhibited about
    engaging in sexual activity.
  d. All of these changes are likely.

19. I am a synthetic stimulant and mild hallucinogen that produces euphoria and social intimacy by triggering the
release of dopamine and serotonin. What am I?

_____

20. Lyndall was in a car accident that required critical surgery
to repair her damaged internal organs. During surgery,
she had a sense of being outside her body, floating above
the operating room. These _____-
_____ experiences are similar to sensations of an LSD "trip."

21. Which of the following statements concerning marijuana
is true?
  a. The by-products of marijuana are cleared from the
    body more slowly than are the by-products of alcohol.
  b. Regular users may need a larger dose of the drug to
    achieve a high than occasional users would need to
    get the same effect.
  c. Marijuana is as addictive as nicotine or cocaine.
  d. Even small doses of marijuana hasten the loss of
    brain cells.

Objective 12: Discuss the biological, psychological, and
social-cultural factors that cause people to abuse mind-
altering drugs.

Drug use among North American youth increased during
the 1970s, then declined for a while. After the early

1990s, the cultural antidrug voice softened. Various studies indicate that some people are biologically more likely
to become dependent on drugs. For example, researchers
have identified genes that are more common among
people and animals predisposed to alcohol dependence.
These genes may produce deficiencies in the brain's natural dopamine reward system. One psychological factor
that contributes to drug use is the feeling that one's life
is meaningless and directionless. Studies reveal that
heavy drug users often have experienced significant
stress or failure and are depressed. Drug use can also
have social roots, evident in differing rates of drug use
across cultural and ethnic groups. In the United States,
drug addiction rates are very low among the Amish,
Mennonites, Mormons, and Orthodox Jews. Peer pressure may lead people, especially teenagers, to experiment with—and become dependent on—drugs. Possible
avenues for treatment and prevention involve education,
boosting people's self-esteem and purpose in life, and
"inoculation" against peer pressure.

22. Adopted individuals are more susceptible to alcohol
dependence if they had a(n) _____
(adoptive/biological) parent with a history of alcohol
dependence. Boys who at age 6 are _____
(more/less) excitable are more likely as teens to
smoke, drink, and abuse other drugs. Genes that are
more common among people predisposed to alcohol
dependence may cause deficiencies in the brain's

_____ _____
system.

Identify some of the psychological and social-cultural
roots of drug use.

23. Among teenagers, drug use _____
(varies/is about the same) across
_____ and _____
groups.

24. African-American high school seniors report
_____ (higher/lower) rates of drug
use than other U.S. teens. A major social influence
on drug use is the _____ culture.

25. State three possible channels of influence for drug
prevention and treatment programs.
  a. _____
  b. _____
  c. _____

STUDY TIP: This chapter discusses three major categories of psychoactive drugs, drugs that when abused may lead to clinically significant impairment or distress. Information about their psychological effects and their actions on the nervous system is best organized in the form of a chart. To help you review this material, complete the missing information in the chart below. To get you started, the first drug category has already been filled in. In combination with text Table 12.6, you should have a useful summary of substance-related disorders.

26. Psychoactive Drug Category	Specific Drugs in This Category	Psychological Effects of These Drugs	How These Drugs Affect the Nervous System
Depressants	alcohol, barbiturates, opiates	disrupt judgment and inhibition, induce sleep, reduce anxiety	decrease neural activity, slow body functions
Stimulants			
Hallucinogens			

Mood Disorders

Objective 13: Identify the main mood disorders, and explain why some people attempt suicide.

Mood disorders are psychological disorders characterized by emotional extremes. In *major depressive disorder,* a person experiences two or more weeks of significantly depressed moods, lethargy, feelings of worthlessness, and reduced interest in family, friends, and activities. *Bipolar disorder* is a mood disorder in which a person alternates between the hopelessness and lethargy of depression and overexcited *manic* episodes (euphoric, hyperactive, wildly optimistic states). Major depressive disorder is much more common than is bipolar disorder.

The risk of suicide is at least five times greater for those who have been depressed than for the general population. People are most at risk when they begin to rebound from depression and become capable of following through.

1. Mood disorders are psychological disorders characterized by _____

_____ . They come in two forms: The experience of prolonged depression with no discernible cause is called _____

_____ disorder. When a person's mood alternates between depression and the hyperactive state of _____ , a

_____ disorder is diagnosed.

2. Although _____ are more common, _____ is the number one reason that people seek mental health services. It is also the leading cause of disability worldwide.

3. The possible signs of depression include

_____

_____ .

4. Major depression occurs when its signs last

_____ _____

or more with no apparent cause. The risk of _____ is at least _____ times greater in those who have been depressed than for the general population.

5. Mania is characterized by _____

_____ .

6. Bipolar disorder is less common among creative professionals who rely on _____

and _____ than among those who rely on _____ expression and vivid _____ .

APPLICATIONS:

7. As a child, Monica was criticized severely by her mother for not living up to her expectations. This criticism was always followed by a beating with a whip. As an adult, Monica is generally introverted and extremely shy. Sometimes, however, she acts more like a young child, throwing tantrums if she doesn't get her way. At other times, she is a flirting, happy-go-lucky young lady. Most likely, Monica is suffering from

_____ _____ .

8. For the past six months, Haeji has complained of feeling isolated from others, dissatisfied with life, and discouraged about the future. Haeji could be diagnosed as suffering from _____

_____ _____ .

9. On Monday, Delon felt optimistic, energetic, and on top of the world. On Tuesday, he felt hopeless and lethargic, and thought that the future looked very grim. Delon would most likely be diagnosed as having

_____ _____ .

Objective 14: Explain the development of mood disorders, paying special attention to the biological and social-cognitive perspectives.

Researchers have suggested that any theory of depression must explain the many behavioral and cognitive changes that accompany the disorder, its widespread occurrence, women's greater vulnerability to depression, the tendency for most major depressive episodes to self-terminate, the link between stressful events and the onset of depression, and the disorder's increasing rate and earlier age of onset.

The biological perspective emphasizes the importance of genetic and biochemical influences. Mood disorders run in families. Certain neurotransmitters, including norepinephrine and serotonin, seem to be scarce in depression. Finally, the brain's left frontal lobe, which is active during positive emotions, is less active during depression.

The *social-cognitive perspective* suggests that self-defeating beliefs, arising in part from *learned helplessness,* and a negative explanatory style feed depression. Depressed people explain bad events in terms that are *global, stable,* and *internal.* This perspective sees the disorder as a vicious cycle in which (1) negative, stressful events are interpreted though (2) a brooding, pessimistic explanatory style, creating (3) a hopeless, depressed state that (4) hampers the way a person thinks and acts. This, in turn, fuels (1) more negative experiences.

10. Depression is accompanied by many

_____ and _____

changes.

11. The commonality of depression suggests that its _____ must also be common.

12. Compared with men, women are _____ (more/less) vulnerable to major depression. In general, women are most vulnerable to disorders involving _____ states, such as

_____ .

13. Men's disorders tend to be more _____ and include _____

_____ .

14. Depressed persons usually _____ (can/cannot) recover without therapy.

15. It often _____ (is/is not) the case that a depressive episode has been triggered by a stressful event. An individual's risk of depression also increases following, for example,

_____ .

16. With each new generation, the rate of depression is _____ (increasing/decreasing) and the disorder is striking _____ (earlier/later). In North America today, young adults are _____ times (how many?) more likely than their grandparents to suffer depression.

17. Mood disorders _____ (tend/do not tend) to run in families. Studies of _____ also reveal that genetic influences on mood disorders are _____ (weak/strong).

18. The brains of depressed people tend to be _____ (more/less) active, especially in an area of the _____ _____ lobe.

19. Depression may also be caused by _____ (high/low) levels of two neurotransmitters, _____ and

_____ .

20. Drugs that relieve depression tend to make more _____ or _____ available to the depressed brain.

21. According to the social-cognitive perspective, depression may be linked with _____ beliefs and a

_____ _____ style.

22. Such beliefs may arise from _____ _____ , the feeling that can arise when the individual repeatedly experiences uncontrollable, painful events.

23. Gender differences in responding to _____ help explain why women have been twice as vulnerable to depression. When trouble strikes, women tend to _____ .

Describe how depressed people differ from others in their explanations of failure and how such explanations tend to feed depression.

24. Being withdrawn, self-focused, and complaining tends to elicit social _____ (empathy/rejection).

Outline the vicious cycle of depression.

25. Complete the following flow chart comparing how a depressed person and a person who is not depressed would deal with this situation.

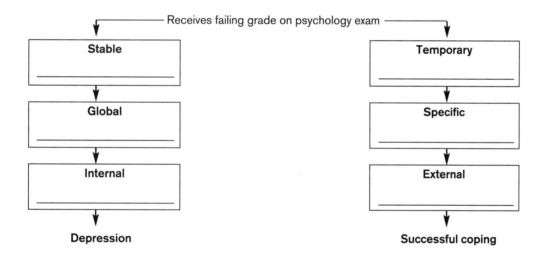

Receives failing grade on psychology exam

Stable → Global → Internal → **Depression**

Temporary → Specific → External → **Successful coping**

Schizophrenia

Objective 15: Describe the symptoms of schizophrenia, and contrast chronic and acute schizophrenia.

Schizophrenia is a group of severe disorders characterized by disorganized and delusional thinking, disturbed perceptions, and inappropriate emotions and actions. Literally, schizophrenia means "split mind," which refers to a split from reality rather than multiple personality. The thinking of people with schizophrenia may be marked by _delusions,_ that is, false beliefs—often of persecution or grandeur. Sometimes, they also experience _hallucinations,_ sensory experiences without sensory stimulation. Hallucinations are usually auditory and often take the form of voices making insulting statements or giving orders.

Schizophrenia patients who are disorganized and deluded in their talk or tend toward inappropriate laugh-ter, tears, or rage are said to have positive symptoms. When appropriate behaviors are absent—for example, patients may be mute or rigid—symptoms are said to be "negative." Other people with schizophrenia show a _flat effect,_ a zombielike state. _Chronic,_ or _process,_ schizophrenia develops gradually, emerging from a long history of social inadequacy. Recovery is doubtful. _Acute,_ or _reactive,_ schizophrenia develops rapidly in response to particular life stresses. Recovery is much more likely.

1. Schizophrenia, or "split mind," refers not to a split personality but rather to a split from _____ .

2. Three manifestations of schizophrenia are disorganized _____ , disturbed _____ , and inappropriate _____ and _____ .

People with schizophrenia who display inappropriate behavior are said to have _____ symptoms, while those with toneless voices and expressionless faces are said to have _____ symptoms.

3. The distorted, false beliefs of schizophrenia patients are called _____ .

4. Disorganized thinking may appear as jumbled ideas that make no sense, called _____ _____ .

5. The disturbed perceptions of people suffering from schizophrenia may take the form of _____ , which usually are _____ (visual/auditory).

6. Some victims of schizophrenia lapse into a zombielike state of apparent apathy, or _____ _____ ; others, who exhibit _____ , may remain motionless for hours and then become agitated.

7. When schizophrenia develops slowly (called _____ schizophrenia), recovery is _____ (more/less) likely than when it develops rapidly in reaction to particular life stresses (called _____ schizophrenia).

APPLICATIONS:

8. Claiming that she heard a voice commanding her to warn other people that eating is harmful, Kelly attempts to convince others in a restaurant not to eat. The psychiatrist to whom she is referred finds that Kelly's thinking and speech are often fragmented and distorted. In addition, Kelly has an unreasonable fear that someone is "out to get her" and consequently trusts no one. Her condition is most indicative of _____ symptoms of schizophrenia.

9. Shawn hears voices; this symptom is a(n) _____ ; Pierre believes that he is Napoleon; this is a(n) _____ .

Objective 16: Outline some abnormal brain chemistry, functions, and structures associated with schizophrenia, and discuss the possible link between prenatal viral infections and schizophrenia.

Researchers have linked certain forms of schizophrenia with brain abnormalities such as an excess number of receptors for the neurotransmitter dopamine. Brain scans indicate that some people with schizophrenia have abnormally low brain activity in the frontal lobes or enlarged, fluid-filled areas and a corresponding shrinkage of cerebral tissue. One area that becomes active dur-

ing hallucinations is the thalamus. A possible cause of these abnormalities is a midpregnancy viral infection that impairs fetal brain development. For example, people are at increased risk of schizophrenia if, during the middle of their fetal development, their country experienced a flu epidemic. People born in densely populated areas, where viral diseases spread more readily, also seem at greater risk for schizophrenia.

10. The brain tissue of schizophrenia patients has been found to have an excess of receptors for the neurotransmitter _____ . Drugs that block these receptors have been found to _____ (increase/decrease) positive symptoms of schizophrenia.

11. Brain scans have shown that many people suffering from schizophrenia have abnormally _____ (high/low) brain activity in the _____ lobes.

12. Enlarged, _____ -filled areas and a corresponding _____ of cerebral tissue is also characteristic of schizophrenia. Schizophrenia patients also show unusual activity in the _____ , which filters incoming _____ signals and transmits them to the cortex.

13. Some scientists contend that the brain abnormalities of schizophrenia may be caused by a prenatal problem, such as _____ _____ _____ ; birth complications, such as lack of _____ during delivery; or a _____ _____ contracted by the mother.

List several pieces of evidence for this theory.

Objective 17: Discuss the evidence for a genetic contribution to the development of schizophrenia.

The nearly 1-in-100 odds of any person developing schizophrenia become about 1 in 10 if a family member has it and close to 5 in 10 if an identical twin has the disorder. Adoption studies confirm the genetic contribution to schizophrenia. An adopted child's probability of developing the disorder is greater if the biological parents have schizophrenia.

The search for specific genes that underlie schizophrenia-related brain abnormalities continues. Multiple genes seem to interact to produce the disorder. A variety of environmental factors such as prenatal viral infections, nutritional deficiencies, and oxygen deprivation at birth may activate the genes that make some people more susceptible to the disease.

14. Twin studies _____ (support/do not support) the contention that heredity plays a role in schizophrenia.

15. The role of the prenatal environment in schizophrenia is demonstrated by the fact that identical twins who share the same _____ , and are therefore more likely to experience the same prenatal _____ , are more likely to share the disorder.

16. Adoption studies _____ (confirm/do not confirm) a genetic link in the development of schizophrenia.

17. It appears that for schizophrenia to develop there must be both a _____ predisposition and other factors such as those listed earlier that turn on the _____ that predispose this disease.

APPLICATIONS:

18. Wayne has been diagnosed with schizophrenia. His doctor attempts to help Wayne by prescribing a drug that blocks receptors for _____ .

19. Lolita, whose class presentation is titled "Current Views on the Causes of Schizophrenia," concludes her talk with the statement
    a. "Schizophrenia is caused by intolerable stress."
    b. "Schizophrenia is inherited."
    c. "Genes may predispose some people to react to particular experiences by developing schizophrenia."
    d. "As of this date, schizophrenia is completely unpredictable and its causes are unknown."

• •
SUMMARY STUDY TIP: This chapter discusses six categories of psychological disorders. To help organize your study of this material, complete the following table. For each category, list the specific disorders discussed. Then, for each disorder, give a description and a brief explanation of possible causes of the disorders. To get you started, portions of the first category of disorders, plus some random information, has been provided.

Category	Specific Disorders	Description of the Disorder	Possible Explanations of Causes
Anxiety disorders	Generalized anxiety disorder Panic disorder Phobias Obsessive-compulsive disorder Post-traumatic stress disorder	Distressing, persistent anxiety or maladaptive behaviors that reduce anxiety	Conditioning and reinforcement of fears. For example, stimulus generalization. Also, observational learning. Pairing of a traumatic event with a genetic predisposition.
Dissociative disorders			
Personality disorders			
Substance-related disorders	Alcohol dependence		
Mood disorders	Major depressive disorder Bipolar disorder		
Schizophrenia			

PROGRESS TEST

Multiple-Choice Questions

Circle your answers to the following questions and check them with the answers beginning on page 235. If your answer is incorrect, read the explanation for why it is incorrect and then consult the text.

1. Gender differences in the widespread occurrence of depression may be partly due to the fact that when stressful experiences occur
   a. women tend to act, while men tend to think.
   b. women tend to think, while men tend to act.
   c. women tend to distract themselves by drinking, while men tend to lose themselves in their work.
   d. women tend to lose themselves in their work, while men tend to distract themselves by drinking.

2. The view that all behavior arises from the interaction of heredity and environment is referred to as the _____ approach.
   a. biopsychosocial
   b. psychoanalytic
   c. medical
   d. conditioning

3. Which of the following is NOT true concerning depression?
   a. Depression is more common in females than in males.
   b. Most depressive episodes appear not to be preceded by any particular factor or event.
   c. Most depressive episodes last less than 3 months.
   d. Most people recover from depression without professional therapy.

4. Which of the following is NOT true regarding schizophrenia?
   a. It occurs more frequently in people born in winter and spring months.
   b. It occurs less frequently as infectious disease rates have declined.
   c. It occurs more frequently in lightly populated areas.
   d. It usually appears during adolescence or early adulthood.

5. Evidence of environmental effects on psychological disorders is seen in the fact that certain disorders, such as _____ , are universal; others, such as _____ , are culture-bound.
   a. schizophrenia; depression
   b. depression; schizophrenia
   c. antisocial personality; anorexia nervosa
   d. depression; anorexia nervosa

6. The effect of drugs that block receptors for dopamine is to
   a. lessen schizophrenia symptoms.
   b. reduce feelings of depression.
   c. increase schizophrenia symptoms.
   d. increase feelings of depression.

7. The diagnostic reliability of DSM-IV-TR
   a. is unknown.
   b. depends on the age of the patient.
   c. is very low.
   d. is relatively high.

8. Phobias and obsessive-compulsive behaviors are classified as
   a. anxiety disorders.
   b. mood disorders.
   c. dissociative disorders.
   d. personality disorders.

9. According to the social-cognitive perspective, a person who experiences unexpected negative events may develop helplessness and manifest a(n)
   a. obsessive-compulsive disorder.
   b. dissociative disorder.
   c. personality disorder.
   d. mood disorder.

10. Which of the following was presented in the text as evidence of biological influences on anxiety disorders?
    a. Identical twins often develop similar phobias.
    b. Brain scans of persons with obsessive-compulsive disorder reveal unusually high activity in brain areas involved in impulse control and habitual behavior.
    c. Brain pathways resulting from fear-learning experiences create easy inroads for more fear experiences.
    d. All of these facts were presented.

11. Most of the hallucinations of schizophrenia patients involve the sense of
    a. smell.
    b. vision.
    c. hearing.
    d. touch.

12. When expecting to be electrically shocked, people with an antisocial personality disorder, as compared with normal people, show
    a. greater bodily arousal and higher levels of stress hormones.
    b. little bodily arousal and lower levels of stress hormones.
    c. greater fear and greater bodily arousal.
    d. greater fear and less bodily arousal.

13. In treating depression, a psychiatrist would probably prescribe a drug that would
    a. increase levels of acetylcholine.
    b. decrease levels of dopamine.
    c. increase levels of norepinephrine.
    d. decrease levels of serotonin.

14. When schizophrenia is slow to develop, called _____ schizophrenia, recovery is _____ .
    a. reactive; unlikely
    b. process; likely
    c. process; unlikely
    d. reactive; likely

15. Which of the following is true concerning disordered behavior?
    a. Definitions of disordered behavior are culture-dependent.
    b. A behavior cannot be defined as disordered unless it is considered harmful to society.
    c. Disordered behavior can be defined as any behavior that is distressful.
    d. Definitions of disordered behavior are based on physiological factors.

16. Research evidence links the brain abnormalities of schizophrenia to _____ during prenatal development.
    a. maternal stress
    b. a viral infection contracted
    c. abnormal levels of certain hormones
    d. the weight of the unborn child

17. Disorders such as schizophrenia are universal and influenced by heredity. Other disorders such as anorexia nervosa are culture-bound. These facts provide evidence for the _____ model of psychological disorders.
    a. medical
    b. biopsychosocial
    c. social-cultural
    d. psychoanalytic

18. In general, women are more vulnerable than men to
    a. external disorders such as anxiety.
    b. internal disorders such as depression.
    c. external disorders such as antisocial conduct.
    d. internal disorders such as alcohol abuse.

19. Which of the following statements concerning the labeling of disordered behaviors is NOT true?
    a. Labels interfere with effective treatment of psychological disorders.
    b. Labels promote research studies of psychological disorders.
    c. Labels may create preconceptions that bias people's perceptions.
    d. Labels may be self-fulfilling.

20. Which neurotransmitter is present in overabundant amounts during the manic phase of bipolar disorder?
    a. dopamine
    b. serotonin
    c. epinephrine
    d. norepinephrine

21. Which of the following provides evidence that human fears have been subjected to the evolutionary process?
    a. Compulsive acts typically exaggerate behaviors that contributed to our species' survival.
    b. Most phobias focus on objects that our ancestors also feared.
    c. It is easier to condition some fears than others.
    d. All of these facts provide evidence.

22. Which of the following is true of the medical model?
    a. In recent years, it has been in large part discredited.
    b. It views psychological disorders as sicknesses that are diagnosable and treatable.
    c. It emphasizes the role of psychological factors in disorders over that of physiological factors.
    d. It focuses on cognitive factors.

23. Psychoanalytic and learning theorists both agree that the symptoms of dissociative identity disorder are the person's attempt to deal with
    a. unconscious conflicts.
    b. anxiety.
    c. unfulfilled wishes.
    d. unpleasant responsibilities.

24. Behavior is classified as disordered when it is
    a. deviant
    b. distressful.
    c. dysfunctional.
    d. all of these answers.

25. Many psychologists criticize the DSM-IV-TR for
    a. its failure to emphasize observable behaviors in the diagnostic process.
    b. its learning theory bias.
    c. including almost any kind of behavior within its scope.
    d. being unreliable.

26. Which of the following is NOT a symptom of schizophrenia?
    a. inappropriate emotions
    b. disturbed perceptions
    c. panic attacks
    d. disorganized thinking

27. Social-cognitive theorists believe that depression is linked with
    a. negative moods.
    b. maladaptive explanations of failure.
    c. self-defeating beliefs.
    d. all of these symptoms.

28. Among the following, which is generally accepted as a possible cause of schizophrenia?
    a. an excess of endorphins in the brain
    b. being a twin
    c. extensive learned helplessness
    d. a genetic predisposition

29. Psychoactive drugs affect behavior and perception through
    a. the power of suggestion.
    b. the placebo effect.
    c. altering neural activity in the brain.
    d. psychological, not physiological, influences.

30. Alcohol has its strongest effect on
    a. the transfer of experiences to long-term memory.
    b. immediate memory.
    c. previously established long-term memories.
    d. all of these answers.

31. A person who requires increasing amounts of a drug in order to feel its effect is said to have developed
    a. tolerance.
    b. physical dependency.
    c. psychological dependency.
    d. withdrawal.

32. Which of the following is NOT a stimulant?
    a. amphetamines
    b. caffeine
    c. nicotine
    d. alcohol

33. Which of the following was NOT cited in the text as evidence that heredity influences alcohol use?
    a. Children whose parents abuse alcohol have a lower tolerance for multiple alcoholic drinks taken over a short period of time.
    b. Boys who are impulsive and fearless at age 6 are more likely to drink as teenagers.
    c. Laboratory mice have been selectively bred to prefer alcohol to water.
    d. Adopted children are more susceptible if one or both of their biological parents has a history of alcohol dependence.

34. THC is the major active ingredient in
    a. nicotine.
    b. MDMA.
    c. marijuana.
    d. cocaine.

35. How a particular psychoactive drug affects a person depends on
    a. the dosage and form in which the drug is taken.
    b. the user's expectations and personality.
    c. the situation in which the drug is taken.
    d. all of these factors.

Matching Items

Match each term with the appropriate definition or description.

Terms

_____ 1. dissociative disorder
_____ 2. medical model
_____ 3. mood disorders
_____ 4. phobia
_____ 5. addiction
_____ 6. mania
_____ 7. obsessive-compulsive disorder
_____ 8. schizophrenia
_____ 9. hallucination
_____ 10. panic attack
_____ 11. antisocial personality
_____ 12. delusion
_____ 13. tolerance
_____ 14. bipolar disorder

Definitions or Descriptions

a. psychological disorders marked by emotional extremes
b. an extremely elevated mood
c. an individual who seems to have no conscience
d. a false sensory experience
e. approach that considers behavior disorders as illnesses that can be diagnosed, treated, and, in most cases, cured
f. a sudden escalation of anxiety often accompanied by a sensation of choking or other physical symptoms
g. a type of mood disorder
h. a disorder in which conscious awareness becomes separated from previous memories, feelings, and thoughts
i. compulsive craving for a drug despite unpleasant consequences and withdrawal symptoms
j. the diminishing of a psychoactive drug's effect with repeated use
k. a false belief
l. a group of disorders marked by disorganized thinking, disturbed perceptions, and inappropriate emotions and actions
m. a disorder characterized by repetitive thoughts and actions
n. an anxiety disorder marked by a persistent, irrational fear of a specific object or situation

Application Essay

Clinical psychologists label people disordered if their behavior is (1) deviant, (2) distressful, and (3) dysfunctional. Demonstrate your understanding of the classification process by giving examples of behaviors that might be considered deviant, distressful, or dysfunctional but, because they do not fit all three criteria, would not necessarily be labeled disordered. (Use the space below to list the points you want to make, and organize them. Then write the essay on a separate piece of paper.)

TERMS AND CONCEPTS

Using your own words, on a separate piece of paper write a brief definition or explanation of each of the following terms.

1. psychological disorder
2. medical model
3. DSM-IV-TR
4. anxiety disorders
5. generalized anxiety disorder
6. panic disorder
7. phobia
8. obsessive-compulsive disorder (OCD)
9. post-traumatic stress disorder (PTSD)
10. dissociative disorders
11. dissociative identity disorder
12. personality disorders
13. antisocial personality disorder
14. substance-related disorders
15. psychoactive drug
16. tolerance
17. addiction
18. withdrawal
19. physical dependence
20. psychological dependence
21. depressants
22. alcohol dependence
23. barbiturates
24. opiates
25. stimulants
26. amphetamines
27. nicotine
28. methamphetamine
29. Ecstasy (MDMA)
30. hallucinogens
31. LSD
32. near-death experience
33. THC
34. mood disorders
35. major depressive disorder
36. bipolar disorder
37. mania
38. schizophrenia
39. delusions

SUMMING UP

See page 232.

ANSWERS

Chapter Review

What Is a Psychological Disorder?

1. thoughts; feelings; actions; deviant; distressful; dysfunctional
2. variable
3. culture
4. deviant; distressful; dysfunctional
5. medical; illness; symptoms; therapy
6. biology; personal; social; cultural
7. depression; schizophrenia; anorexia nervosa; bulimia nervosa; dynamic; anxiety; symptoms
8. biological; biology; psychology; social-cultural. Haya's behavior is directed by a specific situation. Because it does not interfere with her everyday life, it is not considered disordered.
9. DSM-IV-TR; does not; describes
10. show; reliable
11. increased; increased
12. a significant

Psychological labels may be arbitrary. They can create preconceptions that bias our perceptions and interpretations and they can affect people's self-images. Moreover, labels can change reality by being self-fulfilling. Despite these drawbacks, labels are useful in describing, treating, and researching the causes of psychological disorders.

Anxiety Disorders

1. distressing, persistent anxiety or maladaptive behaviors that reduce anxiety; intensity; persistence

SUMMING UP

Soo-Mee often feels tense and uneasy for no apparent reason. She has trouble concentrating on her studies and her thoughts wander from problem to problem. This suggests that

she may suffer from a _____ _____ disorder,

which

may lead to physical problems, such as high _____ _____ .

Because Soo-Mee cannot identify the cause of her tension,

it would be described by Sigmund _____ as _____-_____ ,

while

learning theorists would link her anxiety with _____ _____ of fear, and biological psychologists might link it to an overarousal of _____ areas involved in _____ control.

Soo-Mee's friend Shayna complains of similar feelings, but she also

experiences unexpected episodes of intense dread, indicating _____ attacks,

which

are accompanied by physical symptoms such as irregular _____ , shortness of breath, and choking sensations.

Fearing that she might be having a heart attack when these episodes occur, Shayna avoids situations in which

she fears _____ may be difficult.

So,

Shayna refuses to leave her house, a sure sign that she suffers from _____ .

Soo-Mee and Shayna's friend Randal laughs at their inability to identify the source of their anxiety. He says,

"I know exactly what I fear: snakes. I have a _____ ,

which

I know is _____ , but at least I can deal with it by avoiding areas where snakes are known to be, for example.

My problem may result from my _____ a friend being bitten by a snake."

Percentage of people surveyed

25% 20 15 10 5 0

Being alone | Storms | Water | Closed spaces | Flying | Blood | Heights | Animals

■ Fear ■ Phobia

2. generalized anxiety; free-floating
3. high blood pressure; panic disorder; panic attack
4. panic attack; nicotine
5. phobia; specific phobias
6. social phobia; agoraphobia
7. obsessive-compulsive
8. post-traumatic stress; haunting memories, nightmares, social withdrawal, jumpy anxiety, and insomnia; limbic system
9. survivor resiliency; post-traumatic growth; trauma
10. phobia. Phobias are intense fears of objects or situations that result either from experience or from observing another person's experience.
11. generalized anxiety. The key to identifying this disorder is the fact that the anxiety occurs for no apparent reason.
12. obsessive-compulsive. Showering a couple of times a day could be normal, depending on the situation. Showering 10 times a day is a compulsion resulting from an obsession with dirt and/or germs.
13. post-traumatic stress. Zheina's behavior is a direct result of the traumatic events she experienced during the war.
14. panic attack. These are unpredictable, exaggerated fears that something bad is about to happen.
15. repressed
16. classical; fears
17. stimulus generalization
18. reinforced; observational
19. is
20. impulse; habitual
21. are; survival
22. learning. In the learning perspective, a phobia such as Julia's is seen as a conditioned fear.
23. stimulus generalization. Joseph's fear has generalized from ladders to airplanes.
24. biological. According to the biological perspective, increased activity in areas of the brain involved in impulse control and habitual behavior is a factor in compulsive behavior.
25. a. is the answer. Humans seem biologically prepared to develop a fear a heights and other dangers that our ancestors feared.

Dissociative and Personality Disorders

1. dissociative; memory; identity
2. dissociative identity
3. brain; body

Skeptics point out that the recent increase in the number of reported cases of dissociative identity disorder indicates that it has become a fad. The fact that the disorder is almost nonexistent outside North America also causes skeptics to doubt the disorder's genuineness. Another possible answer is that some think that DID could be an extension of the way we vary the "selves" we present.

4. anxiety; childhood trauma; fantasy-prone; therapist-patient
5. dissociative identity. Unlike schizophrenia, which is a split from reality, dissociative identity disorder involves the existence of multiple personalities.
6. social functioning
7. antisocial; psychopath or sociopath
8. is
9. arousal; stress
10. frontal lobe; impulses
11. is not; childhood abuse
12. antisocial personality. Repeated wrongdoing and aggressive behavior are part of the pattern associated with the antisocial personality disorder, which may also include marital problems and an inability to keep a job.

Substance-Related Disorders

1. psychoactive; biological; expectations; culture
2. tolerance; addiction
3. withdrawal; dependence; psychological
4. depressants; stimulants; hallucinogens; neurotransmitters
5. b. is the answer. Continued use of a drug produces tolerance; to experience the same "high," Dan will have to use larger and larger doses.
6. calm; slow; disinhibitor; judgment; inhibitions
7. sympathetic; reactions
8. long-term; shrink; later dependence

Studies have found that if people believe that alcohol affects social behavior in certain ways, then, when they drink alcohol (or even mistakenly think that they have been drinking alcohol), they will behave according to their expectations, which vary by culture. For example, if people believe alcohol promotes sexual feeling, on drinking they are likely to behave in a sexually aroused way.

9. barbiturates
10. depress; opiates; endorphins
11. caffeine, nicotine, amphetamines, cocaine, Ecstasy, and methamphetamine; can be
12. do; nicotine; central nervous; epinephrine; norepinephrine; appetite; alertness; mental efficiency; dopamine; opioids; anxiety; pain
13. dopamine; serotonin; norepinephrine; methamphetamine; dopamine; energy; mood
14. Ecstasy; stimulant; hallucinogen; dopamine; serotonin; rhythms; immune system; cognitive
15. psychedelics; MDMA (Ecstasy); serotonin; blocking
16. near-death; oxygen
17. THC; much longer than; frontal; limbic; motor

Like alcohol, marijuana relaxes, disinhibits, and may produce a euphoric feeling. Also like alcohol, marijuana impairs perceptual and motor skills. Marijuana is a mild hallucinogen; it can increase sensitivity to colors, sounds, tastes, and smells. Marijuana also interrupts memory formation.

18. **d.** is the answer. Alcohol loosens inhibitions and reduces self-awareness, making people more likely to act on their feelings of anger or sexual arousal. It also disrupts the processing of experiences into long-term memory.

19. MDMA (Ecstasy). As an amphetamine derivative, MDMA releases serotonin and blocks its reuptake, prolonging its feel-good flood. As a mild hallucinogen, it distorts perceptions.

20. near-death

21. **a.** is the answer. Alcohol is eliminated from the body within hours. Marijuana and its by-products may stay in the body for a month or more.

22. biological; more; dopamine reward
A psychological factor in drug use is the feeling that one's life is meaningless and lacks direction. Regular users of psychoactive drugs often have experienced stress or failure and are somewhat depressed. Drug use often begins as a temporary way to relieve depression, anger, anxiety, or insomnia. A powerful social factor in drug use, especially among adolescents, is peer influence. Peers shape attitudes about drugs, provide drugs, and establish the social context for their use.

23. varies; cultural; ethnic

24. lower; peer

25. **a.** education about the long-term costs of a drug's temporary pleasures
b. efforts to boost people's self-esteem and purpose in life
c. attempts to "inoculate" youth against peer pressures

26. Stimulants include caffeine, nicotine, amphetamines, cocaine, Ecstasy, and methamphetamines. They enhance energy and mood and can be addictive. They excite neural activity and speed up body functions.
Hallucinogens include Ecstasy, LSD, and marijuana. They distort perceptions and evoke sensory images in the absence of sensory input. They produce their effects by interfering with the serotonin neurotransmitter system.

Mood Disorders

1. emotional extremes; major depressive; mania; bipolar

2. phobias; depression

3. lethargy, feelings of worthlessness, and loss of interest in family, friends, and activities

4. two weeks; suicide; five

5. an intensely happy, hyperactive, and wildly optimistic state

6. precision; logic; emotional; imagery

7. bipolar disorder. Bipolar disorder is marked by emotional extremes, as seen in Monica's varying behavior.

8. major depressive disorder. Haeji's symptoms are classic symptoms of this disorder. The fact that they have lasted for six months makes them clinically significant.

9. bipolar disorder

10. behavioral; cognitive

11. causes

12. more; internal; depression, anxiety, and inhibited sexual desire

13. external; alcohol abuse, antisocial conduct, and lack of impulse control

14. can

15. is; a family member's death, loss of a job, a marital crisis, or a physical assault

16. increasing; earlier; three

17. tend; twins; strong

18. less; left frontal

19. low; norepinephrine; serotonin

20. norepinephrine; serotonin

21. self-defeating; negative explanatory

22. learned helplessness

23. stress; overthink (ruminate)
Depressed people are more likely than others to explain failures or bad events in terms that are stable (it's going to last forever), global (it will affect everything), and internal (it's my fault). Such explanations lead to feelings of hopelessness, which in turn feed depression.

24. rejection
Depression is often brought on by stressful experiences. Depressed people brood over such experiences with a pessimistic explanatory style that creates a hopeless, depressed state that hampers the way the person thinks and acts. These thoughts and actions fuel social rejection and other negative experiences.

25. There are no right or wrong answers to this. Possible responses of a depressed person might be "I'll never be able to pass this course (stable)," "I'm never going to do well in any college courses (global)," and "It's my fault; I didn't study hard enough (internal)."

Schizophrenia

1. reality

2. thinking; perceptions; emotions; actions; positive; negative

3. delusions

4. word salad

5. hallucinations; auditory

6. flat affect; catatonia

7. chronic (or process); less; acute (or reactive)

8. positive. Kelly's hallucinations (hearing voices), delusions (fearing someone is "out to get her"), and fragmented speech indicate positive symptoms.

9. hallucination; delusion. Hallucinations are false perceptions. Delusions are false beliefs.

10. dopamine; decrease

11. low; frontal

12. fluid; shrinkage; thalamus; sensory

13. low birth weight; oxygen; viral infection

Risk of schizophrenia increases for those who undergo fetal development during a flu epidemic, or simply during the flu season. People born in densely populated areas and those born during winter and spring months are at increased risk. The months of excess schizophrenia births are reversed in the Southern Hemisphere, where the seasons are the reverse of the Northern Hemisphere's. Mothers who were sick with influenza during their pregnancy may be more likely to have children who develop schizophrenia. Blood drawn from pregnant women whose children develop schizophrenia has higher-than-normal levels of viral infection antibodies.

14. support

15. placenta; viruses

16. confirm

17. genetic; genes

18. dopamine. Schizophrenia patients sometimes have an excess of receptors for dopamine. Drugs that block these receptors can therefore reduce symptoms of schizophrenia.

19. **c.** is the answer. Risk for schizophrenia increases for individuals who are related to a schizophrenia victim, and the greater the genetic relatedness, the greater the risk.

Summary Study Tip: Using the text discussion and tables to complete this chart will enhance your understanding of the material in this chapter.

Progress Test

Multiple-Choice Questions

1. **b.** is the answer.
c. & d. Men are more likely than women to cope with stress in these ways.

2. **a.** is the answer.

3. **b.** is the answer. Depression is often preceded by a stressful event related to work, marriage, or a close relationship.

4. **c.** is the answer.

5. **d.** is the answer. Although depression is universal, anorexia nervosa and bulimia nervosa are rare outside Western culture.
a. & b. Schizophrenia and depression are both universal.
c. Although anorexia is mentioned as a culture-bound disorder, antisocial personality is not mentioned as a universal disorder.

6. **a.** is the answer.
b. & d. Thus far, only norepinephrine and serotonin have been implicated in depression and bipolar disorder.
c. Schizophrenia has been associated with an excess of dopamine receptors. Blocking them alleviates, rather than increases, schizophrenia symptoms.

7. **d.** is the answer.
b. The text does not mention DSM-IV-TR's reliability in terms of a person's age.

8. **a.** is the answer.
b. The mood disorders include major depressive disorder and bipolar disorder.
c. Dissociative identity disorder is the only dissociative disorder discussed in the text.
d. Antisocial personality disorder is the only personality disorder discussed in the text.

9. **d.** is the answer. Learned helplessness may lead to self-defeating beliefs, which in turn are linked with depression, a mood disorder.

10. **d.** is the answer.

11. **c.** is the answer.

12. **b.** is the answer. Those with antisocial personality disorders show less autonomic arousal in such situations, and emotions, such as fear, are tied to arousal.

13. **c.** is the answer. Drugs that relieve depression tend to increase levels of norepinephrine.
a. Acetylcholine is a neurotransmitter involved in muscle contractions.
b. It is in certain types of schizophrenia that decreasing dopamine levels is known to be helpful.
d. On the contrary, it appears that a particular type of depression may be related to *low* levels of serotonin.

14. **c.** is the answer.

15. **a.** is the answer. Different cultures have different standards for behaviors that are considered acceptable and normal.
b. Some disordered behaviors are simply maladaptive for the individual.
c. Many individuals who are deviant, such as Olympic gold medalists, are not considered to have psychological disorders. There are other criteria that must be met for behavior to be considered disordered.
d. Although physiological factors play a role in the various disorders, they do not define disordered behavior. Rather, behavior is said to be disordered if it is deviant, distressful, and dysfunctional.

16. **b.** is the answer.

17. **b.** is the answer. The fact that some disorders are universal and at least partly genetic in origin implicates biological factors in their origin. The fact that other disorders appear only in certain parts of the world implicates social-cultural and psychological factors in their origin.

18. **b.** is the answer.
a. Anxiety is an internal disorder.
d. Alcohol abuse is an external disorder.

19. **a.** is the answer. In fact, just the opposite is true. Labels are useful in promoting effective treatment of psychological disorders.

20. **d.** is the answer. In bipolar disorder, norepinephrine appears to be overabundant during mania and in short supply during depression.

a. There is an overabundance of dopamine receptors in some schizophrenia patients.
b. Serotonin sometimes appears to be scarce during depression.
c. Epinephrine has not been implicated in psychological disorders.

21. **d.** is the answer.

22. **b.** is the answer.
    a. This isn't the case; in fact, the medical model has gained credibility from recent discoveries of genetic and biochemical links to some disorders.
    c. & d. The medical perspective tends to place more emphasis on physiological factors.

23. **b.** is the answer. The psychoanalytic explanation is that DID symptoms are defenses against the anxiety caused by unacceptable impulses. According to the learning perspective, the troubled behaviors that result from this disorder have been reinforced by anxiety reduction.
    a. & c. These are true of the psychoanalytic, but not the learning, perspective.

24. **d.** is the answer.

25. **c.** is the answer.
    a. & d. In fact, just the opposite is true. DSM-IV-TR was revised to improve reliability by basing diagnoses on observable behaviors. And it is reliable.
    b. DSM-IV-TR does not reflect a learning or a psychoanalytic bias.

26. **c.** is the answer. Panic attacks are characteristic of certain anxiety disorders, not of schizophrenia.

27. **d.** is the answer.

28. **d.** is the answer. Risk for schizophrenia increases for individuals who are related to a schizophrenia victim, and the greater the genetic relatedness, the greater the risk.
    a. Schizophrenia victims have an overabundance of the neurotransmitter dopamine, not endorphins.
    b. Being a twin is, in itself, irrelevant to developing schizophrenia.
    c. Although learned helplessness has been suggested by social-cognitive theorists as a cause of self-defeating depressive behaviors, it has not been suggested as a cause of schizophrenia.

29. **c.** is the answer. Such drugs work primarily at synapses, altering neural transmission.
    a. What people believe will happen after taking a drug will likely have some effect on their individual reactions, but psychoactive drugs actually work by altering neural transmission.
    b. Since a placebo is a substance without active properties, this answer is incorrect.
    d. This answer is incorrect because the effects of psychoactive drugs on behavior, perception, and so forth have a physiological basis.

30. **a.** is the answer. Alcohol disrupts the processing of experiences into long-term memory but has little effect on either immediate or previously established memories.

31. **a.** is the answer.
    b. Physical dependence may occur in the absence of tolerance. The hallmark of physical dependence is the presence of withdrawal symptoms when the person is off the drug.
    c. Psychological dependence refers to a felt, or psychological, need to use a drug, for example, a drug that relieves stress.
    d. There is no such thing as drug "resistance."

32. **d.** is the answer. Alcohol is a depressant.

33. **a.** is the answer. Compared with other children, children whose parents abuse alcohol have a higher tolerance for multiple drinks, making it more likely that they will, in fact, consume more alcohol.

34. **c.** is the answer.

35. **d.** is the answer.

Matching Items

1. h	**6.** b	**11.** c
2. e	**7.** m	**12.** k
3. a	**8.** l	**13.** j
4. n	**9.** d	**14.** g
5. i	**10.** f	

Application Essay

There is more to a psychological disorder than being different from other people. Gifted artists, athletes, and scientists have deviant capabilities, yet are not considered psychologically disordered. Also, what is deviant in one culture may not be in another, or at another time. Homosexuality, for example, was once classified as a psychological disorder, but it is no longer. Similarly, nudity is common in some cultures and disturbing in others. Deviant behaviors are more likely to be considered disordered when judged as distressful and dysfunctional to the individual. Prolonged feelings of depression or the use of drugs to avoid dealing with problems are examples of deviant behaviors that may signal a psychological disorder if the person is unable to function, to perform routine behaviors (become dysfunctional).

Summing Up

Soo-Mee often feels tense and uneasy for no apparent reason. She has trouble concentrating on her studies, and her thoughts wander from problem to problem. This suggests that she may suffer from a *generalized anxiety disorder*, which may lead to physical problems, such as high *blood pressure*. Because Soo-Mee cannot identify the cause of her tension, it would be described by Sigmund *Freud* as *free-floating*, while learning theorists would link her anxiety with *classical conditioning* of fear, and biological psychologists might link it to an overarousal of *brain* areas involved in *impulse* control.

Soo-Mee's friend Shayna complains of similar feelings, but she also experiences unexpected episodes of intense dread, indicating *panic attacks*, which are accompanied by physical symptoms such as irregular *heartbeat*, shortness of breath, and choking sensations. Fearing that she might be having a heart attack when these episodes occur, Shayna avoids situations in which she fears *escape* may be difficult. So, Shayna refuses to leave her house, a sure sign that she suffers from *agoraphobia*.

Soo-Mee and Shayna's friend Randal laughs at their inability to identify the source of their anxiety. He says, "I know exactly what I fear: snakes. I have a *phobia,* which I know is *irrational,* but at least I can deal with it by avoiding areas where snakes are known to be, for example. My problem may result from my *observing* a friend being bitten by a snake."

Terms and Concepts

1. To be classified as a **psychological disorder,** thoughts, feelings, or behaviors must be deviant, distressful, and dysfunctional.

2. The **medical model** holds that psychological disorders are illnesses that can be diagnosed, treated, and, in most cases, cured, often through treatment in a psychiatric hospital.

3. **DSM-IV-TR** is a short name for the American Psychiatric Association's *Diagnostic and Statistical Manual of Mental Disorders* (Fourth Edition, Text Revision), which provides a widely used system of classifying psychological disorders.

4. **Anxiety disorders** involve distressing, persistent anxiety or maladaptive behaviors that reduce anxiety.

5. In the **generalized anxiety disorder,** the person is continually tense, fearful, and in a state of autonomic nervous system arousal for no apparent reason.

6. A **panic disorder** is an unpredictable episode of intense dread accompanied by chest pain, dizziness, or choking. It is essentially an increase of the anxiety associated with generalized anxiety disorder.

7. A **phobia** is an anxiety disorder in which a person has a persistent, irrational fear and avoidance of a specific object or situation.

8. **Obsessive-compulsive disorder (OCD)** is an anxiety disorder in which the person experiences uncontrollable and repetitive thoughts (obsessions) and/or actions (compulsions).

9. **Post-traumatic stress disorder (PTSD)** is an anxiety disorder characterized by haunting memories, nightmares, social withdrawal, jumpy anxiety, and/or insomnia lasting four weeks or more after a traumatic experience.

10. **Dissociative disorders** involve a separation of conscious awareness from previous memories, thoughts, and feelings.

    Memory aid: To *dissociate* is to separate or pull apart. In the **dissociative disorders** a person becomes dissociated from his or her memories and identity.

11. The **dissociative identity disorder** is a dissociative disorder in which a person exhibits two or more distinct and alternating personalities; formerly called *multiple personality disorder.*

12. **Personality disorders** are characterized by inflexible and enduring maladaptive character traits that impair social functioning.

13. The **antisocial personality disorder** is a personality disorder in which the person (usually a man) shows no sign of a conscience that would inhibit wrongdoing, even toward friends and family members. May be ruthless and aggressive or a clever con artist.

14. **Substance-related disorders** are maladaptive patterns of drug use that lead to clinically significant impairment or distress.

15. **Psychoactive drugs**—which include stimulants, depressants, and hallucinogens—are chemical substances that alter mood and perceptions. They work by affecting or mimicking the activity of neurotransmitters.

16. **Tolerance** is the diminishing of a psychoactive drug's effect that occurs with repeated use, requiring larger and larger doses in order to produce the same effect.

17. An **addiction** is a compulsive craving for a drug despite unpleasant consequences and withdrawal symptoms.

18. **Withdrawal** refers to the discomfort and distress that follow the discontinued use of an addictive drug.

19. **Physical dependence** is a physiological need for a drug that is indicated by the presence of withdrawal symptoms when the drug is not taken.

20. The psychological need to use a drug is referred to as **psychological dependence.**

21. **Depressants** are psychoactive drugs, such as alcohol, opiates, and barbiturates, that reduce neural activity and slow body functions.

22. Popularly known as alcoholism, **alcohol dependence** is characterized by the development of alcohol tolerance, withdrawal symptoms if use is suspended, and a drive to continue use.

23. **Barbiturates** are depressants, sometimes used to induce sleep or reduce anxiety; they depress central nervous system activity and impair memory and judgment.

24. **Opiates** are depressants derived from the opium poppy, such as opium, morphine, and heroin; they reduce neural activity and temporarily lessen pain and anxiety.

25. **Stimulants** are psychoactive drugs, such as caffeine, nicotine, the amphetamines, cocaine, methamphetamine, and Ecstasy, that excite neural activity and speed up body functions.

26. **Amphetamines** are a type of stimulant and, as such, stimulate neural activity, causing speeded-up body functions and associated energy and mood changes.

27. **Nicotine** is the stimulant drug found in tobacco; it is highly addictive.

28. **Methamphetamine** is a powerfully addictive stimulant that speeds up body functions and is associated with energy and mood changes.

29. Classified as both a (synthetic) stimulant and mild hallucinogen, **Ecstasy (MDMA)** produces short-term euphoria and social intimacy. Repeated use may permanently damage serotonin neurons, suppressing immunity and disrupting memory and other cognitive functions.

30. **Hallucinogens** are psychedelic drugs, such as LSD and marijuana, that distort perception and evoke sensory images in the absence of sensory input.

31. **LSD** (*lysergic acid diethylamide*) is a powerful hallucinogen capable of producing perceptual distortions and hallucinations and extreme emotions. LSD produces its unpredictable effects partially because it blocks the action of the neurotransmitter serotonin.

32. The **near-death experience** is an altered state of consciousness that has been reported by some people who have had a close brush with death.

33. The major active ingredient in marijuana, **THC** is classified as a mild hallucinogen.

34. **Mood disorders** are characterized by emotional extremes.

35. **Major depressive disorder** is the mood disorder that occurs when a person exhibits the lethargy, feelings of worthlessness, and loss of interest in family, friends, and activities characteristic of depression for more than a two-week period and for no obvious reason.

36. **Bipolar disorder** is the mood disorder in which a person alternates between depression and the euphoria of a manic state; formerly called *manic-depressive disorder*.

    Memory aid: Bipolar means having two poles, that is, two opposite qualities. In **bipolar disorder,** the opposing states are mania and depression.

37. **Mania** is the wildly optimistic, intensely happy, hyperactive state that alternates with depression in the bipolar disorder.

38. **Schizophrenia** refers to the group of severe disorders whose symptoms may include disorganized and delusional thinking, inappropriate emotions and actions, and disturbed perceptions.

39. **Delusions** are false beliefs that may accompany schizophrenia and other disorders.

13

THERAPY

Chapter 13 discusses the major psychotherapies and biomedical therapies for maladaptive behaviors. The various psychotherapies all derive from the personality theories discussed earlier, namely, the psychoanalytic, humanistic, behavioral, and cognitive theories. The chapter groups the therapies by perspective but also emphasizes the common threads that run through them. In evaluating the psychotherapies, the chapter points out that, although people who are untreated often improve, those receiving psychotherapy tend to improve somewhat more, regardless of the type of psychotherapy.

The biomedical therapies discussed are drug therapies, electroconvulsive therapy and other forms of brain stimulation, and psychosurgery, which is seldom used. By far the most important of these, drug therapies are being used in the treatment of psychotic, anxiety, and mood disorders.

CHAPTER REVIEW

First, skim each text section, noting headings and bold-face items. Review the section by reading the objectives and summaries provided here, then answer the questions that follow. In some cases, STUDY TIPS explain how best to learn a difficult concept and APPLICATIONS help you to know how well you understand the material. Check your understanding of the material by consulting the answers beginning on page 255. Do not continue with the next section until you understand each answer. If you need to, review or reread the section in the textbook before continuing.

Treating Psychological Disorders

Objective 1: Discuss how *psychotherapy, biomedical therapy,* and an *eclectic approach* to therapy differ.

In **psychotherapy,** a trained therapist uses psychological techniques to assist someone seeking to overcome psychological difficulties or achieve personal growth. The **biomedical therapies** use prescribed medications or medical procedures. Half of all psychotherapists describe themselves as taking an *eclectic approach* in which they use techniques from various forms of therapy depending on the client's problem.

1. Mental health therapies are classified as either
   _____ therapies or
   _____ therapies.

2. Psychological therapy is more commonly called
   _____ . This type of therapy is
   appropriate for disorders that are
   _____ -related.

3. Biomedical therapies include the use of
   _____ _____
   and medical procedures.

4. Some therapists blend several psychotherapy techniques and so are said to take an
   _____ approach.

The Psychological Therapies

Objective 2: Discuss the aims, methods, and criticisms of psychoanalysis.

Psychoanalysis is Sigmund Freud's therapeutic approach to help the person release repressed feelings and gain self-insight. The goal of psychoanalysis is to help people gain insight into the unconscious origins of their disorders, to work through the accompanying feelings, and to take responsibility for their own growth.

Psychoanalysts draw on techniques such as *free association* (saying aloud anything that comes to mind), **resistances** (the blocking from consciousness of anxiety-laden material) and their *interpretation,* dream interpretation, and other behaviors such as *transference* (transferring to the therapist long-repressed feelings). Psychoanalysis is criticized because its interpretations are hard to prove or disprove and because it is time-consuming and costly.

1. The goal of Freud's psychoanalysis is to help the
   patient gain _____ .

2. Freud assumed that many psychological problems originate in childhood impulses and conflicts that
   have been _____ .

3. Psychoanalysts attempt to bring
   _____ feelings into
   _____ awareness where they
   can be dealt with.

4. Freud's technique in which a patient says whatever
   comes to mind is called _____
   _____ .

5. When, in the course of therapy, a person omits shameful or embarrassing material,
   _____ is occurring.
   Insight is facilitated by the analyst's
   _____ of the meaning of such
   omissions, of dreams, and of other information revealed during therapy sessions.

6. When strong feelings, similar to those experienced in other important relationships, are developed toward the therapist, _____ has occurred.

7. Critics point out that psychoanalysts' interpretations are hard to _____ and that therapy takes a long time and is very

_____ .

Objective 3: Contrast psychodynamic therapy with traditional psychoanalysis.

Psychodynamic therapists try to understand patients' current symptoms by focusing on themes across important relationships, including childhood experiences and the therapist relationship. They may also help the person explore and gain perspective on defended-against thoughts and feelings. However, they talk with the patient face-to-face, once a week, and for only a few weeks or months. *Interpersonal psychotherapy,* a brief alternative to psychodynamic therapy, emphasizes symptom relief in the present, not overall personality change. The therapist also focuses on current relationships and the mastery of relationship skills. It has been found effective with depressed patients.

8. Therapists who are influenced by Freud's psychoanalysis but who talk to the patient face to face are _____ therapists. These therapists try to understand a patient's current symptoms by focusing on _____ across important _____ . In addition, they work with patients only once or twice a week and for only a few weeks or months.

9. While this approach aims to help people gain _____ into their difficulties, it focuses on _____ _____ rather than on past hurts.

Objective 4: Identify the basic themes of humanistic therapy, and describe the specific goals and techniques of Carl Rogers' client-centered therapy.

Humanistic therapists focus on the present and the future instead of the past, on clients' conscious thoughts, and on clients' taking responsibility for their own growth. In emphasizing people's inherent potential for self-fulfillment, they aim to promote growth rather than to cure illness. In his nondirective **client-centered therapy,** Rogers used **active listening** to express *genuineness, acceptance,* and *empathy.* This technique, he believed, would help clients to increase their self-understanding and self-acceptance. The therapist interrupts only to restate and confirm the client's feelings, to accept what the client is expressing, or to seek clarification. The client-centered counselor seeks to provide a psychological mirror that helps clients see themselves more clearly.

10. Humanistic therapies attempt to help people meet their potential for _____ .

List several ways that humanistic therapy differs from psychoanalysis.

11. The humanistic therapy based on Rogers' theory is called _____-_____ therapy, which is described as _____ therapy because the therapist _____ (interprets/does not interpret) the person's problems.

12. To promote growth in clients, Rogerian therapists exhibit _____ , _____ , and _____ .

13. Rogers' technique of echoing, restating, and clarifying what a person is saying is called

_____ _____ .

14. Given a nonjudgmental environment that provides _____ _____ _____ , patients are better able to accept themselves as they are and to feel valued and whole.

15. Three tips for listening more actively in your own relationships are to _____ , _____ _____ , and _____ _____ .

Objective 5: Explain how the assumptions and techniques of behavior therapy differ from those of traditional psychoanalytic and humanistic therapies, and describe the techniques used in exposure therapies and aversive conditioning.

Traditional psychoanalysts attempt to help people gain insight into their unresolved and unconscious conflicts. Humanistic therapists help clients to get in touch with their feelings. In contrast, **behavior therapists** question the healing power of self-awareness. They assume problem behaviors are the problems and thus do not look for inner causes. Instead, they apply learning principles to eliminate a troubling behavior.

Counterconditioning is based on classical conditioning, and it involves conditioning new responses to stimuli that trigger unwanted behaviors. Two types are exposure therapy and aversive conditioning. *Exposure therapies* treat anxieties by exposing people to the things they fear and avoid. In *systematic desensitization,* a widely used exposure therapy, a pleasant relaxed state is associated with gradually increasing anxiety-triggering stimuli. *Virtual reality exposure therapy* equips patients with a head-mounted display unit that provides vivid simulations of feared stimuli, such as a plane's takeoff. In *aversive conditioning,* an unpleasant state (such as nausea) is associated with an unwanted behavior (such as drinking alcohol). This method works in the short run, but for long-term effectiveness it is combined with other methods.

16. Behavior therapy applies principles of _____ to eliminate troubling behaviors.

Contrast the assumptions of the behavior therapies with those of psychoanalysis and humanistic therapy.

17. One cluster of behavior therapies is based on the principles of _____ _____ , as developed in Pavlov's experiments.

18. The technique, in which a new, incompatible response is substituted for a maladaptive one, is called _____ . Two examples of this technique are _____ _____ and _____ _____ .

19. One widely used exposure therapy is

_____ _____ .

This technique has been most fully developed by the therapist _____ . The idea behind this technique is that a person cannot simultaneously be _____ and relaxed.

20. The first step in systematic desensitization is to make a list of anxiety-arousing stimuli. The second step involves training in _____ _____ . In the final step, the person is trained to associate the _____ state with the _____ -arousing stimuli.

21. A newer option, involving a head-mounted display unit, is _____

_____ _____ therapy.

22. In aversive conditioning, the therapist attempts to substitute a _____ (positive/negative) response to a harmful stimulus for one that is currently _____ (positive/negative). In this technique, a person's unwanted behaviors become associated with _____ feelings.

Objective 6: State the basic concept of operant conditioning therapies.

Operant conditioning therapies are based on the concept that our behaviors are strongly influenced by their consequences. Behavior therapists apply operant conditioning principles by reinforcing desired behaviors while failing to reinforce or punishing undesired behaviors. The rewards used to modify behavior vary from attention or praise to more concrete rewards such as food. In institutional settings, therapists may create a **token economy** in which a patient exchanges a token of some sort, earned for displaying appropriate behavior, for rewards, such as candy or TV time.

23. Reinforcing desired behaviors and withholding reinforcement for or punishing undesired behaviors are key aspects of _____ _____ .

24. Therapies that influence behavior by controlling its consequences are based on principles of _____ conditioning. One application of this form of therapy to institutional settings is the _____ _____ , in which desired behaviors are rewarded.

STUDY TIP/APPLICATION: Each type of behavior therapy discussed is derived from principles of either classical conditioning or operant conditioning. Recall from Chapter 6 that classical conditioning is based on the formation of a learned association between two stimulus situations or events. Operant conditioning is based on the use of reinforcement and punishment to modify the future likelihood of behaviors.

Several problem behaviors are described in the chart below. Test your understanding of behavior therapy by completing the chart and explaining how you would treat the problem behavior using one of the behavior therapies. Be sure to identify any reinforcers, conditioned stimuli, and unconditioned stimuli that you would use. The first example is completed for you.

25. Situation	Type of Conditioning	Procedure
A friend is trying to quit smoking	Aversive conditioning, a type of counterconditioning (classical conditioning)	Each time your friend puffs the cigarette, the taste of the cigarette (conditioned stimulus) is paired with a blast of hot air delivered to his/her face (unconditioned stimulus).
a. A relative has a fear of flying (Hint: use imagined situations)		
b. The parents of a sloppy teenager want to get him to clean up his room		
c. A child is terrified of dogs (Hint: use real situations)		

Objective 7: Describe the goals and techniques of the cognitive therapies.

Cognitive therapists assume that our thinking colors our feelings, and so they try to teach people who suffer psychological disorders new, more adaptive ways of thinking.

In treating depression, Aaron Beck seeks to reverse clients' negative thinking about themselves, their situations, and their futures. His technique is a gentle questioning that aims to help people discover their irrationalities.

Cognitive-behavioral therapists combine cognitive therapy (changing self-defeating thinking) with behavior therapy (changing behavior). They aim to make people aware of their irrational negative thinking, to replace it with new ways of thinking and talking, and to practice the more positive approach in everyday settings.

26. Therapists who teach people new, more constructive ways of thinking are using

_____ therapy.

27. One variety of cognitive therapy attempts to reverse the _____ themes often associated with _____ by helping clients see their irrationalities. This therapy was developed by _____ .

28. Children and adolescents trained to _____ their negative thoughts showed a greatly reduced rate of future depression.

29. Treatment that combines an attack on negative thinking with efforts to modify behavior is known as

_____-_____ therapy.

APPLICATIONS:

30. Given that Don Carlo's therapist attempts to help him by offering genuineness, acceptance, and empathy, she is probably practicing _____ therapy.

31. To help Sam lose weight by eating fewer sweets, his therapist laced a batch of cookies with a nausea-producing drug. Which technique is the therapist using?

_____ _____

32. B.J.'s therapist interprets her psychological problems in terms of repressed impulses. Which type(s) of therapy is she using? _____

33. Ben is a cognitive-behavioral therapist. Compared with Rachel, who is a behavior therapist, Ben is more likely to
a. base his therapy on principles of operant conditioning.
b. base his therapy on principles of classical conditioning.
c. address clients' attitudes as well as behaviors.
d. focus on clients' unconscious urges.

34. To help him overcome his fear of heights, Duane's therapist has him construct a list of anxiety-triggering stimuli and then learn to associate each with a state of deep

relaxation. Duane's therapist is using the technique called

_____ _____ .

35. A patient in a hospital receives poker chips for making her bed, being punctual at meal times, and maintaining her physical appearance. The poker chips can be exchanged for privileges, such as television viewing, snacks, and magazines. This is an example of the
   a. psychodynamic therapy technique called systematic desensitization.
   b. behavior therapy technique called token economy.
   c. cognitive therapy technique called token economy.
   d. humanistic therapy technique called systematic desensitization.

36. After Darnel dropped a pass in an important football game, he became depressed and vowed to quit the team because of his athletic incompetence. The campus psychologist used gentle questioning to reveal to Darnel that his thinking was irrational: His "incompetence" had earned him an athletic scholarship. The psychologist's response was most typical of a _____ therapist.

37. Leota is startled when her therapist says that she needs to focus on eliminating her problem behavior rather than gaining insight into its underlying cause. Most likely, Leota has consulted a _____ therapist.

Objective 8: Discuss the rationale and benefits of group therapy, including family therapy.

The social context provided by group therapy allows people to discover that others have problems similar to their own and to try out new ways of behaving. Receiving honest feedback can be very helpful, and it can be reassuring to find that you are not alone. *Family therapy* assumes that we live and grow in relation to others, especially our families. It views an individual's unwanted behaviors as influenced by or directed at other family members. In an effort to heal relationships, therapists attempt to guide family members toward positive relationships and improved communication.

List several advantages of group therapy.

38. The type of group interaction that focuses on the fact that we live and grow in relation to others is _____ _____ .

39. In this type of group, therapists focus on improving _____ within the family.

STUDY TIP/APPLICATION: To organize your thinking about the psychological therapies discussed in this chapter, complete the following chart. For each category of therapy, state the assumed underlying cause of psychological disorders, the overall goal of therapy, and the role of the therapist. To help you get started, the first example is already filled in.

40. Type of Psychotherapy	Assumed Cause of Psychological Disorder	Goal of Therapy	Role of Therapist
Psychoanalysis	Repression of forbidden impulses and childhood conflicts	Self-insight	Interpreting dreams, free associations, resistances, and transferences
Humanistic Therapies			
Behavior Therapies			
Cognitive Therapies			
Group and Family Therapies			

Evaluating Psychotherapies

Objective 9: Explain why clients and clinicians tend to overestimate the effectiveness of psychotherapy.

Clients tend to overestimate the effectiveness of psychotherapy because they enter therapy in crisis. With the normal ebb and flow of events, the crisis passes and people say the therapy helped them. Clients may also need to believe that the investment of time and money has been worth it. Finally, clients generally speak positively of therapists who have been understanding and who have helped them gain a new perspective.

Clients enter therapy when they are extremely unhappy, usually leave when they are less unhappy, and stay in touch only if satisfied. Thus, therapists, like most clients, testify to therapy's success. Clinicians are mostly aware of other therapists' failures as clients seek new therapists for their recurring problems.

Randomized clinical trials assign people on a waiting list to therapy or no therapy. Statistical methods that combine the results of these studies reveal that people who remain untreated often improve, but those who receive psychotherapy are more likely to improve.

1. In contrast to earlier times, most therapy today _____ (is/is not) provided by psychiatrists.

2. A majority of psychotherapy clients express _____ (satisfaction/dissatisfaction) with their therapy.

Give three reasons why client testimonials are not persuasive evidence for psychotherapy's effectiveness.

3. Clinicians tend to _____ (overestimate/underestimate) the effectiveness of psychotherapy.

4. One reason clinicians' perceptions of the effectiveness of psychotherapy are inaccurate is that clients justify entering therapy by emphasizing their _____ and justify leaving therapy by emphasizing their _____ .

5. In hopes of better assessing psychotherapy's effectiveness, psychologists have turned to _____ research studies.

6. The debate over the effectiveness of psychotherapy began with a study by _____ ; it showed that the rate of improvement for those who received therapy _____ (was/was not) higher than the rate for those who did not.

7. When researchers used statistical methods to combine the results of outcome studies, they found that psychotherapy is _____ (somewhat effective/ineffective). They found that the outcome for _____ (what percentage?) of treated clients surpassed that of untreated clients.

Objective 10: Describe which psychotherapies are most effective for specific disorders.

No one psychotherapy has been shown to be best in all cases, nor is there any relationship between clinicians' experience, training, supervision, and licensing and their clients' outcomes. Some psychotherapies are, however, well suited to particular disorders, such as behavioral conditioning therapies for treating specific problems such as phobias, compulsions, and sexual disorders and cognitive therapy for coping with anxiety, post-traumatic stress disorder, and depression. Unsupported therapies that should be avoided include energy therapies, recovered-memory therapies, rebirthing therapies, facilitated communication, and crisis debriefing.

Who should decide which psychotherapies should be used? Science-oriented clinicians call for *evidence-based* decision making. Thus, they make decisions based on research evidence, clinical expertise, and knowledge of the patient.

8. Comparisons of the effectiveness of different forms of psychotherapy reveal _____ (clear/no clear) differences, that the type of psychotherapy provider _____ (matters greatly/does not matter), and that whether therapy is provided by an individual psychotherapist or within a group _____ (makes a difference/does not make a difference).

9. With phobias, compulsions, and other specific behavior problems, _____ _____ therapies have been the most effective. Other studies have demonstrated that depression may be effectively treated with _____ therapy.

10. There _____ (is/is no) scientific support for therapies such as energy therapies and rebirthing therapies.

11. To determine which psychotherapies are acceptable, science-oriented clinicians call for _____-_____ _____ _____ .

APPLICATION:

12. Your best friend Armand wants to know which type of therapy works best. You should tell him that
  a. psychotherapy does not work.
  b. behavior therapy is the most effective.
  c. cognitive therapy is the most effective.
  d. no one type of therapy is consistently the most successful.

Objective 11: Describe the three benefits shared by all psychotherapies, and discuss the role of values and cultural differences in the relationship between a therapist and a client.

Despite their differences, all psychotherapies offer at least three benefits. First, they all offer the expectation that, with commitment from the patient, things can and will get better. Second, every psychotherapy offers people an explanation of their symptoms and new experiences. Third, no matter what technique they use, effective psychotherapists are empathic people who seek to understand another's experience, whose care and concern the client feels, and who earn the client's trust and respect. In short, all psychotherapies offer hope for demoralized people, a new perspective on oneself and the world, and an empathic, trusting, caring relationship.

Psychotherapists' personal beliefs and values influence their therapy. While nearly all agree on the importance of encouraging clients' sensitivity, openness, and personal responsibility, they differ in cultural and moral matters. Value differences also become important when a client from one culture meets a psychotherapist from another. For example, clients from a collectivist culture may have difficulty with a psychotherapist who requires them to think only of their own well-being. Such differences may help explain the reluctance of some minorities to use mental health services. Another area of potential value conflict is religion. Some psychologists believe that psychotherapists should divulge their values more openly.

13. All forms of effective psychotherapy offer three benefits: _____ for demoralized people; a new _____ on oneself; and a relationship that is _____ , _____ , and _____ .

14. The emotional bond between therapist and client—the _____ _____ — is a key aspect of effective psychotherapy.

15. The importance of a fresh perspective by a caring person is why paraprofessionals _____ (are/are not) able to assist so many troubled people so effectively.

16. In summary, those who do not seek help improve _____ (more than/less than/as much as) those who undergo psychotherapy. And, people with _____-_____ , specific problems tend to improve the most.

17. Generally speaking, psychotherapists' personal values _____ (do/do not) influence their therapy. This is particularly significant when the therapist and client are from _____ (the same/different) cultures.

18. In North America, Europe, and Australia, most therapists reflect their culture's _____ .

19. Differences in values may help explain the reluctance of some _____ populations to use mental health services.

The Biomedical Therapies

Objective 12: Describe the different drug therapies, and discuss some of the side effects of those treatments.

To control for normal recovery and the *placebo effect,* researchers use the *double-blind technique:* Neither staff nor patients know who gets a drug and who gets a placebo. Using this approach, several types of drugs have proven effective in treating psychological disorders.

Antipsychotic drugs, such as chlorpromazine (sold as Thorazine), provide help to people experiencing the positive symptoms of auditory hallucinations and paranoia by reducing their overreaction to irrelevant stimuli. Clozapine (sold as Clozaril) helps schizophrenia patients with the negative symptoms of apathy and withdrawal. Long-term use of some of these drugs blocks dopamine receptors and can produce *tardive dyskinesia,* which is marked by involuntary movements of facial muscles, tongue, and limbs. Many of the newer antipsychotics have fewer such side effects, but they may increase the risk of obesity and diabetes.

Antianxiety drugs such as Xanax and Ativan depress central nervous system activity. Used with psychological therapy, they can help people learn to cope with frightening stimuli. Antianxiety drugs can produce both psychological and physiological dependence.

Antidepressant drugs aim to lift people up. Typically, they work by increasing the availability of the neurotransmitters norepinephrine or serotonin. For example, Prozac slows the reuptake of serotonin, and so Prozac and its cousins Zoloft and Paxil are called *selective-serotonin-reuptake-inhibitors (SSRIs).* They also are increasingly being used to treat anxiety disorders such as obsessive-compulsive disorder. Although antidepressants influence neurotransmitter systems within hours, their full psychological effects may take four weeks. Depression may also be helped by aerobic exercise and cognitive therapy in combination with drugs.

The simple salt *lithium* is often an effective *mood stabilizer* for those suffering the manic-depressive swings of bipolar disorder. Although lithium significantly lowers the risk of suicide, we do not fully understand how it works.

1. The most widely used biomedical treatments are the _____ therapies. Thanks to these therapies, the number of residents in mental hospitals has _____ (increased/ decreased) sharply.

2. To guard against the _____ effect and normal _____ , neither the patients nor the staff involved in a study may be aware of which condition a given individual is in; this is called a _____-_____ study.

3. One effect of chlorpromazine (Thorazine), a type of _____ drug, is to help those experiencing _____ (positive/ negative) symptoms of schizophrenia by decreasing their responsiveness to irrelevant stimuli. Schizophrenia patients who are apathetic and withdrawn may be more effectively treated with the drug _____ .

4. These drugs work by blocking the receptor sites for the neurotransmitter _____ .

5. Long-term use of antipsychotic drugs can produce _____ _____ , which involves involuntary movements of the muscles of the

_____ , _____ , and _____ .

6. Xanax and Ativan are classified as _____ drugs. These drugs depress activity in the _____ _____ .

7. When used in combination with _____ _____ , these drugs can help people cope with frightening situations and fear-triggering stimuli.

8. Antianxiety drugs have been criticized for merely reducing _____ , rather than resolving underlying _____ . These drugs can also cause _____ .

9. Drugs that are prescribed to alleviate depression are called _____ drugs. These drugs also work by increasing levels of the neurotransmitters _____ or _____ .

10. One example of this type of drug is _____ , which works by partially blocking the normal reuptake (b) of excess _____ from synapses (c) and is therefore called a _____-_____-_____ drug.

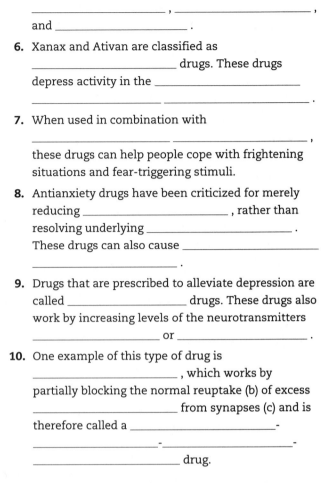

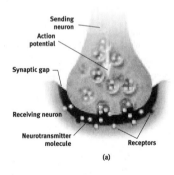

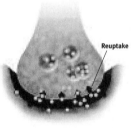

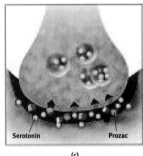

Sending neuron
Action potential
Synaptic gap
Receiving neuron
Neurotransmitter molecule
Receptors
(a)

Reuptake
(b)

Serotonin   Prozac
(c)

11. Equally effective in calming anxious people and energizing depressed people is _____ _____ , which has positive side effects. Even better is to use drugs, which work from the _____ (bottom up/top down), in conjunction with _____-_____ therapy, which works from the _____ (bottom up/top down).

12. Although people with depression often improve after one month on antidepressants, studies demonstrate that a large percentage of the effectiveness is due to _____ _____ or a _____ .

13. The mood-stabilizing drug _____ , which was originally used to treat epilepsy, was found effective in controlling the _____ episodes associated with bipolar disorder.

14. To stabilize the mood swings of a bipolar disorder, the simple salt _____ is often prescribed.

APPLICATIONS:

15. Seth enters therapy to talk about some issues that have been upsetting him. The therapist prescribes medication to help him. The therapist is most likely a

    _____ .

16. In an experiment testing the effects of a new antipsychotic drug, neither Dr. Vargas nor her patients know whether the patients are in the experimental or the control group. This is an example of the _____-_____ technique.

17. Zuza's doctor prescribes medication that blocks the activity of dopamine in her nervous system. Evidently, Zuza is being treated with an _____ drug.

18. Donovan's doctor prescribes medication that increases the availability of norepinephrine or serotonin in his nervous system. Evidently, Donovan is being treated with an _____ drug.

19. A psychiatrist has diagnosed a patient as having bipolar disorder. It is likely that she will prescribe

    _____ .

Objective 13: Describe the use of brain stimulation techniques and psychosurgery in treating specific disorders.

Electroconvulsive therapy (ECT), or shock treatment, is used for severely depressed patients. A brief electric current is sent through the brain of an anesthetized patient. Although ECT is credited with saving many from suicide, no one knows for sure how it works. Some patients with chronic depression have found relief through a chest implant that intermittently stimulates the vagus nerve, which sends signals to the brain's mood-related limbic system. Another new experimental procedure is *deep stimulation,* which is administered by a pacemaker. *Repetitive transcranial magnetic stimulation (rTMS)* is performed on wide-awake patients. Magnetic energy penetrates only to the brain's surface (although tests are underway with a higher energy field that penetrates more deeply). Unlike ECT, the rTMS procedure produces no seizures, memory loss, or other side effects. Studies have confirmed its therapeutic effect.

   Psychosurgery removes or destroys brain tissue in an effort to change behavior. For example, the *lobotomy* was once used to calm uncontrollably emotional or violent patients. The nerves that connect the frontal lobes to the emotion-controlling centers of the inner brain are cut. The lobotomy usually produced a permanently lethargic, immature, impulsive personality. Because of these effects and the introduction of drug treatments in the 1950s, the procedure has been abandoned. Other psychosurgery is used only in extreme cases. For example, for patients who suffer uncontrollable seizures, surgeons may deactivate the specific nerve clusters that cause or transmit the convulsions. MRI-guided precision surgery may also be used to cut the circuits involved in severe obsessive-compulsive disorder.

20. The therapeutic technique in which the patient receives an electric shock to the brain is referred to as _____ therapy, abbreviated as _____ .

21. ECT is most often used with patients suffering from severe _____ . Research evidence _____ (confirms/does not confirm) ECT's effectiveness with such patients. However, the mechanism by which ECT works is _____ .

22. A gentler alternative is a chest _____ that intermittently stimulates the _____ nerve. Similarly, implanted electrodes are controlled by a pacemaker in a procedure called _____ _____ .

23. Another gentler procedure called _____ _____ _____ aims to treat depression by presenting pulses through a magnetic coil held close to a person's skull. Unlike ECT, this procedure produces no _____ , _____ loss, or other side effects. This procedure may work by energizing the brain's left _____ _____ , which is relatively inactive during depression.

24. The biomedical therapy in which a portion of brain tissue is removed or destroyed is called

    _____ .

25. In the 1930s, Moniz developed an operation called the _____ . In this procedure, the _____ lobe of the brain is disconnected from the rest of the brain.

26. Today, most psychosurgery has been replaced by the use of _____ or some other form of treatment.

Objective 14: Discuss the value of adopting a healthier life-style as a way to gain relief from depression.

Everything psychological is also biological: Stress affects body chemistry and health. And chemical imbalances can produce schizophrenia and depression. This suggests that it is no longer valid to treat mind and body separately. Stephen Ilardi and his colleagues are promoting therapeutic life-style change, which involves aerobic exercise, adequate sleep, light exposure, social connection, anti-rumination, and nutritional supplements.

Research, which has to be replicated, suggests that their program provides relief from depressive symptoms.

27. When considering the effectiveness of therapy, it is important to remember that everything psychological is also _____ . The neat separation of _____ and _____ that prevailed in the past no longer is valid.

28. Stephen Ilardi has developed training seminars that promote _____ _____-_____ change. The elements of this program include _____ _____ _____ .

29. Research reveals that regular _____ _____ rivals the healing power of antidepressant drugs. Regular _____ also boosts mood and energy.

Preventing Psychological Disorders

Objective 15: Discuss ways of preventing psychological disorders.

Faced with unforeseen trauma, most adults exhibit *resilience*. Research has shown that those who suffer often develop a greater-than-usual sensitivity to suffering, greater empathy for those who suffer, an increased sense of responsibility, and enlarged capacity for caring. Other evidence shows that struggling with challenging crises can lead to *post-traumatic growth*. Preventive mental health workers, including *community psychologists*, view many psychological disorders as an understandable response to a disturbing and stressful society. It is not only the person who needs treatment but also the person's social context. Thus, the aim of preventive mental health is to identify and wipe out the conditions that cause the problem, the situations that undermine a person's sense of competence, personal control, and self-esteem.

Among the upstream prevention workers are *community psychologists*, who focus on creating environments that support psychological health.

1. One way to prevent some disorders is by building individuals' _____ , their ability to cope with stress and recover from adversity. _____ (Most/Few) adults exhibit this ability.

2. Research indicates that those who have suffered develop, among other things, a greater _____ for others who suffer, an increased sense of _____ , and an enlarged capacity for _____ . Taken together, these indicate _____ .

3. Psychotherapies and biomedical therapies locate the cause of psychological disorders within the _____ .

4. An alternative viewpoint is that many psychological disorders are responses to _____ .

5. According to this viewpoint, it is not just the _____ who needs treatment, but also the person's _____ .

6. Preventive mental health seeks to wipe out the social stresses that undermine people's sense of _____ , _____ , and _____ . These stresses include _____ , work that is _____ , constant _____ , _____ , _____ , and _____ .

7. One group of psychologists who focus on creating environments that support psychological health are _____ _____ .

8. These views remind us that disorders are not just biological and not just environmental or psychological because we are all an _____ _____ system.

PROGRESS TEST

Multiple-Choice Questions

Circle your answers to the following questions and check them with the answers beginning on page 257. If your answer is incorrect, read the explanation for why it is incorrect and then consult the text.

1. Electroconvulsive therapy is most useful in the treatment of
   a. schizophrenia.
   b. depression.
   c. personality disorders.
   d. anxiety disorders.

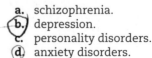

2. The technique in which a person is asked to report everything that comes to his or her mind is called _____ ; it is favored by_____ therapists.
   a. active listening; cognitive
   b. spontaneous recovery; humanistic
   c. free association; psychoanalytic
   d. systematic desensitization; behavior

3. Of the following categories of psychotherapy, which is known for its nondirective nature?
   a. psychoanalysis
   b. humanistic therapy
   c. behavior therapy
   d. cognitive therapy

4. Which of the following is NOT a common criticism of psychoanalysis?
   a. It emphasizes the existence of repressed memories.
   b. It provides interpretations that are hard to disprove.
   c. It is generally a very expensive process.
   d. It gives therapists too much control over patients.

5. Which of the following types of therapy does NOT belong with the others?
   a. cognitive therapy
   b. family therapy
   c. behavior therapy
   d. psychosurgery

6. Which of the following is NOT necessarily an advantage of group therapies over individual therapies?
   a. They tend to take less time for the therapist.
   b. They tend to cost less money for the client.
   c. They are more effective.
   d. They allow the client to test new behaviors in a social context.

7. Which biomedical therapy is MOST likely to be practiced today?
   a. psychosurgery
   b. electroconvulsive therapy
   c. drug therapy
   d. counterconditioning

8. The effectiveness of psychotherapy has been assessed both through clients' perspectives and through controlled research studies. What have such assessments found?
   a. Clients' perceptions and controlled studies alike strongly affirm the effectiveness of psychotherapy.
   b. Clients' perceptions strongly affirm the effectiveness of psychotherapy, but studies point to more modest results.
   c. Studies strongly affirm the effectiveness of psychotherapy, but many clients feel dissatisfied with their progress.
   d. Clients' perceptions and controlled studies alike paint a very mixed picture of the effectiveness of psychotherapy.

9. Cognitive-behavioral therapy aims to
   a. alter the way people act.
   b. make people more aware of their irrational negative thinking.
   c. alter the way people think and act.
   d. countercondition anxiety-provoking stimuli.

10. The results of outcome research on the effectiveness of different psychotherapies reveal that
    a. no single type of therapy is consistently superior.
    b. behavior therapies are most effective in treating specific problems, such as phobias.
    c. cognitive therapies are most effective in treating depressed emotions.
    d. all of these answers are correct.

11. The antipsychotic drugs appear to produce their effects by blocking the receptor sites for
    a. dopamine.
    b. epinephrine.
    c. norepinephrine.
    d. serotonin.

12. Psychologists who believe in a _____ approach to mental health contend that many psychological disorders could be prevented by changing the disturbed individual's _____ .
    a. biomedical; diet
    b. family; behavior
    c. humanistic; feelings
    d. preventive; environment

13. An eclectic psychotherapist is one who
    a. takes a nondirective approach in helping clients solve their problems.
    b. views psychological disorders as usually stemming from one cause, such as a biological abnormality.
    c. uses one particular technique, such as psychoanalysis or counterconditioning, in treating disorders.
    d. uses a variety of techniques, depending on the client and the problem.

14. The technique in which a therapist echoes and restates what a person says in a nondirective manner is called
    a. active listening.
    b. free association.
    c. systematic desensitization.
    d. transference.

15. One reason that aversive conditioning may only be temporarily effective is that
    a. for ethical reasons, therapists cannot use sufficiently intense unconditioned stimuli to sustain classical conditioning.
    b. patients are often unable to become sufficiently relaxed for conditioning to take place.
    c. patients know that outside the therapist's office they can engage in the undesirable behavior without fear of aversive consequences.
    d. most conditioned responses are elicited by many nonspecific stimuli and it is impossible to countercondition them all.

16. The technique of systematic desensitization is based on the concept that maladaptive symptoms are
    a. a reflection of irrational thinking.
    b. conditioned responses.
    c. expressions of unfulfilled wishes.
    d. all of these things.

17. The operant conditioning technique in which desired behaviors are rewarded with points or poker chips that can later be exchanged for various rewards is called
    a. counterconditioning.
    b. systematic desensitization.
    c. a token economy.
    d. exposure therapy.

18. One variety of _____ therapy is based on the finding that depressed people often attribute their failures to _____ .
    a. humanistic; themselves
    b. behavior; external circumstances
    c. cognitive; external circumstances
    d. cognitive; themselves

19. A person can benefit from psychotherapy simply by believing in it. This illustrates the importance of
    a. spontaneous recovery.
    b. the placebo effect.
    c. the transference effect.
    d. interpretation.

20. Before 1950, the main mental health providers were
    a. psychologists.
    b. clinicians.
    c. psychiatrists.
    d. the clergy.

21. Carl Rogers was a _____ therapist who was the creator of _____ .
    a. behavior; systematic desensitization
    b. psychoanalytic; insight therapy
    c. humanistic; client-centered therapy
    d. cognitive; cognitive therapy for depression

22. Using techniques of classical conditioning to develop an association between unwanted behavior and an unpleasant experience is known as
    a. aversive conditioning.
    b. systematic desensitization.
    c. transference.
    d. electroconvulsive therapy.

23. Which type of psychotherapy emphasizes the individual's inherent potential for self-fulfillment?
    a. behavior therapy
    b. psychoanalysis
    c. humanistic therapy
    d. biomedical therapy

24. Which type of psychotherapy focuses on changing unwanted behaviors rather than on discovering their underlying causes?
    a. behavior therapy
    b. cognitive therapy
    c. humanistic therapy
    d. psychoanalysis

25. The techniques of counterconditioning are based on principles of
    a. observational learning.
    b. classical conditioning.
    c. operant conditioning.
    d. behavior modification.

26. In which of the following does the client learn to associate a relaxed state with a hierarchy of anxiety-arousing situations?
    a. cognitive therapy
    b. aversive conditioning
    c. counterconditioning
    d. systematic desensitization

27. Principles of operant conditioning underlie which of the following techniques?
    a. counterconditioning
    b. systematic desensitization
    c. aversive conditioning
    d. the token economy

28. Which type of therapy focuses on eliminating irrational thinking?
    a. rTMS
    b. client-centered therapy
    c. cognitive therapy
    d. behavior therapy

29. Some antidepressant drugs are believed to work by affecting serotonin and
    a. dopamine.
    b. lithium.
    c. norepinephrine.
    d. acetylcholine.

30. Long-term use of antipsychotic drugs can result in a condition in which facial muscles sometimes twitch involuntarily. This condition is called
    a. tardive dyskinesia.
    b. spontaneous recovery.
    c. repetitive transcranial magnetic stimulation.
    d. the placebo effect.

31. Which of the following is the mood-stabilizing drug most commonly used to treat bipolar disorder?
    a. Ativan
    b. chlorpromazine
    c. Xanax
    d. lithium

32. The type of drugs criticized for reducing symptoms without resolving underlying problems are the
    a. antianxiety drugs.
    b. antipsychotic drugs.
    c. antidepressant drugs.
    d. amphetamines.

33. Which form of therapy is MOST likely to be successful in treating depression?
    a. behavior modification
    b. psychoanalysis
    c. cognitive therapy
    d. humanistic therapy

34. Although Moniz won the Nobel Prize for developing the lobotomy procedure, the technique is not widely used today because
    a. it produces a listless, immature personality.
    b. it is irreversible.
    c. calming drugs became available in the 1950s.
    d. of all of these reasons.

35. Among the common ingredients of the psychotherapies is(are)

    a. the offer of a therapeutic relationship.

    b. the expectation among clients that the therapy will prove helpful.

    c. the chance to develop a fresh perspective on oneself and the world.

    d. all of these answers.

36. Family therapy differs from other forms of psychotherapy because it focuses on

    a. using a variety of treatment techniques.

    b. conscious rather than unconscious processes.

    c. the present instead of the past.

    d. how family tensions may cause individual problems.

37. The idea that mind and body are inseparable is the basis for

    a. client-centered therapy.

    b. evidence-based decision making.

    c. therapeutic life-style change.

    d. resilience.

Matching Items 1

Match each term with the appropriate definition or description.

Terms

_____ **1.** cognitive therapy
_____ **2.** behavior therapy
_____ **3.** systematic desensitization
_____ **4.** cognitive-behavioral therapy
_____ **5.** client-centered therapy
_____ **6.** exposure therapy
_____ **7.** aversive conditioning
_____ **8.** psychoanalysis
_____ **9.** preventive mental health
_____ **10.** biomedical therapy
_____ **11.** counterconditioning

Definitions or Descriptions

    a. associates unwanted behavior with unpleasant experiences

    b. associates a relaxed state with anxiety-arousing stimuli

    c. emphasizes the social context of psychological disorders

    d. integrated therapy that focuses on changing self-defeating thinking and unwanted behavior

    e. category of therapies that teach people more adaptive ways of thinking and acting

    f. a widely used method of behavior therapy

    g. therapy developed by Carl Rogers

    h. therapy based on Freud's theory of personality

    i. treatment with psychosurgery, electroconvulsive therapy, or drugs

    j. classical conditioning procedure in which new responses are conditioned to stimuli that trigger unwanted behaviors

    k. category of therapies based on learning principles

Matching Items 2

Match each term with the appropriate definition or description.

Terms

_____ **1.** active listening
_____ **2.** token economy
_____ **3.** placebo effect
_____ **4.** lobotomy
_____ **5.** lithium
_____ **6.** double-blind technique
_____ **7.** Xanax
_____ **8.** free association
_____ **9.** therapeutic life-style change
_____ **10.** resilience

Definitions or Descriptions

    a. type of psychosurgery

    b. mood-stabilizing drug

    c. empathic technique used in client-centered therapy

    d. ability to cope with stress

    e. antianxiety drug

    f. technique of psychoanalytic therapy

    g. an operant conditioning procedure

    h. experimental procedure in which both the patient and staff are unaware of a patient's treatment condition

    i. intervention focusing on regular exercise, sleep, social interaction, and healthy patterns of thinking

    j. the beneficial effect of a person's expecting that treatment will be effective

Application Essay

Willie has been diagnosed as suffering from major depressive disorder. Describe the treatment he might receive from a psychoanalyst, a cognitive therapist, and a biomedical therapist. (Use the space below to list points you want to make, and organize them. Then write the essay on a separate sheet of paper.)

TERMS AND CONCEPTS

Using your own words, on a separate piece of paper write a brief definition or explanation of each of the following terms.

1. psychotherapy
2. biomedical therapy
3. eclectic approach
4. psychoanalysis
5. resistance
6. interpretation
7. transference
8. psychodynamic therapy
9. client-centered therapy
10. active listening
11. unconditional positive regard
12. behavior therapy
13. counterconditioning
14. exposure therapies
15. systematic desensitization
16. virtual reality exposure therapy
17. aversive conditioning
18. token economy
19. cognitive therapy
20. cognitive-behavioral therapy
21. family therapy
22. antipsychotic drugs
23. antianxiety drugs
24. antidepressant drugs
25. electroconvulsive therapy (ECT)
26. repetitive transcranial magnetic stimulation (rTMS)
27. psychosurgery
28. lobotomy
29. resilience

SUMMING UP

BEHAVIOR THERAPY

Trish, who lives in Canada, is so afraid of flying that she can never visit her closest friend, who lives 3000 miles away. Because this fear interferes with her life,

it is considered a
_____ ,

and so

Trish seeks a therapist trained in
_____ ,

which

uses _____ conditioning to pair new responses with the stimuli that trigger her fear.

The therapy shown to be most effective in treating Trish's problem is

a technique called systematic
_____ ,

which is

a type of _____ therapy that pairs
_____

with

gradually increasing _____-triggering stimuli (going to the airport, going to the gate, getting on the plane, learning about flight procedures, actually taking a flight).

Because of her limited time, Trish decides to try another route to curing her problem.

She decides that vivid simulation through
_____ _____

_____ therapy would work just as well

because

within the confines of a room, she can experience her

fears through _____ sensors that adjust the scene as she turns her head.

COGNITIVE THERAPY

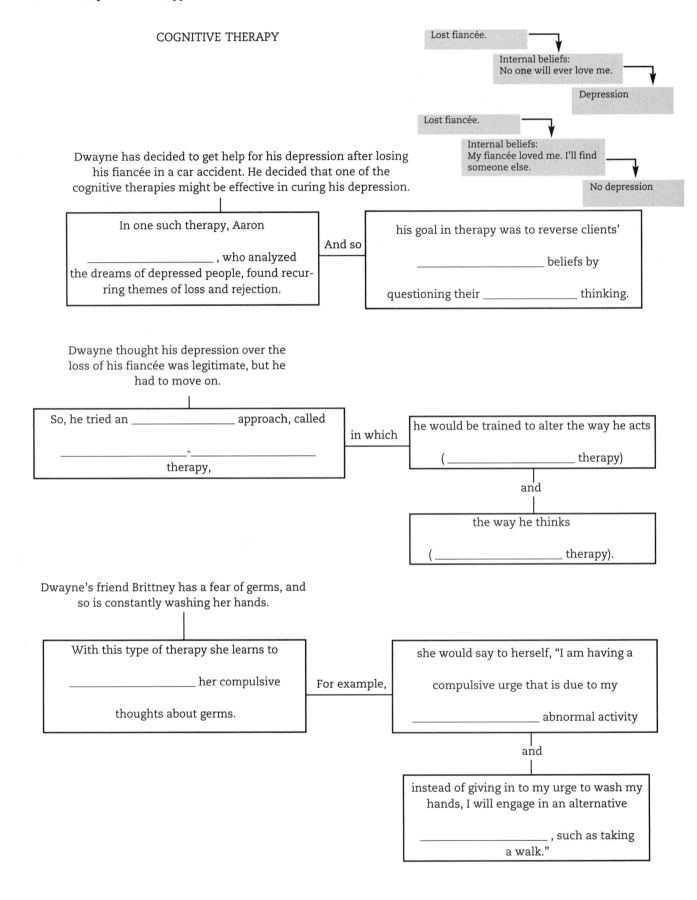

Lost fiancée.

Internal beliefs:
No one will ever love me.

Depression

Lost fiancée.

Internal beliefs:
My fiancée loved me. I'll find someone else.

No depression

Dwayne has decided to get help for his depression after losing his fiancée in a car accident. He decided that one of the cognitive therapies might be effective in curing his depression.

In one such therapy, Aaron _____ , who analyzed the dreams of depressed people, found recurring themes of loss and rejection.

And so

his goal in therapy was to reverse clients' _____ beliefs by questioning their _____ thinking.

Dwayne thought his depression over the loss of his fiancée was legitimate, but he had to move on.

So, he tried an _____ approach, called _____-_____ therapy,

in which

he would be trained to alter the way he acts (_____ therapy)

and

the way he thinks (_____ therapy).

Dwayne's friend Brittney has a fear of germs, and so is constantly washing her hands.

With this type of therapy she learns to _____ her compulsive thoughts about germs.

For example,

she would say to herself, "I am having a compulsive urge that is due to my _____ abnormal activity

and

instead of giving in to my urge to wash my hands, I will engage in an alternative _____ , such as taking a walk."

ANSWERS

Chapter Review

Treating Psychological Disorders

1. psychological; biomedical
2. psychotherapy; learning
3. prescribed medications
4. eclectic

The Psychological Therapies

1. insight
2. repressed
3. repressed; conscious
4. free association
5. resistance; interpretation
6. transference
7. disprove; expensive
8. psychodynamic; themes; relationships
9. insight; current relationships
10. self-fulfillment

Unlike psychoanalysis, humanistic therapy is focused on the present and future instead of the past, on conscious rather than unconscious processes, on promoting growth and fulfillment instead of curing illness, and on helping clients take immediate responsibility for their feelings and actions rather than on uncovering the obstacles to doing so.

11. client-centered; nondirective; does not interpret
12. genuineness; acceptance; empathy
13. active listening
14. unconditional positive regard
15. summarize; invite clarification; reflect feelings
16. learning

Psychoanalysis and humanistic therapies assume that problems diminish as self-awareness grows. Behavior therapists doubt that self-awareness is the key. Instead of looking for the inner cause of unwanted behavior, behavior therapy applies learning principles to directly attack the unwanted behavior itself.

17. classical conditioning
18. counterconditioning; exposure therapy; aversive conditioning
19. systematic desensitization; Joseph Wolpe; anxious
20. progressive relaxation; relaxed; anxiety
21. virtual reality exposure
22. negative; positive; unpleasant
23. behavior modification
24. operant; token economy
25. **a.** Virtual reality exposure therapy, a type of counterconditioning (classical conditioning).
    b. Token economy, based on operant conditioning principles.

c. Systematic desensitization, an exposure therapy, which is a form of counterconditioning.

Specific procedures may vary. Refer to the text for general descriptions.

26. cognitive
27. negative; depression; Aaron Beck
28. dispute
29. cognitive-behavioral
30. humanistic. According to Rogers' client-centered therapy, the therapist must exhibit genuineness, acceptance, and empathy if the client is to move toward self-fulfillment.
31. aversive conditioning. Aversive conditioning is the classical conditioning technique in which a positive response is replaced by a negative response. (In this example, the US is the nausea-producing drug, the CS is the taste of the sweets, and the intended CR is aversion to sweets.)
32. psychoanalysis and psychodynamic therapy. Both psychoanalysis and psychodynamic therapy seek insight into a patient's unconscious feelings. The analysis of dreams, slips of the tongue, and resistances are considered a window into these feelings.
33. **c.** is the answer. Cognitive therapists attempt to change a person's way of thinking about themselves. Cognitive-behavioral therapists also try to change the behaviors that result from that thinking.
34. systematic desensitization. This type of exposure therapy assumes that you cannot be simultaneously relaxed and anxious. Whenever Duane begins to feel anxious, the therapist moves him back to a less anxiety-triggering stimulus and focuses on relaxation.
35. **b.** is the answer. The token economy is an application of operant conditioning principles. Rewarding desired behavior gets the person to repeat that behavior.
36. cognitive. Because the psychologist is focusing on Darnel's irrational thinking, this response is most typical of Beck's cognitive therapy for depression.
37. behavior. Behavior therapists believe that the problem behavior is the problem. They do not try to uncover unconscious, repressed impulses.

Group therapy saves therapists time and clients money. The social context of group therapy allows people to discover that others have similar problems and to try out new ways of behaving.

38. family therapy
39. communication
40. Humanistic therapies focus on the present and future, conscious thoughts, and having the person take responsibility for his or her feelings and actions. The goal is self-fulfillment. The therapist is genuine, accepting, and empathic and uses active listening in this nondirective therapy.

Behavior therapies focus on the problem behavior. The goal is to change undesirable behaviors to desirable behaviors. They use techniques based on classical and operant conditioning principles—for example, exposure therapies, aversive conditioning, and token economies.

Cognitive therapies focus on the person's way of thinking about himself or herself. Self-blaming and overgeneralized explanations of bad events cause the problem. The goal is to change the person's negative thinking. They use gentle questioning to reveal the patient's irrational thinking and persuade a depressed person, for example, to adopt a more positive attitude.

Group and family therapies assume that problems arise from social interactions. They help people to see that others have similar problems and that communication can resolve most problems. During sessions, for example, they try to guide family members toward positive relationships and improved communication.

Evaluating Psychotherapies

1. is not
2. satisfaction

People often enter therapy in crisis. When the crisis passes, they may attribute their improvement to the therapy. Clients, who may need to believe the therapy was worth the effort, may overestimate its effectiveness. Clients generally find positive things to say about their therapists, even if their problems remain.

3. overestimate
4. unhappiness; well-being
5. controlled
6. Hans Eysenck; was not
7. somewhat effective; 80
8. no clear; does not matter; does not make a difference
9. behavioral conditioning; cognitive
10. is no
11. evidence-based decision making
12. d. is the answer. Behavioral conditioning therapies work best with specific problems, and cognitive therapy is effective in treating depression. But no one therapy is consistently superior.
13. hope; perspective; caring; trusting; empathic
14. therapeutic alliance
15. are
16. less than; clear-cut
17. do; different
18. individualism
19. minority

The Biomedical Therapies

1. drug; decreased
2. placebo; recovery; double-blind
3. antipsychotic; positive; clozapine (Clozaril)
4. dopamine
5. tardive dyskinesia; face; tongue; limbs
6. antianxiety; central nervous system
7. psychological therapy
8. symptoms; problems; psychological dependence
9. antidepressant; norepinephrine; serotonin
10. fluoxetine (Prozac); serotonin; selective-serotonin-reuptake-inhibitor
11. aerobic exercise; bottom up; cognitive-behavioral; top down
12. spontaneous recovery; placebo effect
13. depakote; manic
14. lithium
15. psychiatrist. Only a psychiatrist is a medical doctor who can prescribe drugs.
16. double-blind. To control for the influences of the placebo effect and normal recovery rates, researchers give half the patients the drug and half a similar-appearing placebo. The double-blind technique prevents the researchers' biases from affecting the results.
17. antipsychotic. These drugs are used in treating severe disorders such as schizophrenia.
18. antidepressant. SSRI drugs increase the availability of the neurotransmitters norepinephrine and serotonin, which increase more positive moods.
19. lithium. This simple salt seems to act as a mood stabilizer in people with bipolar disorder.
20. electroconvulsive; ECT
21. depression; confirms; unknown
22. implant; vagus; deep stimulation
23. repetitive transcranial magnetic stimulation (rTMS); seizures; memory; frontal lobe
24. psychosurgery
25. lobotomy; frontal
26. drugs
27. biological; body; mind
28. therapeutic life-style; aerobic exercise, adequate sleep, light exposure, social connection, anti-rumination, and nutritional supplements
29. aerobic exercise; sleep

Preventing Psychological Disorders

1. resilience; Most
2. empathy; responsibility; caring; post-traumatic growth
3. person
4. a disturbing and stressful society
5. person; social context
6. competence; personal control; self-esteem; poverty; meaningless; criticism; unemployment; racism; sexism
7. community psychologists
8. integrated biopsychosocial

Progress Test

Multiple-Choice Questions

1. **b.** is the answer. Although no one is sure how ECT works, one possible explanation is that it increases release of norepinephrine, the neurotransmitter that elevates mood.

2. **c.** is the answer.
   a. Active listening is a Rogerian technique in which the therapist echoes, restates, and clarifies the client's statements.
   b. Spontaneous recovery refers to improvement without treatment.
   d. Systematic desensitization is a process in which a person is conditioned to associate a relaxed state with anxiety-triggering stimuli.

3. **b.** is the answer.

4. **d.** is the answer. This is not among the criticisms commonly made of psychoanalysis. (It would more likely be made of behavior therapies.)

5. **d.** is the answer.
   a., b., & c. Each of these is a type of psychological therapy.

6. **c.** is the answer. Outcome research on the relative effectiveness of different therapies reveals no clear winner; the other factors mentioned are advantages of group therapies.

7. **c.** is the answer.
   a. The fact that its effects are irreversible makes psychosurgery a drastic procedure, and with advances in psychopharmacology, psychosurgery was largely abandoned.
   b. ECT is still widely used as a treatment of severe depression, but in general it is not used as frequently as drug therapy.
   d. Counterconditioning is not a biomedical therapy.

8. **b.** is the answer. Clients' testimonials regarding psychotherapy are generally very positive. The research, in contrast, seems to show that therapy is only *somewhat* effective.

9. **c.** is the answer.

10. **d.** is the answer.

11. **a.** is the answer. By occupying receptor sites for dopamine, these drugs block its activity and reduce its production.

12. **d.** is the answer.

13. **d.** is the answer. Today, half of all psychotherapists describe themselves as eclectic—as using a blend of therapies.
    a. An eclectic therapist may use a nondirective approach with certain behaviors; however, a more directive approach might be chosen for other clients and problems.
    b. In fact, just the opposite is true. Eclectic therapists generally view disorders as stemming from many influences.
    c. Eclectic therapists, in contrast to this example, use a combination of treatments.

14. **a.** is the answer.

15. **c.** is the answer. Although aversive conditioning may work in the short run, the person's ability to discriminate between the situation in which the aversive conditioning occurs and other situations can limit the treatment's effectiveness.
    a., b., & d. These were not offered in the text as limitations of the effectiveness of aversive conditioning.

16. **b.** is the answer.
    a. This reflects a cognitive perspective.
    c. This reflects a psychoanalytic perspective.

17. **c.** is the answer.
    a. & b. Counterconditioning is the replacement of an undesired response with a desired one by means of aversive conditioning or systematic desensitization.
    d. Exposure therapy exposes a person, in imagination or in actuality, to a feared situation.

18. **d.** is the answer.

19. **b.** is the answer.
    a. Spontaneous recovery refers to improvement without any treatment.
    c. Transference is the psychoanalytic phenomenon in which a client transfers feelings from other relationships onto his or her analyst.
    d. Interpretation is the psychoanalytic procedure through which the analyst helps the client become aware of resistances and understand their meaning.

20. **c.** is the answer.

21. **c.** is the answer.
    a. This answer would be a correct description of Joseph Wolpe.
    b. There is no such thing as insight therapy.
    d. This answer would be a correct description of Aaron Beck.

22. **a.** is the answer.
    b. In systematic desensitization, a hierarchy of anxiety-provoking stimuli is gradually associated with a relaxed state.
    c. Transference refers to a patient's transferring of feelings from other relationships onto his or her psychoanalyst.
    d. Electroconvulsive therapy is a biomedical shock treatment.

23. **c.** is the answer.
    a. Behavior therapy focuses on behavior, not self-awareness.
    b. Psychoanalysis focuses on bringing repressed feelings into awareness.
    d. Biomedical therapy focuses on physical treatment through drugs, ECT, or psychosurgery.

24. **a.** is the answer. For behavior therapy, the problem behaviors *are* the problems.
    b. Cognitive therapy teaches people to think and act in more adaptive ways.
    c. Humanistic therapy promotes growth and self-fulfillment by providing an empathic, genuine, and accepting environment.
    d. Psychoanalytic therapy focuses on uncovering and interpreting repressed feelings.

25. **b.** is the answer. Counterconditioning techniques involve taking an established stimulus, which

triggers an undesirable response, and pairing it with a new stimulus in order to condition a new, and more adaptive, response.

a. As indicated by the name, counterconditioning techniques are a form of conditioning; they do not involve learning by observation.

c. & d. The principles of operant conditioning are the basis of behavior modification, which, in contrast to counterconditioning techniques, involves use of reinforcement.

26. **d.** is the answer.

a. This is a confrontational therapy, which is aimed at teaching people to think and act in more adaptive ways.

b. Aversive conditioning is a form of counterconditioning in which unwanted behavior is associated with unpleasant feelings.

c. Counterconditioning is a general term, including not only systematic desensitization, in which a hierarchy of fears is desensitized, but also other techniques, such as aversive conditioning.

27. **d.** is the answer.

a. & b. These techniques are based on classical conditioning.

c. Aversive conditioning is a form of counterconditioning in which unwanted behavior is associated with unpleasant feelings.

28. **c.** is the answer.

a. rTMS is a gentler method of brain stimulation for treating people who are depressed.

b. In this humanistic therapy, the therapist facilitates the client's growth by offering a genuine, accepting, and empathic environment.

d. Behavior therapy concentrates on modifying the actual symptoms of psychological problems.

29. **c.** is the answer.

30. **a.** is the answer.

31. **d.** is the answer. Lithium works as a mood stabilizer.

a. & c. Ativan and Xanax are antianxiety drugs.

b. Chlorpromazine is an antipsychotic drug.

32. **a.** is the answer.

33. **c.** is the answer.

a. Behavior modification is most likely to be successful in treating specific behavior problems, such as bed wetting.

b. & d. The text does not single out particular disorders for which these therapies tend to be most effective.

34. **d.** is the answer.

35. **d.** is the answer.

36. **d.** is the answer.

a. This is true of most forms of psychotherapy.

b. & c. This is true of humanistic, cognitive, and behavior therapies.

37. **c.** is the answer. Therapeutic life-style change involves treating both mind and body through aerobic exercise, plentiful sleep, and nutritional supplements, for example.

a. Client-centered therapy is Rogers' nondirective form of therapy.

b. Evidence-based decision making is suggested by science-oriented clinicians as the most appropriate way of selecting acceptable therapies.

d. Resilience is the ability to cope with stress.

Matching Items 1

1. e	**5.** g	**9.** c
2. k	**6.** f	**10.** i
3. b	**7.** a	**11.** j
4. d	**8.** h	

Matching Items 2

1. c	**5.** b	**9.** i
2. g	**6.** h	**10.** d
3. j	**7.** e	
4. a	**8.** f	

Application Essay

Psychoanalysts assume that psychological problems such as depression are caused by unresolved, repressed, and unconscious impulses and conflicts from childhood. A psychoanalyst would probably attempt to bring these repressed feelings into Willie's conscious awareness and help him gain insight into them. He or she would likely try to interpret Willie's resistance during free association, the latent content of his dreams, and any emotional feelings he might transfer to the analyst.

Cognitive therapists assume that a person's emotional reactions are influenced by the person's thoughts in response to the event in question. A cognitive therapist would probably try to teach Willie new and more constructive ways of thinking in order to reverse his negative beliefs about himself, his situation, and his future.

Biomedical therapists attempt to treat disorders by altering the functioning of the patient's brain. A biomedical therapist would probably prescribe an antidepressant drug such as fluoxetine to increase the availability of norepinephrine and serotonin in Willie's nervous system. If Willie's depression is especially severe, a psychiatrist might treat it with several sessions of electroconvulsive therapy.

Summing Up

Behavior Therapy

Trish, who lives in Canada, is so afraid of flying that she can never visit her closest friend, who lives 3000 miles away. Because this fear interfers with her life, it is considered a *phobia*, and so Trish seeks a therapist trained in *counterconditioning*, which uses *classical* conditioning to pair new responses with the stimuli that trigger her fear. The therapy shown to be most effective in treating Trish's problem is a technique called systematic *desensitization*, which is a type of *exposure* therapy that pairs *relaxation* with gradually increasing *anxiety*-triggering stimuli (going to the airport, going to the gate, getting on the plane, learning about flight procedures, actually taking a flight). Because of her limited time, Trish decides to try another route to curing her problem. She decides that vivid simulation through *virtual reality exposure* therapy would work just as well because within the confines of a room, she can experience her fears through *motion* sensors that adjust the scene as she turns her head.

Cognitive Therapy

Dwayne has decided to get help for his depression after losing his fiancée in a car accident. He decided that one of the cognitive therapies might be effective in curing his depression. In one such therapy, Aaron *Beck,* who analyzed the dreams of depressed people, found recurring themes of loss and rejection. And so his goal in therapy was to reverse clients' *catastrophizing* beliefs by questioning their *irrational* thinking. Dwayne thought his depression over the loss of his fiancée was legitimate, but he had to move on. So, he tried an *integrated* approach, called *cognitive-behavioral* therapy, in which he would be trained to alter the way he acts (*behavior* therapy) and the way he thinks (*cognitive* therapy).

Dwayne's friend Brittney has a fear of germs, and so is constantly washing her hands. With this type of therapy, she learns to *relabel* her compulsive thoughts about germs. For example, she would say to herself, "I am having a compulsve urge that is due to my *brain's* abnormal activity and instead of giving in to my urge to wash my hands, I will engage in an alternative *behavior,* such as taking a walk."

Terms and Concepts

1. **Psychotherapy** is an interaction between a trained therapist and someone who suffers from psychological difficulties or wants to achieve personal growth.

2. **Biomedical therapy** is the use of prescribed medications or medical procedures that act on a patient's nervous system to treat psychological disorders.

3. With an **eclectic approach,** therapists are not locked into one form of psychotherapy, but draw on whatever combination seems best suited to a client's needs.

4. **Psychoanalysis,** the therapy developed by Sigmund Freud, attempts to give clients self-insight by bringing into awareness and interpreting previously repressed feelings.

   Example: The tools of the **psychoanalyst** include free association, the analysis of dreams and transferences, and the interpretation of repressed impulses.

5. **Resistance** is the psychoanalytic term for the blocking from consciousness of anxiety-laden memories. Hesitation during free association may reflect resistance.

6. **Interpretation** is the psychoanalytic term for the analyst's helping the client to understand resistances and other aspects of behavior, so that the client may gain deeper insights.

7. **Transference** is the psychoanalytic term for a patient's redirecting to the analyst emotions from other relationships.

8. **Psychodynamic therapy** is a Freud-influenced approach that sees behavior, thinking, and emotions in terms of unconscious motives but focuses on a patient's current symptoms and relationships.

9. **Client-centered therapy** is a humanistic nondirective therapy developed by Carl Rogers, in which growth and self-awareness are facilitated in an environment that offers genuineness, acceptance, and empathy.

10. **Active listening** is a nondirective technique of Rogers' client-centered therapy, in which the listener echoes, restates, and clarifies, but does not interpret, clients' remarks.

11. **Unconditional positive regard** is an accepting, nonjudgmental attitude toward others, which Carl Rogers believed promoted self-acceptance and self-awareness.

12. **Behavior therapy** is therapy that applies learning principles to the elimination of unwanted behaviors.

13. **Counterconditioning** is a category of behavior therapy in which new responses are classically conditioned to stimuli that trigger unwanted behaviors.

14. **Exposure therapies** treat anxiety by exposing people to things they normally fear and avoid. Among these therapies are systematic desensitization and virtual reality exposure therapy.

15. **Systematic desensitization** is a type of exposure therapy in which a state of relaxation is classically conditioned to a hierarchy of gradually increasing anxiety-provoking stimuli.

    Memory aid: This is a form of **counterconditioning** in which sensitive, anxiety-triggering stimuli are **desensitized** in a progressive, or **systematic,** fashion.

16. **Virtual reality exposure therapy** progressively exposes people to electronic simulations of feared situations to treat their anxiety.

17. **Aversive conditioning** is a form of counterconditioning in which an unpleasant state becomes associated with an unwanted behavior.

18. A **token economy** is an operant conditioning procedure in which desirable behaviors are promoted in people by rewarding them with tokens, or positive reinforcers, which can be exchanged for privileges or treats. For the most part, token economies are used in hospitals, schools, and other institutional settings.

19. **Cognitive therapy** focuses on teaching people new and more adaptive ways of thinking and acting. The therapy is based on the idea that our feelings and responses to events are strongly influenced by our thinking, or cognition.

20. **Cognitive-behavioral therapy** is an integrated therapy that focuses on changing self-defeating thinking (cognitive therapy) and unwanted behaviors (behavior therapy).

21. **Family therapy** views problem behavior as partially engendered by the client's family system and environment. Therapy therefore focuses on relationships and problems among the various members of the family.

22. **Antipsychotic drugs,** such as chlorpromazine, are used to treat schizophrenia and other severe thought disorders.

23. **Antianxiety drugs,** such as Xanax, help control anxiety and agitation by reducing central nervous system activity.

24. **Antidepressant drugs,** such as Prozac, treat depression and some anxiety disorders by altering the availability of various neurotransmitters.

25. In **electroconvulsive therapy (ECT)**, a biomedical therapy often used to treat severe depression, electric shock is passed through the brain.

26. **Repetitive transcranial magnetic stimulation (rTMS)** is the delivery of repeated pulses of magnetic energy to stimulate or suppress brain activity.

27. **Psychosurgery** is a biomedical therapy that attempts to change behavior by removing or destroying brain tissue. Since drug therapy became widely available in the 1950s, psychosurgery has been infrequently used.

28. Once used to control violent patients, the **lobotomy** is a form of psychosurgery in which the nerves linking the emotion centers of the brain to the frontal lobes are severed.

29. **Resilience** is the personal strength that helps people cope with stress and recover from traumatic events.

14

SOCIAL PSYCHOLOGY

Chapter 14 demonstrates the powerful influences of social situations on the behavior of individuals. The social principles that emerge help us understand how individuals are influenced by advertising, political candidates, and the various groups to which they belong. Although social influences are powerful, we need to remember the significant role of individuals in choosing and creating the social situations that influence them.

The chapter also discusses how people relate to one another, from the negative—developing prejudice and behaving aggressively—to the positive—being attracted to people who are nearby and/or similar and behaving altruistically. The chapter concludes with a discussion of situations that provoke conflict and techniques that have been shown to promote conflict resolution.

CHAPTER REVIEW

First, skim each text section, noting headings and bold-face items. Review the section by reading the objectives and summaries provided here, then answer the questions that follow. In some cases, STUDY TIPS explain how best to learn a difficult concept and APPLICATIONS help you to know how well you understand the material. Check your understanding of the material by consulting the answers beginning on page 275. Do not continue with the next section until you understand each answer. If you need to, review or reread the section in the textbook before continuing.

Introduction and Social Thinking

Objective 1: Identify the three main focuses of social psychology, and explain how the fundamental attribution error can affect our analyses of behavior.

Social psychology scientifically studies how (1) we *think about*, (2) *influence*, and (3) *relate to* one another.

We may explain people's behavior in terms of internal traits or in terms of the external situation. For example, a teacher may explain a child's hostility in terms of an aggressive personality or as a reaction to stress or abuse. The *fundamental attribution error*—our tendency to underestimate situational influences and to overestimate the influence of personal traits—can lead us to unwarranted conclusions about other people's behavior. For example, we may blame the poor and the unemployed for their own misfortune.

1. Psychologists who study how we think about, influence, and relate to one another are called

   _____ _____ .

2. Most people tend to_____
   (overestimate/underestimate) the extent to which people's actions are influenced by social situations and _____ (overestimate/underestimate) the influence of personality. This tendency is called the _____

   _____ _____ .

   When explaining our own behavior, or that of someone we know well, this tendency is _____ (stronger/weaker).

Give an example of the practical consequences of attributions.

STUDY TIP: To drive home the concept of the fundamental attribution error, think about a recent embarrassing moment. Perhaps you made an unkind remark that you later regretted. In explaining your behavior, you likely would say, "I was caught up in the moment," or "It was the people I was with." These are *external* (situational) attributions. Now think about how you would explain the same type of behavior in another person, especially someone you have just met. If you committed the fundamental attribution error, you would be less likely to "forgive" the person by making an external attribution. Instead, you would attribute it to personality and expect the person to behave similarly in the future.

APPLICATION:

3. Professor Vargas' students did very poorly on the last exam. The tendency to make the fundamental attribution error might lead her to conclude that the class did poorly because
   a. the test was unfair.
   b. students didn't have enough time to complete the test.
   c. students were distracted by some social function on campus.
   d. students were unmotivated.

Objective 2: Define *attitude*, and explain how attitudes and actions affect each other.

Attitudes are feelings, often based on our beliefs, that predispose us to respond in a particular way to objects, people, and events. For example, we may *feel* dislike for a person because we *believe* he or she is mean, and, as a result, *act* unfriendly toward that person.

Attitudes have a strong impact on actions when (1) outside influences on what we say and do are minimal; (2) the attitude is stable, specific to the behavior; and (3) the attitude is easily recalled. Attitudes also follow behavior. For example, the *foot-in-the-door phenomenon* is the tendency for people who have first agreed to a small request to comply later with a larger request. Because doing becomes believing, a trivial act makes the next act easier. Similarly, the behaviors associated with a new *role* may at first feel phony. However, play-acting soon becomes real as we adopt attitudes in keeping with our roles. *Cognitive dissonance theory,* proposed by Leon Festinger, argues that we feel discomfort when two of our thoughts (cognitions) clash. For example, when our actions conflict with our feelings and beliefs, we reduce the discomfort by bringing our attitudes more in line with our actions.

4. Feelings, often based on our beliefs, that predispose our responses are called _____ .

List three conditions under which our attitudes do predict our actions. Give examples.

5. Many research studies demonstrate that our attitudes are strongly influenced by our _____ . One example of this is the tendency for people who agree to a small request to comply later with a larger one. This is the _____-_____-_____ _____-_____ phenomenon.

6. When you follow society's expectations for how you should act as, say, a student, you are adopting a _____ .

7. Taking on a set of behaviors, or acting in a certain way, generally _____ (changes/does not change) people's attitudes.

8. According to _____ _____ theory, thoughts and feelings change because people are motivated to justify actions that would otherwise not match their attitudes. This theory was proposed by _____ .

9. Dissonance theory predicts that people made to feel responsible for behavior that clashes with their attitudes will be motivated to reduce the resulting _____ by changing their _____ .

STUDY TIP/APPLICATION: Cognitive dissonance theory and the foot-in-the-door phenomenon are two powerful exam-

ples of our attitudes following our actions. Think about these examples as you complete the following exercises.

10. **a.** Using the foot-in-the-door technique, how might you persuade a friend to take on an important, time-consuming task such as becoming treasurer of a ski club?

b. Suppose your roommate thinks climate change is nothing more than a hoax foisted by politicians on a gullible public. Using cognitive dissonance theory, how might you go about changing your roommate's attitude?

APPLICATIONS:

11. Which of the following is an example of the foot-in-the-door phenomenon?

a. To persuade a customer to buy a product a store owner offers a small gift.

b. After agreeing to wear a small "Enforce Recycling" lapel pin, a woman agrees to collect signatures on a petition to make recycling required by law.

c. After offering to sell a car at a ridiculously low price, a car salesperson is forced to tell the customer the car will cost $1000 more.

d. All of these are examples.

12. Which of the following situations should produce the GREATEST cognitive dissonance?

a. A soldier is forced to carry out orders he finds disagreeable.

b. A student who loves animals has to dissect a cat in order to pass biology.

c. As part of an experiment, a participant is directed to deliver electric shocks to another person.

d. A student volunteers to debate an issue, taking the side he personally disagrees with.

Social Influence

Objective 3: Describe what experiments on conformity and obedience reveal about the power of social influence.

We all have a natural tendency to mimic others, called the *chameleon effect.* Unconsciously mimicking others' expressions, postures, and voice tones helps us to *empathize* with others. Research participants in an experiment tend to rub their own face when confederates rub their face; similarly, the participants shake their own foot when they are with a foot-shaking person. The most empathic people mimic and are liked the most.

Conformity is adjusting our behavior or thinking toward some group standard. Solomon Asch found that under certain conditions, people will conform to a group's judgment, even when it is clearly incorrect. Experiments indicate that conformity increases when we feel incompetent or insecure, admire the group's status and attractiveness, have made no prior commitment to a response, are being observed by other group members, come from a culture that encourages respect for social standards, and are in a group with at least three people who agree in their judgment.

In the Milgram studies, the experimenter ordered "teachers" to deliver shocks to a "learner" for wrong answers. Torn between obeying the experimenter and responding to the learner's pleas, the people usually chose to obey orders, even though it supposedly meant harming the learner.  Obedience was highest when the person giving the orders was close at hand and was perceived to be a legitimate authority; when the authority figure was supported by a respected, well-known institution; when the victim was depersonalized or at a distance; and when there were no role models for defiance.

1. The chameleon effect refers to our natural tendency to unconsciously _____ others' expressions, postures, and voice tones. This helps us to feel what they are feeling, referred to as _____ .

2. The term that refers to the tendency to adjust one's behavior to coincide with an assumed group standard is _____ .

3. The psychologist who first studied the effects of group pressure on conformity is _____ .

4. In this study, when the opinion of other group members was contradicted by objective evidence, research participants _____ (were/were not) willing to conform to the group opinion.

List some of the conditions under which people are more likely to conform.

5. The classic social psychology studies of obedience were conducted by _____ .
   When ordered by the experimenter to electrically shock the "learner," the majority of participants (the "teachers") in these studies _____ (complied/refused). More recent studies have found that women's compliance rates in similar situations were _____ (higher than/lower than/similar to) men's.

List the conditions under which obedience was highest in Milgram's studies.

APPLICATIONS:

6. José is the one student member on the board of trustees. At the board's first meeting, José wants to disagree with the others on several issues but in each case decides to say nothing. Studies on conformity suggest all except one of the following are factors in José's not speaking up. Which one is not a factor?
   a. The board is a large group.
   b. The board is respected and most of its members are well known.
   c. The board members are already aware that José and the student body disagree with them on these issues.
   d. Because this is the first meeting José has attended, he feels insecure and not fully competent.

7. Twenty-year-old Marge belonged to a sorority. During pledge week, she was ordered to force potential members to strip in front of their friends. Although Marge disapproved of asking fellow students to embarrass themselves, she did it anyway. She respected the sorority officers, and all her fellow sisters were also hazing the pledges. How would Milgram explain Marge's behavior?

Objective 4: Explain what social influence studies teach us about ourselves and about the power of the individual.

The Asch and Milgram experiments demonstrate that social influences can be strong enough to make people conform to falsehoods or give in to cruelty. The studies, because of their design, also illustrate how great evil sometimes grows out of people's acceptance of lesser evils. Evil does not require devilish villains but ordinary people corrupted by an evil situation.

In studying the power of the individual, social psychologists have learned that *social control* and *personal control* interact. A minority that consistently holds to its position can sway the majority. This is especially true if the minority's self-confidence stimulates others to consider why the minority reacts as it does. Even when a minority's influence is not yet visible, it may be convincing members of the majority to rethink their views.

8. In getting people to administer increasingly larger shocks, Milgram was in effect applying the

   _____-_____

   _____-_____

   technique.

9. The Asch and Milgram studies demonstrate that strong _____ influences can make _____ people _____ to falsehoods and _____ orders to commit cruel acts.

10. In considering the power of social influence, we cannot overlook the interaction of

    _____ _____

    (the power of the situation) and

    _____ _____

    (the power of the individual).

11. The power of one or two individuals to sway the opinion of the majority is called

    _____ _____ .

12. A minority opinion will have the most success in swaying the majority if it takes a stance that is _____ (unswerving/flexible).

Objective 5: Describe conditions in which the presence of others is likely to result in social facilitation, social loafing, or deindividuation.

Experiments on **social facilitation** reveal that the presence of observers can arouse individuals, strengthening the most likely response and so boosting their performance on easy or well-learned tasks but hindering it on difficult or newly learned ones. When people pool their efforts toward a group goal, **social loafing** may occur as individuals free-ride on others' efforts. When a group experience arouses people and makes them anonymous, they become less self-aware and self-restrained, a psychological state known as **deindividuation.**

13. The tendency to perform a task better when other people are present is called _____ _____ . In general, people become aroused in the presence of others, and

arousal enhances the correct response on a(n) _____ (easy/difficult) task. Later research revealed that arousal strengthens the response that is most _____ in a given situation.

14. Researchers have found that the reactions of people in crowded situations are often _____ (lessened/amplified).

15. Researchers found that people worked _____ (harder/less hard) in a team tug-of-war than they had in an individual contest. This phenomenon has been called

    _____ _____ .

16. The feeling of anonymity and loss of self-restraint that an individual may develop when in a group is called _____ .

••
STUDY TIP: To help solidify the idea of social facilitation in your mind, think about sports you play—or don't play (because you do not do well). Think about your friends in similar situations, your children if you are a parent. Then think about professional athletes. Does the same hold true for the performing arts (acting, playing a musical instrument, dancing)? What about your everyday activities?
••

Objective 6: Discuss how group interaction can facilitate group polarization and groupthink.

Within groups, discussions among like-minded members often produce **group polarization,** a strengthening of the group's preexisting attitudes. Group polarization can have beneficial results, as when low-prejudice students become even more accepting while discussing racial issues. But it can also have dire consequences, as it can strengthen a terrorist mentality. Sometimes, group interaction distorts important decisions. In **groupthink,** the desire for harmony overrides a realistic appraisal of alternatives.

17. Over time, the initial differences between groups usually _____ (increase/decrease).

18. The strengthening of each group's preexisting attitudes over time is called _____ _____ . A current source for the development of this tendency is the _____ .

19. When the desire for group harmony overrides realistic thinking in individuals, the phenomenon known as _____ has occurred.

••
STUDY TIP: Have you ever served in a leadership role in a group of people? Perhaps you have been a club president, or other officer, who had to lead group discussions. Based on

the information in this section, how might a group leader in such a situation promote groupthink? What steps could a leader take to discourage groupthink from developing?

•••

APPLICATIONS:

20. Which of the following would MOST likely be subject to social facilitation?
    a. proofreading a page for spelling errors
    b. typing a letter with accuracy
    c. playing a difficult piece on a musical instrument
    d. running quickly around a track

21. Concluding her presentation on deindividuation, Renée notes that deindividuation is less likely in situations that make a person feel aroused and _____ .

22. Jane and Sandy were best friends as freshmen. Jane joined a sorority; Sandy didn't. By the end of their senior year, they found that they had less in common with each other than with the other members of their respective circles of friends. Their change in feelings is most likely due to _____ _____ .

Social Relations

Objective 7: Identify the three parts of prejudice, and describe how prejudice has changed over time.

Prejudice is a mixture of *beliefs* (often overgeneralized and called *stereotypes*), *emotions* (hostility, envy, or fear), and predispositions to *action* (to discriminate). Prejudice is a negative attitude; *discrimination* is a negative behavior.

As overt prejudice has waned since the 1930s, *subtle* prejudice lingers. Modern studies indicate that, with our two-track mind, prejudice is often on the track that is out of sight. In other words, prejudice is often implicit, an automatic attitude that does not involve thought.

1. Prejudice is an _____ and usually _____ attitude toward a group that involves overgeneralized beliefs known as _____ .

2. Like all attitudes, prejudice is a mixture of _____ , _____ , and predispositions to _____ .

3. Prejudice is a negative _____ , and _____ is a negative _____ .

4. Americans today express _____ (less/the same/more) racial and gender prejudice than they did 50 years ago.

5. As overt prejudice _____ (increases/decreases/remains), subtle prejudice _____ (increases/decreases/remains).

6. (Close-Up) Even people who deny holding prejudiced attitudes may carry negative _____ . Studies of prejudice indicate that it is often an unconscious, or _____ , action.

7. (Close-Up) Our perceptions are influenced by our _____ . In one study, people (Blacks and Whites) perceived Blacks to be the most threatening.

8. (Close-Up) Neuroscientists have detected implicit prejudice in people's _____ muscles and in their brain's _____ .

Objective 8: Discuss the factors that contribute to the social roots of prejudice, and explain how scapegoating illustrates the emotional component of prejudice.

Prejudice often arises as those who enjoy social and economic superiority attempt to justify the status quo by the *just-world phenomenon,* the idea that good is rewarded and evil is punished. Through our *social identities* we also associate ourselves with some groups and contrast ourselves with others. Mentally drawing a circle that defines "us" (the *ingroup*) also excludes "them" (the *outgroup*). Such group identifications promote an *ingroup bias,* that is, a favoring of one's own group. Even creating an "us-them" distinction by the toss of a coin leads people to show ingroup bias.

Facing the fear of death tends to heighten patriotism and produce anger and aggression toward those who threaten one's world. *Scapegoat theory* suggests that prejudice offers an outlet for anger by providing someone to blame.

9. For those with money, power, and prestige, prejudice often serves as a means of _____ social inequalities.

10. The view that good is rewarded and evil is punished is called the _____-_____ _____ .

11. Through our _____ _____ , we associate ourselves with certain groups.

12. Prejudice is also fostered by the _____ _____ , a tendency to favor the group to which one belongs—called the _____—while excluding others, or the _____ .

13. The terror of facing death tends to produces anger and _____ toward people who threaten our _____ .

14. That prejudice derives from attempts to blame others for one's frustration is proposed by the _____ theory.

15. People who feel loved and supported become more _____ to and _____ of those who differ from them.

Objective 9: Describe how cognitive processes help create and maintain prejudice.

One way we simplify the world is to *form categories*. In categorizing others we often stereotype them, overestimating the similarity of those within another group. We also estimate the frequency of events by *vivid cases* (violence, for example) that come to mind more readily than the less vivid events involving the same group. Third, we can believe the *world is just* and that people get what they deserve and deserve what they get (as noted earlier, the just-world phenomenon).

16. Prejudice may also result from our attempts to simplify our world by classifying people into groups, that is, by _____ them. One by-product of this process is that people tend to _____ the similarity of those within a group.

17. Another factor that feeds prejudice is the tendency to _____ the frequency of events because of vivid or memorable cases.

18. The belief that people get what they deserve—the _____ -_____ phenomenon—is a third factor.

APPLICATIONS:

19. Students at State University are convinced that their school is better than any other; this most directly illustrates an _____ _____ .

20. Alexis believes that all male athletes are self-centered and sexist. Her beliefs are an example of _____ .

21. Ever since their cabin lost the camp softball competition, the campers have become increasingly hostile toward one camper in their cabin, blaming her for every problem in the cabin. This behavior is best explained by _____ _____ .

22. Given the tendency of people to categorize information according to preformed schemas, which of the following stereotypes would Juan, a 65-year-old political liberal and fitness enthusiast, be most likely to have?
   a. "People who exercise regularly are very extraverted."
   b. "All political liberals are advocates of a reduced defense budget."
   c. "Young people today have no sense of responsibility."
   d. "Older people are lazy."

Objective 10: Describe various biological influences on aggression.

In psychology, *aggression* is any physical or verbal behavior intended to hurt or destroy. Psychology's definition recognizes a verbally assaultive person or one who spreads a vicious rumor as aggressive.

Biological influences on aggression operate at the genetic, neural, and biochemical levels. Animals have been bred for aggressiveness, and twin studies suggest that genes also influence human aggression. Animal and human brains have neural systems that, when stimulated, either inhibit or produce aggression. For example, studies of violent criminals have revealed diminished activity in the frontal lobes, which play an important role in controlling impulses. Finally, studies of the effect of hormones (e.g., testosterone) and alcohol in the blood show that biochemical influences contribute to aggression.

23. Aggressive behavior is defined by psychologists as _____ .

24. Like other behaviors, aggression emerges from the interaction of _____ and _____ .

25. Today, most psychologists _____ (do/do not) consider human aggression to be instinctive.

26. In humans, aggressiveness _____ (varies/does not vary) greatly from culture to culture, era to era, and person to person.

27. That there are genetic influences on aggression can be shown by the fact that many species of animals have been _____ for aggressiveness. Twin studies suggest that genes _____ (do/do not) influence human aggression.

28. Implanting an electrode in the brain's _____ of a mild-mannered woman's brain caused her to behave aggressively. Studies of violent criminals reveal diminished activity in the brain's _____ _____ , which play an important role in controlling _____ .

29. In humans and animals, aggression is facilitated by _____ systems, which are in turn influenced by _____ in the blood.

30. The aggressive behavior of animals can be manipulated by altering the levels of the hormone _____ . When this level is _____ (increased/decreased), aggressive tendencies are reduced.

31. One drug that unleashes aggressive responses to provocation is _____ .

Objective 11: Outline psychological triggers of aggression, noting the relationship between viewing multimedia violence and aggressive behavior.

A variety of aversive events, including being miserable and rejection, evoke aggression. The *frustration-aggression principle* states that the blocking of an attempt to reach some goal creates anger, which can generate aggression. Aggression also can be triggered in those who have been rewarded for aggression in the past. People can learn aggression by observing models who act aggressively, for example, in the family or in the media (watching violence or sexual aggression on TV or in film). Media depictions of violence also trigger aggression by providing *social scripts* (mental tapes for how to act provided by our culture). One *aggression-replacement program* has been successful in bringing down rearrest rates of juvenile offenders and gang members. To summarize, aggressive behavior has biological, psychological, and social influences.

Playing violent video games can heighten aggressive behavior by providing social scripts and opportunities to observe modeled aggression. Recent studies have found that playing violent video games primes aggressive thoughts, decreases empathy, and increases aggression. The studies also reject the idea that we feel better if we vent our emotions. The same is true for viewing depictions of sexual violence—"it increases punitive behavior toward women."

32. The idea that the inability to achieve a goal leads to anger, which may generate aggression, is the

_____-_____

principle.

33. Research has shown that people led to feel socially excluded, or _____ , are more likely to put down those who insult them.

34. Aggressive behavior can be learned through _____ , as shown by the fact that people use aggression where they've found it pays, and through _____ of others.

35. Programs that teach juvenile offenders and their parents new ways to control anger, called

_____-_____

programs, have been successful in bringing down re-arrest rates of juvenile offenders.

36. Crime rates are higher in countries in which there is a large disparity between those who are _____ and those who are _____ . In the United States, high violence rates also are typical of cultures and families in which there is minimal

_____ _____ .

37. (Thinking Critically) Kids who play a lot of violent video games see the world as more _____ , get into more _____ and _____ , and get worse _____ .

38. (Thinking Critically) Research studies of the impact of violent video games _____ (confirm/do not confirm) the idea that we feel better if we "blow off steam" by venting our emotions. Instead, playing violent video games _____ (increases/decreases) aggressive thoughts, emotions, and behaviors.

39. On-screen violence tends to _____ people to cruelty and _____ them to respond aggressively when they are provoked.

40. Repeatedly viewing violence also teaches

_____ _____

to which people respond when they are in new situations or are uncertain how to act.

Describe how repeated viewing of X-rated films affects people's attitudes and behavior.

Summarize the findings of the study in which undergraduates either did or did not view sexually explicit films for six weeks.

41. Experiments have shown that it is not the sexual content but depictions by the media of

_____ _____

that most directly affect men's acceptance and performance of aggression against women.

42. Many factors contribute to aggression, including _____ factors, such as an increase in testosterone; _____ factors, such as frustration; and _____ factors, such as media violence.

APPLICATIONS:

43. Summarizing his report on the biology of aggression, Sam notes that
   a. biology does not significantly influence aggression.
   b. when one identical twin has a violent temperament, the other member of the twin pair rarely does.
   c. hormones and alcohol influence the neural systems that control aggression.
   d. testosterone reduces dominance behaviors in animals.

44. After waiting in line for an hour to buy concert tickets, Teresa is told that the concert is sold out. In her anger she pounds her fist on the ticket counter, frightening the clerk. Teresa's behavior is best explained by the

_____ - _____

_____ .

Objective 12: Describe the influence of proximity, physical attractiveness, and similarity on interpersonal attraction.

Three factors are known to influence our liking for one another. Geographical *proximity* is conducive to attraction, partly because of the *mere exposure effect*: Repeated exposure to novel stimuli enhances liking of them. *Physical attractiveness* influences social opportunities and the way one is perceived. We view attractive people as healthier, happier, more sensitive, more successful, and more socially skilled. However, attractiveness is unrelated to self-esteem and happiness. As we move toward friendship, *similarity* of attitudes, beliefs, and interests greatly increases liking. The factors that foster attraction are explained by *reward theory*: We like those whose behavior is rewarding to us, and we will continue relationships that offer more rewards than costs.

45. A prerequisite for, and perhaps the most powerful predictor of, attraction is _____ .

46. When people are repeatedly exposed to unfamiliar stimuli, their liking of the stimuli _____ (increases/decreases).

This phenomenon is the _____ _____ effect.

It had _____ value for our ancestors, for whom the unfamiliar was often dangerous. One implication of this is that _____ against those who are culturally different may be a primitive, _____ , emotional response.

47. Our first impression of another person is most influenced by the person's _____ .

48. In a sentence, list several of the characteristics that physically attractive people are judged to possess:

_____ .

49. A person's attractiveness _____ (is/is not) related to his or her self-esteem or happiness.

50. Cross-cultural research reveals that men judge women as more attractive if they have a _____ appearance. Women judge men who appear _____ , _____ , and _____ as more attractive.

51. Compared with strangers, friends and couples are more likely to be similar in _____

_____

_____ .

Explain what a reward theory of attraction is and how it can account for the three predictors of liking—proximity, attractiveness, and similarity.

Objective 13: Describe the effect of physical arousal on passionate love, and identify two predictors of enduring companionate love.

We can view *passionate love* as an aroused state of intense positive absorption in another. The strong affection of *companionate love*, which often emerges as a relationship matures, is enhanced by *equity*, a condition in which both parties receive in proportion to what they give. Another vital ingredient of loving relationships is mutual *self-disclosure*, in which partners reveal to each other intimate details about themselves.

52. An aroused state of intense positive absorption in another is called _____ love.

53. According to the two-factor theory, emotions have two components: physical _____ plus thoughtful _____ .

54. When college men were placed in an aroused state, their feelings toward an attractive woman _____ (were/were not) more positive than those of men who had not been aroused.

55. As love matures, it becomes _____ love. This type of love is promoted by _____—mutual sharing and giving by both partners. Another key ingredient of loving relationships is the revealing of intimate aspects of ourselves through _____ .

APPLICATION:

56. Ahmed and Monique are on a blind date. Which of the following will probably be most influential in determining whether they like each other?
    a. their personalities
    b. their beliefs
    c. their social skills
    d. their physical attractiveness

57. Opening her mail, Joan discovers a romantic greeting card from her boyfriend. According to the two-factor theory, she is likely to feel the most intense romantic feelings if, prior to reading the card, she has just
    a. completed her daily run.
    b. finished reading a chapter in her psychology textbook.
    c. awakened from a nap.
    d. finished eating lunch.

58. Having read the chapter, which of the following is best borne out by research on attraction?
    a. Birds of a feather flock together.
    b. Opposites attract.
    c. Familiarity breeds contempt.
    d. Absence makes the heart grow fonder.

Objective 14: Define *altruism,* and describe the steps in the decision-making process involved in bystander intervention.

Altruism is unselfish concern for the welfare of others. Risking one's life to save people in trouble with no expectation of personal reward is an example of altruism.

The *bystander effect* is the tendency for any given bystander to an emergency to be less likely to give aid if other bystanders are present. Research on the bystander effects indicates that to decide to help we must (1) notice the event, (2) interpret it as an emergency, or (3) assume responsibility for helping. We are most likely to help if the person appears to need and deserve help, the person is similar to us, and we are not in a hurry, for example.

59. An unselfish concern for the welfare of others is called _____ .

60. According to Darley and Latané, people will help only if a three-stage decision-making process is completed: Bystanders must first _____ the incident, then _____ it as an emergency, and finally assume _____ for helping.

61. When people who overheard a seizure victim calling for help thought others were hearing the same plea, they were _____ (more/less) likely to go to his aid than when they thought no one else was aware of the emergency.

62. In a series of staged accidents, Latané and Darley found that a bystander was _____ (more/less) likely to help if other bystanders were present. This phenomenon has been called the _____ _____ .

Identify the circumstances in which a person is most likely to offer help during an emergency.

....

STUDY TIP: As with other concepts, altruism is best understood by relating it to your own experiences. Can you think of instances of altruism in your home town? At school? Have you personally stopped to help a person who seemed to be in need—for example, an older woman struggling to carry groceries to her car? What are some other examples of truly altruistic behavior?

....

Objective 15: Identify the social processes that fuel conflict, and discuss effective ways of encouraging peaceful cooperation and reducing that conflict.

A *conflict* is a perceived incompatibility of actions, goals, or ideas. The spiral of conflict also feeds and is fed by distorted *mirror-image perceptions,* in which each party views itself as moral and the other as unworthy and evil-intentioned.

Research suggests that noncompetitive contact between parties of equal status may help reduce prejudice. More important, the discovery of *superordinate,* or shared, *goals* that require cooperation can turn enemies into friends.

63. A perceived incompatibility of actions, goals, or ideas is called _____ . This perception can take place between individuals, _____ , or _____ .

64. The distorted images people in conflict form of each other are called _____-_____ perceptions.

65. In most situations, establishing contact between two conflicting groups _____ (is/is not) sufficient to resolve conflict.

66. In Mozafer Sherif's study, two conflicting groups of campers were able to resolve their conflicts by working together on projects in which they shared _____ goals. Shared _____ breed solidarity, as demonstrated by a surge in use of the word _____ in the weeks after 9/11.

APPLICATIONS:

67. Mr. and Mrs. Samuels are constantly fighting, and each perceives the other as hard-headed and insensitive. Their conflict is being fueled by _____-_____ _____ .

68. Which of the following strategies would be most likely to foster positive feelings between two conflicting groups?
    a. Take steps to reduce the likelihood of mirror-image perceptions.
    b. Separate the groups so that tensions diminish.
    c. Increase the amount of contact between the two conflicting groups.
    d. Have the groups work on a superordinate goal.

PROGRESS TEST

Multiple-Choice Questions

Circle your answers to the following questions and check them with the answers beginning on page 277. If your answer is incorrect, read the explanation for why it is incorrect and then consult the text.

1. In his study of obedience, Stanley Milgram found that the majority of subjects
   a. refused to shock the learner even once.
   b. complied with the experiment until the "learner" first indicated pain.
   c. complied with the experiment until the "learner" began screaming in agony.
   d. complied with all the demands of the experiment.

2. According to cognitive dissonance theory, dissonance is most likely to occur when
   a. a person's behavior is not based on strongly held attitudes.
   b. two people have conflicting attitudes and find themselves in disagreement.
   c. an individual does something that is personally disagreeable.
   d. an individual is coerced into doing something that he or she does not want to do.

3. Which of the following statements is true?
   a. Groups are almost never swayed by minority opinions.
   b. Group polarization is most likely to occur when group members frequently disagree with one another.
   c. Groupthink provides the consensus needed for effective decision making.
   d. A group that is like-minded will probably not change its opinions through discussion.

4. Conformity increased under which of the following conditions in Asch's studies of conformity?
   a. The group had three or more people.
   b. The group had high status.
   c. Individuals were made to feel insecure.
   d. All of these situations increased conformity.

5. Violent criminals often have diminished activity in the _____ of the brain, which play(s) an important role in _____ .
   a. occipital lobes; aggression
   b. hypothalamus; hostility
   c. frontal lobes; controlling impulses
   d. temporal lobes; patience

6. The phenomenon in which individuals lose their identity and relinquish normal restraints when they are part of a group is called
   a. groupthink.   c. empathy.
   b. cognitive dissonance.   d. deindividuation.

7. Participants in Asch's line-judgment experiment gave the same answers as the rest of the group, even when they knew the answers were wrong. This behavior is referred to as
   a. social facilitation.
   b. overjustification.
   c. scapegoating.
   d. conformity.

8. Based on findings from Milgram's obedience studies, participants would be *less* likely to follow the experimenter's orders when
   a. they hear the "learner" cry out in pain.
   b. they merely administer the test while someone else delivers the shocks.
   c. the "learner" is an older person or mentions having some physical problem.
   d. they see another subject disobey instructions.

9. *Aggression* is defined as behavior that
   a. hurts another person.
   b. is intended to hurt another person.
   c. is hostile, passionate, and produces physical injury.
   d. has all of these characteristics.

10. Which of the following is true about aggression?
    a. It varies too much to be instinctive in humans.
    b. It is just one instinct among many.
    c. It is instinctive but shaped by learning.
    d. It is the most important human instinct.

11. Research studies have found a positive correlation between aggressive tendencies in animals and levels of the hormone
    a. estrogen.
    b. adrenaline.
    c. noradrenaline.
    d. testosterone.

12. Research studies have indicated that the tendency of viewers to see the world as more sexual, devalue their partners, and trivialize rape is
    a. increased by exposure to pornography.
    b. not changed after exposure to pornography.
    c. decreased in men by exposure to pornography.
    d. decreased in both men and women by exposure to pornography.

13. Increasing the number of people that are present during an emergency tends to
    a. increase the likelihood that people will cooperate in rendering assistance.
    b. decrease the empathy that people feel for the victim.
    c. increase the role that social norms governing helping will play.
    d. decrease the likelihood that anyone will help.

14. Which of the following was NOT mentioned in the text discussion of the roots of prejudice?
    a. people's tendency to overestimate the similarity of people within groups
    b. people's tendency to assume that exceptional, or especially memorable, individuals are unlike the majority of members of a group
    c. people's tendency to assume that the world is just and that people get what they deserve
    d. people's tendency to discriminate against those they view as "outsiders"

15. The mere exposure effect demonstrates that
    a. familiarity breeds contempt.
    b. opposites attract.
    c. birds of a feather flock together.
    d. familiarity breeds fondness.

16. In one experiment, college men were physically aroused and then introduced to an attractive woman. Compared with men who had not been aroused, these men
    a. reported more positive feelings toward the woman.
    b. reported more negative feelings toward the woman.
    c. were ambiguous about their feelings toward the woman.
    d. were more likely to feel that the woman was "out of their league" in terms of attractiveness.

17. The deep affection that is felt in long-lasting relationships is called _____ love; this feeling is fostered in relationships in which _____ .
    a. passionate; there is equity between the partners
    b. passionate; traditional roles are maintained
    c. companionate; there is equity between the partners
    d. companionate; traditional roles are maintained

18. Which of the following is associated with an increased tendency on the part of a bystander to offer help in an emergency situation?
    a. being in a good mood
    b. having recently needed help and not received it
    c. observing someone as he or she refuses to offer help
    d. being a female

19. The belief that those who suffer deserve their fate is expressed in the
    a. just-world phenomenon.
    b. phenomenon of ingroup bias.
    c. fundamental attribution error.
    d. mirror-image perception principle.

20. Which of the following phenomena is best explained by cognitive dissonance theory?
    a. group polarization
    b. the foot-in-the-door phenomenon
    c. ingroup bias
    d. scapegoating

21. (Close-Up) Which of the following is an example of implicit prejudice?
    a. Jake, who is White, gives higher evaluations to essays he believes to be written by Blacks than to White-authored essays.
    b. Carol believes that White people are arrogant.
    c. Brad earns more than Jane, despite having the same job skills, performance level, and seniority.
    d. In certain countries, women are not allowed to drive.

22. We tend to perceive the members of an ingroup as _____ and the members of an outgroup as _____ .
    a. similar to one another; different from one another
    b. different from one another; similar to one another
    c. above average in ability; below average in ability
    d. below average in ability; above average in ability

23. Regarding the influence of alcohol and testosterone on aggressive behavior, which of the following is true?
    a. Drinking alcohol increases aggressive behavior; injections of testosterone reduce aggressive behavior.
    b. Drinking alcohol reduces aggressive behavior; injections of testosterone increase aggressive behavior.
    c. Drinking alcohol and injections of testosterone both promote aggressive behavior.
    d. Drinking alcohol and injections of testosterone both reduce aggressive behavior.

24. Most people prefer mirror-image photographs of their faces. This is best explained by
    a. the principle of equity.
    b. the principle of self-disclosure.
    c. the mere exposure effect.
    d. mirror-image perceptions.

25. Research studies have shown that frequent exposure to sexually explicit films
    a. makes a woman's friendliness seem more sexual.
    b. diminishes the attitude that rape is a serious crime.
    c. may lead individuals to devalue their partners.
    d. may produce all of these effects.

26. Research studies indicate that in an emergency situation, the presence of others often
    a. prevents people from even noticing the situation.
    b. prevents people from interpreting an unusual event as an emergency.
    c. prevents people from assuming responsibility for assisting.
    d. leads to all of these situations.

27. Two neighboring nations are each stockpiling weapons. Each sees its neighbor's actions as an act of aggression and its own actions as self-defense. Evidently, these nations are victims of
    a. prejudice.
    b. groupthink.
    c. group polarization.
    d. the fundamental attribution error.

28. Which of the following factors is the MOST powerful predictor of friendship?
    a. similarity in age
    b. common racial and religious background
    c. similarity in physical attractiveness
    d. physical proximity

29. Most researchers agree that
    a. media violence is a factor in aggression.
    b. media violence and aggressiveness are negatively correlated.
    c. frequently watching X-rated films ultimately diminishes an individual's aggressive tendencies.

    d. media violence is too unreal to promote aggression in viewers.

30. When male students in an experiment were told that a woman to whom they would be speaking had been instructed to act in a friendly or unfriendly way, most of them subsequently attributed her behavior to
    a. the situation.
    b. the situation *and* her personal traits.
    c. her personal traits.
    d. their own skill or lack of skill in a social situation.

31. Which of the following is true?
    a. Attitudes and actions rarely correspond.
    b. Attitudes predict behavior about half the time.
    c. Attitudes are excellent predictors of behavior.
    d. Attitudes predict behavior under certain conditions.

32. People with power and status may become prejudiced because
    a. they tend to justify the social inequalities between themselves and others.
    b. those with less status and power tend to resent them.
    c. those with less status and power appear less capable.
    d. they feel proud and are boastful of their achievements.

33. Which of the following most accurately states the effects of crowding on behavior?
    a. Crowding makes people irritable.
    b. Crowding sometimes intensifies people's reactions.
    c. Crowding promotes altruistic behavior.
    d. Crowding usually weakens the intensity of people's reactions.

34. Research has found that for a minority to succeed in swaying a majority, the minority must
    a. make up a sizable portion of the group.
    b. express its position as consistently as possible.
    c. express its position in the most extreme terms possible.
    d. be able to convince a key majority leader.

35. Which of the following conclusions did Milgram reach as a result of his studies of obedience?
    a. Even ordinary people, without any particular hostility, can become agents in a destructive process.
    b. Most people are able, under the proper circumstances, to suppress their natural aggressiveness.
    c. The need to be accepted by others is a powerful motivating force.
    d. He reached all of these conclusions.

36. Which of the following is important in promoting conformity in individuals?

  a. whether an individual's behavior will be observed by others in the group
  b. whether the individual is male or female
  c. the size of the room in which a group is meeting
  d. whether the individual is of a higher status than other group members

37. Which of the following is MOST likely to promote groupthink?

  a. The group's leader fails to take a firm stance on an issue.
  b. A minority faction holds to its position.
  c. The group consults with various experts.
  d. Group polarization is evident.

Matching Items

Match each term with the appropriate definition or description.

Terms

_____ **1.** social facilitation
_____ **2.** social loafing
_____ **3.** bystander effect
_____ **4.** conformity
_____ **5.** ingroup bias
_____ **6.** group polarization
_____ **7.** stereotype
_____ **8.** altruism
_____ **9.** mere exposure effect

Definitions or Descriptions

  a. a generalized belief about a group of people
  b. people work less hard in a group
  c. performance is improved by an audience
  d. the tendency to favor one's own group
  e. adjusting one's behavior to coincide with a group standard
  f. group discussion enhances prevailing tendencies
  g. unselfish concern for others
  h. the tendency that a person is less likely to help someone in need when others are present
  i. the increased liking of a stimulus that results from repeated exposure to it

Application Essay

The Panhellenic Council on your campus has asked you to make a presentation on the topic "Social Psychology" to all freshmen who have signed up to "rush" a fraternity or sorority. In a fit of cynicism following your rejection last year by a popular fraternity or sorority, you decide to speak on the negative influences of groups on the behavior of individuals. What will you discuss? (Use the space below to list the points you want to make, and organize them. Then write the essay on a separate sheet of paper.)

TERMS AND CONCEPTS

Using your own words, on a separate piece of paper write a brief definition or explanation of each of the following terms.

 1. social psychology
 2. fundamental attribution error
 3. attitude
 4. foot-in-the-door phenomenon
 5. role
 6. cognitive dissonance theory
 7. conformity
 8. social facilitation
 9. social loafing
 10. deindividuation
 11. group polarization
 12. groupthink
 13. prejudice
 14. stereotype
 15. discrimination
 16. just-world phenomenon
 17. ingroup

18. outgroup
19. ingroup bias
20. scapegoat theory
21. other-race effect
22. aggression
23. frustration-aggression principle
24. social script
25. mere exposure effect
26. passionate love

27. companionate love
28. equity
29. self-disclosure
30. altruism
31. bystander effect
32. conflict
33. mirror-image perceptions
34. superordinate goals

SUMMING UP

A person who is the victim of an unjustifiable (usually negative) attitude is being subjected to _____ ,

which is a mixture of

usually overgeneralized beliefs called _____ ,

negative _____ (envy, hostility, or fear), and

unjustifiable negative behavior called _____ .

Where do these attitudes come from? Several possibilities exist.

Social roots include

believing that the good are rewarded and the bad are punished, called the _____ - _____ phenomenon;

favoring our own group, called the _____ - _____ ; and thinking of other groups as _____ .

Emotional roots include

looking for someone to blame when things go wrong, called _____ .

Cognitive roots include

simplifying the world by sorting things into _____ ,

judging the frequency of events by remembering _____ cases, and

believing that people get what they deserve, that is, that the world is _____ .

ANSWERS

Chapter Review

Introduction and *Social Thinking*

1. social psychologists
2. underestimate; overestimate; fundamental attribution error; weaker

Our attributions—to individuals' dispositions or to situations—have important practical consequences. A hurtful remark from an acquaintance, for example, is more likely to be forgiven if it is attributed to a temporary situation than to a mean disposition.

3. **d.** is the answer. The fundamental attribution error refers to the tendency to underestimate situational influences in favor of this type of personal attribution when explaining the behavior of other people.
4. attitudes

Attitudes predict actions when other influences on the attitudes and actions are minimized; when the attitude is stable, specific to the behavior, and easily recalled. Thus, our attitudes are more likely to predict behavior when we are not attempting to adjust our behavior to please others, when we are in familiar situations in which we don't have to stop and think about our attitudes, and when the attitude pertains to a specific behavior, such as purchasing a product or casting a vote.

5. actions or behavior; foot-in-the-door
6. role
7. changes
8. cognitive dissonance; Leon Festinger
9. dissonance; attitudes
10. No single answer is correct. A possible answer for a. is to ask the friend to check some figures from the monthly expenses. For b., you might get your roommate to debate the issue and have him or her argue that climate change is a major concern.
11. **b.** is the answer. In the foot-in-the-door phenomenon, compliance with a small initial request, such as wearing a lapel pin, later is followed by compliance with a much larger request, such as collecting petition signatures.
12. **d.** is the answer. In this situation, the student has volunteered to argue against his opinion, and so the behavior cannot be attributed to the demands of the situation.

Social Influence

1. mimic; empathy
2. conformity
3. Solomon Asch
4. were

People are most likely to conform when they are made to feel incompetent or insecure, they are in a group with at least three people, they are in a group in which everyone else agrees, they admire the group's status and attractiveness, they have not already committed to any response, they know that others in the group are observing them, and they are from a culture that encourages respect for social standards.

5. Stanley Milgram; complied; similar to

Obedience was highest when the person giving the orders was close at hand and perceived to be a legitimate authority figure; the authority figure was supported by a respected, well-known institution; the victim was depersonalized or at a distance; and there were no role models for defiance.

6. **c.** is the answer. Prior commitment to an opposing view generally tends to work against conformity. In contrast, large group size, respect for the group, and an individual's feelings of incompetence and insecurity all strengthen the tendency to conform.
7. Milgram would say that Marge's behavior was a product of the situation, not her personal traits. She respected the officers of the sorority and everyone else was participating in the hazing.
8. foot-in-the-door
9. social; ordinary; conform; obey
10. social control; personal control
11. minority influence
12. unswerving
13. social facilitation; easy; likely
14. amplified
15. less hard; social loafing
16. deindividuation
17. increase
18. group polarization; Internet
19. groupthink
20. **d.** is the answer. Social facilitation, or better performance in the presence of others, occurs for easy tasks but not for more difficult ones. For tasks such as proofreading, typing, or playing an instrument, the arousal resulting from the presence of others can lead to mistakes.
21. anonymous. Deindividuation refers to the loss of self-restraint and self-awareness that sometimes occurs in group situations where people are aroused and feel anonymous.
22. group polarization. Group polarization means that the tendencies within a group—and therefore the differences among groups—grow stronger over time. Thus, because the differences between the sorority and nonsorority students have increased, Jane and Sandy are likely to have little in common.

Social Relations

1. unjustifiable; negative; stereotypes
2. beliefs; emotions; action
3. attitude; discrimination; behavior
4. less
5. decreases; remains

6. associations; implicit
7. expectations
8. facial; amygdala
9. justifying
10. just-world phenomenon
11. social identities
12. ingroup bias; ingroup; outgroup
13. aggression; world
14. scapegoat
15. open; accepting
16. categorizing; overestimate
17. overestimate
18. just-world
19. ingroup bias. In viewing students from other schools as the outgroup, State University students have formed an ingroup and are exhibiting the ingroup bias by favoring their own group.
20. stereotyping. This is an often overgeneralized belief about a group of people, which describes Alexis' view of male athletes.
21. scapegoat theory. According to the scapegoat theory, when things go wrong, people look for someone on whom to take out their frustration and anger.
22. c. is the answer. People tend to overestimate the similarity of people within groups other than their own. Thus, Juan is not likely to form stereotypes of fitness enthusiasts (a.), political liberals (b.), or older adults (c.), which are groups to which he belongs.
23. any physical or verbal behavior intended to hurt or destroy
24. biology; experience
25. do not
26. varies
27. bred; do
28. amygdala; frontal lobes; impulses
29. neural; hormones
30. testosterone; decreased
31. alcohol
32. frustration-aggression
33. rejected
34. rewards; observation (or imitation)
35. aggression-replacement
36. rich; poor; father care
37. hostile; arguments; fights; grades
38. do not confirm; increases
39. desensitize; prime
40. social scripts

Repeatedly watching X-rated films makes one's partner seem less attractive, makes extramarital sex seem less troubling, makes a woman's friendliness seem more sexual, and makes sexual aggression seem less serious.

The research study found that after viewing sexually explicit films for several weeks, undergraduates were more likely to recommend a lighter prison sentence for a convicted rapist than were those who viewed nonerotic films.

41. sexual violence
42. biological; psychological; social
43. c. is the answer. Just the opposite is true of a., b., and d.
44. frustration-aggression principle. According to this principle, the blocking of an attempt to achieve some goal—in Teresa's case, buying concert tickets—creates anger and can generate aggression.
45. proximity
46. increases; mere exposure; survival; prejudice; automatic
47. appearance
48. Attractive people are perceived as healthier, happier, more sensitive, more successful, and more socially skilled.
49. is not
50. youthful; mature; dominant; affluent
51. attitudes, beliefs, interests, religion, race, education, intelligence, smoking behavior, economic status, age

A reward theory of attraction says that we are attracted to, and continue relationships with, those people whose behavior provides us with more benefits than costs. Proximity makes it easy to enjoy the benefits of friendship at little cost, attractiveness is pleasing, and similarity is reinforcing to us.

52. passionate
53. arousal; appraisal
54. were
55. companionate; equity; self-disclosure
56. d. is the answer. Hundreds of experiments indicate that first impressions are most influenced by physical appearance.
57. a. is the answer. According to the two-factor theory, physical arousal can intensify whatever emotion is currently felt. Only in the situation described in a. is Joan likely to be physically aroused.
58. a. is the answer. Friends and couples are much more likely than randomly paired people to be similar in views, interests, and a range of other factors.
59. altruism
60. notice; interpret; responsibility
61. less
62. less; bystander effect

People are most likely to help someone when they have just observed someone else being helpful, when they are not in a hurry, when the victim appears to need and deserve help, when they are in some way similar to the victim, when in a small town or rural area, when feeling guilty, when not preoccupied, and when in a good mood.

63. conflict; groups; nations
64. mirror-image
65. is not
66. superordinate; predicaments; "we"

67. mirror-image perceptions. The couple's similar, and presumably distorted, feelings toward each other fuel their conflict.

68. **d.** is the answer. Sherif found that hostility between two groups could be eliminated by giving the groups superordinate, or shared, goals.

Progress Test

Multiple-Choice Questions

1. **d.** is the answer. In Milgram's initial experiments, 63 percent of the subjects fully complied with the experiment.

2. **c.** is the answer. Cognitive dissonance is the tension we feel when we are aware of a discrepancy between our thoughts and actions, as would occur when we do something we find distasteful.
   a. Dissonance requires strongly held attitudes, which must be perceived as not fitting behavior.
   b. Dissonance is a personal cognitive process.
   d. In such a situation the person is less likely to experience dissonance, since the action can be attributed to "having no choice."

3. **d.** is the answer. In such groups, discussion usually strengthens prevailing opinion; this phenomenon is known as group polarization.
   a. Minority opinions, especially if consistently and firmly stated, can sway the majority in a group.
   b. Group polarization, or the strengthening of a group's prevailing tendencies, is most likely in groups where members agree.
   c. When groupthink occurs, there is so much consensus that decision making becomes less effective.

4. **d.** is the answer.

5. **c.** is the answer.

6. **d.** is the answer.
   a. Groupthink refers to the mode of thinking that occurs when the desire for group harmony overrides realistic and critical thinking.
   b. Cognitive dissonance refers to the discomfort we feel when two thoughts (which include the knowledge of our *behavior*) are inconsistent.
   c. Empathy is feeling what another person feels.

7. **d.** is the answer. People are most likely to conform when they are unsure of themselves, are in a group of three or more, and have no models for defiance.
   a. Social facilitation involves performing tasks better or faster in the presence of others.
   b. Overjustification occurs when a person is rewarded for doing something that is already enjoyable.
   c. Scapegoating is finding someone to blame as an outlet for your anger when things go wrong.

8. **d.** is the answer. Role models for defiance reduce levels of obedience.
   a. & c. These did not result in diminished obedience.
   b. This "depersonalization" of the victim resulted in increased obedience.

9. **b.** is the answer. Aggression is any behavior, physi-

cal or verbal, that is intended to hurt or destroy.
   a. A person may accidentally be hurt in a nonaggressive incident; aggression does not necessarily prove hurtful.
   c. Verbal behavior, which does not result in physical injury, may also be aggressive. Moreover, acts of aggression may be cool and calculated, rather than hostile and passionate.

10. **a.** is the answer. The very wide variations in aggressiveness from culture to culture indicate that aggression cannot be considered an unlearned instinct.

11. **d.** is the answer.

12. **a.** is the answer.

13. **d.** is the answer. This phenomenon is known as the bystander effect.
   a. This answer is incorrect because individuals are less likely to render assistance at all if others are present.
   b. Although people are less likely to assume responsibility for helping, this does not mean that they are less empathic.
   c. This answer is incorrect because norms tend to encourage helping others, yet people are less likely to help with others around.

14. **b.** is the answer. In fact, people tend to overestimate the frequency of an event based on vivid cases, rather than assume that such cases are unusual.
   a., c., & d. Each of these is an example of a cognitive (a. & c.) or a social (d.) root of prejudice.

15. **d.** is the answer. Being repeatedly exposed to novel stimuli increases our liking for them.
   a. For the most part, the opposite is true.
   b. & c. The mere exposure effect concerns our tendency to develop likings on the basis, not of similarities or differences, but simply of familiarity, or repeated exposure.

16. **a.** is the answer. This result supports the two-factor theory of emotion and passionate attraction, according to which arousal from any source can facilitate an emotion, depending on how we label the arousal.

17. **c.** is the answer. Deep affection is typical of companionate love, rather than passionate love, and is promoted by equity. Traditional roles may be characterized by the dominance of one sex.

18. **a.** is the answer.
   b. & c. These factors would most likely decrease a person's altruistic tendencies.
   d. There is no evidence that one sex is more altruistic than the other.

19. **a.** is the answer.
   b. Ingroup bias is the tendency of people to favor their own group.
   c. The fundamental attribution error is the tendency of people to underestimate situational influences when observing the behavior of other people.

d. The mirror-image perception principle is the tendency of conflicting parties to form similar, diabolical images of each other.

20. **b.** is the answer.
a. Group polarization involves group opinions.
c. Ingroup bias is the tendency to favor groups to which you belong.
d. Scapegoating is finding someone to blame as an outlet for your anger.

21. **a.** is the answer.
b. This is an example of overt prejudice.
c. & d. These are examples of discrimination.

22. **b.** is the answer.
a. We are keenly sensitive to differences within our group, less so to differences within other groups.
c. & d. Although we tend to look more favorably on members of the ingroup, the text does not suggest that ingroup bias extends to evaluations of abilities.

23. **c.** is the answer.

24. **c.** is the answer. The mere exposure effect refers to our tendency to like what we're used to, and we're used to seeing mirror images of ourselves.
a. Equity refers to equality in giving and taking between the partners in a relationship.
b. Self-disclosure is the sharing of intimate feelings with a partner in a loving relationship.
d. Although people prefer mirror images of their faces, mirror-image perceptions are often held by parties in conflict. Each party views itself favorably and the other negatively.

25. **d.** is the answer.

26. **d.** is the answer.

27. **d.** is the answer. In this case, each nation has mistakenly attributed the other's action to a *personal trait*, whereas its own action is viewed as a *situational* response.

28. **d.** is the answer. Because it provides people with an opportunity to meet, proximity is the most powerful predictor of friendship, even though, once a friendship is established, the other factors mentioned become more important.

29. **a.** is the answer.

30. **c.** is the answer. In this example of the fundamental attribution error, even when given the situational explanation for the woman's behavior, students ignored it and attributed her behavior to her personal traits.

31. **d.** is the answer. Our attitudes are more likely to guide our actions when other influences are minimal, when there's a specific connection between the two, and when we're keenly aware of our beliefs. The presence of other people would more likely be an outside factor that would lessen the likelihood of actions being guided by attitude.

32. **a.** is the answer. Such justifications arise as a way to preserve inequalities. The just-world phenomenon presumes that people get what they deserve. According to this view, someone who has less must deserve less.

33. **b.** is the answer.
a. & c. Crowding may amplify irritability or altruistic tendencies that are already present. Crowding does not, however, produce these reactions as a general effect.
d. In fact, just the opposite is true. Crowding often intensifies people's reactions.

34. **b.** is the answer.
a. Even if they made up a sizable portion of the group, although still a minority, their numbers would not be as important as their consistency.
c. & d. These aspects of minority influence were not discussed in the text; however, they are not likely to help a minority sway a majority.

35. **a.** is the answer.

36. **a.** is the answer. As Solomon Asch's experiments demonstrated, individuals are more likely to conform when they are being observed by others in the group. The other factors were not discussed in the text and probably would not promote conformity.

37. **d.** is the answer. Group polarization, or the enhancement of a group's prevailing attitudes, promotes groupthink, which leads to the disintegration of critical thinking.
a. Groupthink is more likely when a leader highly favors an idea, which may make members reluctant to disagree.
b. A strong minority faction would probably have the opposite effect: It would diminish group harmony while promoting critical thinking.
c. Consulting experts would discourage groupthink by exposing the group to other opinions.

Matching Items

1.	c	**4.**	e	**7.**	a
2.	b	**5.**	d	**8.**	g
3.	h	**6.**	f	**9.**	i

Application Essay

Your discussion might focus on some of the following topics: conformity, obedience, group polarization, and groupthink.

As a member of any group with established social norms, individuals will often act in ways that enable them to avoid rejection or gain social approval. Thus, a fraternity or sorority pledge would be likely to conform to the attitudes and norms projected by the group—or be rejected socially. In extreme cases of pledge hazing, acute social pressures may lead to atypical and antisocial individual behaviors—for example, on the part of pledges complying with the demands of senior members of the fraternity or sorority. Over time, meetings and discussions will probably enhance the group's prevailing attitudes (group polarization). This may lead to the unrealistic and irrational decision making that is groupthink. The potentially negative consequences of groupthink depend on the issues being discussed, but may include a variety of socially destructive behaviors.

Summing Up

A person who is the victim of an unjustifiable (usually negative) attitude is being subjected to *prejudice*, which is a mixture of usually overgeneralized beliefs called *stereotypes*, negative *emotions* (envy, hostility, or fear), and unjustifiable negative behavior called *discrimination*. Where do these attitudes come from? Several possibilities exist. Social roots include believing that the good are rewarded and the bad are punished, called the *just-world* phenomenon; favoring our own group, called the *ingroup bias*; and thinking of other groups as *outgroups*. Emotional roots include looking for someone to blame when things go wrong, called *scapegoating*. Cognitive roots include simplifying the world by sorting things into *categories*, judging the frequency of events by remembering *vivid* cases, and believing that people get what they deserve, that is, that the world is *just*.

Terms and Concepts

1. **Social psychology** is the scientific study of how we think about, influence, and relate to one another.

2. The **fundamental attribution error** is our tendency to underestimate the impact of situations and to overestimate the impact of personal traits on the behavior of others.

3. **Attitudes** are feelings, often based on our beliefs, that may predispose us to respond in particular ways to objects, people, and events.

4. The **foot-in-the-door phenomenon** is the tendency for people who have first agreed to a small request to comply later with a larger request.

5. A **role** is a set of explanations (norms) about how people in a specific social position ought to behave.

6. **Cognitive dissonance theory** refers to the theory that we act to reduce the psychological discomfort (dissonance) we experience when two of our thoughts (cognitions) clash. This is often done by changing our attitude rather than our behavior.

   Memory aid: Dissonance means "lack of harmony." **Cognitive dissonance** occurs when two thoughts, or cognitions, are at variance with one another.

7. **Conformity** is the tendency to change our thinking or behavior to coincide with a group standard.

8. **Social facilitation** is stronger performance of simple or well-learned tasks that occurs when other people are present.

9. **Social loafing** is the tendency for individual effort to be diminished when one is part of a group working toward a common goal.

10. **Deindividuation** refers to the loss of self-restraint and self-awareness that sometimes occurs in group situations that foster arousal and anonymity.

    Memory aid: As a prefix, *de-* indicates reversal or undoing. To **deindividuate** is to undo one's individuality.

11. **Group polarization** refers to the strengthening of a group's preexisting attitudes through discussion, which often has the effect of accentuating the group's differences from other groups.

    Memory aid: To *polarize* is to "cause thinking to concentrate about two poles, or contrasting positions."

12. **Groupthink** refers to the unrealistic thought processes and decision making that occur within groups when the desire for group harmony overrides a realistic appraisal of alternatives.

    Example: The psychological tendencies of self-justification, conformity, and group polarization foster the development of the "team spirit" mentality known as **groupthink**.

13. **Prejudice** is an unjustifiable and usually negative attitude toward a group and its members.

14. A **stereotype** is a generalized (sometimes accurate but often overgeneralized) belief about a group of people.

15. **Discrimination** is unjustifiable negative behavior toward a group and its members.

16. The **just-world phenomenon** is people's tendency to believe that good is rewarded and evil is punished. The logic is indisputable: "If I am rewarded, I must be good."

17. The **ingroup** refers to the people and groups with whom we share a common identity.

18. The **outgroup** refers to the people and groups perceived as different or apart from our group.

19. The **ingroup bias** is the tendency to favor our own group.

20. The **scapegoat theory** proposes that prejudice provides an outlet for anger by finding someone to blame.

21. The **other-race effect** is the tendency to recall faces of one's own race more accurately than faces of other races.

22. **Aggression** is any physical or verbal behavior intended to hurt or destroy.

23. The **frustration-aggression principle** states that aggression is triggered when people become angry because their efforts to achieve a goal have been blocked.

24. **Social scripts** are culturally modeled guides for how to act in various situations.

25. The **mere exposure effect** refers to the fact that repeated exposure to an unfamiliar stimulus increases our liking of it.

26. **Passionate love** refers to an aroused state of intense positive absorption in another person, especially at the beginning of a relationship.

27. **Companionate love** refers to a deep, affectionate attachment.

28. **Equity** refers to the condition in which there is mutual giving and receiving between the partners in a relationship.

29. **Self-disclosure** refers to a person's sharing intimate feelings with another.

30. **Altruism** is unselfish concern for the welfare of others.

31. The **bystander effect** is the tendency of a person to be less likely to offer help to someone if there are other people present.

32. **Conflict** is a perceived incompatibility of actions, goals, or ideas between individuals or groups.

33. **Mirror-image perceptions** are mutual views of each other often held by people in conflict

34. **Superordinate goals** are mutual goals that require the cooperation of individuals or groups otherwise in conflict.

appendix A

PSYCHOLOGY AT WORK

> Research on worker motivation reveals that workers who view their careers as a meaningful calling, those working in jobs that optimize their skills, and those who become absorbed in activities that result in flow find work satisfying and enriching. Effective leaders recognize this and develop management styles that focus on workers' strengths and adapt their leadership style to the situation. Research on achievement motivation underscores the importance of self-discipline and persistence in achieving one's goals.

APPENDIX REVIEW

First, skim each text section, noting headings and bold-face items. Review the section by reading the objectives and summaries provided here, then answer the questions that follow. In some cases, STUDY TIPS explain how best to learn a difficult concept. Check your understanding of the material by consulting the answers on page 270. Do not continue with the next section until you understand each answer. If you need to, review or reread the section in the textbook before continuing.

Work and Life Satisfaction

Objective 1: Explain the concept of flow.

Work supports us, connects us to others, and helps define us. People may view their work as a *job*, a *career*, or a *calling*. When work fully engages our skills, we experience *flow*. We are completely involved and have a diminished awareness of self and time. Flow experiences boost our sense of self-esteem, competence, and well-being.

1. Most people _____ (have/do not have) a predictable career path. People who work to make money for other activities see work as a _____ , those who see their present position as a rung on the ladder to a better position view it as a _____ , and those view work as a fulfilling and socially useful activity see it as a _____ .

2. Psychologist Mihaly Csikszentmihalyi formulated the concept of _____ , which is defined as an intense, _____ state and diminished awareness of _____ and time. People who experience this state also experience increased feelings of _____ , _____ , and _____ .

3. People who are unemployed _____ (report/do not report) lower well-being. People who view their work as a _____ report the greatest satisfaction.

4. (Close-Up) Satisfied and successful people devote less time to _____ _____ than to _____ _____ .

•••
STUDY TIP: Think about relatives and other people you know who have been employed for a period of years. Of these, which person's attitude toward work best represents the concept of a calling? A career? A job?
•••

Industrial–Organizational Psychology

Objective 2: Identify the three main subfields of industrial-organizational psychology.

Industrial-organizational (I/O) psychology applies psychology's principles to the workplace through its primary subfields of personnel psychology, organizational psychology, and human factors psychology. *Personnel psychology* applies the discipline's methods and principles to selecting, placing, training, and evaluating workers. *Organizational psychology* considers how an organization's goals, work environments, and management styles influence worker motivation, satisfaction, and productivity. *Human factors psychology* explores how machines and environments can be optimally designed to fit human abilities and expectations.

1. The nature of work has changed, from _____ to _____ to "_____ _____ ."

2. The field of _____ - _____ psychology applies psychology's principles to the workplace. The subfield of _____ _____ focuses on selecting, placing, training, and

evaluating workers. Another subfield, _____
_____ , examines how work environments and _____
styles influence worker motivation, satisfaction, and productivity. A third subfield, _____
_____ psychology, focuses on how machines and work environments can be made safe and easy to use.

Motivating Achievement

Objective 3: Explain why it is important for managers to motivate achievement among workers.

People who score high in *achievement motivation* have a desire for significant accomplishment; for mastering things, people, or ideas; for control; and for meeting a high standard. Researchers refer to passionate dedication to a long-term goal as *grit.* Employee satisfaction contributes to successful organizations. Positive moods at work foster creativity, persistence, and helpfulness. Engaged workers know what's expected of them, have what they need to do their work, feel fulfilled in their work, have regular opportunities to do what they do best, perceive that they are part of something significant, and have opportunities to learn and to develop. Worker satisfaction and engagement are associated with less employee turnover, higher productivity, and greater profits.

1. A desire for significant accomplishment; for mastery of things, people, or ideas; and for attaining a high standard is called _____
_____ .

2. The best predictor of school performance, attendance, and graduation honors among high school and college students is _____
rather than _____
_____ . This motivation also _____ talent.

3. Passionate dedication to an ambitious long-term goal has been called _____ .

4. Training students in resilience under stress, or _____ , leads to better grades.

5. Positive moods at work contribute to worker _____ , _____ , and _____ . Researchers have also found a positive correlation between measures of organizational success and employee _____ , or the extent of workers' involvement, identification, and enthusiasm.

Identify the characteristics of engaged workers.

•••
STUDY TIP: Research studies have shown that people who possess a low need for achievement tend to prefer situations and tasks that are either very easy or impossibly hard. Conversely, people with a high need for achievement tend to prefer tasks that are moderately difficult. Why do you think this might be? Which types of tasks (e.g., college courses) do you prefer?
•••

Leadership

Objective 4: Identify the characteristics of effective leaders.

Effective leaders engage their employees' interests and loyalty, figure out their natural talents and adjust their work roles to suit those talents, and develop those talents into great strengths. They care about how their people feel about their work and reinforce positive behaviors through recognition and reward. To improve productivity, managers work with people to define specific, challenging goals; make a plan to achieve those goals; and provide feedback on progress.

Some managers excel at *task leadership*—setting standards, organizing work, and focusing attention on goals. They keep a group centered on its mission. Task leaders typically have a directive style, which can work well if they are bright enough to give good orders. Other managers excel at *social leadership*—solving conflicts, building high-achieving teams, and offering support. Social leaders often delegate authority and welcome the participation of team members. Research suggests that effective managers exhibit a high degree of both task and social leadership.

1. The best managers help people to _____ and _____ their talents, match tasks to their _____ , care how their people feel about their work, and _____ positive behaviors.

2. Higher worker achievement is motivated by a leader who sets _____ , _____ goals.

3. Experts once believed that all great leaders _____ (share/do not necessarily share) certain traits.

4. Effective leaders tend to exude a self-confident _____ that is a mix of a _____ of some goal, an ability to _____ the goal clearly, and enough optimism to _____ others to follow. Leadership that inspires others to transcend their own self-interests for the sake of the group is called _____ leadership. _____ (Women/Men) more than _____ (women/men) tend to be this type of leader.

5. The most effective style of leadership _____ (varies/does not vary) with the situation and/or the person. In some situations, the _____ style of a commanding leader may be needed. In other situations, a _____ style that shares power is best.

6. Managers who are directive, set clear standards, organize work, and focus attention on specific goals are said to employ _____ _____ . More democratic managers who aim to build teamwork and mediate conflicts in the work force employ _____ _____ .

7. Effective managers _____ (rarely/often) exhibit a high degree of both task and social leadership. Giving workers a chance to voice their opinion before a decision is made _____ them in the process. This _____ decision making takes longer but increases worker _____ to the decision.

•••

STUDY TIP: Think about several leaders you know. These might be group leaders, employers, teachers, and relatives. Of these people, whose leadership skills do you admire the most? Why? What type of leadership style (e.g., social leadership, task leadership) best characterizes this person?

•••

PROGRESS TEST

Multiple-Choice Questions

Circle your answers to the following questions and check them with the answers beginning on page 270. If your answer is incorrect, read the explanation for why it is incorrect and then consult the appropriate pages of the text (in parentheses following the correct answer).

1. In almost every industrialized nation, unemployed people report
   a. better health.
   b. lower well-being.
   c. being bored.
   d. enjoying time to travel.

2. To increase employee productivity, managers should
   a. adopt a directive leadership style.
   b. adopt a democratic leadership style.
   c. instill competitiveness in each employee.
   d. deal with employees according to their individual motives.

3. Because Brent believes that his employees are intrinsically motivated to work for reasons beyond money, Brent would be described as a _____ manager.
   a. directive   c. task-oriented
   b. social-oriented d. charismatic

4. Which of the following individuals would be characterized as experiencing flow?
   a. Sheila, who, despite viewing her work as merely a job, performs her work conscientiously
   b. Larry, who sees his work as an artist as a calling
   c. Arnie, who views his present job as merely a stepping stone in his career
   d. Montel, who often becomes so immersed in his writing that he loses all sense of self and time

5. Darren, a sales clerk at a tire store, enjoys his job, not so much for the money as for its challenge and the opportunity to interact with a variety of people. The store manager asks you to recommend a strategy for increasing Darren's motivation. Which of the following is most likely to be effective?
   a. Create a competition among the salespeople so that whoever has the highest sales each week receives a bonus.
   b. Put Darren on a week-by-week employment contract, promising him continued employment only if his sales increase each week.
   c. Leave Darren alone unless his sales drop and then threaten to fire him if his performance doesn't improve.
   d. Involve Darren as much as possible in company decision making and use rewards to inform him of his successful performance.

6. For as long as she has been the plant manager, Juanita has welcomed input from employees and has delegated authority. Bill, in managing his department, takes a more authoritarian, iron-fisted approach. Juanita's style is one of _____ leadership, whereas Bill's is one of _____ leadership.
   a. task; social
   b. social; task
   c. directive; democratic
   d. democratic; participative

7. Dr. Iverson conducts research focusing on how management styles influence worker motivation. Dr. Iverson would most accurately be described as a(n)
   a. motivation psychologist.
   b. personnel psychologist.
   c. organizational psychologist.
   d. human factors psychologist.

Matching Items

Match each term with its definition or description.

Terms

_____ 1. transformational leadership
_____ 2. personnel psychology
_____ 3. organizational psychology
_____ 4. human factors psychology
_____ 5. task leadership
_____ 6. social leadership
_____ 7. flow
_____ 8. industrial-organizational (I/O) psychology

Definitions or Descriptions

a. an intense, focused state
b. applies psychological concepts and methods to human behavior in the workplace
c. applies psychological methods and principles to selecting, placing, training, and evaluating workers
d. goal-oriented leadership that sets standards, organizes work, and focuses attention on goals
e. group-oriented leadership that builds teamwork, solves conflict, and offers support
f. examines organizational influences on worker satisfaction and productivity
g. motivates others to commit themselves to the group's mission
h. explores how people and machines interact

TERMS AND CONCEPTS

Using your own words, write on a separate piece of paper a brief definition or explanation of each of the following terms.

1. flow
2. industrial-organizational (I/O) psychology
3. human factors psychology
4. personnel psychology
5. organizational psychology
6. achievement motivation
7. task leadership
8. social leadership

ANSWERS

Chapter Review

Work and Life Satisfaction

1. do not have; job; career; calling
2. flow; focused; self; self-esteem, competence, well-being
3. report; calling
4. correcting weaknesses; sharpening skills

Industrial-Organizational Psychology

1. farming; manufacturing; knowledge work
2. industrial-organizational; personnel psychology; organizational psychology; management; human factors

Motivating Achievement

1. achievement motivation
2. self-discipline; intelligence score; refines
3. grit
4. hardiness
5. creativity; persistence; helpfulness; engagement

Researchers found that engaged workers know what's expected of them, have what they need to do their work, feel fulfilled in their work, have regular opportunities to do what they do best, perceive that they are part of something significant, and have opportunities to learn and develop.

Leadership

1. identify; measure; talents; reinforce
2. specific; challenging
3. share
4. charisma; vision; communicate; inspire; transformational; Women; men
5. varies; directive; democratic
6. task leadership; social leadership
7. often; engages; shared; commitment

Progress Test

Multiple-Choice Questions

1. **b.** is the answer.
2. **d.** is the answer. As different people are motivated by different things, to increase motivation and thus productivity, managers are advised to learn what motivates individual employees and to challenge and reward them accordingly.
   a. & b. The most effective management style will depend on the situation.

c. This might be an effective strategy with some, but not all, employees.

3. **b.** is the answer.
   a. & c. Directive, or task-oriented, managers are likely to assume that worker motivation is low.
   d. The most effective leaders are generally charismatic, which has nothing to do with whether they are directive or democratic leaders.

4. **d.** is the answer.

5. **d.** is the answer. Because Darren appears to resonate with the principle that people are intrinsically motivated to work for reasons beyond money, giving him feedback about his work and involving him in decision making are probably all he needs to be very satisfied with his situation.
   a., b., & c. Creating competitions and using controlling, rather than informing, rewards may have the opposite effect and actually undermine Darren's motivation.

6. **b.** is the answer.
   a. Bill's style is one of task leadership, whereas Juanita's is one of social leadership.
   c. Juanita's style is democratic, whereas Bill's is directive.
   d. Participative is another term used to refer to the social or group-oriented style of leadership.

7. **c.** is the answer.

Matching Items

1.	g	**5.**	d
2.	c	**6.**	e
3.	f	**7.**	a
4.	i	**8.**	c

Terms and Concepts

1. **Flow** is a completely involved, focused state that engages a person's skills, often accompanied by a diminished awareness of self and time.

2. **Industrial-organizational (I/O) psychology** applies psychological concepts and methods to human behavior in the workplace.

3. **Human factors psychology** is a subfield of I/O psychology that explores how people and machines interact and how machines and physical environments can be made safe and easy to use. (p. 408)

4. **Personnel psychology** is a subfield of I/O psychology that focuses on employee selection, placement, training, and appraisal.

5. **Organizational psychology** is a subfield of I/O psychology that examines organizational influences on worker satisfaction and productivity and facilitates organizational change.

6. **Achievement motivation** is the desire for significant accomplishment; mastery of things, people, or ideas; and for attaining a high standard.

7. **Task leadership** is goal-oriented leadership that sets standards, organizes work, and focuses attention on goals.

8. **Social leadership** is group-oriented leadership that builds teamwork, mediates conflict, and offers support.